Beyond Religious Tolerance
Muslim, Christian and Traditionalist
Encounters in an African Town

Series information:
RELIGION IN TRANSFORMING AFRICA
ISSN 2398-8673

Series Editors
Barbara Bompani, Joseph Hellweg, Ousmane Kane and **Emma Wild-Wood**

Editorial Reading Panel
Robert Baum (Dartmouth College)
Dianna Bell (University of Cape Town)
Ezra Chitando (University of Zimbabwe)
Martha Frederiks (Utrecht University)
Paul Gifford (SOAS)
David M. Gordon (Bowdoin College)
Jörg Haustein (University of Cambridge)
Paul Lubeck (Johns Hopkins University-SAIS)
Philomena Mwaura (Kenyatta University, Nairobi)
Ebenezer Obadare (University of Kansas)
Benjamin Soares (University of Florida & University of Amsterdam)
Abdulkader I. Tayob (University of Cape Town)
Stephen Wooten (University of Oregon)

Series description
The series is open to submissions that examine local or regional realities on the complexities of religion and spirituality in Africa. Religion in Transforming Africa will showcase cutting-edge research into continent-wide issues on Christianity, Islam and other religions of Africa; Traditional beliefs and witchcraft; Religion, culture & society; History of religion, politics and power; Global networks and new missions; Religion in conflict and peace-building processes; Religion and development; Religious rituals and texts and their role in shaping religious ideologies and theologies. Innovative, and challenging current perspectives, the series provides an indispensable resource on this key area of African Studies for academics, students, international policy-makers and development practitioners.

Please contact the Series Editors with an outline or download the proposal form at www.jamescurrey.com.

Dr Barbara Bompani, Reader in Africa and International Development, University of
    Edinburgh: b.bompani@ed.ac.uk
Dr Joseph Hellweg, Associate Professor of Religion, Department of Religion, Florida State
    University: jhellweg@fsu.edu
Professor Ousmane Kane, Prince Alwaleed Bin Talal Professor of Contemporary Islamic
    Religion & Society, Harvard Divinity School: okane@hds.harvard.edu
Dr Emma Wild-Wood, Senior Lecturer, African Christianity and African Indigenous
    Religions, University of Edinburgh: emma.wildwood@ed.ac.uk

Previously published title in the series are listed at the back of this volume.

Beyond Religious Tolerance
Muslim, Christian and Traditionalist Encounters in an African Town

Edited by
INSA NOLTE, OLUKOYA OGEN and REBECCA JONES

Adeyemi College Academic Press

James Currey
is an imprint of
Boydell & Brewer Ltd
PO Box 9, Woodbridge
Suffolk IP12 3DF (GB)
www.jamescurrey.com
and of
Boydell & Brewer Inc.
668 Mt Hope Avenue
Rochester, NY 14620-2731 (US)
www.boydellandbrewer.com

Nigeria (paperback) edition first published 2017 under the title
Ede is One Room: Encounters between Muslims, Christians and Traditionalists in a Yoruba Town
by
Adeyemi College Academic Press
Adeyemi College of Education,
P.M.B. 520, Ondo-Ore Road, Ondo, Nigeria

© Contributors 2017
First published 2017
Paperback edition 2020

All rights reserved. No part of this book may be reproduced in any form, or by electronic or mechanical means, including information storage and retrieval systems, without permission in writing from the publishers, except by a reviewer who may quote brief passages in a review.

British Library Cataloguing in Publication Data
A catalogue record for this book is available on request from the British Library

ISBN 978-1-84701-153-4 (James Currey cloth)
ISBN 978-1-84701-251-7 (James Currey paperback)
ISBN 978-978-904-802-1 (Adeyemi College Academic Press Nigeria edition paperback)

The publisher has no responsibility for the continued existence or accuracy of URLs for external or third-party internet websites referred to in this book, and does not guarantee that any content on such websites is, or will remain, accurate or appropriate

Typeset by Double Dagger Book Production in 9.5/13pt Georgia

Contents

List of Illustrations	vii
List of Contributors	ix
Acknowledgements	xii
Note on Orthography	xv
Glossary of Yoruba and Arabic Terms	xvii

1 Beyond Religious Tolerance: Muslims, Christians and Traditionalists in a Yoruba Town
Insa Nolte and Olukoya Ogen — 1

2 Kingship and Religion: An Introduction to the History of Ede
Siyan Oyeweso — 31

3 Ambivalence and Transgression in the Practice of Ṣàngó
Aderemi Suleiman Ajala and Insa Nolte — 57

4 Ṣàngó's Thunder: Poetic Challenges to Islam and Christianity
George Olusola Ajibade — 75

5 Compound Life and Religious Control in Ede's Muslim Community
Amusa Saheed Balogun — 95

6 Challenges and Affirmations of Islamic Practice: The Tablighi Jamaat
Adeyemi Balogun — 123

7 The Baptist Church in Ede: Christian Struggles over Education and Land
Olukoya Ogen and Amusa Saheed Balogun — 151

8 **Freedom and Control:
Islam and Christianity at the Federal Polytechnic**
Akin Iwilade and Oladipo Fadayomi   173

9 **Religious Accommodation in Two Generations of
the Adeleke Family**
Ibikunle H. Tijani   189

10 **Marrying Out: Gender and Religious Mediation
in Interfaith Marriages**
Insa Nolte and Tosin Akinjobi   207

11 **Everyday Inter-Religious Encounters and Attitudes**
Rebecca Jones and Insa Nolte   227

12 **Outlook: Religious Difference, the Yoruba and Beyond**
Insa Nolte and Olukoya Ogen   257

Appendix 1: Ede Anthem   267
Appendix 2: Songs of Ede   269
Appendix 3: Oríkì *of the* Tìmì *of Ede, Present and Past*   277
Bibliography   297
Index   309

Illustrations

Photographs

1. The view over Ede from the south, towards palace, central mosque and river © Insa Nolte 2013 — 6
2. The royal palace of Ede © Insa Nolte 2012 — 10
3. The central mosque of Ede © Insa Nolte 2013 — 18
4. Organisers and participants of workshop on 'Everyday religion and tolerance in Ede' © Insa Nolte 2012 — 25
5. His Royal Majesty, the *Tìmì* of Ede, *Ọba* Muniru Adesola Lawal, leading townspeople to the prayer ground during *Iléyá* 2012 © Insa Nolte 2012 — 32
6. Chief Imam *Alhaji* Mas'ud Husain Akajewole entering the prayer ground during *Iléyá* 2012 © Insa Nolte 2012 — 46
7. *Egúngún* Adinimodo before the central mosque with spectators, 2012 © Insa Nolte 2012 — 66
8. Alfa Lagunju during *Egúngún* festival 2012 © Insa Nolte 2012 — 66
9. The statue of *Tìmì* Agbale with *Ṣàngó* paraphernalia, located behind the royal palace © Insa Nolte 2012 — 77
10. The view over Ede from Imole compound © Insa Nolte 2015 — 97
11. Salam Basit of Imole compound points to the mosque well © Insa Nolte 2015 — 106
12. 'Healing Jesus Crusade' propaganda in Ede © Insa Nolte 2012 — 141
13. Islamic counterpropaganda to 'Healing Jesus Crusade' in Ede © Insa Nolte 2012 — 142
14. First Baptist Church Ede © Insa Nolte 2015 — 161
15. Team member Kehinde Akinduro discussing the survey with potential respondents © Insa Nolte 2012 — 228

Maps

1. Ede in south-west Nigeria — 5
2. The town of Ede — 19

Contributors

Aderemi Suleiman Ajala is an Associate Professor of Cultural Anthropology at the Department of Archaeology and Anthropology, University of Ibadan, Nigeria. He is a recipient of a British Academy Visiting Research Fellowship (2006), an Alexander von Humboldt Fellowship (2009) and a Rockefeller Foundation Fellowship (2011) among others. He has authored and edited books and published in journals including *African Identities* and *Ethnic and Racial Studies*. His research interests include culture and health, ethnography and identity, and nationalism and the state in Nigeria.

George Olusola Ajibade is an Associate Professor and the Head of Department of Linguistics and African Languages, Obafemi Awolowo University, Ile-Ife, Nigeria, where he teaches Yoruba language, literature and culture. He is an alumnus of the Alexander von Humboldt Research Fellow at the University of Bayreuth, Germany, and was a Research Fellow at the Institute for African Studies, University of Bayreuth, Germany, under the project 'Imagination, Aesthetic and the Global Art World (B4)' carried out at the Humanities Collaborative Research Centre of University of Bayreuth, Germany, 2000–2004. Olusola's research interests are in African Cultural Studies, critical social and literary theories and folklore. He is also author of a number of articles on Yoruba cultural studies.

Tosin Akinjobi-Babatunde is a Lecturer II in the Department of History and International Relations at Elizade University, Ilara-Mokin, Ondo State, Nigeria and a PhD student at Obafemi Awolowo University, Ile-Ife, Nigeria. She was a member of the 'Knowing Each Other' project in 2012 and is now a Fellow of the SSRC's Next-Generation Social Science in Africa programme. Tosin has published articles and book chapters on gender in contemporary police history and in peace and security studies, and she is specifically interested in the history of Nigerian women peacekeepers in the UN peacekeeping operations in Africa.

Saheed Balogun Amusa is a Lecturer Grade I in the Department of History, Obafemi Awolowo University (OAU), Ile-Ife, Nigeria since 2008, where he is teaching courses in Nigerian and African history. Saheed obtained his bachelor's degree in History at the Adekunle Ajasin University Akungba-Akoko, Nigeria, in 2005, and a Master's and PhD in History at Obafemi Awolowo University, Ile-Ife, Nigeria, in 2010 and 2015 respectively. He is a winner of a 2015 African–German Network of Excellence in Science (AGNES) Grant for Junior Researchers, a member of the Historical Society of Nigeria, the International Research Network on AIDS and Religion in Africa (IRNARA) and the International Society for Studies in Oral Traditions. Saheed has published journal articles and book chapters, most of which focus on Nigeria's social and political history since the colonial period.

Adeyemi Balogun is a Junior Fellow at the Bayreuth International Graduate School of African Studies (BIGSAS), University of Bayreuth, Germany, where he is currently pursuing his doctorate. Before that he completed undergraduate and graduate studies at Obafemi Awolowo University, Ile-Ife, Nigeria, and he was a member of the 'Knowing Each Other' project between 2012 and 2015. His research interests are in youth, nation-building and religion.

Oladipo Fadayomi works at the Ministry of Foreign Affairs, Abuja. He holds an MSc in International Relations from Obafemi Awolowo University, Ile-Ife, Nigeria. His main research interests are in the areas of inter-faith dialogue, human rights and Nigerian foreign policy.

Akin Iwilade is a Lecturer in International Relations at Obafemi Awolowo University, Ile-Ife, Nigeria. He is currently ENI Scholar and doctoral candidate in International Development at St Antony's College, University of Oxford. His main research interests are in the broad areas of political and everyday violence, youth politics and regional security frameworks in West Africa.

Rebecca Jones is a Research Fellow on the 'Knowing Each Other' project based at the Department of African Studies and Anthropology, University of Birmingham. In 2014, she was awarded her PhD from the University of Birmingham, for which she researched Nigerian travel writing in Yoruba and English. Prior to this, she received a BA in English from the University of Cambridge and an MA in African Studies from the School of Oriental and African Studies, London, where she first studied Yoruba. Her research interests centre on ideas of encounter, knowledge and travel, and on Yoruba and English print culture in Nigeria, drawing on literary, anthropological and historical studies.

Insa Nolte is a Reader in the Department of African Studies and Anthropology, University of Birmingham, UK, and a Visiting Research Professor at Osun State University, Osogbo, Nigeria. She is the Reviews Editor of *Africa: Journal of the International African Institute*, and the Vice President of the African Studies Association of the UK for 2014–16. Her research focuses on the importance of everyday encounters and interpersonal relationships for wider social and political processes in Nigeria. She is the Principal Investigator of a European Research Council (ERC) project entitled 'Knowing Each Other: Everyday Religious Encounters, Social Identities and Tolerance in Southwest Nigeria', which explores the way in which differences and encounters between Yoruba Muslims, Christians and traditionalists inform social identities shaped by locality, gender and generation.

Olukoya Ogen is the Provost of Adeyemi College of Education, Ondo, Nigeria. Olukoya is also a Professor of History at Osun State University, Osogbo; an Associate Expert at the UNESCO Institute for African Culture and Understanding, Olusegun Obasanjo Presidential Library, Abeokuta; and a Visiting Senior Research Fellow at the Department of African Studies and Anthropology, University of Birmingham, UK. He has held a range of UK- and US-based fellowships and published widely on Nigerian history and the history and politics of Ikale and Yorubaland more generally. He is the Nigerian Coordinator of the ERC 'Knowing Each Other' project.

Siyan Oyeweso is a Professor of History at Osun State University, Osogbo, Nigeria. He holds PhD in History from Obafemi Awolowo University, Ile-Ife, and is a former Head of Department of History and International Studies and Dean, Faculty of Arts, at Lagos State University. He has also served as the Provost, College of Humanities and Culture, and Chairman, Committee of Provosts, Deans and Directors at Osun State University, Osogbo, Nigeria. Siyan is a Fellow of the Historical Society of Nigeria, member of the Nigerian Academy of Letters and several other professional bodies. His areas of research interests include Islam in Yorubaland, culture and history of Nigeria, Nigeria`s intellectual history, Yoruba inter-state warfare and the Nigerian Civil War.

Ibikunle Tijani is the Deputy Vice Chancellor of Adeleke University, Nigeria. He was formerly the pioneer Dean of the Faculty of Arts at the same university. After first and higher degrees in Nigeria, the UK and South Africa, he taught at various universities in the United States as a professor of African history and African Diaspora. He is a member of the General Labour History of Africa (GLHA) project based at Leiden University, The Netherlands. His areas of research include decolonisation, labour and social history, urban studies and historical biographies.

Acknowledgements

This book owes its existence to many individuals and institutions.

We are grateful to His Royal Majesty the *Tìmì* of Ede, *Ọba* Muniru Adesola Lawal, who graciously allowed us to carry out our research in his domain. We also thank *Alhaji* Mas'ud Husain Akajewole, the Chief Imam of Edeland; *Alhaji* Ibraheem Tijani Dende Adekilekun, the Chief Imam of Ansar-Ud-Deen; Chief Oyebanji Sangodokun, the Chief Priest of *Ṣàngó* in Edeland; and the late Professor (Revd.) Joseph Abiodun Ilori, the former President of the Nigerian Baptist Theological Seminary in Ogbomoso for all assistance rendered.

We also greatly appreciate the assistance of Professor Siyan Oyeweso, a 'native son' of Ede and the first Provost of the College of Humanities and Culture at Osun State University, who offered us hospitality and support throughout our research. *Alhaji* Rasheed Adio and *Alhaji* Nureni Lawal, our local gatekeepers, offered tireless help during our time in Ede.

Work on this book was supported by a Starting Researcher Grant awarded by the European Research Council and led by Dr Insa Nolte in close collaboration with Professor Olukoya Ogen. Our book is part of a larger research project entitled 'Knowing Each Other: Everyday Religious Encounters, Social Identities and Tolerance in Southwest Nigeria' (Grant No. 283466) and based at the University of Bimingham, UK, and Osun State University, Nigeria.

At Osun State University, we thank Professor Olusola Akinrinade, the founding Vice-Chancellor of Osun State University, who oversaw the start of the 'Knowing Each Other' project. Both Professor Ganiyu Olatunji Olatunde, who took over from him as the Acting Vice Chancellor, and Professor Adekunle Bashiru Okesina, the subsequent Vice Chancellor, supported the project. We are grateful to all the members of the Department of History and International Studies, Osun State University, for their interest in our project: Dr Emmanuel Ibiloye, Dr Kemi Adeshina, Dr Tunde Decker, Mr Ranti Afowowe, Mr Isiaka Raifu, the late Mr Olawale Idowu, Mr Adewole Adeleke, Mr Ben Akobi and Mr Sunday Akande. We also thank Professor Folorunso Abayomi Kizito, the Provost of the College of Humanities and Culture, Dr Rotimi Fasan and Dr Temitayo Amao of the Department of English and Mr Komolafe of the Department of Linguistics.

ACKNOWLEDGEMENTS

We are very grateful to the Nigerian team members who carried out the 'Knowing Each Other' project survey, interviews and archival research: Mr Adebayo Adewusi, Miss Rita Ajayi, Miss Kehinde Akinduro, Mrs Tosin Akinjobi, Mr Joseph Ayodokun, Mr Adeyemi Balogun and Mr Charles Omotayo. Dr Amusa Balogun provided valuable assistance to the team during this period. Mr Adeyemi Balogun in particular assisted with numerous queries and extra research for this book, including help with the description of the images selected for the book, and we are grateful for his thorough and reliable work.

In the UK, we must thank the 'Knowing Each Other' team members Dr David Kerr, Mr Jovia Salifu, Mrs Oluwakemi Olabode, Mr Olufemi Ogundayo and Mrs Omolara Fasanmi for all their work on the project. We are also grateful to Nick Ward, who helped to format the images, and Miles Irving, who produced the maps for this book.

The Department of African Studies and Anthropology (DASA) at the University of Birmingham provided a collegial environment in which to discuss the ideas behind the book, and we thank all our DASA colleagues for their insight: Professor Karin Barber, Dr Maxim Bolt, Dr Stewart Brown, Dr Lynne Brydon, Dr Reginald Cline-Cole, Dr Juliet Gilbert, Dr Leslie James, Dr David Kerr (again!), Dr Paulo Fernando de Moraes Farias, Professor Tom McCaskie, Dr Katrien Pype, Dr Benedetta Rossi, Dr Keith Shear and Dr Kate Skinner. We particularly thank our colleagues Karin Barber and Paulo Fernando de Moraes Farias for reading the manuscript of this book and offering detailed and thorough comments and suggestions, and we are grateful for the feedback on an early draft of the book by our anonymous reviewers.

Earlier versions of most of the chapters in this book were first presented at the workshop on 'Everyday Religion and Tolerance in Ede, Southwest Nigeria' held at Adeleke University on 5–6 December 2012, hosted by the 'Knowing Each Other' project. We appreciate Professor Ayandiji Aina, the Pioneer President/Vice Chancellor of Adeleke University, and Professor Ibikunle Tijani, Adeleke's first Dean of the Faculty of Arts and Education, for their enthusiastic support – both practical and intellectual – for the workshop. We also appreciate all the participants in the workshop, both presenters and audience members, academics and non-academics, who helped us develop our ideas about religious tolerance and co-existence in Ede, and whose support for and interest in our research encouraged us to pursue it further.

Later versions of chapters of this book were presented at the conference 'Crossroads in African Studies' at the Department of African Studies and Anthropology (DASA), University of Birmingham in 2013; and the African Studies Association 2014 conference in Indianapolis, USA, in the panel 'The Limits of Tolerance: Understanding the Dynamics of Religious Conflict in Yorubaland, SW Nigeria'. We are grateful to our co-panelists, discussants and audience members for their questions, ideas and suggestions, particularly Professor Toyin Falola.

The editors and publisher gratefully acknowledge the permission granted by the following individuals to reproduce the copyright material in this book: Hameed Nasiru Akinlade and Adeniyi Moshood Raiji for permission to publish excerpts from songs written and performed by Hameed Nasiru Akinlade, Adeniyi Moshood Raiji and the Akinlade cultural group on Mapo Arogun day (Ede annual festival) held on 30 November 2013; Dr John Adelekan Olunlade on behalf of Pa E.A. Olunlade for permission to publish excerpts from E.A. Olunlade, *Ede: A Short History*, originally published in 1961 by the Ministry of Education of the now defunct Western Region of Nigeria; Prince Laoye Adewale, on behalf of late Tìmì John Adetoyese Laoye, for permission to publish translations of Ede's royal *oríkì* by Tìmì John Adetoyese Laoye, which originally appeared in E.A. Olunlade, *Ede: A Short History*; and Chief Mrs M. Olayinka Babalola for permission to publish excerpts from A. Babalola, *Awon Oriki Borokinni*, originally published in 1975 by Hodder & Stoughton in Ibadan and London. Every effort has been made to trace copyright holders and to obtain their permission for the use of copyright material. The publisher and editors apologise for any errors or omissions in the above list and would be grateful to be notified of any corrections that should be incorporated in future reprints or editions of this book.

Rebecca Jones would like to thank Dr Insa Nolte and Professor Olukoya Ogen for the opportunity to work on this book and the 'Knowing Each Other' project. In Nigeria, thanks to Joseph Osuolale and Abiola Oladunjoye Ayodokun; Dr Olusola Ajibade, Dr (Mrs) Bolaji Ajibade and family; and Dr (Mrs) Olaide Sheba for continued hospitality.

Olukoya Ogen would like to express his immense gratitude to Insa Nolte for the confidence and trust reposed in him to coordinate the Nigerian end of the 'Knowing Each Other' project. At Osun State University, the Bursar, Mr Bayo Lasisi and the Registrar, Dr J.O. Faniran deserve accolades for being very supportive of the research on everyday religious encounter in Yorubaland. In the UK, he would like to thank the family of Insa Nolte and Simon Green for their warm hospitality.

Insa Nolte would like to thank the Research and Innovation Services team at the University of Birmingham, the Research and Knowledge Transfer Office (College of Arts and Law), and Ms Sue Bowen, Ms Caroline Marshall and Ms Parminder Kaur, who have provided valuable support for the 'Knowing Each Other' project. In Nigeria, thank you to HRM Ọba Dr Adedayo Olusino Adekoya and *Olorì* Mistura Adekoya, and especially to Olukoya Ogen and Iyabo Ekundayo-Ogen for their ongoing hospitality and friendship. It has been essential to the success of the project.

Birmingham and Ibadan, May 2016

Note on Orthography

Yoruba

Standard Yoruba uses diacritics: tone marks on vowels and sub-dots below particular letters. In this book, we use full diacritics for quotations from Yoruba, and individual Yoruba words (including the names of Yoruba òrìṣà or deities).

However, we have made an exception for names of people and places, which are presented without diacritics, not only for the purposes of legibility, but also since these names have now been incorporated into Nigerian English, so full Yoruba diacritics may appear overly elaborate.

Yoruba words are capitalised where they appear as part of proper nouns (e.g. as titles) but not where they are used as common nouns. For instance, 'ọba' (ruler of a town) refers to the ruler in general, while 'Ọba' is used in the title of a particular ruler.

Arabic

Arabic words have been spelt in an Anglicised form for words commonly used in English-language speech (e.g. *Qur'an, hijab, Allah*), and in a local form where commonly used this way in south-western Nigeria (e.g. *Alhaji, wa'azi*), but otherwise follow standard Arabic transliteration.

Where some Arabic terms could be translated into English – such as *Allah* or God – we have used the English form.

However, all quotations from Yoruba and Arabic (including survey responses, as well as published texts) are preserved with the writer's original diacritics and transliteration.

Interviews

We have endeavoured to provide as much information as possible regarding the interviews carried out in the course of research for this book, but since interviews were undertaken by many different researchers at different times, the amount of information they recorded about their interviews differs. Where possible, we provide the name of the interviewee, their occupation or role, the date of interview, the place of interview and the interviewer (if someone other than the author of the chapter).

Glossary of Yoruba and Arabic Terms

Yoruba and Arabic terms are translated into English on their first appearance in this book, and in some cases on subsequent appearances. For ease of reference we also present some of the most frequently used or important terms in this glossary.

Adhān – Islamic call to prayer
Ajágemọ – an *Ọbàtálá* priest in Ede
Àlàáfíà – peace, good health
Aláàfin – title of the ruler of the old Oyo empire
Alfa – a Muslim cleric
Alhaja – title for a woman who has completed the *hajj* pilgrimage
Alhaji – title for a man who has completed the *hajj* pilgrimage
Àṣà – custom, tradition
Balógun – title for a war leader
Da'wa – proselytising or invitation to Islam
Ẹbí – immediate family (blood relations)
Ẹdẹ yàrá kan – Ede is one room
Egúngún – ancestor masquerade
Eid al-Fitr – Islamic festival, the celebration of completion of Ramadan
Eid al-Kabir or *Eid al-Adha* – Islamic festival, the celebration of Ibrahim's willingness to sacrifice Ishmael
Hajj – Islamic pilgrimage to Mecca
Hijab – Islamic head covering or veil
Ifá – the god of divination, also used to refer to divination itself
Ijtimā' – annual gathering of the Tablighi Jamaat
Ilé aiyé – the world
Iléyá – the Islamic festival of *Eid al-Kabir/Eid al-Adha* (the celebration of Ibrahim's willingness to sacrifice Ishmael)
Imam – Islamic cleric who leads congregational prayers
Ìmọ̀le – term for 'Muslim', sometimes perceived as slightly pejorative
Ipedi – festival to commemorate the founding of Ede and the Yam season

Ìyá Ṣàngó – priestess of Ṣàngó
khurūj – Tablighi Jamaat missionary tours
Markaz – Arabic word for 'centre', i.e. religious centre
Mọgbà – chief priest of Ṣàngó
Mọ̀lé – relatives or extended family
Ọba – king of a town
Ọbàtálá – an òrìṣà, the god of creation and the arch-divinity
Odò Ṣàngó – Ṣàngó's river
Ọdún – festival
Ògún – an òrìṣà, god of iron and war
Oníbàtá – bàtá drummer
Oríkì – oral praise or attributive poetry
Òrìṣà – any Yoruba deity
Ọ̀sun – an òrìṣà, the goddess of the river Ọsun
Ọya – an òrìṣà, the goddess of the river Niger and the wife of Ṣàngó
Ramadan – the Islamic month of fasting
Ṣalāt – Islamic prayer
Ṣalāt al-'aṣr – Islamic afternoon prayers
Ṣalāt al-jum'a – Islamic congregational Friday prayers
Ṣalāt al-zuhr – Islamic noon prayers
Ṣàngó – an òrìṣà, the god of thunder and lightning
Sharia – Islamic law
Shirk – Islamic term for the sin of idolatry, polytheism or associating others with God
Sunna – the practices of Prophet Muhammed
Tìmì – title of the ruler (ọba) of Ede
'Ulamā' – Islamic scholar
Umma – the global Islamic community
Wa'azi – open-air Islamic lectures
Zakat – Islamic annual obligatory payment for charity and religious purposes

CHAPTER 1

Beyond Religious Tolerance: Muslims, Christians and Traditionalists in a Yoruba Town

Insa Nolte and Olukoya Ogen

Since the end of the Cold War, and especially since September 2001, religion has been recognised as an increasingly important factor in personal and group identification and mobilisation. In a global environment increasingly dominated by economic neoliberalism, tensions between Islam and Christianity have become especially salient. However, a detailed understanding of the dynamics of religious conflict – and accommodation – is obscured by the overwhelming focus of analysts and commentators on the global North. In this context, attacks by Islamic groups and the perception and treatment of Muslim minorities in the culturally Christian societies in the US and Europe are often seen to confirm the existence of a 'faultline' between 'Western civilisations' and 'Islamic civilisations',[1] which has been transposed somewhat uncritically to different African contexts.[2] In this way, Africa is treated as little more than a 'reservoir of raw fact', which is made to fit the theories and truths produced on the basis of European and North American knowledge and praxis.[3]

But although the social and political transformations following the end of the Cold War reflected the politics of the global North, the complexity of their implications reveals itself more fully in the societies in the South. While Africa has its share of Muslim–Christian conflicts, not all religious violence on the continent takes place across a religious divide. In Uganda and neighbouring countries, the Christian Lord's Resistance Army has terrorised communities for many decades irrespective of religion. In the Sudan, the self-consciously

---

[1] S.P. Huntington, 'The clash of civilizations?', *Foreign Affairs* 72:3 (1993), 22–49.
[2] cf. E. Griswold, *The Tenth Parallel: Dispatches from the Faultline between Christianity and Islam* (London: Penguin Books, 2010).
[3] J. Comaroff and J. Comaroff, *Theory from the South or, How Euro-America is Evolving Toward Africa* (London and Boulder: Paradigm Publishers, 2012), p. 1.

Muslim Janjaweed militia has committed large-scale violence against co-religionists.[4] Similarly, Islamic insurgent groups in Mali and northern Nigeria have targeted fellow Muslims far more frequently than Christians and other non-Muslims.[5] While the implications of this phenomenon cannot be explored in detail here, the high incidence of intra-Muslim violence certainly challenges the notion that conflict is necessarily associated with religious difference.

But the opposite also applies: even in highly religious societies, religious difference is not necessarily associated with conflict. Thus Africa is also home to several states and regions where Muslims and Christians coexist without large-scale conflict. In South Africa, the country's liberal post-Apartheid Constitution has enabled a diverse Muslim minority to pursue religiously distinctive rights.[6] In West Africa, Muslims and Christians have sought insight and inspiration from debates about the merits and content of their respective religions in different contexts over the course of the twentieth century.[7] Although Ghanaian popular culture has been transformed by the growing influence of Pentecostalism,[8] mobilisation for conflict by Muslims or by Christians purely on the basis of religion alone is rare.[9] In the Yoruba-speaking south-west of Nigeria, including Ede, the town at the centre of this book, Muslims and Christians – and often smaller groups of traditional religionists[10] – also live closely together.

The intricate patterns of Muslim–Christian relations in Africa suggest that here, adaptation to the global changes is far more diverse than in Europe or North America, confirming the Comaroffs' suggestion that 'the history of the

---

[4] J. Haynes 'Religion, ethnicity and civil war in Africa: The cases of Uganda and Sudan', *The Round Table* 96:390 (2007), 305–17.

[5] A.R. Mustapha, ed., *Sects & Social Disorder: Muslim Identities & Conflict in Northern Nigeria* (Oxford: James Currey, 2014).

[6] G. Vahed and S. Jeppie, 'Multiple communities: Muslims in post-apartheid South Africa', *State of the Nation: South Africa 2004–2005*, ed. J. Daniel, R. Southall and J. Lutchman (Cape Town: HSRC Press, 2004), pp. 252–4.

[7] Lamin Sanneh, *Piety and Power: Muslims and Christians in West Africa* (Maryknoll, NY: Orbis Books, 1996).

[8] B. Meyer, '"Praise the Lord": Popular cinema and pentecostalite style in Ghana's new public sphere', *American Ethnologist* 31:1 (2004), 92–110.

[9] A. Langer, 'Situational importance of ethnicity and religion in Ghana', *Ethnopolitics* 9:1 (2010), 9–29.

[10] Given that traditional practice includes areas of social life that are excluded from the field of the religious in most areas of academic discourse, we use the term religion reluctantly. As important aspects of traditional practice are considered – and debated – as 'religious' in south-west Nigeria, it would however complicate matters unnecessarily to refuse this description. It is perhaps most useful to understand the 'religiousness' of traditional practice as cultural work in progress.

present reveals itself more starkly in the antipodes'.[11] It is therefore imperative to explore the wide range of Muslim-Christian relationships globally also from a Southern, and indeed African, vantage point. And while religious conflict in Africa deserves attention, it is equally important to study those contexts where different groups live with each other without resorting to large-scale violence. As Shobana Shankar's evocation of early Christianity in colonial northern Nigeria illustrates, the encounter between Muslims and Christians can inspire mutual fascination even where religious hierarchies are explicit and politically legitimated.[12] Similarly, Barbara Cooper's study of evangelical churches in Niger shows that even as Islam constrained Christianity, it also helped to define Christian practice and expression.[13] But only a study of successful Muslim–Christian coexistence can show the limits of existing approaches that understand religious difference as inherently problematic, and thus illustrate the possibilities for further reflection and theorising.

In the European context, relations between Muslims and Christians are often understood within the paradigm of tolerance, which has been theoretically developed by the German philosopher Rainer Forst. Forst sets out convincingly that tolerance, derived from the Latin *tolerare*, i.e. to countenance, endure or suffer, only applies with regard to practices seen as wrong or displeasing, but nonetheless considered acceptable. Tolerance is therefore aimed at practices located between that which is 'good' and therefore not in need of toleration, and that which is 'bad', and cannot be tolerated. Forst suggests that the spectrum of tolerance is complex and ranges from toleration by authoritarian permission at one end to toleration on the basis of mutual respect at the other.[14] All forms of toleration are normatively dependent, i.e. reflective of values and norms that define that which is to be tolerated. Aiming to produce mutually respectful dialogue, most academic (and non-academic) engagement with Muslim–Christian and interfaith relations therefore takes place at the liberal end of the tolerance spectrum.

Despite the limited amount of work on non-conflictual Muslim–Christian relations in Africa (and, with important exceptions, beyond[15]), the analytical limitations to approaches highlighting the existence of Muslims and Christians as distinct religious communities are obvious. Benjamin Soares points out that

---

[11] Comaroff and Comaroff, *Theory from the South*, p. 7.
[12] S. Shankar, *Who Shall Enter Paradise? Christian Origins in Muslim Northern Nigeria, ca. 1890–1975* (Athens OH: Ohio University Press, 2014).
[13] B. Cooper, *Evangelical Christians in the Muslim Sahel* (Bloomington and Indianapolis: Indiana University Press, 2006).
[14] R. Forst, 'The limits of toleration', *Constellations* 11:3 (2004), 315–16.
[15] cf. S. Bayly, *Saints, Goddesses and Kings: Muslims and Christians in South Indian Society, 1700–1900* (Cambridge: Cambridge University Press, 1989).

such studies struggle to take into account 'the broad range of ways in which Muslims and Christians have interacted with each other over time', because they assume stable religious boundaries and a static social order, which often do not exist in reality. Where African Muslims and Christians live side by side, they do more than tolerate each other: they reject, borrow and appropriate each other's practices, and sometimes they convert to each other's religions.[16] In such contexts, the subsumption of largely peaceful religious coexistence under the notion of tolerance obscures the multiple ways in which people engage with religions other than their own.

J.D.Y. Peel's pioneering study of the interplay between Christianity, Islam and traditional religion in Yorubaland emphasises that religious boundaries in south-west Nigeria crosscut ethnic and communal identities. Peel illustrates that both Islam and Christianity have made important contributions not only to Yoruba social life, language and dress, but also to Yoruba notions of community.[17] While his argument centres on the religions as coherent traditions rather than on their everyday mobilisation by individuals, occasional references to private practices are illuminating. Descriptions of the enthusiastic participation of Muslim guests in the celebration of the New Year in church and the participation of a Christian child in the early breakfast of his fasting Muslim relatives during Ramadan illustrate that exchanges between Muslims and Christians can extend beyond notions of tolerance to joyful, educational, or otherwise beneficial encounters and to different personal and interpersonal strategies and ambitions.[18]

By focusing on the town of Ede, albeit in the context of Yoruba history, politics and practice, this book illustrates in detail the social implications of religious pluralism in everyday life. But how individuals draw on the knowledge and experience of religions other than their own to navigate their lives, authority, gender and social identity more generally cannot be captured by a focus on one religious community alone. Presently, anthropological work on religion and social identity in Africa focuses on either Muslim or Christian societies. It tends to explore the importance of religion in the creation of social roles either in the context of conversion to a world religion or as an aspect of religious change or reform.[19] However, such approaches must also recognise

---

[16] B. Soares, 'Introduction: Muslim–Christian encounters in Africa', *Muslim–Christian Encounters in Africa*, ed. B. Soares (Leiden: Brill, 2006), pp. 1–16.

[17] J.D.Y. Peel, *Christianity Islam and Orisha Religion: Three Traditions in Comparison and Interaction* (Oakland CA: University of California Press: 2016), p. 12.

[18] Peel, *Christianity, Islam, and Orisha Religion*, p. 134.

[19] Exemplary studies of different approaches in this field include R. Loimeier, *Islamic Reform and Political Change in Northern Nigeria* (Evanston IL: Northwestern University Press, 1997); D. Maxwell, *African Gifts of the Spirit: Pentecostalism & the Rise*

Map 1 Ede in south-west Nigeria

that where members of different religions are intimately familiar with important aspects of each other's religions, meaning is created both by religious expression and by the absence of other forms of expression.

This book's focus on the different ways in which Ede's citizens put religion and religious difference to work resonates with Jane Guyer's argument that Yoruba societies actively foster and encourage their members' potential for originality and difference. She suggests that this reflects both the practical importance of adaptability and potentiality, and the moral and aesthetic

---

of a Zimbabwean Transnational Religious Movement (Oxford: James Currey, 2006); J.D.Y. Peel, *Religious Encounter and the Making of the Yoruba* (Bloomington: Indiana University Press, 2000).

pleasures associated with the creation of diverse life trajectories.[20] In the context of religious plurality, this implies that religious difference is valued in itself, as difference. Shaping the town beyond appearances at first glance, the religious diversity of Ede confirms the town's cosmopolitanism, attractiveness and complexity, conferring status both on the community as a whole and on its individual members.

1 The view over Ede from the south, towards palace, central mosque and river

Guyer's emphasis on the intrinsic value of multiplicity helps us explain not only the widespread acceptance of Ede's religious pluralism but also the fact that Ede's citizens manage and engage with religious difference in multiple ways, often depending on context. Thus different forms of traditionally legitimated authority in the town – especially ọbaship and the power of Ede's deity Ṣàngó – partly rely on the ability to transcend or even transgress religious boundaries (chapters 2–4). In such contexts, reference to tolerance, as the 'suffering' or acceptance of the other, obscures the fact that transcendence and transgression draw their symbolic and political power from difference.

Yet on a different scale, some extended families, associations or churches that define themselves as distinctly Muslim or Christian police their boundaries closely and try to limit the influence of religious others (chapters 5–7). Even in the ostensibly secular space of Ede's polytechnic, the management of

[20] J. Guyer, 'Traditions of invention in Equatorial Africa', *African Studies Review* 39:3 (1996), 1–28.

inter- and intra-faith relations is intrinsically linked to institutional authority (chapter 8). Here an engagement with how others are tolerated is helpful in understanding the degree to which religious boundaries are put to social use.

But as chapter 7 illustrates, the usefulness of the tolerance paradigm as an objective measure must take into account that toleration itself has its own competitive appeal: while Ede's Christians rely on the 'tolerance' of the predominantly Muslim townspeople, they assert their moral (and spiritual) superiority by exceeding their hosts in tolerance. Moreover, even as the coexistence of Muslims with traditionalists and Christians at the private level is sometimes conflictual, it enables individuals to navigate religious difference in the pursuit of individual ambitions (chapters 9–11). Private participation in multiple religions and mediation between different religions are linked to particular political or gendered identities, and therefore they clearly complicate notions of tolerance as forms of engagement based on abstract normative values.

As the chapters of this book offer an insight into the many ways in which both religion and religious difference are invested with social meaning 'beyond tolerance' in Ede, they offer a tentative and fluid categorisation at best. Where we, and other authors of this book, are drawn towards macro-sociological arguments in order to step back from the complexity of local practice and debate, such arguments do not imply the existence of a stable social order based on clear categories of religious practice. This is perhaps best illustrated by the different roles played by religion in Ede's Muslim compounds (chapter 5) and in the locally prominent Adeleke family (chapter 9). Here individual chapters, read in the wider context of the book, illustrate that engagement with religion at different levels of social practice reflects a capacity for creative adaptation and ongoing change.

Importantly, the personal navigation of a shifting and complex religious landscape is not primarily driven by an instrumental engagement with religion. While not all citizens of Ede consider religion equally important (chapter 8), it is more than a categorical identity or an ideological tool. But just as religion is not 'a message about something else', it is not primarily a site of action in the realm of the political either.[21] Most people engage with religion as a frame of reference that enables individuals to understand, manage and recast their relationships with others, but also with themselves and the truth. Thus personal engagements with the religious enable – and perhaps require – a high degree of both self-examination and recognition of others.[22] As all

---

[21] R. Marshall, *Political Spiritualities: The Pentecostal Revolution in Nigeria* (Chicago and London: University of Chicago Press, 2009), p. 5.
[22] C. Taylor, *Sources of the Self: The Making of the Modern Identity* (Cambridge: Cambridge University Press, 1992).

our chapters illustrate, religious practices in Ede are intricately bound up with social hierarchies and political agency, but they are also mobilised in earnest debates about the meaning of life.

Despite Ede's clear Muslim majority, then, Ede is a religiously plural town both because it is home to a multiplicity of religious practices, and because the difference between the religions takes on very different forms and meanings. In some contexts, an emphasis on religious boundaries is strong and sustained, in others it is fleeting, and in others the importance of celebrating and transcending religious difference is emphasised. The complexity of these meanings is condensed in the local proverb, '*Ẹdẹ yàrá kan ni*,' meaning 'Ede is one room'. Often used to remind quarrelling or complaining parties to consider the other side's interest, the proverb suggests that Ede constitutes a community both *despite* and *because of* its religious diversity.

The next two sections of this introduction bring in two discussions relevant to this book, namely the study of religious multiplicity and coexistence, and debates about Yoruba Islam. The final part of the introduction includes an overview of Ede's religious landscape as local context for the following chapters, a description of the genesis of this book, and a short outlook.

Religious Encounter and Pluralism in Yorubaland

The Yoruba validation of multiplicity and difference has historical roots both in religious and in political practice. In 1939 the sociologist N.A. Fadipe described traditional Yoruba religious practice as a 'veritable welter of objects of worship apportioned out among individuals and extended-families on no very clearly defined principles'.[23] In addition to the worship of ancestors, many deities – locally known as *òrìṣà* – are linked either to natural phenomena (hills, rivers, thunder) or to important personalities. However, categories of divine beings are loosely defined. Thus, *òrìṣà* also include material objects such as royal crowns or, in the case of *orí*, the worshipper's own fate (literally, her or his own head). Even the deities themselves often exist in loosely defined conceptual categories, such that a deity that is male in one context can be female in another.[24]

Although the complex and fluid web of ancestors, deities and other spiritual forces does not reflect a hierarchical or clearly categorised cosmology, it

---

[23] N.A. Fadipe, *The Sociology of the Yoruba* (Ibadan: Ibadan University Press, 1970 [1939]), p. 261.

[24] J.D.Y. Peel, 'A comparative analysis of Ogun in precolonial Yorubaland', *Africa's Ogun: Old World and New*, ed. Sandra T. Barnes, 2nd edn (Bloomington: Indiana University Press, 1997), pp. 263–89.

is nonetheless understood as part of a greater system of belief. The very multiplicity of the divine is brought together and celebrated in the *Ifá* divination system. Based on the understanding that all events have roots and precedents in the past, *Ifá* offers guidance in the present by accessing a large oral corpus of stories, songs and riddles about gods, spirits and cultural heroes, all of which are anchored in past divinations. Assuming the position of a mediator between human beings and spiritual forces, *Ifá*'s advice to its patrons often includes suggestions about the deities and cults they should worship.[25] While the long presence of Islam in West Africa has likely influenced the shape of *Ifá*,[26] Islam (and more recently Christianity) also appears explicitly in its corpus. Thus, when the pattern called *Odù Òtura Méjì*, also known as *Odù Ìmọ̀le* or *Odù* of Muslims, appears during the divination held for a newborn child, this child should be brought up as a Muslim.[27] As the early history of Islam in Ede illustrates, this link between *Ifá* and Islam contributed both to the spread and the legitimacy of Islam (chapters 2 and 3).[28]

Like *Ifá*, the spiritual power of Yoruba kings, or ọbas, is associated with their ability to stand above the many spiritual practices within the town. In historical Yoruba discourse, ọbas are understood as the founders or conquerors of towns. The emergence of centralised urban settlements is therefore inextricably linked to ọbaship.[29] Political power tended to be anchored in the spiritual, and ọbas, established their political superiority partly by emphasising their independence from local cults. But at the same time, as long as land for new settlements remained available, the rulers of Yoruba towns could not prevent the emigration of disenfranchised groups and individuals from their towns. Because the inability to maintain consent among a diverse population could lead to the decline or death of a community, rulers needed to acknowledge the

---

[25] W.R. Bascom, *Ifa Divination: Communication between Gods and Men in West Africa* (Bloomington: Indiana University Press, 1969), pp. 11–12.

[26] L. Brenner, 'Muslim divination and the history of religion of Sub-Saharan Africa', *Insight and Artistry in African Divination*, ed. J. Pemberton III (Washington and London: Smithsonian Institution Press, 2000), pp. 45–59.

[27] T.G.O. Gbadamosi, '"Odu Imale": Islam in Ifa divination and the case of predestined Muslims', *Journal of the Historical Society of Nigeria* 8:4 (1977), 77–93.

[28] For a more detailed presentation of the argument presented in this paragraph, see I. Nolte 'Spirit: Histories of religion and the Word', *West Africa: Cultures of the Word*, ed. G. Casely-Hayford, J. Topp Fargion and M. Wallace (London: British Library, 2015), pp. 48–71.

[29] P.C. Lloyd, 'Yoruba myths: A sociologist's interpretation', *Odù: Journal of Yoruba and Related Studies* 2 (1955), 20–8.

validity of local practices.³⁰ Addressing the town both as a collectivity and as a locus of difference, ọbas were (and remain) recognised as the 'heads' of all religions. This claim represents both an ideology of power that projects the ọba's authority over all sections of the community, and a reminder of the need to respect, and even empathise with, all those who share in its making.³¹

2 The royal palace of Ede

Below the level of ọbaship, the validation of diversity and difference remains important for men and women who hold positions of power within society. While such leaders may be strict regarding their own religious adherence, they are aware that actions perceived as violent or as discriminating against others tend not to attract popular support beyond the short term (cf. chapters 2 and 6). The widely shared ethos of diversity is closely linked to an appreciation of enlightened progress, or ọ̀làjú. As Peel has argued, ọ̀làjú is associated with different forms of knowledge, but it is perhaps most strongly associated with education and trade or other links to the world beyond the town. Emphasising

---

³⁰ For a more detailed description and analysis of these processes, see E. Renne, *Population and Progress in a Yoruba Town* (Edinburgh: Edinburgh University Press, 2003), pp. 26–39; and I. Nolte, *Obafemi Awolowo and the Making of Remo: The Local Politics of a Nigerian Nationalist* (Edinburgh: Edinburgh University Press for the International Africa Institute, 2009), pp. 58–88.

³¹ cf. I. Nolte, 'Transformations of the customary: Christianity, Islam and traditional rulers in Yorubaland, Nigeria', *Chiefship and the Customary in Contemporary Africa*, ed. J. Comaroff and J. Comaroff (Bloomington: Indiana University Press, forthcoming).

the importance and moral value of carefully considered choice, ọ̀làjú reflects the ability to locate the self, and one's own community, in the context of wider networks of knowledge and practice in order to increase one's own power and wellbeing.[32] Thus ọ̀làjú shapes agency both at the political and at the private level, because it offers an understanding of 'otherness' not as a threat but as a potential resource.

Certainly the openness towards others associated with *Ifá*, and the emphasis on consent and ọ̀làjú, helped the establishment of Islam and later Christianity in Yorubaland. In many towns the first arrival of Islam is associated with protection or healing through prayer.[33] As Muslim communities expanded, they were usually organised at the town level under the leadership of a Chief Imam. T.G.O. Gbadamosi explains that like a Yoruba ọba, the Chief Imam held a life-long office of religious as well as political significance, in which he would not only lead the community in prayer but also resolve disputes between different factions of the (Muslim) community. Often the chief imam was drawn into the circles that advised the ọba, enabling Yoruba Muslims to maintain a close engagement with town politics and civic life.[34] While Muslim scholars seldom took traditional offices, all communities appreciated the contribution of Muslim rulers to the cause of Islam. Beyond the town, Muslims offered ọ̀làjú by linking the town to wider Muslim networks in Nigeria, West Africa and the world.

The early links between education, modernity and mission Christianity in Yorubaland meant that Christianity was associated with forms of orientation that transcended town politics. As most converts were attracted to Christianity through the establishment of local schools, they became part of the community of their individual mission churches and the wider networks formed by literacy and education. Early Christian converts often acted as cultural brokers between Europeans and local culture. Drawing on the vast archive of local practices and traditions, they imagined and confirmed a Yoruba nation that could stand in opposition to European culture.[35] Building on enlightenment values within the European tradition as well the local appreciation of ọ̀làjú,

---

[32] J.D.Y. Peel, 'Olaju: A Yoruba concept of development', *The Journal of African Studies* 2 (1978), 139–65.

[33] I. Adebayo, 'The role of traditional rulers in the Islamization of Osun State (Nigeria)', *Journal for Islamic Studies* 30 (2010), 60–77.

[34] T.G.O. Gbadamosi, *The Growth of Islam among the Yoruba, 1841–1908* (London: Longman, 1978), pp. 5–6, 37–8.

[35] K. Barber, 'Discursive strategies in the texts of Ifá and in the "Holy Book of Odù" of the African Church of Òrúnmìlà', *Self-Assertion and Brokerage: Early Cultural Nationalism in West Africa*, ed. K. Barber and P.F. de Moraes Farias (Birmingham: Birmingham University African Studies Series, 1990), pp. 196–224.

the imagination of the Yoruba nation relied on widely shared values to transcend the town level.[36]

The Yoruba encounter between Islam, Christianity, and local spiritual and political practices has inspired a number of distinct scholarly arguments. While David Laitin's study of Ile-Ife highlights the differences between Yoruba Muslims and Christians, he argues that these are subsumed under more important forms of local belonging, both to the hometown and to the Yoruba (ethnic) nation. However, his suggestion that while religious cleavages are real, other forms of belonging and identification primarily reflect colonial manipulation, simply does not ring true.[37] As Wale Adebanwi has convincingly demonstrated, the notion of a Yoruba culture has certainly been subject to political and other forms of manipulation. However, this has only been possible because Yorubaness remains crucial to Yoruba self-perception and political agency.[38]

Peel's analysis of the historical encounter between mission Christianity and the Yoruba illustrates that beyond providing the spark for the imagination of the modern Yoruba nation, the introduction of Christianity offered converts a complex perspective on local traditional practices, which could be understood either as culture or as religion. While the 'making of the Yoruba', led by the region's educated elite, privileged the former, the growing importance of religion since the 1970s and 1980s has also encouraged more negative views of traditional practice.[39] This is exemplarily highlighted in a more recent study of Yoruba religious interaction by Jacob Olupona, who explores the pressures of the two monotheist religions on the adaptation and reform of traditional practices.[40]

Taking up the imperative to consider all three religious practices in the Yoruba context, Peel's most recent book focuses on the relationship between Christianity, Islam and traditional practice. Emphasising the importance of both Muslim and Christian contributions to the making of community in Yorubaland, Peel suggests that conversion to the monotheist religions was compatible with the Yoruba belief that order existed within diversity, as expressed in the logic of *Ifá*. Tracing appropriations and adaptations that

---

[36] J.D.Y. Peel, *Religious Encounter and the Making of the Yoruba* (Bloomington: Indiana University Press, 2000).

[37] D.D. Laitin, *Hegemony and Culture: Politics and Religious Change among the Yoruba* (Chicago and London: University of Chicago Press, 1986).

[38] W. Adebanwi, *Yorùbá Elites and Ethnic Politics in Nigeria: Ọbáfẹmi Awólowo and Corporate Agency* (Cambridge: Cambridge University Press, 2014).

[39] Peel, *Religious Encounter*.

[40] J. Olupona, *City of 201 Gods: Ilé-Ifẹ̀ in Time, Space, and the Imagination* (Berkeley: University of California Press, 2011).

have transformed Yoruba Islam and Christianity over the twentieth century, he argues convincingly that the monotheist religions are shaped both by their own foundational practices, texts and traditions of interpretation, and by the cultural context in which they are realised.[41] Peel's magisterial study provides the context and foil for our own study of the cultural embedment of religion in Ede.

Importantly, the study of religious coexistence and multiplicity in Ede shifts the primary point of view away from the cultural realisation of religion and instead illustrates how the existence of these religions is put to work in one particular locality. In Ede, the emphasis on strict adherence and clear boundaries and distinctions in some contexts challenges the suggestion, sometimes implicit in the focus on larger patterns visible at the ethno-regional level, that because the practice of Islam and Christianity was included into a framework that celebrated diversity, it was subject to processes of processes of 'blending', i.e. the incorporation of non-Muslim or non-Christian practices. While critics of such approaches have pointed out that the implicit assertion of the existence of 'pure' forms of religion is normative rather than objective and reflects a Western bias towards belief rather than practice,[42] this book also avoids such assessments because they privilege the study of Islam and Christianity as clearly circumscribed practices.

In the context of Ede, the realisation of both monotheist religions takes numerous, and sometimes contradictory, forms. Thus the ability of Yoruba ọbas and òrìṣà to transcend religious difference contrasts with the grassroots practices through which Ede's Muslims tolerate Christians (and vice versa) in other social contexts, and with the bridging of religious gaps in mixed-religious families, in marriage and in friendships. While such forms may be locally discussed in terms of 'mixing' or 'blending', this book explores such discourses in the context of social reproduction and meaning-making. Illustrating that the religious life of a Yoruba town is shaped both by strict adherence to religion in some contexts, and by the transgression, transcendence and mediation of religious boundaries in other contexts, this book emphasises that both forms of engagement with the other – tolerance and practices beyond tolerance – have multiple meanings. The drawing of clear religious boundaries is not a denial but a recognition of the religious agency of others, and transgression or transcendence do not imply that religious boundaries do not matter: in fact,

---

[41] Peel, *Christianity, Islam, and Orisha Religion*.

[42] cf. A. Talal, 'Anthropological conceptions of religion: Reflections on Geertz', *Man* 18:2 (1983), 237–59; and R. McCutcheon, 'The category "religion" in recent publications: A critical survey', *Numen* 42:3 (1995), 284–309.

the agency that derives from such practices is only meaningful as long as religious boundaries exist.

Studying Yoruba Islam among Ede's Muslims

By focusing on a predominantly Muslim town, this book addresses the study of Yoruba Islam; a topic that has been shockingly under-researched. Most research on Islam in the region has been focused on northern Nigeria. And despite the significant presence of Islam in south-west Nigeria, most research on Yoruba religion has concentrated on the Yoruba deities, the complex *Ifá* divination system,[43] and Christianity.[44] While some scholarly attention has focused on the Yoruba town of Ilorin,[45] Yoruba Islam outside of Ilorin has only attracted limited research.[46]

T.G.O. Gbadamosi, the only historian to produce a book on Islam that does not centre primarily on Ilorin, discusses the emergence of the Muslim community at the town level. He suggests that the inclusion of the chief imam into the traditional hierarchy in most Yoruba towns reflects a permeation of Islam by 'Oyo [Yoruba] custom'.[47] This description has been taken up by other authors, and Islam in south-west Nigeria is often described as having been subject to a 'Yorubacisation'.[48] This assessment is problematic both because it suggests that there is such a thing as a 'pure' Islam, and because it assigns ontological

---

[43] For Ifá, see W.R. Bascom, *Ifa Divination: Communication between Gods and Men in West Africa* (Bloomington: Indiana University Press, 1969); W. Abimbola, *Ifa: An Exposition of Ifa Literary Corpus* (Ibadan: Oxford University Press, 1976).

[44] Outstanding examples include J.A. Ajayi, *Christian Missions in Nigeria, 1841–1891: The Making of a New Elite* (London: Longman, 1965); H. Turner, *History of an African Independent Church: The Church of the Lord (Aladura)* (Oxford: Clarendon Press, 1967); and Peel, *Religious Encounter*.

[45] S. Reichmuth, *Islamische Bildung und soziale Integration in Ilorin (Nigeria) seit ca. 1800* (Münster: LIT Verlag, 1998).

[46] The most widely read texts on Yoruba Islam are Gbadamosi, *The Growth of Islam among the Yoruba*; and P. Clarke, *Mahdism in West Africa: The Ijebu Mahdiyya Movement* (New York: Weatherhill Incorporated, 1995). For a contextualised discussion of Islam in Ibadan politics and Igboho ritual practice respectively see K. Post and G. Jenkins, *The Price of Liberty: Personality and Politics in Colonial Nigeria* (Cambridge: Cambridge University Press, 1973), and J.L. Matory, 'Rival empires: Islam and the religions of spirit possession among the Ọ̀yọ́-Yorùbá', *American Ethnologist* 21:3 (1994), 495–515.

[47] Gbadamosi, *Growth of Islam among the Yoruba*, p. 6.

[48] See Laitin, *Hegemony and Culture*, p. 41. This term is also quoted in H.O. Danmole, 'Religious encounter in southwestern Nigeria: The domestication of Islam among the Yorùbá', *Òrìṣà Devotion as World Religion: The Globalization of Yorùbá Religious Culture*, ed. J.K. Olupona and T. Rey (Madison: University of Wisconsin Press, 2007), pp. 202–17: 205–6.

primacy to a non-religious 'Oyoness' or 'Yorubaness' without exploring in what ways conversion to Islam has itself shaped Oyo and Yoruba practices.

Beyond academia, such views sometimes find expression in engagements between northern and southern Nigerian Muslims. Rivalry between northern Nigerian and Yoruba Muslims has a root in historical conflict. When the jihadist Sokoto Caliphate expanded southwards from northern Nigeria during the first half of the nineteenth century, it contributed to the collapse of the powerful Oyo Empire and the destruction of many of its towns. While the Yoruba town of Ilorin became part of the Caliphate, most Yoruba Muslims converted only after the local defeat of the Caliphate's (Ilorin) armies in the battle of Osogbo in 1838. As the experience of Ilorin remained both exceptional and subject to resentment from the rest of Yorubaland, it is certainly possible that the conflict between Ilorin and the rest of Yorubaland played a role in the widespread adoption of Islam as a predominantly private religion in southwest Nigeria.[49]

However, the fact that (apart from Ilorin), Yoruba towns did not adopt Islamic structures does not mean that Muslims were unable to draw distinctions between themselves and non-Muslims. As explained in chapter 5, the creation of explicitly Muslim compounds enabled Ede's Muslims to live largely separately from non-Muslims. Important especially in Oyo towns like Ede, where Islam has played a significant role since the nineteenth century, compounds are large areas or sections of the town, often populated by many hundreds of people, which belong to, and are controlled by, extended families or lineages. As forms of corporate identity beyond the town level, compound leaders play a central role in facilitating access to land and housing, and also in town politics. The social and religious lives of compound members tend to be shaped by the compound's history and leadership. As the existence of different Muslim compounds illustrates, the compound system also accommodated the existence of difference within the Muslim community.

Additionally, many Yoruba Muslims explain their ability to coexist with non-Muslims with reference to Surah 109 (al-Kāfirūn), which is understood as legitimating the existence of religions other than Islam, and as allowing Muslims to live in non-Islamic societies and communities. Such interpretations resonate with the Islamic tradition of the late fifteenth-century Malian scholar *Alhaji* Salim Suwari, whose influence extended across West Africa.[50] As there is some evidence for contact between Yorubaland and Mali, the

---

[49] Gbadamosi, *Growth of Islam among the Yoruba*, pp. 1–110.
[50] R. Launay, *Beyond the Stream: Islam and Society in a West African Town* (Berkeley: University of California Press, 1992).

Suwarian influence may have extended to this area either directly or indirectly.[51] Equally, Yoruba practices may reflect more general West African Islamic traditions of peaceful coexistence with non-Muslims.[52]

Even so, the example of the Emirate of Ilorin illustrates that, if such non-conflictual traditions shaped Yoruba Islam, they coexisted with more forceful visions of Islam. And as Ilorin was a centre of learning that attracted many Yoruba Muslims, any suggestion of a clear separation between Ilorin and other Yoruba interpretations of Islam seems artificial. In the history of Ede, both seem to have a place. Chapters 2 and 3 of this book describe the violent transformations associated with the introduction of Islam to Ede under *Tìmì* Abibu Lagunju (1847–1900), who had converted to Islam in Ilorin, as well as the eventual lack of political support for his Muslim grandson who lost the contest over the throne of Ede to the town's first and only Christian ruler, *Tìmì* John Adetoyese Laoye (1946–75).

Today, doctrinal differences certainly exist and reflect the ongoing appropriation, construction and deconstruction of Islamic trends and debates by groups and individuals engaging in meaningful attempts to take control of their lives and make practical sense of their world.[53] As chapters 5 to 9 especially illustrate, as in other parts of Africa, Muslim debates and disagreements in Ede reveal 'multiple ways' of 'being Muslim',[54] transcending the stereotypical dichotomy between Sufism or and reformist Islam.[55] As a result, intra-Muslim harmony remains an ongoing project, produced both through communally shared practices and through engagement, and competition, with religious others.

Inspired both by West African Islamic intellectual traditions and the competition with mission-educated Christians, many Yoruba Muslims embraced a modernist and enlightened Islam. The great value placed by Yoruba Muslims on Western as well as Arabic education during the twentieth century is likely to have contributed to the fact that relations between Yoruba Muslims and Christians have remained peaceful overall. Even though the introduction of

---

[51] However we disagree with J.D.Y. Peel, who suggests that Yoruba Islam has been exclusively shaped by the Suwarian tradition. Peel, *Christianity, Islam, and Orisa Religion*, p. 170.

[52] R.T. Ware, *The Walking Qur'an: Islamic Education, Embodied Knowledge, and History in West Africa* (Chapel Hill NC: University of Carolina Press, 2014), p. 89.

[53] See for example J.S. Schielke and L. Debevec, eds., *Ordinary Lives and Grand Schemes: An Anthropology of Everyday Religion* (Oxford and New York: Berghahn, 2012).

[54] A. Masquelier, *Women and Islamic Revival in a West African Town* (Bloomington: Indiana University Press, 2009).

[55] M. Mamdani, *Good Muslim, Bad Muslim: America, the Cold War, and the Roots of Terror* (New York: Pantheon, 2004).

Western education was often conflictual because it was linked to Christian conversion, Muslims caught up by building their own schools (cf. chapters 3, 7). As the provision of education was also emphasised by several leading Yoruba politicians, Yoruba Muslims and Christians today share the understanding that learning is an important aspect of both individual spirituality and collective self-assertion.

But importantly, religion is also understood as a central form of knowledge and ọ̀làjú. Possibly also because of the relative importance of Christian schooling for older generations, many Muslims are familiar with the Bible, and some Muslims use the Bible in order to illustrate the universal nature of Islam to both Muslims and non-Muslims. At the same time, learned Muslims continue to draw authority explicitly from the intellectual and physical efforts associated with the study of the Qur'an and other Islamic texts in Arabic. It is a source of great pride to many Ede Muslims that the Islamic scholarship of several of their townspeople has been recognised outside of Ede. Perhaps most emblematic of this appreciation of knowledge is the career of the town's late *Alhaji* Daud Adekilekun Tijani (1942–2006), whose attainments in Islamic and Western education enabled him to become a lecturer in the Arabic and Islamic Studies Department of the University of Ibadan as well as the university's Chief Imam.[56]

Ede's Pluralist Religious Landscape

Ede's religious topography illustrates the different spaces occupied by Islam, Christianity and traditional practice. At the heart of the town is the central market place over which the town's Muslim ruler, HRM *Tìmì* Muniru Adesola Lawal, presides. Next to the market place is the *Tìmì*'s palace, faced across the market place by the town's majestic central mosque. Public and private mosques can be seen from the roads and footpaths leading from the centre to the town's different quarters, which house Muslim schools as well as a Muslim hospital in prominent locations.

By contrast, most churches and Christian schools are located in the newer parts of the town. Beyond the town proper, but still on Ede land, the state-owned polytechnic has been joined by two private Christian universities, and recently by a planned Muslim institution. Only a deeper knowledge of the town reveals the enduring presence of the Yoruba traditional deities or òrìṣà: hidden from public view behind the royal palace and in special rooms of their owners' compounds and houses for most of the year, they transform

---

[56] Interview with *Alhaji* Ibraheem Tijani Dende Adekilekun, Chief Imam of Ansar-Ud-Deen Society, Ede. 17 April 2012. Ile Imole, Ede.

3 The central mosque of Ede

Ede, and even its central mosque, on festival days. This topography reflects not only the apparent dominance of Islam, but also the important roles played by Christianity and traditional practices in Ede.

Only a century and a half ago, the vast majority of people in Ede sought attainment for themselves and their communities through links to Ògún, Ṣàngó or one of the many other local deities or òrìṣà, and they turned to Ifá divination to prepare for the future. Understanding the material and the spiritual as closely entwined, the religious was inseparable from local economic, social and political institutions. However, the dramatic rise of Islam (and to a lesser degree Christianity) in Ede since the nineteenth century does not mean an equal reduction of traditional practice. As Lorand Matory has pointed out, initiates of the òrìṣà priesthoods have always been a relatively small section of the population even as their worship and celebration was part of everyday life.[57] This has helped to legitimise the enduring appeal of the òrìṣà as 'culture' (chapter 11). The town's prominent forms of traditional practice remain deeply embedded in its historical institutions, and especially that of its ọba. Whether the Tìmì is a Muslim or a Christian, he is also the 'owner' of the town's deity Ṣàngó.

Despite the large and complex verbal and symbolic repertoire of Ede's Ṣàngó worshippers (chapter 4), a comparison of present-day practice with Ulli Beier's vibrant description of the regular celebration of traditional festivals in

---

[57] Matory, 'Rival empires', p. 499.

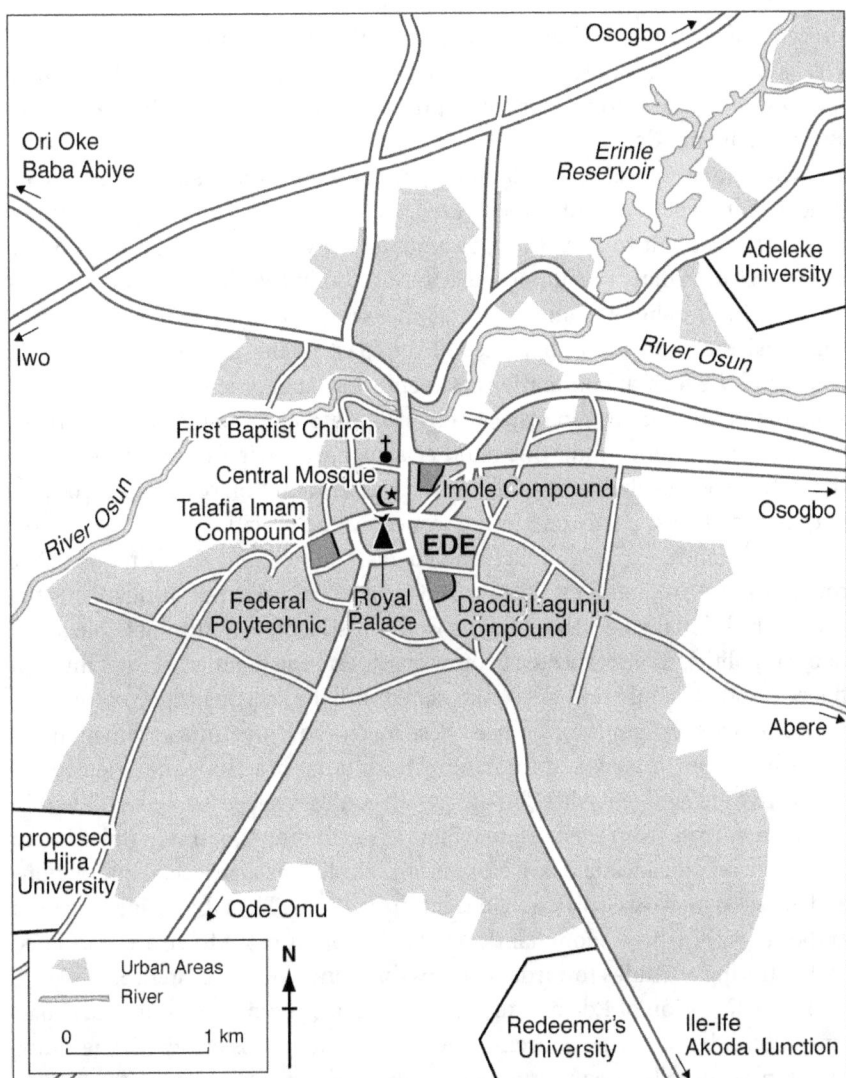

Map 2 The town of Ede

1959 suggests that the celebration of traditionalist events in Ede has declined.[58] In some Yoruba towns traditional practice is of little importance today, but in many others a younger generation has revitalised traditional worship. In Ede's neighbouring town of Osogbo, the celebration of the annual festival of the deity *Òsun* draws large numbers of national and international visitors. But

---

[58] See U. Beier, *A Year of Sacred Festivals in One Yoruba Town*, ed. D.W. MacRow (Lagos: Nigeria Magazine Special Publication, 1959).

present-day practice in Ede may at least partly be linked to the fact that Chief Oyebanji Sangodokun, the town's senior priest of the royal deity of Ṣàngó, is a very senior man who was already a prominent worshipper at the time of Ulli Beier's visits to Ede.

While some of Ede's Muslims emphasise Islam's aversion to polytheist practices in order to reduce the presence of the town's traditional deities or òrìṣà, others point to Surah 109, mentioned above, to argue that it would be disrespectful to deny the importance of the òrìṣà in the history of the town. As a result, Ede's religious landscape includes forms of practice which, through their insistence on the importance of the 'past in the present',[59] obscure or transcend the formal boundaries between traditional practice and Islam (and sometimes Christianity) in order to ensure communal wellbeing. While these religions do not encounter one another as equals, their shared concern over the rightful acknowledgement of the past reflects a notion of religious coexistence based at least partly on mutual respect or reciprocity.

In addition to explicitly religious debates, the religious dispositions of the town's leaders frequently reflect institutional roles and expectations. Thus the town's traditional ruler, the *Tìmì*, as well as its leading traditional chiefs and popular politicians are expected to draw on widespread popular consent through their extended social networks.[60] Associated with the representation of the community beyond religious difference, these men (and, sometimes, women) often argue in favour of an Islam tolerant of traditional practices and open to the productive engagement with Christianity. In contrast, those whose status within the town derives from their Islamic identity, including the town's Chief Imam and other religious leaders, are often more selective in their social interactions and insist on more exclusive religious interpretations. Thus the various forms of authority within the predominantly Muslim hierarchy of the town are associated with differing attitudes towards religious difference and coexistence.

The delineation of Ede as a unified Muslim community is potentially challenged both by Christian churches and by Muslim groups critical of the status quo. Linked closely to communities of fellow believers beyond the town, such groups emphasise the importance of personal belief and practice rather than the town's overall wellbeing. But as the wider networks on which especially Christian groups draw also enable them to establish local institutions, particularly schools and institutions of higher education, the negotiation of institutional practice both forces and enables them to participate in the social and political life of the town. As the continued Christian dominance of such resources both suggests

---

[59] J.D.Y. Peel, 'Making history: The past in the Ijesha present', *Man* 19:1 (1984), 111–32.
[60] For a discussion of the importance of consent in Yoruba local politics, see Nolte, *Obafemi Awolowo and the Making of Remo*.

alternative notions of community and confirms the importance of the town, the ongoing competition between Christianity and Islam reflects a multiplicity of local hierarchies of belonging and ownership (chapters 2, 7).

The fact that most of Ede's indigenes are Muslims puts Christians at a disadvantage when it comes to public activities or to finding land for churches and religious institutions. But the practices by which Christian agency is limited are not considered wrong in themselves: it is generally accepted that the town's old families control the use of public places as well as the sale (and sometimes use) of land, especially in the heart of the town. In towns with an almost exclusively Christian identity, for example in Ondo and Okitipupa in eastern Yorubaland, Christians might behave in a similar way. Moreover, outside the town centre, Ede's Christians have been highly successful in building churches and even setting up two Christian universities (chapter 9). As a result it would be misleading to discuss the limits placed on Ede's Christians in the context of tolerance: rather than understanding the Christian disadvantage in Ede as the result of rejection of Christianity, it is perhaps more usefully understood as reflecting concerns about the religion's symbolic presence.

A comparison of Ede with other towns shows that Ede experienced a particularly early and dramatic Islamisation, and as such the limitation of Christianity in the town may partly reflect an exceptionally strong shared commitment to an Islamic identity for the town. Like Ede, nearby towns such as Iwo and Ikirun were religiously transformed by nineteenth-century Islamic rulers, but many other predominantly Muslim towns adopted Islam more gradually. The presence of Christian churches and schools in central locations in other Oyo towns suggests that in towns with a slower conversion process and fewer exclusively Muslim compounds, Christians have found it easier to assert their presence at the heart of the town.

The spatial control of Christianity in Ede also contrasts with practices in most of Lagos and Ibadan, where such localised forms of religious control have been undermined by rapid population growth. In some sections of these cities, the large number of immigrants has meant that original landholding families lost control over the use of land or public spaces. It is therefore likely that the greater success of Christianity in both cities owes something to those cities' greater commodification and anonymity. But it is also possible that the appeal of Pentecostal Christianity, which often emphasises the need to break with the past,[61] is more convincing in the context of migrant communities in Lagos and Ibadan than in the more conservative environment of Ede.

---

[61] B. Meyer, '"Make a complete break with the past." Memory and post-colonial modernity in Ghanaian Pentecostalist discourse', *Journal of Religion in Africa* 28:3 (1998), 316–49.

Belonging is also an important distinction at the compound level, where the importance of local family networks for the establishment of Christian communities has led to the slow growth of churches associated with immigrants and the success of unusual forms of worship linked to local leaders, such as the prayer mountain Ori-Oke Baba Abiye of the Christ Apostolic Church established by Oladeji Akande or Baba Abiye (chapters 5, 7). But as in the town more generally, outsiders coming into a compound – whether as wives, tenants or visitors – must recognise the rights of the compound leaders to determine the use of public and private spaces. In self-consciously Islamic compounds, this means that the religious self-expression of non-Muslim outsiders, especially Christians, is often limited. But again, such practices do not reflect an abstract or general judgement of Christianity, but simply the concern that it would be, for want of a better expression, expressed in the wrong place.

Muslim–Christian relations at the town and compound level contrast with those in the Federal Polytechnic of Ede, where the staff manages and controls Muslims and Christians groups of students. But the association of religion with hierarchical relationships between staff and students stands at odds with the institution's existence as an apparently secular centre of knowledge production. The treatment of Muslims and Christians as equal religious groups highlights differences between more and less intensely religious individuals, which in other contexts rarely appear relevant (chapter 8).

At the individual level, religion is primarily experienced as a site of personal practice and activity.[62] As a result, the engagement with religious difference is clearly shaped by considerations of status, and especially age and gender (chapter 10). In the context of corporate family life, conversion and inter-faith marriage therefore often first appear as a challenge to a person's elders and especially their extended family or patrilineage. However, such choices become more acceptable when the individuals who made them fulfil important social responsibilities, such as the continuation of the family through childbirth. As women carry the burden of both social and religious mediation between families linked through inter-religious marriages, religious difference is often resolved through the wife's conversion to the religion of her husband. While this does not always happen, the notion that the husband – irrespective of religion – holds religious authority over his wife indicates that the experience of religious difference at the personal level is strongly shaped by gendered expectations of marriage and familial position. Thus, while friendship and collaboration with members of other religions is a part of ordinary life for

---

[62] M.B. McGuire, *Lived Religion: Faith and Practice in Everyday Life* (Oxford: Oxford University Press, 2008).

most citizens of Ede (chapter 11), these encounters are predicated upon the social differences implicit in the ostensibly natural hierarchies of everyday life.

As the engagement with religious difference is associated with the sometimes contrasting pressures of leadership, belonging and status, there is no exclusive way in which Ede's citizens negotiate their coexistence. Drawing on dispositions associated with a range of social fields, ranging from institutional leadership roles to the control and membership of corporate social groups and the interpersonal hierarchies of everyday life, Ede's citizens have at their command a multiplicity of repertoires for confrontation as well as cooperation and conciliation. Transcending boundaries between the private and the public, personal disagreements with members of other religions are sometimes interpreted in the light of the perceived position of their religion in the town. But at the same time, a group's sense of grievance over another's perceived transgression is often diffused with reference to the burdens shouldered, and achievements attained, by them.[63] While religious difference is clearly often linked to potentially conflicting interests, it is perhaps the openness of this repertoire to emotional moments of solidarity that has enabled the successful coexistence of Ede's different religions so far.[64]

The Genesis of this Book

This book arose out of work for a larger research project funded by the European Research Council (ERC) as a Starting Researcher Grant awarded to Insa Nolte. Under the title 'Knowing Each Other: Everyday Religious Encounters, Social Identities and Tolerance in Southwest Nigeria', this project focuses on the reasons for the relatively peaceful coexistence of Islam, Christianity and traditional practice in the Yoruba-speaking parts of Nigeria. The project investigates in what way the existence of religious difference, and in particular the practices associated with peaceful religious coexistence, is linked to particular social identities.

The project relies strongly on historical and anthropological methodologies, but in order to address the scarcity of quantitative data on religion in Yorubaland, research also included a large-scale ethnographic survey. Under the leadership of Olukoya Ogen, this survey was carried out by a dedicated team of researchers based at Osun State University. Eventually, the survey was completed by 2,819 respondents in 18 local government areas in both

---

[63] A. Honneth, 'Integrity and disrespect: Principles of a conception of morality based on the theory of recognition', *Political Theory* 20: 2 (1992), 187–201: 192.

[64] Honneth, 'Integrity and disrespect', p. 195.

rural and urban areas of the seven main Yoruba-speaking states of Nigeria.[65] Reflecting the team's base at Osun State University, we decided to carry out the pilot study for this survey in two local government areas within the state, and eventually settled on the local government areas of Ede North and Ede South, which make up the important and historically Muslim town of Ede.

In Ede, we obtained the permission of His Royal Majesty the *Tìmì* of Ede, *Ọba* Muniru Adesola Lawal, who graciously allowed us to carry out our research in his domain. It is in recognition of his support that the book includes a collection of praise poems, or *oríkì*, of the *Tìmì* of Ede in an appendix. We also relied strongly on the support and hospitality of Siyan Oyeweso, the first Provost of the College of Humanities and Culture at Osun State University, and on the tireless support of our two local gatekeepers, *Alhaji* Rasheed Adio and *Alhaji* Nureni Lawal. Thanks to their help and encouragement, we administered the questionnaire to a total number of 291 respondents in Ede and interviewed a large number of individuals able to comment on particular aspects of the research between February and June 2012. Most enjoyably, we also participated in the celebration of both traditional and Islamic festivals in Ede during that period and afterwards.

As we worked and celebrated with different local groups and institutions in Ede, many people encouraged us to turn our work for the pilot study into a separate aspect of our project. Thanks to the welcoming attitude of Ayandiji Aina, the Pioneer President/Vice Chancellor of Adeleke University, and the initiative of Ibikunle Tijani, Adeleke's first Dean of the Faculty of Arts and Education, we eventually decided to hold a workshop on 'Everyday Religion and Tolerance in Ede, Southwest Nigeria' at Adeleke University on 5–6 December 2012. The workshop included both academic presentations and a 'community' day of town–gown exchanges, and it attracted about 300 participants from academia, civil society and Ede's traditional and religious elite. It was in the context of this discussion that the idea for this book was first mooted, and selected workshop contributions and the preliminary findings from the survey of the town form the kernel of the contributions to this edited volume.

Like many edited volumes, this book brings together chapters written from different disciplinary and personal perspectives. However, given the close focus of the book on one community, editors and authors were committed to ensuring that all chapters had a distinct focus, while at the same time engaging with each other. This required a high degree of collaboration from editors as well as contributors. In some cases, editors and authors of chapters – and even fellow authors – were involved in ardent exchanges with each other before

---

[65] These include Ekiti, Kwara, Lagos, Ogun, Ondo, Osun and Oyo States.

4 Organisers and participants of workshop on 'Everyday religion and tolerance in Ede'

chapters could be completed. Apart from editorial suggestions, many chapters were refined and improved through the exchange of material between authors, making such chapters the result of group engagement rather than individual authorship. Acknowledging the collaborative work that went into all the chapters, we retained a conventional system of authorship to accept that the thrust of each chapter primarily represents the work of its named author(s). Reflecting the results of intense debate and engagement between the contributing authors and its editors, the book's chapters now offer a coherent discussion of religious coexistence in different social constellations.

Finally, while important chapters of this book were produced by established historians, anthropologists and linguists, we also wanted to offer the members of our research team, both in Nigeria and the UK, the opportunity of participating in the book project. Having got to know Ede 'from below' through survey and interview work, the members of our research team were eminently qualified to contribute to the book. Most of them were, at the time of writing, junior scholars or graduate students hoping to pursue academic careers eventually, and we consider the experience of preparing a paper for publication in a closely edited volume an important aspect of their professional training. Like many research projects, our research would have been impossible without the young scholars whose idealism, commitment and enthusiasm contributed to its success. As the editors, we are proud and grateful to have been part of this time-intensive and yet deeply satisfying process of mutual learning.

Outlook

Exploring the social life of one town, the contributors to this book rely on detailed observations and fine-grain descriptions to analyse both the realisation of religions in existing social formations and individual dispositions, and the inspiration they provide to the constitution of new forms of community and institutions beyond, but especially within, the town. The book's multidisciplinary approach illuminates the fluid and contradictory role played by religious difference in both the production and the transcendence of social difference. While all chapters of this book are linked to each other, their order offers a range of gradually shifting perspectives on religious encounter and coexistence. Starting with an introduction to the religious history of Ede and its important institutions (chapters 2 to 4), the book later explores the role of religious difference for different institutions within the town (chapters 5 to 8) and eventually moves on to the importance of religious difference in individual lives and interpersonal relationships (chapters 9 to 11).

The chapter that follows this introduction offers an overview of the religious history of Ede by focusing on the role of the *Tìmì*, the town's historical traditional ruler or *ọba*, in shaping the town's changing religious identity. Siyan Oyeweso explores the role of *Tìmì* Bamigbaye, who is associated with the introduction of *Ṣàngó* worship in Ede during the eighteenth century, and *Tìmì* Lagunju, who played an instrumental role during the nineteenth century in turning Ede into a Muslim town. Reigning in the twentieth century, *Tìmì* Laoye, Ede's first Christian ruler, was not able to transform Ede's religious identity, but by emphasising the importance of Western education he was able to greatly strengthen the position of the Baptist church in the town. Oyeweso suggests that while successive *Tìmì* have played an important role in facilitating religious change in Ede, their ability to control other religions has been limited by the expectations of their subjects: while the *Tìmì* could play a powerful role in encouraging religious change, they have been expected, as the purported 'head of all religions', to do so without disadvantaging existing practices.

Engaging with chapter 2 through a critical exploration of the significance of precedent, Aderemi Ajala and Insa Nolte discuss the enduring importance of *Ṣàngó* worship for the institution of *ọba*ship in Ede in chapter 3. Focusing on *Ṣàngó*'s association with contradictory, ambivalent and transgressive positions in Ede, the chapter understands transgression as a site and a strategy of power and domination, on the part of both *Ṣàngó* and the *Tìmì*. As both draw on the ability to challenge religious boundaries, they are empowered by religious difference. By examining transgression in the context of royal agency, the chapter also engages with Jacob Olupona's argument that the Yoruba *ọba* presides over the town's religious practices by transforming them into a unified 'civil religion'.[66] The authors suggest that because many ọbas are closely associated with òrìṣà, and can be seen as òrìṣà in their own right, the potential for religious transgression may also be a widely shared aspect of ọbaship.

The verbal arts associated with Ṣàngó reflect the tension between the deity's historical importance for the town and its current existence as a minority religious practice. In chapter 4, Olusola Ajibade points out that some of the songs, chants and proverbs associated with Ṣàngó advocate Ṣàngó's coexistence with Islam and Christianity. But at the same time, other texts appear to reject or mock these monotheist faiths. Indeed, often the same texts can be understood as celebrating Ṣàngó both as tolerating other religions and as an òrìṣà that challenges and surpasses them. Ṣàngó is imagined – by his supporters – as a supreme power, without which the world religions would not exist as they do. The author argues that as Ṣàngó's alterity illuminates Islam and Christianity as ultimately cognate, the deity's existence may contribute to their relatively peaceful coexistence.

The next two chapters illuminate a different and explicitly Muslim perspective on coexistence with, and indeed tolerance of, religious others. In chapter 5, Amusa Saheed Balogun discusses three of the town's important Islamic compounds, which played significant roles in the historical establishment and spread of Islam. Drawing on observations as well as oral data from the Imole, Talafia Imam and Daodu Lagunju compounds, the chapter reflects on the ways in which the dominant Muslims in these compounds expect their dependants, tenants and visitors of other religions to behave. The insistence on the specifically Muslim character of the compound reflects the hierarchical relationship between those born into the extended family that owns the compound and those married into the compound, or renting rooms in it. Conscious of their role as examples to Ede's Muslim community, the owners of the town's Muslim compounds ensure that even where there is a strong influx of non-Muslims, this does not change the fundamental Islamic character of the space.

Despite the exemplary role of the historically Muslim compounds within Ede, the town's Muslim community is not homogenous. In chapter 6, Yemi Balogun offers a short discussion of the different Muslim groups that have contributed to the town's debates about Islam since the 1930s and suggests that notions of tolerance apply here too. Balogun explores current debates about Islamic reform and innovation through the beliefs and everyday practices of the Tablighi Jamaat, a conservative reformist movement with a small

---

[66] J.O. Olupona, *Kingship, Religion, and Rituals in a Nigerian Community: A Phenomenological Study of Ondo Yoruba Festivals* (Stockholm: Alimquist & Wiksell, 1991), p. 84.

but significant following. The Tablighi Jamaat's practices are often seen as challenging local forms of Muslim practice, thus contributing to local debates about the relationship between culture and religion. While this development echoes important trends in Pentecostal practice, the author remains critical about the purported 'Pentecostalisation of Islam', which foregrounds the engagement with Christianity. He suggests that it is more productive to understand the Tablighi Jamaat's critique of existing Muslim practices and dispositions as an illustration of the Yoruba Muslim community's ability to engage in self-examination and religious innovation.

The complex relationship between religion and belonging explored in chapter 5 is re-examined from a different perspective in chapter 7 by Olukoya Ogen and Amusa Saheed Balogun. Focusing on Ede's Baptist Church, the authors examine the relationships between Baptists, other Christians and the town's Muslim majority. Historically, schooling was instrumental in achieving conversions in the community. But by drawing on resources outside the town and offering access to opportunities beyond the locality, education was also associated with mobility, and thus often with the arrival of outsiders or non-indigenes. Muslim attempts to limit the spread and impact of Christianity drew on the control of local resources. Today Christian activities in Ede continue to be constrained by limited access to land and living space, e.g. through the refusal of some Muslims to sell land, or rent their rooms or houses to Christians. But the conflation of tolerance and religious competition has unexpected outcomes: even as Ede's Christians rely on the tolerance of the predominantly Muslim townspeople, they assert their moral (and spiritual) superiority by exceeding their hosts in tolerance.

In chapter 8, Akin Iwilade and Oladipo Fadayomi explore the management of religious difference on the campus of the Federal Polytechnic of Ede. Established at the outskirts of Ede in 1992, the Federal Polytechnic is an ostensibly secular institution of higher education. But the polytechnic has attracted a significant number of Christians, both staff and students, to Ede. As all Muslim and Christian student associations are subsumed into religion-based structures of authority, conflict between Muslims and Christians has been avoided through the close control of all religious students. The tensions inherent in this hierarchical system led to an unsuccessful bid for independence by one Muslim group in 2002, but the mediation and reconciliation process, supported by Islamic leaders from Ede, successfully reasserted Muslim commitment to religious unity. But while the investment into religious control ensures unity within and tolerance across the Muslim–Christian divide, it is also linked to the institutional alienation and discontent of those students who are not intensely religious, pointing to tensions between the polytechnic's reliance on religious politics and its ostensibly secular educational mission.

The last three chapters of the book focus on the role of religious difference in the everyday lives of families, couples and individuals. Ibikunle Tijani discusses the personalities and practices of the religiously mixed Adeleke family in chapter 9. He argues that the ability of its founding bi-religious couple, Raji and Esther Adeleke, to overlook religious and ethnic difference drew strongly on their shared commitment to unionism and redistributive politics. Their commitment to the town and its community continues to drive the activities of their descendants. Facilitating close relationships and mutual understanding between people of different religions in Ede, members of the Adeleke family understand their family as exemplary for the town. The apparent unity of all family members irrespective of their religious identity challenges notions of an exclusively Muslim or Christian community.

In chapter 10, Insa Nolte and Tosin Akinjobi explore inter-religious marriage as a point of tension between the social institutions shaped by religion and everyday inter-religious sociality. While inter-religious marriages are relatively frequent in Ede, they are nonetheless often viewed with reservation, both by the respective faith communities and by the members of the bride's family. As a women is expected to submit to her husband's religious authority, interfaith marriages often involve conversion or at least close familiarity with the husband's religion for women, which can be perceived as challenging paternal status. Often the acceptance of inter-religious marriages begins with childbirth, and it relies on the ability of women to facilitate her children's familiarity both with her husband's religion and with her own or her father's religion. Often familiar with a range of religious practices, debates and discourses, women in inter-religious marriages are not only social but also religious mediators.

In the book's final chapter, Rebecca Jones and Insa Nolte discuss the complexity of attitudes towards religious difference illuminated by a survey of Ede. Survey results confirm the dominance of Islam in the old and central sections of the town and the greater importance of Christianity in the town's newer sections and tertiary educational institutions. The survey also reveals that the number of Christians and converts is higher among those who have greater exposure to education. Conversely, Muslims and indigenes of the town are more likely to tolerate traditional practices than Christians. But despite these differences, Muslim and Christian views about the other monotheist religion imply strong congruity and sympathy. Emphasising qualities shared by virtue of being Yoruba, and observed in everyday encounters, mutually positive views of the other religion reflect the importance of family, friendship and other social ties between members of different religions. In Ede, engagement with other religions reflects notions of wellbeing that include, but are not limited to, toleration, but it also refers to forms of community both above and below the town level.

The book ends with a short outlook that focuses on the wider insights that can be drawn from the book's exploration of the various forms of religious coexistence in Ede. It suggests that the multiplicity of practices within the town arises from the fact that no religion is exclusively associated with power. As each religion remains subject to the multiple pull of the other two, religious practice is not primarily shaped by large-scale identification but by the creative and differential engagement with different religious others. Reflecting on the findings of this book in the context of cognate studies and wider debates, the outlook also offers suggestions for further research on religious coexistence and encounter, both in Africa and beyond.

CHAPTER 2

Kingship and Religion:
An Introduction to the History of Ede

Siyan Oyeweso

Located in the heart of the Yoruba-speaking south-west of Nigeria, Ede is a town with a distinctive military, political and religious history. A former outpost of the powerful Oyo Empire, the town remains an important centre of political activity in south-west Nigeria today.[1] Ede also has a traditional administration headed by a ruler, or ọba, who holds the title of Àgbàlé Ọlọ́fà Iná, or Tìmì. The current Tìmì, HRM Ọba Muniru Adesola Lawal, Laminisa I, is assisted by a council of twelve traditional chiefs whose members represent the main traditional quarters of the town.[2] Building on a multi-layered history of religious change and transformation, Tìmì Lawal presides over a town whose complex ritual and religious life was largely shaped by his predecessors.

Today, Ede is famous for its flamboyant annual celebration of the traditional deity Ṣàngó, which is associated with the reign of Ede's powerful ọba, Tìmì Ajeniju Bamigbaye (c.1780–1843), who is widely believed to have been born as a follower of Ṣàngó. But thanks to the efforts of Tìmì Sangolami Abibu Lagunju (1847–1900), a Muslim convert also held by some to have been predestined to adopt Islam, Ede today is a predominantly Muslim town.[3] In addition to the worship of Ṣàngó and Islam, the town also has a significant

---

[1] Ede is located close to Osogbo, the capital of Osun State, and it is the administrative headquarters of two Local Government Areas: Ede North (Faosun) and Ede South (Oke Iresi).

[2] The traditional chiefs are headed by the military high chief, the Balógun of Ede, who is the second in command to the Tìmì. See also A. Adegbola, Ile-Ife: The Source of Yoruba Civilisation (Lagos: Oduduwa International Communications, 2009), pp. 505–8.

[3] In E. Olunlade's Ede: A Short History (Ibadan: General Publications Section, Ministry of Education, 1961), the end date of Tìmì Lagunju's reign is given as 1892, which is when he was deposed. However, since in many Yoruba traditions an ọba is considered to reign until his death, we have given the dates of his reign here (and throughout the book) as ending with his death in 1900.

5 His Royal Majesty, the *Tìmì* of Ede, *Ọba* Muniru Adesola Lawal, leading townspeople to the prayer ground during *Iléyá* 2012

Christian minority, which was much strengthened during the reign of *Tìmì* John Adetoyese Laoye (1946–75), Ede's first – and only – Christian *ọba*.

Offering an introduction to Ede's history through the activities of its rulers, this chapter focuses on the religious politics of the three *Tìmì* whose names are today associated with the popularisation of Ṣàngó worship, Islam and Christianity. Exploring the different historical and political processes mobilised by these three rulers, the chapter reflects on the importance of royal success and destiny in the justification of religious change. As all Yoruba *ọba*s are considered to hold spiritual power that they must use for the good of the whole community, an *ọba* – and especially an *ọba* fated to follow a particular religion – is certainly able to provide religious leadership to his subjects. Reflecting on the difficulties experienced especially by the two later *Tìmì*, the chapter also considers the popular expectations that shaped these rulers' engagement with religion. The reign of *Tìmì* Lagunju illustrates that tolerance of other religions is an absolute requirement for a ruler wishing to retain political legitimacy. Beyond tolerance, as confirmed by events during *Tìmì* Laoye's reign, the *ọba* is also expected to represent and support members of all religions in their ambitions.

Ede's Early History

Like other Yoruba kingdoms and states, the early history of Ede is contained in numerous Yoruba traditions of origin, myths and legends, which are sometimes contradictory. The most popularly and generally accepted tradition states that Ede was founded during the reign of an early *Aláàfin* or ruler of the old Oyo Empire, in the fifteenth or sixteenth century C.E. A detailed version of Ede's foundation is presented in Samuel Johnson's *The History of the Yorubas*,[4] but this chapter will offer the slightly different version generally believed to be true in Ede.[5] Several local authors assert that Ede was founded by an Oyo military general named Agbale Olofa Ina,[6] who had been given a military mandate to curb the excesses of marauders from the nearby Ijesa kingdom and to safeguard the territories of the settlements of Awo, Ara and Ojo in the Oyo borderlands. After Agbale had left Oyo-Ile, the capital, he established his military base at a site called Idi-Ede, located not far from the present-day location of Ede but on the northern bank of the river Osun. This site was so named because it contained many 'Ede' trees, and the town has retained the reference to these trees in its name.[7]

Within a short period of time, Agbale succeeded in establishing control over Idi-Ede and its environs. Agbale's leadership attracted traders and settlers to Idi-Ede, and as the military settlement expanded it was renamed Ede-Ile, or Ede town. Agbale also collected of a toll of five cowries per head from the traders who passed through Ede-Ile. A portion of the collected tolls was meant to be sent to the royal treasury at Oyo as a proof of loyalty and vassalage, but as Ede-Ile began to expand, Agbale endeavoured to assert the independence of his town and stopped the payment of tributes to the *Aláàfin*. The ensuing disagreement between the *Aláàfin* and Agbale Olofa Ina eventually led to the death of both men.[8] In Ede it is believed that the *Aláàfin* who died in this manner was *Aláàfin* Sango, who was later deified.[9] After Agbale's death, the Ijesa resumed their attacks and eventually *Aláàfin* Kori, the successor of *Aláàfin* Sango, sent another Oyo warrior called Alapo Tiemi Tiemi to pacify the area. Alapo Tiemi Tiemi finally put an end to Ijesa incursions into this part

---

[4] S. Johnson, *The History of the Yorubas: From the Earliest Times to the Beginning of the British Protectorate* (Lagos: CMS Bookshops, 1921), pp. 156–7.

[5] See also G. Oyeweso, 'Traditions of origin and growth of Ede up to 1960', BA Long Essay (Ile-Ife: Department of History, University of Ife, 1982), pp. 1–5.

[6] Translation: Agbale, the expert and fiery archer.

[7] cf. Olunlade, *Ede: A Short History*, pp. 1–12.

[8] S. Oyeweso, *Ede in Yoruba History* (Lagos: Multi Vision Publishing House, 2002), pp.1–16.

[9] According to Johnson, *History of the Yorubas*, pp. 149–52, *Aláàfin* Sango was not directly associated with the foundation of Ede, and while he died violently he did so as a result of a different conflict.

of Oyo and established the title of the Ede rulers, who are called *Tìmì* after him to this day.¹⁰

Thus, Ede grew out of the desire of the Oyo Empire to protect its southern boundary. As an important border town, Ede also featured prominently in the struggles that followed the destruction of old Oyo in the war with its former vassal Ilorin and the Sokoto Empire. In fact, Ede was one of very few Oyo towns that maintained political independence from Ilorin during that period,¹¹ and it participated actively in both the battle of Osogbo, during which Ilorin was defeated, and in the peace-making process that reordered the politics of the Yoruba-speaking area at the end of the nineteenth century.¹² By the beginning of colonial rule, Ede had maintained and strengthened its position as an important Oyo town in central Yorubaland, with significant military and political influence within the region and beyond.

For most of its history as a frontier town of Oyo, Ede's most important deity (*òrìṣà*) is said to have been *Ògún*, who was the main deity of the *Tìmì*.¹³ Widely worshipped throughout Yorubaland, *Ògún* was associated with iron, war and metal working. However, worship of *Ògún* was by no means exclusive. In Yoruba cosmology *Ògún* is a powerful, fearless and brave warrior who possesses the power of conquest and victory. He is said to have been one of the first of the *òrìṣà*, or deities, to descend to the realm of *ilé aiyé* – the earth – to find suitable habitation for future human life. This explains why one of his praise names is *Ọ̀ṣín Ìmọlẹ̀*, i.e. the first of the *òrìṣà* to descend from heaven to earth.¹⁴ He is the Yoruba deity of iron and all users of instruments or equipment made of iron appease him. As the deity of iron technology and conquest, *Ògún* was widely worshipped throughout Yorubaland (before the arrival of Islam and Christianity).¹⁵ The reason for his pre-eminence in Ede was probably due to the fact that Ede was a frontier town where hunting, warfare and the provision of justice played an important role.

In Ede, *Ògún*'s association with hunting is illustrated by the fact that the head of the *Ògún* worshippers was called *Olú-Ọdẹ*, i.e. the head of the hunters.

---

[10] The founder and first ruler of the town, Agbale Olofa Ina, was simply known as *Elẹ́dẹ*, i.e. 'Owner of Ede' or 'Ruler of Ede'. See Olunlade, *Ede: A Short History*, p. 12.

[11] R. Law, *The Oyo Empire, c. 1600–c. 1836: A West African Imperialism in the Era of the Atlantic Slave Trade* (Oxford: Clarendon Press, 1977).

[12] Oyeweso, *Ede in Yoruba History*, pp. 38–76.

[13] Olunlade, *Ede: A Short History*, p. 54.

[14] See J.O. Awolalu, *Yoruba Beliefs and Sacrificial Rites* (London: Longman, 1979).

[15] J.D.Y. Peel points out that there was considerable variation in the worship of Ogun, which also remains the case today. J.D.Y. Peel, 'A comparative analysis of Ogun in pre-colonial Yorubaland', *Africa's Ogun: Old World and New*, ed. S.T. Barnes, 2nd edn (Bloomington: Indiana University Press, 1997), pp. 263–89.

The major items used in daily or weekly *Ògún* worship or sacrifice included cooked beans, kola nut and roasted yam. During the annual *Ògún* worship in the seventh month of every year, a dog had to be slaughtered at the *Ògún* shrine.[16] The importance of *Ògún* is still attested today by the names of several traditional compounds in Ede. These include not only Ologun compound (the compound of *Ògún* devotees), but also Olode Ibadehin, Olode Afenle and Olode Olokuta (compounds of hunters) and Alagbede (a compound of blacksmiths). It should be noted that some other compounds have changed their names following their embrace of a new religion, particularly Islam. However, even today, *Ògún* is worshipped in Ede by professionals such as hunters, blacksmiths, drivers, goldsmiths and other artisans who make use of iron and other metals.

Other important traditional deities and masquerades in Ede included Ṣàngó, Ọbàtálá, Ìpedì, Ajágemọ, Egúngún, Ọ̀sun and Ọya. In fact, there is hardly any form of Yoruba traditional worship that did (and does) not have adherents in Ede town.[17] The *Egúngún* masquerade in particular remains popular today. It is believed that people's ancestors reincarnate through the *Egúngún* masquerade, and this explains why they speak in an unnatural guttural tone. *Egúngún* worship is usually accompanied by festivities that include singing and dancing with masqueraders parading the market centres in colourful costumes, and it is known to most townspeople through an annual festival.[18] The annual *Egúngún* festival is held for seven consecutive days in April, when masquerades of various statures come out to perform and pray for the people. It climaxes with the appearance of *Orídorù*, the most powerful and important masquerade in Ede, which is regarded as *Egúngún Ọba*, or the king's masquerade.[19] Other important masquerades in Ede include *Àlùpè*,

---

[16] The sacrificial dog was held lengthwise by two people while the third person cut it into two in one stroke. Failure to achieve this was considered as unacceptable sacrifice. The dog's blood was poured on *Ògún*'s shrine. L. Dokun, 'Islam in Ede', BA Long Essay (Ibadan: Department of Arabic and Islamic Studies, University of Ibadan, 1974), p. 15.

[17] The late *Tìmì* John Adetoyese Laoye of Ede introduced the German scholar Ulli Beier and his Austrian wife Susanne Wenger, later the *Àdùnní Olóriṣà* of Osun Osogbo, to important aspects of Yoruba traditional practice in the early 1950s, thereby laying a foundation for the wider academic, literary and artistic engagement with Yoruba *òrìṣà* traditions. See W. Ogundele, 'Ulli Beier', *Centre for Black Culture and Understanding* (n.d.), <http://www.centreforblackculture.org/Ulli.htm>, accessed 8 September 2014.

[18] However, its chief priest, the *Ẹlẹgbára*, and some of its primary devotees engage in daily or weekly worship. The main sacrificial animal for *Egúngún* worship is fowl, the blood of which is put on the grave of the ancestor who is believed to have reincarnated through the masquerade.

[19] Dokun, 'Islam in Ede', p. 17.

Atéré, Iyekíye and Gbájéró, and the compounds of Ile Sanyin and Ile Eleegun are, or were, traditionally renowned for *Egúngún* worship.[20]

Tìmì Ajeniju Bamigbaye (c.1825–43) and the Rise of *Ṣàngó* as the *Ọba*'s Religion in Ede

Ògún was replaced by *Ṣàngó* as the principal *òrìṣà* of the *Tìmì* of Ede during the reign of *Tìmì* Lalemo, who reigned in Ede-Ile. An important reason for this was that according to legend, Ajeniju Bamigbaye, one of *Tìmì* Lalemo's sons, likely to have been born in or around 1780,[21] came into the world with both fists closed. Upon investigation and after elaborate ceremonies conducted by an invited *Ṣàngó* priest, the child opened his fists, which contained a cowry shell and a small thunder stone, both of which are traditionally associated with *Ṣàngó*. This was interpreted to mean that this child was destined to be a worshipper of *Ṣàngó*.[22] *Ṣàngó* is the Yoruba deity of thunder, lightning, justice, force and male sexuality. In some *Ifá* divination verses, *Ṣàngó* is described as one of the sixteen principal Yoruba divinities who descended from heaven.[23] This understanding has also shaped some recent academic discussions of the deity among Yoruba scholars.[24] However, local histories of Ede describe *Ṣàngó* as a former ruler of the old Oyo Kingdom whose extraordinary power derived from Nupeland, his mother's birthplace.[25] After his death as a human being, *Ṣàngó* was deified.[26]

[20] The former Eleegun Compound had since changed its name to Adini Islam Compound to reflect the embrace of Islam by the majority of its inhabitants. See Dokun, 'Islam in Ede', p. 15.

[21] As he was born several years after the installation of *Aláàfin* Abiodun, usually dated to c.1770, and before Abiodun's failed campaign against Borgu in c.1783, several oral historians of Ede have suggested c.1780 as a likely birthdate for *Tìmì* Bamigbaye.

[22] Olunlade, *Ede: A Short History*, p. 15.

[23] This narrative is contained in the *Odù Ifá* called *Òsà Ẹlẹyẹ*.

[24] See J. Tishken, T. Falola and A. Akinyemi, *Ṣàngó in Africa and the African Diaspora* (Bloomington: Indiana University Press, 2009).

[25] For a detailed discussion of the historical relationship between Oyo and Nupe, and some of the implications of this relationship for the worship of *Ṣàngó* (and other Oyo cults), see B.A. Agiri, 'Early Oyo history reconsidered', *History in Africa* 2 (1975), 1–16; and R. Law, 'How many times can history repeat itself? Some problems in the traditional history of Oyo', *International Journal of African Historical Studies* 18:1 (1985), 33–51. *Ṣàngó* is mentioned as the fourth Aláàfin of Oyo in Johnson, *History of the Yorubas*, p. 34.

[26] This is what Adejumo calls the 'apotheosized or deified' *Ṣàngó*. A. Adejumo, 'The practice and worship of Ṣàngó in contemporary Yorubaland', *Ṣàngó in Africa and the African Diaspora*, ed. J. Tishken, T. Falola and A. Akinyemi (Bloomington: Indiana University Press, 2009), p. 60.

As set out above, Ede's historians assert that *Aláàfin* Sango played an important role in the history of the town by sending both the original founder of Ede, Agbale, and later the warrior Gbonka Ebiri to the town.²⁷ But more importantly, they argue that after Gbonka Ebiri had killed Ede's founder Agbale, he also disobeyed *Aláàfin* Sango and demanded his abdication.²⁸ Eventually, *Aláàfin* Sango gave in to Gbonka, vacated the throne and hanged himself on an Ayan tree outside the town of Oyo.²⁹ Perhaps due to the stigma of suicide, some argue that he only disappeared into the ground.³⁰ Sango's followers and admirers, led by the *Mọgbà*, who later became *Ṣàngó*'s chief priest, began to pray to him to punish his enemies, and this happened.³¹ This led to *Ṣàngó*'s deification and it marked the origin of *Ṣàngó* worship in Yorubaland, and eventually also among the Yoruba in the diaspora.³²

The worship of *Ṣàngó* in Ede also reflects the town's political history within the Oyo Empire in another way. The rise of *Ṣàngó* as the *ọba*'s deity in Ede is likely to have taken place during a period of expansion of Oyo's royal powers under *Aláàfin* Abiodun (c.1770–89). After having successfully removed Baṣọrun Gaa, the kingdom's powerful councillor of state, Abiodun replaced Gaa's provincial representatives with his own messengers, eunuchs, royal wives and also possession priests of *Ṣàngó*, thus contributing to a systematic

---

²⁷ For a discussion of some discrepancies in the version of this history presented by Johnson and the versions rooted in Ede, see P.F. de Moraes Farias, '"Yoruba Origins" Revisited by Muslims: An interview with the Arókin of Òyó and a reading of the Aṣl Qabā'il Yūrubā of Al-Ḥājj Ādam al-Ilūrī', *Self-Assertion and Brokerage. Early Cultural Nationalism in West Africa*, ed. K. Barber and P.F de Moraes Farias (Birmingham: Birmingham University African Studies Series, 1990), pp. 117–21.

²⁸ Some traditions suggest that *Ṣàngó* kept his powerful *èdùn àrá* (thunderstones) with *Ọya*, his last wife, whose menstrual period had however neutralised his weapon so that *Ṣàngó* could not put Gbonka to death. An attempt to restore the efficacy of his thunderstone by *Ṣàngó* only resulted in the burning of his palace. See O.T. Oladipo, 'SANGO; The god of Thunder', *TIA-This is Africa* (17 April 2011), <http://tia-thisisafrica.blogspot.co.uk/2011/04/sango-god-of-thunder_17.html>, accessed 27 July 2013.

²⁹ Olunlade, *Ede: A Short History*, p. 12.

³⁰ See Oladipo, 'SANGO; The god of Thunder'.

³¹ To show that *Ṣàngó* was not dead and that his power to strike thunder was still strong even after his physical disappearance, the houses of all his enemies were razed by fire, probably by *Ṣàngó*'s loyalists. People therefore changed their tune from 'Ọba so', i.e. 'the king hanged himself' to 'Ọba kò so' or 'Olú kò so', meaning 'the King (*Ṣàngó*) did not hang himself'.

³² See A. Akinyemi, 'The place of Ṣàngó in the Yorùbá pantheon', *Ṣàngó in Africa and the African Diaspora*, ed. J. Tishken, T. Falola and A. Akinyemi (Bloomington: Indiana University Press, 2009), pp. 23–43.

spread of Ṣàngó worship throughout Oyo.³³ Thus the birth of Tìmì Bamigbaye, believed to have been revealed to be a predestined Ṣàngó worshipper, took place precisely at the moment when Ṣàngó worship took on new symbolic and political meaning within the Oyo Empire.

The notion that some people are predestined to worship a particular deity or religion is widely accepted in Yorubaland, and it is usually revealed through divination. In Tìmì Bamigbaye's case, the personal religious predestination was generalised for the town because of the matter of his birth to a reigning ọba and his eventual ascension to the throne. As the Tìmì was seen as holding important spiritual powers for the good of the community, it is certainly possible that the belief that fate had ordained Tìmì Bamigbaye's worship of Ṣàngó made him a popular choice as a ruler at a time when Ṣàngó was increasingly associated with Oyo's power. At the same time, it is likely that once Tìmì Bamigbaye was installed, his identity as a Ṣàngó priest, or even an incarnation of Ṣàngó, drew support for his championing of the deity.

Nonetheless, it is unlikely that the rise of Ṣàngó worship under Tìmì Bamigbaye was a complete innovation for Ede. Ongoing excavations at Ede-Ile, the location of Ede until the reign of reign of Tìmì Kubolaje Agbonran Gbakoya (Bamigbaye's elder brother), suggest a strong presence of artefacts tentatively linked to the worship of Ṣàngó.³⁴ Ede's historical association with Aláàfin Sango certainly suggests that Ṣàngó was an important òrìṣà in Ede even before the reign of Bamigbaye.³⁵ This illustrates Barber's argument that the worship of Yoruba òrìṣà was highly personal and often idiosyncratic. Thus, even before Ajeniju Bamigbaye adopted 'his' Ṣàngó and generalised its veneration for the town, other worshippers in Ede may have worshipped Ṣàngó, probably in subtly different ways, and possibly arising out of different encounters and relationships that were only indirectly linked to the town's history.³⁶

Tìmì Ajeniju Bamigbaye became Ede's ruler in c.1825. By then the worship of Ṣàngó, which was originally strengthened during the reign of Aláàfin Abiodun, had taken on a new symbolic and political meaning as conflict between Oyo and

---

[33] See J.L. Matory, *Sex and the Empire that is no more: Gender and the Politics of Metaphor in Oyo Yoruba Religion* (Minneapolis and London: University of Minnesota Press, 1994), p. 12.

[34] Akin Ogundiran, personal communication to Dr S.A. Ajala. The artefacts are yet to be dated.

[35] It is of course also possible that the prominence given to *Aláàfin* Sango in Ede's history of origin reflects the expansion of Ṣàngó worship under Tìmì Bamigbaye. However, given the depth of time that has passed and the wide agreement on this detail, both in Ede and in neighbouring communities, this would be very difficult to reconstruct.

[36] K. Barber, 'Oríkì, women and the proliferation and merging of Òrìṣà', *Africa* 60:3 (1990), 313–37.

the expanding Muslim power of Ilorin intensified. From the 1790s onwards,[37] Oyo had had to contend with internal disintegration and rebellion from powerful provincial commanders. The most powerful of these commanders was based in Ilorin and, in alliance with mainly Muslim groups, had seceded from Oyo in 1817. By 1823, Ilorin had become part of the Sokoto Caliphate and started attacking towns and villages in Oyo, eventually destroying the capital Oyo-Ile in 1835. The empire collapsed in 1836, and the new capital, New Oyo, was only a minor force in the ensuing wars between Ilorin and the new warrior cities of Ibadan and Ijaye, largely settled by Oyo refugees. In this context, we can imagine that Ṣàngó was, or became, a champion of Oyo against the Muslim armies that threatened (and ended) the existence of its empire.

Reflecting this political opposition, the relationship between Ṣàngó and Islam in nineteenth- and early twentieth-century Ede is often remembered as confrontational. Certainly the greatest challenges to Islam in its early years in Ede came from Ṣàngó worshippers.[38] However, this opposition was not always directed against Muslim practices, but primarily focused on the challenge of Islam to established institutions of town and social life. In Oyo and the warrior cities that succeeded it, the number of Muslims increased fairly steadily throughout the nineteenth century. But as Ṣàngó remained a powerful deity, none of these towns adopted Islamic political structures.

It is possible that the rejection of clearly identifiable Islamic structures throughout Oyo, and the continued influence of Ṣàngó in many Oyo towns, was a form of political nostalgia and self-assertion directed at the new Islamic power of Ilorin.[39] This might also explain why Aláàfin Atiba, the founder of New Oyo, and other nineteenth-century leaders who at one time professed Islam, renounced the religion when they attained important political offices in Oyo.[40] But even as he stands for Oyo's political resistance to Ilorin, Ṣàngó is sometimes still referred to as a Muslim today.[41] Indeed, Ṣàngó himself was addressed as Akéwú-gbẹrú, an appellation describing one who is versed in

---

[37] Some authors suggest that the decline of Oyo had already begun by the 1750s. See R. Law, 'Making sense of a traditional narrative: Political disintegration in the Kingdom of Oyo', *Cahiers d'études africaines* 22:87/88 (1982), 387–401.

[38] For some details, see S. Oyeweso, *Eminent Yoruba Muslims of the 19th and Early 20th Centuries* (Ibadan: Rex Charles Publications in association with Connel Publications, 1999), pp. 11–33.

[39] I am grateful to Insa Nolte for this suggestion.

[40] Law, 'How many times can history repeat itself?', p. 42.

[41] J.D.Y. Peel, 'Review of *Sango in Africa and the African Diaspora*', *Africa* 81:2 (2011), 340–1: 340.

Arabic to the extent that he could win a slave (see also chapter 4).⁴² Ogunmola also suggests that *Ṣàngó* was associated with the material and intellectual innovations associated with Islam in the Oyo Empire, from trade and cotton-growing to healing and divinatory practices. As these innovations and practices were associated with an increase in health and wellbeing, the state of wellbeing is, until today, expressed in Yoruba through the Arabic-root word *àlààfíà*.⁴³ As will be explored in greater detail in the next two chapters, the historical and contemporary links between *Ṣàngó* and Islam are too intricate to be reduced to antagonism.

In Ede, too, *Ṣàngó*'s relationship to Islam was complex. Thus, the *Ṣàngó* devotee *Tìmì* Ajeniju Bamigbaye (c.1825–43) himself was one of the first in the town to recognise the power of Islam. According to local historians, *Tìmì* Bamigbaye was looking for a potent power to assist the town in a battle against Ibadan, where the newly appointed *Balógun* Oderinlo wanted to prove his mettle as a military chief and had decided to fight against Ede.⁴⁴ To defend the town, *Tìmì* Bamigbaye brought the first Muslim, called Buremo Owon-la-a-rogo, to Ede. Buremo helped to secure the victory,⁴⁵ and *Tìmì* Bamigbaye granted him permission to settle in Ede so that he could continue to protect the town in subsequent battles (see also chapter 3).

Despite, or perhaps because of, *Ṣàngó*'s elaborate relationship with Islam, the military victory of *Tìmì* Bamigbaye against Ibadan strengthened both his political and his spiritual influence within Ede. After the battle, Ede and Ibadan became allies and Ede fought on the Ibadan side in many campaigns. In recognition of *Tìmì* Bamigbaye's powers, he was allowed to lead the Ibadan armies against the Bariba (Borgu).⁴⁶ Military prowess and success, which had always been an important factor in Ede's politics owing to its location on the Oyo frontier, enabled *Tìmì* Bamigbaye to enjoy a splendid reign. As a great warrior and one of Ede's wealthiest men,⁴⁷ *Tìmì* Bamigbaye's reign clearly confirmed the expectations that the deity he was predestined to worship had brought good fortune to him and, by extension, to his town. While Bamigbaye did not forbid or limit other cults, his successes spoke for themselves, and many people adopted *Ṣàngó* worship during his reign, sometimes in addition to other deities worshipped in their compounds.

---

⁴² M. Ogunmola, *A New Perspective to Oyo Empire History, 1530–1944* (Ibadan: Vantage Publishers, 1985), p. 67.
⁴³ Ogunmola, *A New Perspective to Oyo Empire History*, pp. 67–8.
⁴⁴ Oyeweso, *Ede in Yoruba History*, p. 78.
⁴⁵ Olunlade, *Ede: A Short History*, pp. 22–3.
⁴⁶ Olunlade, *Ede: A Short History*, p. 23.
⁴⁷ Johnson described *Tìmì* Bamigbaye as 'the richest Timi that ever ruled Ede'. See Johnson, *History of the Yorubas*, p. 212.

Tìmì Sangolami Abibu Lagunju (1847–1900) and the Spread of Islam in Ede

The earliest introduction of Islam into Ede is associated with the arrival of Muslim families and individuals who were displaced by the wars that predated the destruction of Oyo-Ile. However, these migrants did not win many converts. It was only after the success of the Muslim Buremo Owon-la-a-rogo in the battle against Ibadan, and after his settlement in Ede, that Islam began to grow. As the townspeople were aware of Buremo's supernatural powers, he attracted a number of people who requested his assistance in attending to one problem or the other. Buremo often used this opportunity to preach Islam to his host community, and a number of people converted to Islam.

However, many traditional worshippers strongly opposed the rising influence of the new religion. They feared that the new religion and its followers could become so influential as to overshadow the town's traditional practices, which provided a link to the town's history and ancestors. Equally importantly, many saw Islam as a threat to the powers of the *Tìmì*, who was not only the political head of the town but also the custodian of the *Ṣàngó* cult. As a result, the first generation of Muslims in the town experienced some discrimination at the hands of the traditionalists.[48] Many parents and relatives refused to accommodate converts to Islam in their houses or compounds because they were regarded as rebels. Most converts were also disowned and had to seek refuge in Buremo's house. Moreover, these early Muslims could not practise their religion in public. Their call to prayer (*adhān*) had to be said into a keg in order not to ring out and arouse the anger of the traditionalists.[49]

The gradual acceptance of Muslims and their religion into mainstream Ede society was achieved under *Tìmì* Sangolami Abibu Lagunju.[50] In his youth Lagunju, born as a *Ṣàngó* worshipper, travelled to Ilorin, where Islam had gained its most important foothold in Yorubaland. He converted to Islam and remained at Ilorin for some time to learn Arabic and study Islam, before returning to Ede around or shortly after 1840. There he retreated to an uninhabited place now known as Agbongbe or Sooro, during an interregnum in Ede. He lived in a thatched hut that also served as a mosque and gained numerous converts and friends who admired his adventurous spirit, strength of character and spiritual conviction. As he was also very successful in playing

---

[48] Interview with *Alhaji* Mas'ud Husain Akajewole, Chief Imam of Edeland. 20 March 2013.
[49] Dokun, 'Islam in Ede', p. 25.
[50] S. Oyeweso, 'Historical development of Islam in Ede', *Islam and Society in Osun State: Essays in Honour of HRM Oba Raufu Olayiwola Olawale Adedeji II, Akinrun of Ikirun*, ed. S. Oyeweso and R.O. Olawale (Abuja: Mega Press, 2012), pp. 1–18.

other candidates and the kingmakers off against each other, Lagunju eventually became the *Tìmì* in 1847.[51]

There are fewer stories about *Tìmì* Lagunju's religious predestination than about *Tìmì* Bamigbaye's, but it has been claimed that *Tìmì* Lagunju was revealed as a 'predestined' Muslim by *Ifá* divination after his birth, and that his parents ignored the prophecy. Later Lagunju fulfilled his own fate by travelling to Ilorin and converting to Islam. This narrative opens the door to another – necessarily short – reflection on the complex relationship between Yoruba pre-Islamic practices and Islam.[52] Drawing on a large repertoire of stories, songs and riddles about different gods, spirits and cultural heroes, all of which are anchored in past divinations, *Ifá* offers predictions and revelations about the present and future. As a supreme intermediary between human beings and spiritual forces, *Ifá*'s advice often includes suggestions about the deities and cults that an individual should worship,[53] and according to some Ede historians, it was *Ifá* that revealed *Tìmì* Bamigbaye's destiny of *Ṣàngó* worship (see chapter 3). But it is also documented for many parts of Yorubaland that *Ifá* has revealed the religious destiny of conversion to Islam through the *Ifá* verse *Odù Òtura Méjì*, also known as the *Odù* of Muslims. As in the relationship between *Ṣàngó* and Islam, this implies again that the spread of Islam in Yorubaland owes at least some of its success to the way in which it was appropriated by, and included into, non-Islamic practice.[54]

As the first Muslim ruler of the nearby town of Iwo in 1860 was believed to be a predestined Muslim, this 'traditional' legitimation of Islam through *Ifá* may also have played a role in garnering acceptance for the installation of a Muslim *Tìmì* as the ruler of Ede.[55] It is certainly likely that belief in *Tìmì* Lagunju's preordained Islamic identity encouraged and legitimised conversion among the townspeople. In addition, given the importance of *Tìmì* Bamigbaye's predestination for Ede's acceptance of large-scale *Ṣàngó* worship, it is also possible that the ostensibly fated nature of *Tìmì* Lagunju's Islamic identity repeated a form of royal agency that had served the town well in the past. In many Yoruba communities, the 'stereotypic reproduction' of

---

[51] Olunlade, *Ede: A Short History*, pp. 24–5.
[52] See L. Brenner, 'Muslim divination and the history of religion of sub-Saharan Africa', *Insight and Artistry in African Divination*, ed. John Pemberton III (Washington and London: Smithsonian Institution Press, 2000), pp. 45–59, for a discussion about the relationship between *Ifá* and Islamic divination.
[53] W.R. Bascom, *Ifa Divination: Communication Between Gods and Men in West Africa* (Bloomington: Indiana University Press, 1969), pp. 11–12.
[54] T.G.O. Gbadamosi, '"Odu Imale": Islam in Ifa divination and the case of predestined Muslims', *Journal of the Historical Society of Nigeria* 8:4 (1977), 77–93.
[55] Gbadamosi, 'Odu Imale', pp. 91–2.

local events explains, legitimises and incorporates recent transformations into existing understandings of past and present.[56]

As the town's ruler, *Tìmì* Lagunju gave his support to the growth of Islam and his protection to the Muslims. One of the strategies he employed was to ensure the conversion of his immediate family, relatives and friends to Islam. His other method was to encourage the conversion of influential chiefs by giving out his daughters in marriage to them. Among these chiefs were Gbamolada in Isale Osi and Alfa Lawani in Saki, both of whom were influential men.[57] He further gave free chieftaincy titles to wealthy individuals,[58] many of whom embraced the religion to gain his favour. One other method he used was to act as patron for many craft guilds, which relied on his protection and goodwill. Enforcing Islamic religious and aesthetic practices, *Tìmì* Lagunju insisted that his chiefs wore turbans in the palace and that his followers performed the five daily ṣalāt (prayers) and the Friday congregational prayers at their appropriate times. After he had raised the profile of Islam and ensured that Muslims enjoyed the freedom to practise their religion in public, the religion attracted both the rich and the poor.

Tìmì Abibu Lagunju consolidated the practice of Islam in Ede with the appointment of one of his friends, Nuhu Adekilekun, as the Chief Imam of Ede. Sheikh Noah Adekilekun, as he was later called, was well-versed in Arabic and Islamic knowledge and had attracted many followers before his appointment. He accommodated many of the Muslims who were rejected by their families in his house, which later became known as Imole Compound.[59] Lagunju also built a town mosque where the current central mosque is located and invited other itinerant mallams, often as teachers and preachers, to Ede. Many of these mallams settled permanently in the town, built up families and successfully converted other people to Islam. Among the notable mallams of this period were Alfa Sado from Ilorin, who settled at Daodu Compound and Alfa Abudu, also from Ilorin, who first settled at Asafa Compound and later moved to a place known as Talafia Imam Compound (for a detailed discussion of Ede's Muslim compounds, see chapter 5).

But in addition to attracting followers to Islam, *Tìmì* Lagunju also insisted on an end to òrìṣà worship. Serious attempts were made to purge local Islamic

---

[56] See J.D.Y. Peel, 'Making history: The past in the Ijesha present', *MAN* 19:1 (1984), 111–32: 113–14, 118; P.F. de Moraes Farias, 'History as consolation: Royal Yorùbá bards comment on their craft', *History in Africa* 19 (1992), 263–97.

[57] T.G.O. Gbadamosi, *The Growth of Islam among the Yoruba, 1841–1908* (London: Longman, 1978), p. 72.

[58] Recipients of chieftaincy titles and other honours were (and are) normally expected to reciprocate by giving the ọba a handsome gift.

[59] A. Oyedeji, 'History of Imamship in Ede', unpublished manuscript (n.p., n.d.).

practice of accretions, syncretism, and adulteration, and *Tìmì* Lagunju insisted that those who accepted Islam should bring their 'idols' out to the public to be burnt or dumped in the Osun River. His stance against the traditional religion was later eulogised with the talking drums: 'Lágúnjú paná ẹbọ pátápátá / Ó fó igbá ẹbọ wómúwómú' ('Lagunju extinguished the fire of idol-worship totally / He crushed it completely').[60]

Tìmì Lagunju's opposition to traditional practice also found expression in his employment of Islamic law in the administration of the town. The law was aimed at wiping out vices such as adultery, theft, back-biting etc. However, *Tìmì* Lagunju insisted on a very firm, and possibly idiosyncratic interpretation of the law. For example, if anyone was caught stealing, *Tìmì* Lagunju not only sold the offender but also his whole family into slavery.[61] While some welcomed the introduction of Islamic law and Lagunju's uncompromising attitude towards anti-social practices more generally, many townspeople regarded Lagunju's application of Islamic law as too authoritarian and cruel.

Like *Tìmì* Bamigbaye, *Tìmì* Lagunju was however able to boost his political authority within the town through his abilities as a warrior. In the 1860s, *Tìmì* Lagunju led a battle against Ijesa forces that had previously challenged the Ibadan (and Ede) armies. The Ede side was victorious in the ensuing battle, also known as the *Alágbára* war, and *Tìmì* Lagunju returned home bolstered by his military victories.[62] After these victories, however, Lagunju became more of an absolute ruler, and made decisions increasingly without the consent of the town's civic leaders. Popular opposition to Lagunju's rule was captured in a nineteenth-century song, here offered in translation:

> In the days of [*Tìmì*] Arohanran[63] we were wealthy,
> Everyone bought at least seven shawls.
> Please note that in the reign of [*Tìmì*] Ajeniju[64] we were not too badly-off,
> Everyone bought at least six shawls.
> Please note that in the reign of [*Tìmì*] Lagunju we are all famished,
> Even foodstuffs are costly and we are underfed.
> Please note that you, *Tìmì*, a despised Muslim, are unwanted in Ede,
> You have to go beyond the Osun River.[65]

---

[60] A.F.K. Makinde, 'The institution of Shari'ah in Oyo and Osun States, Nigeria, 1890–2005', unpublished PhD thesis (Ibadan: Department of Arabic and Islamic Studies, University of Ibadan, 2007), p. 69.

[61] Olunlade, *Ede: A Short History*, p. 25.

[62] Olunlade, *Ede: A Short History*, p. 25.

[63] *Tìmì* Ojo Arohanran was *Tìmì* Bamigbaye's younger brother and ruled after his death.

[64] *Tìmì* Ajeniju Bamigbaye.

[65] Taken and slightly adapted from Olunlade, *Ede: A Short History*, p. 26.

As *Tìmì* Lagunju's reign continued, the town was increasingly divided by civil conflict and he was deposed three times. His good military connections to Ibadan helped him reclaim the throne twice, but he was finally exiled to Ibadan in 1893, where he died in 1900.[66] His exile was clearly related to his uncompromising insistence on exclusive Islamic practice, because it was associated with a short-lived but sharp setback to the spread of Islam in Ede. Many of those who had accepted Islam under his reign returned to their traditional deities after his departure. There was also a renewed persecution of some Muslims by their family members. Most of these Muslims fled to Buremo Owon-la-rogo's compound, now Imole Compound, and to other Muslim-dominated compounds where they were able to practise their religion freely and under the guidance of learned Muslims.

But independently of the *Tìmì*, the Muslim clerics whom Lagunju had invited during his reign provided leadership and guidance to Ede's Muslim community.[67] The Chief Imam and his officers had become an important force within the town's traditional political system, and in this capacity they continued to represent the Muslims of Ede. They also continued to operate the Islamic court, which existed until 1913, i.e. into the early years of colonial rule, under the direction of Qadi Sidiq.[68] Children continued to be taught in Islamic places of learning, which had been established in several Muslim compounds. As a result, the Muslim community continued to thrive and after a while to expand again, even after *Tìmì* Lagunju's deposition.

By the early twentieth century, Muslim groups that were organised independently from the town's main Muslim community were also established. Early groups included the Tijaniyya and Qadiriyya as well as the Ahmadiyya and the Ansar-ud-Deen Society. More recent Muslim groups include the Zumratul-Mu'minin Society, the Nasrullahi al-Fatih Society of Nigeria (NASFAT), Tablighi Jamaat and Fatihu Quareeb. The principles of these groups differ on important issues such as the conduct of social ceremonies like marriage, birth and funerals, but also on other forms of behaviour and religious practices and belief. The early Ahmadis in the town were severely criticised and at times drawn into violent conflict for not accepting the Prophet Muhammed as the seal of prophets in Islam. It was only after the intervention

---

[66] 1903 is the date given by *Tìmì* Laoye. Agiri suggests that he was exiled earlier, namely in 1890. See J.A. Laoye, *The Story of My Installation* (Ede: Aafin Timi Ede, 1956), p. 18; and Agiri, 'Early Oyo history reconsidered', p. 3.

[67] They included Zulu Qarnain, a son of Noah Adekilekun, who turned the Imole compound into a learning centre for Islamic studies and became the first indigenous Alfa Tafsir in the town. Dokun, 'Islam in Ede', p. 33.

[68] Makinde, 'The institution of Shari'ah', p. 69.

of *Tìmì* Laoye that the group was allowed to be formally inaugurated in the town in August 1970.[69] Today the group still remains somewhat isolated from other Muslim groups.[70]

6 Chief Imam *Alhaji* Mas'ud Husain Akajewole entering the prayer ground during *Iléyá* 2012

As the Muslim community has grown, the coexistence of Islam and the town's traditional religions has involved both friction and mutual engagement. *Tìmì* Abibu Lagunju's insistence on the public destruction of converts' idols echoed the concerns of early Christian missionaries elsewhere in Yorubaland. It was an enormous challenge for many Muslims not to continue to perform the rituals associated with local deities, and some Muslims still continue to participate in such practices. Giving up their *òrìṣà* was especially difficult for converts who were *Ifá* diviners or who consulted *Ifá* regularly, even though some *Ifá* diviners were very attracted to Islam and eventually converted.[71] In more practical terms, hunters and blacksmiths often found that they could not practise their profession without *Ògún*, and faced the choice between giving up their profession or maintaining the *òrìṣà*.

The abandonment of traditional practice was also difficult where it was associated with the traditional deities of their families and compounds. These

---

[69] Dokun, 'Islam in Ede', p. 111.
[70] Interview with Mutiu Lawal, Timi Road, Ede. 20 July 2013.
[71] J.D.Y. Peel, *Religious Encounter and the Making of the Yoruba* (Bloomington: Indiana University Press, 2000), pp. 114–21.

òrìṣà were believed to govern the life of every member of the compound, and the failure to appease them could spell doom to the entire family. Thus when traditionalists tried as much as possible to oppose the spread of Islam, they were often acting out of concern for the town or their family. Conflicts arose in many families when Muslim sons attempted to convert their traditionalist parents to Islam or to destroy the family deity, which was usually kept in the compound. To prevent such conflicts, many parents initiated one of their sons into the family cult while they allowed others to join the new religion. Parents often pressurised their initiates not to abandon their family cults, but over time this strategy also failed, as many of the initiates nonetheless embraced Islam.[72]

Overall, as people have converted to Islam, a growing number of Muslims has refused to be involved in traditional practices. This trend was encouraged by *wa'azi*, or open-air lectures, organised by Muslim clerics to educate the Muslim community. Especially during the colonial period, these open-air lectures recorded some successes, and many Muslims abandoned their traditional deities.[73] In the past, some traditionalists attacked the Muslim preachers in public for condemning their religion. However, while individual traditional priests are still unhappy about such sermons, such conflicts have not taken place for a long time. The main reason for this is that the number of people who remain involved in òrìṣà worship is declining, and many of those who still pay homage to the òrìṣà would not like to admit in public that they do so.

Today there are very few self-declared traditionalists in Ede. However, the òrìṣà remain important in the search for solutions by some individuals, and as the anchors of important town festivals. For this reason the relationship between Islam and traditional practice remains shaped by the tension between the desire for exclusive Islamic practice and the recognition of the òrìṣà as important links between past and present. As townspeople and descendants of local families, Muslims can participate in such celebrations of community in different ways, including in ways that assert their identity as Muslims.

Christianity as a Minority Religion and the Rule of *Timì* John Adetoyese Laoye (1946–75)

Despite the dominance of Islam in Ede, Christianity also has a significant presence in the town. But like the relationship between Islam and traditional worship, the relationship between Islam and Christianity is in many ways ambiguous. Thus, the first encounter of the people of Ede with Christianity

---

[72] Makinde, 'The institution of Shari'ah', pp. 35–6.
[73] Ibid.

took place in 1856 when the Baptist missionary W.H. Clarke visited *Tìmì* Abibu Lagunju (1847–1900) during his travels in Yorubaland. In recognition of the shared monotheism of Islam and Christianity, and possibly also with a view to the potential political importance of European goodwill, W.H. Clarke was given a warm reception. He used the opportunity of his visit to preach Christianity to the people; they allowed him to speak and listened to him carefully,[74] though no-one embraced Christianity. Today, some Muslims and traditionalists are united in their scepticism of Christianity. This is captured in the locally popular Yoruba proverb,

> Ayé la bá 'fá
> Ayé la bá 'mọ̀le
> Ọsán gangan nì gbàgbọ́ wọlé.

> *Ifá*, we met in the world
> Islam, we met in the world
> But Christianity is a latter-day entrant.[75]

The actual introduction of (Baptist) Christianity into Ede can be traced to Jacob Oyeboade Akerele, an indigene of Ede born to parents who were practitioners of traditional religions. Akerele had spent the years between 1892 and 1900 in Ogbomoso, then a stronghold of the Baptist mission in Yorubaland. Living with guardians who were staunch Baptists, Akerele attended Baptist schools and converted to Christianity. In 1900, he returned to Ede,[76] where his missionary work was greatly assisted by his literacy. Jacob Akerele organised classes for young men and women under a tree in front of his house, where he taught them to read and write in the English language and instructed them in Bible verses and messages. While many people opposed him, he managed to attract about thirty converts, who included both former Muslims and traditionalists.[77] Impressed with his success, the *Tìmì* gave him some land to build a Baptist Church at Babasanya compound. However, the members of the first

---

[74] W.H. Clarke, *Travels and Explorations in Yorubaland, 1854–1858*, ed. J.A. Atanda (Ibadan: Ibadan University Press, 1972), p. 115.
[75] Dokun, 'Islam in Ede', p. 38.
[76] Ibid.
[77] I thank all my informants and interviewees at various branches of the Baptist Church in Ede. These include interviews with Reverend Sunday Olu Ogunwale, Pastor of Mercyland Baptist Church. 1 February 2013; Reverend (Dr) S.A. Alabi, Pastor of First Baptist Church Apaso. 1 February 2013; Reverend G.J. Oladele, Pastor of Oore-Ofe Baptist Church. 5 February 2013; Reverend S.A. Olawale, Pastor of Christ Baptist Church. 6 February 2013; Reverend Jesugbemi, Pastor of New Glory Baptist Church. 20 February 2013; and Reverend G.R. Olorode, Pastor of Good News Baptist Church. 28 February 2013.

Baptist Christian congregation at Babasanya Church soon divided into factions and the young Christian community collapsed.

After the collapse of Babasanya Church, many Christians reverted to their earlier religions, i.e. Islam and traditional practice.[78] This return to past practices was similar to the reversion of some Muslim converts to traditional practice after *Tìmì* Lagunju went into exile. There are probably many reasons for such relapses among converts, but apart from suggesting that conversion is a longer-term process than often assumed, they point to the social importance of religious practice for many converts. Personal conviction certainly played an important role for the conversion of early Muslims and Christians; however, the social nature of religious practice for many individuals is illustrated by the fact that both religions attracted followers when they could offer royal patronage and a well-organised and locally recognised communal life, and lost them when their patronage declined or the congregation faced problems.

Even so, a faction of the former community at Babasanya Church that had remained Christian eventually established the First Baptist Church at Oke Apaso (see Figure 14),[79] and the Baptist church began to wax stronger in the town. Other Christian denominations that found their way into Ede included the Anglican Church Mission, which arrived in Ede in 1911 and built its first church in 1920.[80] The Roman Catholic Church was established in the town in 1921,[81] and the African Church first arrived in Ede in 1926. While many of these churches were led by migrants to the town, the founder of the local Christ Apostolic Church, the late Prophet Samson Oladeji Akande of Kusi compound, was – like Jacob Akerele – a native of Ede. Originally a Muslim, his conversion to Christianity in 1938 attracted some converts from within the town. As discussed in greater detail in chapters 3 and 8, many of these churches built primary schools and eventually secondary schools in Ede. However, while schools and churches were able to draw some converts, it was the installation

---

[78] J.A. Atanda, *Baptist Churches in Nigeria, 1850–1950: Accounts of Their Foundation and Growth* (Ibadan: University of Ibadan Press, 1988), pp. 156–8.

[79] The First Baptist Church was founded in 1900 by the Jacob Akerele-led faction of the former Babasanya congregation in 1914. See *First Baptist Church, Oke Apaso, Ede: A Century of Practical and Expansive Evangelism in Edeland, 1900–2000* (n.d.), p. 1.

[80] The Anglican Mission was one of the five oldest European Christian missions that came to Nigeria under Henry Townsend in the 1840s; cf. J.A. Ajayi, *Christian Missions in Nigeria, 1841–1891: The Making of a New Elite* (London: Longman, 1965), p. 1.

[81] As a means of winning converts, the Catholic Church established a seminary in Ede in 1955 and Our Lady and St Kizito Catholic Minor Seminary in 1975. Today, there are many Catholic churches in Ede, including Catholic Church of Christ Sagba, Ojularede Road, Ede and St Anthony Catholic Church, Alagbede, Ede.

of Ede's first Christian ọba, Tìmì John Adetoyese Laoye, that really encouraged the growth of Christianity in Ede.

After losing his father young, Laoye had spent much of his childhood in the family of a maternal uncle who taught him drumming. Later he was sent to the palace to learn to read and write under the tutelage of a Christian scribe, J.O. Aboderin. One day, Baptist missionaries visited the palace and invited him to follow them to Osogbo, where he attended school and Baptist services. When his father's younger brother decided to send him to a Qur'anic school instead, John ran away to Saki to complete his studies. Eventually he became a dispenser and entered the civil service, spending years in places as far away as Kano and Maiduguri but also Benin City, Warri, Sapele, Jos, Lagos, Ibadan and Akure. Popular, cosmopolitan and relatively wealthy, John Adetoyese Laoye returned to his hometown to be installed as the Tìmì in 1946. Apart from his own Baptist denomination, he supported many Christian groups during his reign, especially those that promised to bring Western education to the town.

A few years after his installation, Tìmì Laoye leased 107.8 acres of land to the Seventh Day Adventist Mission, whose leaders wanted to establish a secondary school. The Seventh Day Adventist (SDA) Grammar School was opened on 29 February 1960.[82] The SDA Church and Secondary School won many converts from the majority Muslims of the town, including Adedeji Adeleke, the founder of Ede's Adeleke University (see chapter 9). Prince S.B. Oniye, a soldier in the Nigerian Army, established the first Parish of the Celestial Church of Christ (CCC) in 1968. It started at a rented room at 1 Elerin Street that belonged to one of the wives of Tìmì Laoye. As time went on, the congregation began to grow and the olorì (queen), Mrs Laoye, generously donated a place on the ground floor of her house to the Church.[83] The CCC moved to its first site at 17 Ibadehin Road (behind the old National Bank), Ede in 1969.[84] Today there are numerous other Christian denominations in Ede, including

---

[82] The school was originally under the headship of Pastor G.M. Ellstrom and later Messer Cross from the United States, who became the first substantive principal succeeded by Mr Cecil Boram. The first indigenous principal of the school was Mr E.O. Dare, who emerged in 1964. See A.A. Adesegun, 'Christian education in the Seventh-Day Adventist Church in Remo, Ogun State, Nigeria, 1959–2004', unpublished PhD thesis (Ibadan: Department of Religious Studies, University of Ibadan, 2009), p. 55.

[83] The pioneers of the church engaged in public announcements of the wonders of God through the church in different parts of Ede and the founder travelled wide in consultation with leaders of the CCC across the country to towns such as Ibadan, Lagos, Okitipupa, Ijebu Ode and Abeokuta.

[84] After several years of opposition from members of a secret society who dominated the area where the church was sited, the church grew stronger as more prayers were performed and more miracles happened. Interview with Prophet J. Segun Oniye, Leader and Presiding Shepherd. 22 March 2013. Ede Parish, Celestial Church of Christ, Ede.

the Cherubim and Seraphim Church, Redeemed Christian Church of God (RCCG), Deeper Life Christian Ministry and a host of other new-generation Pentecostal movements.

But *Tìmì* John Adetoyese Laoye's apparently selective support of Christian activity in general, and education in particular, also contributed to Muslim–Christian rivalry. As Christian missions in Ede established institutions of learning as well as hospitals, maternity homes and dispensaries, these were used as direct and indirect instruments of evangelisation. Muslims were especially affected by the relative advantage that Christians had owing to their excellent access to Western education. Many Muslims refused to send their children and wards to mission schools. Instead of putting them in a position where they might be converted, people insisted that their children attend only Arabic and Islamic schools to acquire Qur'anic education and learn a trade.

The educational distance between Muslims and Christians was further heightened in 1949, when Laoye supported the Baptist Church in establishing a Teacher Training College in the town. The Teacher Training College provided job opportunities for educated Christians to the exclusion of dominant Muslim population, and it gave Christians a further edge by enabling them to produce even more of the town's teachers. To be on a par with the Christians in educational advancement, the overwhelmingly Muslim community of the town raised money to build a community secondary school that would accommodate every child without any pressure for conversion to Christianity. However, when the school was completed in 1963, the only local qualified teachers were Christians. Instead of trying to retain at least some Muslim teachers, *Tìmì* Laoye employed mostly Baptist teachers at this community school. This decision meant that many Muslims who had contributed to the school now feared that their children would yet again be subject to pressure to convert. Their suspicions were confirmed when the school's name was changed to Baptist High School.

It is possible that Muslim resentment over this development was linked to the fact that in the early years of his reign, *Tìmì* Laoye's allocation of town land appeared somewhat biased against the Muslim community. In 1958, the Muslim community had felt the need to expand the mosque located at the central market place, Oja Timi, to accommodate the growing Muslim population in a new Central Mosque. *Tìmì* Laoye gave them a piece of land located adjacent to the old mosque. While some Muslims were prepared to accept the offer because land in the town centre was hard to come by, the majority thought that the plot given to the community was too small. They found the *ọba*'s conservative allocation of space especially galling because he had supported the Christian community with generous gifts of land. As a result, *Tìmì* Laoye had to contend with local unrest and opposition, including threatening protest songs directed at him. The lyrics of one of these songs highlight his perceived attempt to contain the predominance of Islam and, like the songs directed against *Tìmì* Lagunju, point to the limits of religious manipulation by an *ọba*: 'Ọba tí ó jẹ, tí kò fẹ́ 'mọ̀le, ẹ lé l'Ẹ́dẹ̀' ('The reigning king who hates Muslims should be banished from Ede').

Unlike those of his predecessors who were associated with the introduction or consolidation of new religions, *Tìmì* Laoye was not known for the fierceness of his character. But nor was he able to draw on military prowess or connections to defend his reign against those who were opposed to his religious politics. With colonial rule, Yorubaland had been subjected to the *pax Britannica*, and the role of Ede's *ọbas* changed dramatically. While colonial policy, and especially Indirect Rule, empowered traditional rulers in many ways, it was also based on the idea that *ọbas* could (and should) represent all their subjects. As this idea resonated with the historical notion that the *ọba* is the head of all cults, or religions, it was shared by many Yoruba speakers. For that reason, petitions and complaints regarding unpopular rulers often referred to their bias, and colonial officials, as well as their postcolonial successors, were prepared to take such complaints seriously. As those rulers who could not maintain control over their communities were subjected to inquiries or even dethroned, *ọba*ship remained based, at least in part, on consent from the population. Unlike under previous *Tìmì*, the disagreement between the Christian *Tìmì* Laoye and his predominantly Muslim subjects was therefore settled in a colonial court of law, with a ruling in favour of those Muslims who supported the use of the old site at Oja-Timi.[85]

Unlike the many war-like rulers who had preceded him, the progress *Tìmì* Laoye brought to Ede was linked to his commitment to development along lines also recognised by the colonial and postcolonial state. Much of his popularity rested on his ability and willingness to mobilise the resources to build motorable roads and to provide better access to water and electricity. He was also acutely aware of the importance of education, and in the later period of his reign increased his acceptance by supporting the establishment of Muslim schools such as the Bamigbaye Memorial School, now called the Tajudeen School.[86] The Muslim community also raised money for a second time and built a new school called Ede Muslim Grammar School in 1974. These schools finally succeeded in motivating Muslims to take up Western education in

---

[85] See Dokun, 'Islam in Ede', p. 52.

[86] *Tìmì* Laoye's commitment to modernisation and education is clearly set out in his autobiography: Laoye, *Story of My Installation*.

larger numbers.[87] The establishment of private Muslim schools for the education of their children also helped to ease competition between Muslims and Christians.[88]

Even so, the relationship between Islam and Christianity has remained competitive, and it continues to centre on Christians' control of resources including education and health (see chapters 2 and 7). In the debates and compromises that surround the attempts to come to mutually acceptable solutions, competing notions of community are often at play. While Christians sometimes offer access to their resources with the expectation that the beneficiaries of such goods would join their community, many Muslims imply that such goods should be made available to the whole town without any pressure or temptation regarding conversion. This expectation clearly reflects the majority position of the Muslims, who find it easier than the minority groups to see the boundaries between the religious community and the community of descent and residence – Ede – as overlapping.

Conclusion

The *Tìmì* of Ede have played an important role in establishing the influence and reach of religions throughout the town's history. *Tìmì* Bamigbaye and *Tìmì* Lagunju are associated with the introduction of Ṣàngó and Islam as the town's dominant religions respectively, and *Tìmì* Laoye entrenched the position of Christianity and especially the Baptist Church. But while Bamigbaye and Lagunju were successful in attracting large sections of the town to new religious practices, Laoye was unable, or unwilling, to do so. There are many reasons for these differences, and the fact that both Bamigbaye and Lagunju were believed to be predestined followers of a new religion may have both strengthened and (retrospectively) legitimised their success. However, the fact that *Tìmì* Laoye reigned in a very different context, in which he could not draw on military success to legitimise religious change and where the colonial state limited religious discrimination, also restricted his ability to effect large-scale religious change.

A closer look at the involvement of these *Tìmì* in religious conflicts also suggests that there are some enduring expectations associated with ọbaship in Ede. If *Tìmì* Bamigbaye offered others the chance to experience the efficacy

---

[87] Interview with *Alhaja* Lateefat Giwa, former *Amirah*, Federation of Muslim Women Association of Nigeria (FOMWAN), Osun State Chapter. 22 March 2013. Lati Rental Service, Olaiya Junction, Osogbo.

[88] These Muslim schools include Al-Fareed Nursery and Primary School, An-Nuur Primary School, Ahmadiyyah Schools, Muslim Grammar School, Ansarul-Il-Islam Grammar School, etc.

of the Ṣàngó he worshipped, it was by example. Because the Tîmì was both a political and a spiritual leader, the power and success of the Ṣàngó he was predestined to worship was more than simply an asset to the town – it meant that both the ọba and the townspeople had an obligation towards the deity. And while Ṣàngó may indeed have offered a powerful symbol of Oyo identity and its complex engagement with Islam, the deity won widespread acceptance in Ede primarily owing to its work for and in the community. Ṣàngó became the town's most important òrìṣà because it enabled Tîmì Bamigbaye to achieve victory against Ibadan, because it provided powerful protection to the town and its leaders, and because it was found efficacious by those who adopted it for themselves or their families.

As Tîmì Bamigbaye's change of the town's dominant religion focused on public and royal practices, it did not forcibly interfere with the family and personal practices of other worshippers, even as many were convinced of Ṣàngó's efficacy. Given that Ṣàngó worship is not predicated on the non-existence of other deities, and that Ṣàngó even draws some of its strength from the ability to transgress religious boundaries – as illustrated by his reliance on Islamic prayer to defend the town – it would however be misleading to consider Ṣàngó's coexistence with other deities as a form of toleration. Instead of simply 'tolerating' other practices, Ṣàngó appropriated them for his own benefit.

Tîmì Lagunju's conversion to Islam was, like Bamigbaye's, legitimated through predestination, but Lagunju set out to transform the community much more radically than his predecessor. Tîmì Lagunju's harsh rule and his suppression of pre-Islamic practices transformed both the public institutions of the town, such as its laws, and the private religious practices of its citizens. The exclusive demands of Islam meant that its establishment was fraught with potential for social and political conflict. This suggests that Tîmì Lagunju's approach challenged widespread expectation that the ọba should, at a minimum, not disadvantage those who practiced other religions. While Tîmì Lagunju used his traditionally legitimated office to lay the foundations for a large-scale conversion to Islam, the repeated and eventually successful attempts to depose him suggest that his lack of toleration for non-Islamic practice eventually undermined his own traditional legitimacy.

By the time Tîmì Laoye became Ede's ruler, the colonial and later postcolonial state strongly discouraged the kinds of coercive actions that Tîmì Lagunju had undertaken to establish Islam. However, given the instability that coercion brought to Tîmì Lagunju's reign, the colonial state's limitation of religious manipulation may have echoed precolonial notions of the ọba's need to tolerate all forms of worship. But Laoye was, by most accounts, also a congenial man with a less forceful – or divisive – personality than Lagunju. Moreover, by the time of his reign, private Muslim and Christian religious identities were relatively firmly established, making large-scale conversion a potentially very conflictual process. While *Tìmì* Laoye was free to encourage the activities of Christian groups, the Muslim community expected him not just to tolerate them but to offer them similar encouragement. When Laoye's greater generosity to Christians than to Muslims with regard to land was seen to put Muslims at a relative disadvantage, he had to face – and acceded to – internal criticism.

Overall, the acceptance of royal involvement in the town's religious life over the past two centuries illustrates the importance of the traditional political system, and especially the *Tìmì*, for the spiritual wellbeing of the town. The fact that in all reigns examined here, conflict was linked to the perceived unfair treatment of another religious group suggests that townspeople accept their rulers' leadership in religious or spiritual terms, but at the same time they expect them not to put other groups at a disadvantage, or even a relative disadvantage. The *ọba* satisfies the expectation that he should act as the head of all religions in his town – a notion whose implications are explored in more detail in the following chapter – not only by tolerating religions other than his own, but by encouraging and supporting them. As the next chapter sets out, such support often involves the expectation that the *ọba* participates in multiple religious practices.

CHAPTER 3

Ambivalence and Transgression in the Practice of Ṣàngó

Aderemi Suleiman Ajala[1] and Insa Nolte

This chapter explores the ambivalent role of Ṣàngó in Ede by focusing on the deity's association with the transgression of boundaries in different contexts. Connected with the foundation of the town, Ṣàngó was always an important historical and civic power in Ede, but with Tìmì Bamigbaye Ṣàngó also became closely identified with Ede's ruler (chapter 2). This association has continued to this day because the successive ọbas of a town are seen as one persona, each individual a continuation of his predecessors.[2] As a result, Ede's Tìmìs are understood as having greater powers than ordinary mortals because they are ọbas and thus imbued with the spiritual power that derives from the history and community of the town.[3] In this capacity, they act as the heads, or patrons, of all religions practised within the town. However, the Tìmìs also represent Ṣàngó, a transgressive deity in his own right.

Focusing on Ṣàngó's association with contradictory, ambivalent and transgressive positions in Ede, the chapter understands transgression as a site and a strategy of power and domination, on the part of both Ṣàngó and the Tìmì.[4]

[1] Aderemi Suleiman Ajala's contribution to this chapter draws on ethnographic support from Mr Tunde Olayiwola Olosun, who conducted additional fieldwork in Ede in October 2012, while Ajala was in Germany for a three-month research residence. In addition, Ajala conducted online interviews with a number of Ede indigenes, many of whom were facilitated by his friends – Sangosakin Ajala (a Ṣàngó priest in Osogbo) and Onifade (an Ifa priest in Ede). Among his respondents Ajala especially appreciates Alhaji Adewolu, Chief Onifade and Mrs Munirat. The rich library resources and the anthropologists of Anthropos Institut, Sankt Augustin, Germany, were helpful in writing the draft paper and seminar discussion in Germany.

[2] I. Nolte, 'Chieftaincy and the state in Abacha's Nigeria: Kingship, political rivalry and competing histories in Abeokuta during the 1990s', Africa 72:3 (2002), 368–90.

[3] The Yoruba people refer to their ọbas as Aláṣẹ Èkejì Òrìṣà (owners of authority that is second to the gods or deities). J. Pemberton and F. Afolayan, Yoruba Sacred Kingship: "a power like that of the gods" (Washington: Smithsonian Institution Press, 1996).

[4] The authors are grateful to Wale Adebanwi for suggesting this point.

It therefore highlights forms of religious encounter and engagement that challenge notions of tolerance as the only form of peaceful or productive religious coexistence. By examining transgression in the context of royal agency, the chapter also engages with Jacob Olupona's argument, based on his study of ọbaship in Ondo, that 'the king's role as the patron of all the town's gods and religions forges the cults of these separate religious groups into a unified civil religion', which however draws on and embraces traditional practices – such as widespread historical understandings of the ruler as the head of all religions (chapter 1).[5]

Building on and qualifying Olupona's work, this chapter argues that in Ede ọbaship is associated both with the civic practice of multiple religious participation, which represents all religions as equally valid in their own context and, inspired by the character of Ṣàngó, with the charismatic transgression of the boundaries that separate different religions. As practices and strategies of power, both multiple religious participation and charismatic transgression reveal religious boundaries as more ambivalent than implied in the concept of tolerance.

The ambivalent powers of royal and divine agency are explored through the narratives surrounding the rise of Ṣàngó (already an important civic deity in Ede) as the personal deity of the town's ruler, and especially in Ṣàngó's ambivalent role in the introduction of Islam to Ede. The chapter also explores the ambivalent practices that serve to contain and celebrate Ṣàngó today, in the context of the town's overwhelming Muslim identity. Focusing on the attempts of Ede's only Christian Tìmì, John Adetoyese Laoye, to establish shared territory between Ṣàngó and Christianity in the town, the last section illustrates in what way charismatic transgression may be implicit in the royal practice of civil religion. The conclusion considers the sometimes contradictory pulls of 'civil religion' and the transgressive appropriation associated with Ṣàngó more generally.

Ṣàngó as a Civic and a Royal Deity

Like all popular Yoruba deities, Ṣàngó is believed to fulfil his devotees' wishes, including requests for a child, success in trading or recovery from a protracted illness. But Ṣàngó also has more specific attributes. He is usually portrayed with a double axe (the symbol of thunder) on his head, called Oṣé Ṣàngó, i.e. Ṣàngó's wand. Just as lightning flashes unexpectedly in the dark

[5] J.O. Olupona, *Kingship, Religion, and Rituals in a Nigerian Community: A Phenomenological Study of Ondo Yoruba Festivals* (Stockholm: Alimquist & Wiksell, 1991), p. 84.

to show up otherwise indistinguishable landscapes, Ṣàngó has the ability to disrupt appearances and to illuminate the hidden truth quickly and violently. He reveals theft, lies and other crimes, and imposes severe punishments on the perpetrators of such acts. As the master of strategy and tactics, Ṣàngó has an ability to move people and things with his words, and rises to confront and meet great challenges. Revealing hidden truths, punishing evildoers and changing the course of events, Ṣàngó is a deity associated with courage and justice, but also with violence, challenges to the appearance of things and transgression.

Ṣàngó's ability to challenge established boundaries or categories is reflected in his own character. Thus he is known, through the *Ifá* divination system, both as one of sixteen principal or primordial deities and as a former ruler of Oyo. It was in this human form, as the *Aláàfin* of Oyo who was later deified as Ṣàngó, that he played a distinctive and important role in the foundation of Ede. Subsequent *Aláàfin* of Oyo were also worshippers of Ṣàngó, and he also remained important as a deity until the fall of Old Oyo Empire in the 1830s.[6] Ṣàngó devotees from Oyo and elsewhere settled in the town.

But while Ṣàngó was always a deity associated with the civic and political history of the town, his influence in Ede expanded greatly when *Tìmì* Kofoworola Ajeniju Bamigbaye came to the throne. According to local historians, Ajeniju Bamigbaye born with closed fists. Upon consultation, *Ifá* divination revealed that he was predestined to be a Ṣàngó devotee (see chapter 2). Following *Ifá*'s revelation, a message was sent to the *Mọgbà* (chief priests of Ṣàngó) at Oyo, who performed certain rituals so that his fists might open. Upon doing this, a small pebble[7] was found in his right palm and a cowry in the left. As both were signs of Ṣàngó, it was then revealed that he had been sent to earth as a *Mọgbà*, or Ṣàngó priest.

When Ajeniju Bamigbaye became the *Tìmì* himself, he instituted the worship of Ṣàngó as an important part of the town's political calendar.[8] *Tìmì* Ajeniju Bamigbaye had become a member of the inner cult of Ṣàngó before becoming the ọba of Ede, and he built a Ṣàngó shrine in the palace, occasionally wore Ṣàngó regalia and lived by Ṣàngó's taboos and obligations. As a result of his success in warfare, he commanded strong respect not only among existing adherents of Ṣàngó, but also among other traditional religious

---

[6] A. Ogundiran, 'Material life and domestic economy in a frontier of the Oyo Empire during the Mid-Atlantic Age', *The International Journal of African Historical Studies* 42:3 (2009), 351–85.

[7] This was a miniature of the stone called *Ẹdun Àrá*, or 'thunderbolt'.

[8] Interview with Ọba Muniru Adesola Lawal, Lamonisa I, the *Tìmì* of Ede. 23 May 2012. *Tìmì*'s palace, Ede.

adherents who admired the spiritual powers he commanded. He was widely seen as an incarnation of Ṣàngó, and the now annual celebration of Ṣàngó as the cult of the Ede monarch began during his reign.[9]

Conflating the boundaries between Ṣàngó as a civic and a personal deity, Tìmì Ajeniju Bamigbaye established the festival of Ṣàngó not as the exclusive preserve of his worshippers but as a festival for the whole town. Today, the annual Ṣàngó Tìmì festival is the most prominent traditional festival in Ede, and it is celebrated with pomp and pageantry for over a week. The Ṣàngó festival comes up during the dry season, usually in late October or early November (a more detailed discussion follows in chapter 4).[10] The date of the festival is announced twenty-one days in advance and is heralded by dancing to the main market square (Oja-Timi) where Ṣàngó's devotees perform symbolic and magical feats and actions. According to His Royal Majesty, Ọba Muniru Adesola Lawal, Laminisa I, 'the festival is the principal event in Ede that is held every October at Odò Ṣàngó on the first day and the rest at the palace and Ọjà Tìmì Market Square'.[11]

As Karin Barber has pointed out, Yoruba deities are maintained and kept in existence by the attention of humans.[12] But this attention does not always have to be explicitly religious, in the sense of being directly linked to firm positions of belief and clearly outlined rituals. On one level, the ongoing celebration of Ṣàngó in Ede simply recognises the importance of the deity for the history of the town. For those who have deep family roots in Ede, Ṣàngó's powerful and war-like character, as well as his promise to deliver swift justice, represent their community as well as themselves. As a concentration of Ede's history and characteristics, Ṣàngó appears a spiritual patron of the community, and the celebration of the deity over which the Tìmì presides can be seen as a central aspect of the town's 'civic religion'.[13] In a more Durkheimian understanding of local practice, the celebration of Ṣàngó is a way in which the community celebrates itself.

---

[9] S. Oyeweso, 'Keynote address', *Everyday Religion and Tolerance in Ede, Southwest Nigeria* conference, Adeleke University, Ede, 5–6 December 2012.

[10] This may not be applicable to all Yoruba towns as Ṣàngó worship also comes up in the rainy season in some parts of Yorubaland. See A. Adejumo, 'The practice and worship of Ṣàngó in contemporary Yorubaland', *Ṣàngó in Africa and the African Diaspora*, ed. J. Tishken, T. Falola and A. Akinyemi (Bloomington: Indiana University Press, 2009), p. 53.

[11] Interview with Ọba Muniru Adesola Lawal, Lamonisa I, the Tìmì of Ede. 23 May 2012. Tìmì's palace, Ede.

[12] K. Barber, 'How man makes God in West Africa: Yoruba attitudes towards the Orisa', *Africa* 51:3 (1981), 724–45.

[13] Olupona, *Kingship, Religion and Rituals in a Nigerian Community*.

In many Yoruba towns, royal festivals centre on the regular renewal of the ọba's – and the town's – power through the worship or celebration of locally important òrìṣà or historical or spiritual forces. Andrew Apter argues cogently that these forces are normally understood as different or separate from the ruler. As a source of rejuvenation, but also a potential form of danger for the community, they represent 'power *ultra vires* and structurally opposed to authority'.[14] But as the popular assertion 'Ṣàngóo Tìmì' (meaning 'Ṣàngó belongs to the Tìmì') illustrates, the townspeople consider that the link between the Tìmì and Ṣàngó is deeply personal: the deity is personally owned by the ruler rather than by the community.[15] All Tìmì, irrespective of personal religious identification, have been identified with Ṣàngó since Tìmì Lagunju's reign.[16] Clearly, Ṣàngó's influence extends beyond that of a purely civic deity.

The double presence of Ṣàngó as both the Tìmì himself and the power *ultra vires* that imbues him with authority challenges the symbolic opposition of power and authority that informs royal festivals in many Yoruba towns. Yet the Ṣàngó festival is celebrated as if the two were separate: as chapter 4 illustrates, the Tìmì offers a sacrifice to Ṣàngó, irrespective of the fact that he also represents Ṣàngó himself. The overdetermined and yet ambivalent role of Ṣàngó in the ritual and symbolic life of Ede indicates the deity's power both to exist within, and to transgress, boundaries.

Ṣàngó as a Facilitator and Rival of Early Islam

A closer look at Ṣàngó's role in the introduction of Islam to Ede illustrates that the deity's ambivalent and potentially transgressive capacity also shapes his relationship with Islam. In the nineteenth century, Ṣàngó competed with and challenged Islam, but the deity also appropriated and even occasionally supported the new religion. As explained in the previous chapter, it was Tìmì Ajeniju Bamigbaye, an incarnation of Ṣàngó himself, who invited Buremo Owon-la-a-rogo (also known as Owonlarogo), Ede's first Muslim, to defend the town against the Ibadan army. The narrative surrounding this encounter further illuminates the complex relationship between Ṣàngó and Islam. According to Olunlade, when Buremo came to Ede:

---

[14] A. Apter, *Black Critics and Kings: The Hermeneutics of Power in Yoruba Society* (Chicago and London: University of Chicago Press, 1992), p. 108.

[15] Ṣàngó is worshipped by some townspeople in a slightly different way, but in that context he is not considered 'Ṣàngóo Tìmì'. For a more detailed reflection on this phenomenon, see K. Barber, 'Oríkì, women and the proliferation and merging of Òrìṣà', *Africa* 60:3 (1990), 313–37.

[16] Interview with Ọba Muniru Adesola Lawal, Lamonisa I, the Tìmì of Ede. 23 May 2012. Tìmì's palace, Ede.

[He] was given all that he needed. When he had prepared his concoction, he ploughed it in the soil as one would plough manure. On that spot he planted cotton seeds. On the same day seeds sprouted, grew to maturity, budded, bloomed and produced cotton stuffs which were the same day made into cotton fibres. These fibres were the same day woven into a big cloth. [...] Owonlarago lifted the cloth gently with all solemnity and then quickly shook it in a way that all the dirts and stuffs hanging on the cloth would shake off in the direction of Ibadan [...]

In no time rain clouds gathered and heavy rains started to fall. Heavy lumps of frozen water started to fall on the Ibadan camp and so heavy were these lumps that they killed every man they hit. These continued for three days in succession and decimated the Ibadan hosts. The Ibadan [...] therefore started on a disorderly retreat shouting as they left "We are retreating for the fear of your strength, you Sango, the mighty protector of Timi."[17]

Clearly the story of *Tìmì* Bamigbaye's invitation and recognition of Muslim help on behalf of the town can be read in several ways. While Buremo's magical feats may seem strange to some Muslims today, they nonetheless illuminate aspects of the contribution of Islam to the town and region. While cotton long predates this period in West Africa, its provenance and trade is clearly associated with Muslim trading networks.[18] Buremo's association with superior agricultural knowledge as well as cloth production points to the many innovations and improvements brought to African communities in association with Islam. As Buremo also produces the hail that terrifies Ede's enemies, one could even interpret this story to suggest that it is Islam that really defends the town.

However, the fact that the Muslim Buremo Owonlarogo served under a *Tìmì* personally marked by, and therefore identified with, Ṣàngó suggests that Islam was introduced to Ede as a 'client religion' of Ṣàngó. Certainly, in this narrative, the powers associated with Islam are understood as subservient to Ṣàngó by both the townspeople and their enemies, the Ibadans, who run away from Buremo's hailstones, acknowledging Ṣàngó's power rather than that of Islam. Indeed, by saving the town through enormous hailstones that strike people dead instantly, the forces unleashed by Buremo evoke both the thunder and lightning with which Ṣàngó strikes, and the stones through which he is worshipped. It is almost as if Ṣàngó's power is revealed in its ability to

---

[17] E. Olunlade, *Ede: A Short History* (Ibadan: General Publications Section, Ministry of Education, 1961), pp. 22–3.

[18] C.E. Kriger, 'Mapping the history of cotton textile production in precolonial West Africa', *African Economic History* 33 (2005), 87–116.

marshal, and partly penetrate, the superior powers and 'outside' origins associated with Islam.[19]

The ambivalent relationship between Ṣàngó and Islam also informed the reign of Tìmì Sangolami Abibu Lagunju, and it supported the establishment of Islam in Ede during the second half of the nineteenth century. Tìmì Lagunju was a Ṣàngó worshipper before his conversion, and even though he is remembered for his insistence on pure Islamic practices among those he could convince to convert to his religion, he was nonetheless installed as the town's Tìmì in the traditional manner. Like his predecessors, Tìmì Lagunju lived in the palace, where daily and weekly obeisance and sacrifices were offered to Ṣàngó by his devotees, some of whom also lived in the royal compound.[20] Thus the power and authority on which Tìmì Lagunju drew to introduce Islam was derived in no small measure from Ṣàngó.

Moreover, Islam's association with Ṣàngó meant that it could be perceived as form of power that could be accessed or controlled through existing practices.[21] Tìmì Lagunju's claim to being a predestined Muslim suggests that his Islamic identity relied on legitimation through Ifá divination.[22] It was additionally justified because it repeated Tìmì Bamigbaye's precedent of having a preordained religion. The introduction of Islam on the basis of this double traditional legitimation meant that like the worship of Ṣàngó, Islam became a royal religion. (And it is certainly possible that the fierceness and violence with which Lagunju introduced Islam to Ede owed something to the ferocity generally associated with Ṣàngó.)

The complex relationship between Ṣàngó and Islam continues to be reflected in Ede's religious topography. Tìmì Lagunju built Ede's first central mosque directly next to the central Ṣàngó shrine, facing the royal palace across Ede's royal market. While both the central mosque and some of Ṣàngó's paraphernalia have moved slightly over the years, they still remain in close proximity and stand facing the Tìmì's palace. This arrangement was surely intended to assert the importance of Islam to the town, albeit in slippery ways. While the proximity of Ede's central mosque could be understood as a challenge to Ṣàngó, it also implied a closeness or comparability between Islam and Ṣàngó. Along with the royal palace, the two buildings associated with the most

---

[19] See S. Barnes, 'Ritual, power, and outside knowledge', *Journal of Religion in Africa* 20:3 (1990), 248–68.

[20] Others live in the compound of Ṣàngó worshippers in the town, Ile Onisango.

[21] A similar point is made for Oyo history in P.F. de Moraes Farias, 'History as consolation: Royal Yorùbá bards comment on their craft', *History in Africa* 19 (1992), 263–97.

[22] This claim is discussed in detail in T.G.O. Gbadamosi, '"Odu Imale": Islam in Ifa divination and the case of predestined Muslims', *Journal of the Historical Society of Nigeria* 8:4 (1977), 77–93: 91–3.

important spiritual powers in Ede's history dominate the town's centre and market place. While all three buildings represent Ede's community in slightly different ways, all appear to ensure the town's wealth and wellbeing.

Despite its emergence in the context of distinctly local dynamics, Ṣàngó's contradictory relationship with Islam is not unique to Ede. Like the Tìmì, the Aláàfin of Oyo is considered a descendant of Ṣàngó, and while the first Muslim Aláàfin was only enthroned in 1905, Oyo's traditional elite overwhelmingly converted to Islam during the twentieth century. Oyo's Aláàfin Adeniran Adeyemi II (1945–56) placed strong emphasis on his Muslim identity and is remembered as someone who did not show great support for traditional practice. Even so, his conferral of a chieftaincy title on the Bahia High Priestess Senhora for her services to the worship of Ṣàngó in Brazil implies that he understood himself also as at least a representative – if not an incarnation – of Ṣàngó.[23] Further study of the relationship between Islam and Ṣàngó would undoubtedly illuminate aspects of Yoruba òrìṣà practice that have remained unexamined to date.

Contemporary Celebration and Containment of Ṣàngó

Although most of Ede's citizens today identify as Muslims, the relationship between Ṣàngó and Islam remains complex. While Islam is firmly established as the dominant personal religion of the town, there are still specialists who carry out traditional practices on behalf of family and residential groups. As the number of priests, or experts, in Ṣàngó worship was never as high as the number of people who would turn to Ṣàngó in times of difficulty, it is not entirely obvious to what degree the worship of Ṣàngó has declined (though the decline itself is not in question).[24] Many Muslims denounce practices they consider to be syncretic and refuse to participate in worship or sacrifice associated with the òrìṣà or other spiritual powers. But even so, a significant number of people who are practising Muslims find it useful to turn to Ṣàngó when they are faced with a persisting problem. This is also true for Christians. An even larger number of people participate in the activities surrounding the

---

[23] P.F. de Moraes Farias, '"Yoruba Origins" Revisited by Muslims: An interview with the Arọ́kin of Ọ̀yọ́ and a reading of the Aṣl Qabā'il Yūrubā of Al-Ḥājj Ādam al-Ilūrī', *Self-Assertion and Brokerage: Early Cultural Nationalism in West Africa*, ed. K. Barber and P.F. de Moraes Farias (Birmingham: University of Birmingham African Studies Series, 1990), p. 115.

[24] A similar point was made in J.L. Matory, 'Rival empires: Islam and the religions of spirit possession among the Ọ̀yọ́-Yorùbá', *American Ethnologist* 21:3 (1994), 495–515: 499.

Ṣàngó festival, or support the òrìṣà financially in order to fulfil family or civic obligations.

The Ṣàngó festival remains important despite the fact that most of Ede's citizens are Muslims. Many associations of Ede townspeople who are based outside Ede hold their home meetings in Ede during the Ṣàngó festival. This enables them to show patriotism and to felicitate with the Tìmì,[25] who is the chief host during the celebration. As a result the Ṣàngó festival always induces a boom in local trading activities. Because Ṣàngó's annual celebration brings home large numbers of Ede people who live abroad, many people like to arrange marriage celebrations for the period. Some believe that such marriages will be blessed by the spirit of Ṣàngó that looms large in the town during its festival, and that the couple will therefore be strongly covenanted and difficult to be torn asunder. Furthermore, the large number of returning townspeople means that new relationships are often begun during the Ṣàngó festival. As large numbers of Ede's Muslims and Christians attend the annual Ṣàngó festival in Ede together, such relationships often cut across religious divides.

During the celebration of traditional festivals more generally, Muslim spaces and concerns take on an interesting position. Thus, when observers of the 2012 Egúngún festival in Ede climbed the walls of the central mosque, the mosque was appropriated by the masquerade for its audience. But equally it became a place of refuge from which a Muslim could safely view the activities of the masquerades, some of which might even represent his or her own ancestors.

During this particular festival, the close mutual implication of traditional practice and Islam was also illustrated by the appearance of Alfa Lagunju, a descendant of the famous Muslim Tìmì Lagunju. Joining the throng that surrounded the masquerades while riding on a camel, he made a distinctly Muslim appearance that competed in majesty and appeal with the town's Egúngún masquerades in order to protest against the ongoing political marginalisation of his family. By using the traditional festival as a forum for communal politics and debate that was open to him as a native of the town, Alfa Lagunju's appearance illustrates that Ede's history cannot be reduced to religious practice.

During traditional festivals, the celebration of Ṣàngó (or Egúngún) is a celebration of both the deity and the town's history and community. While most festivals are open to visitors, it is especially the native Ede people who feel as one with the other townspeople on such occasions. Enjoying the festival

---

[25] Interview with the President, Ede Socialite Club, Osogbo. 22 October 2012. Oke Gada, Ede. Conducted by Tunde Olayiwola-Olosun.

7 *Egúngún* Adinimodo before the central mosque with spectators, 2012

8 Alfa Lagunju during *Egúngún* festival 2012

as a celebration of a shared history and shared commitment to the town, Ede indigenes have reason to appreciate the deity that represents much of their pre-Islamic community. The strength of the bond that Ṣàngó still constitutes is illustrated by an example from the 2012 Ṣàngó festival. Following the conclusion of the traditional part of the Ṣàngó festival in Ede, an additional event was held just for the indigenes of Ede, which was attended by large numbers of both Christians and Muslims. Thus, *Tìmì*'s *Ṣàngó* ties all Ede indigenes together, irrespective of religion.

But in other contexts, the close relationship between *Ṣàngó* and the town's Muslim majority worship has created anxiety and opposition. An example of this is the crisis over the relocation of the *Ṣàngó* statue to the *Tìmì*'s palace during the reign of *Tìmì* Tijani Oladokun Oyewusi, Agbonran II (1976–2007). At some stage in the past, a statue of *Tìmì* Agbale in the incarnation of *Ṣàngó* had been erected in the centre of the market, a strategic public space linking *Tìmì* Palace Road, Poly Road, Alapa/Oluobinu Road and Agunyan Masesu/Apaso Road. The statue was placed very close to a small *ratibi* mosque (compound mosque) located next to the Ede Central Mosque, and electric power sourced from this *ratibi* mosque was used to light a bulb in the statue's mouth, making it seem as if *Ṣàngó* was actually spitting fire. One day the popular Yoruba poet and critic Olanrewaju Adepoju visited the town and saw the statue. He made jest of the people in one of his albums by saying:

Nígbà tí èyàn ò gọ̀ bí ará Ẹdẹ?
wọ́n kọ́ mọ́sálásí, wọ́n fi Ṣàngó jẹ lèmọmù.

When are people not as foolish as the citizens of Ede?
They built a mosque, and made *Ṣàngó* their Imam.[26]

Piqued by this remark, some members of the Muslim community, led by Sheikh Salahudeen Olayiwola and Abdul-Ganiyu Olagunju as well as other members of the Joint Association of Ede Muslim Youth Organizations (JAEMYO), decided to get rid of the *Ṣàngó* statue. They removed the statue in a late-night operation, which attracted the attention of people close to the market. Protests by the traditionalists against this action were led by one of the *Ṣàngó* priests, Prince Jimoh of the Ajeniju ruling house. The crisis was resolved when both groups agreed that the statue should be moved to the palace of the *Tìmì*, where it stands today (see Figure 9, in the next chapter).[27]

These examples suggest that *Ṣàngó* has retained a double aspect in relation to Islam, and he appears both as an accommodating basis for the town's community and as potentially transgressive by infringing on the practices and obligations as Muslims (a similar relationship to Islam may be partly shared by other *òrìṣà*, such as *Egúngún*). However, as in an old marriage, the ongoing tension between *Ṣàngó* and Islam illustrates both the possibilities for mutual acceptance, especially in the context of communal feeling and respect based

---

[26] O. Adepoju, *Esin* (n.p., 1978).
[27] Interviews with *Alhaji* Nureni Lawal. 27 July 2013. Saw Mill Area, Ede; *Alhaji* Adio. 27 July 2013. Saw Mill Area, Ede. Conducted by Yemi Balogun.

on shared history, and the potential for conflict in the context of the ongoing Muslim concern with purity of practice.

Ṣàngó in the Church: Multiple Religious Practice and Transgression

The emergence of a Christian *Tìmì* in the person of Ọba John Adetoyese Laoye in 1946 produced an ọba who did not, at least in the first instance, explicitly identify with either of the two great sources of spiritual power – Ṣàngó and Islam – historically associated with the office of the *Tìmì*. His personal faith seems to be illustrated by the fact that he rarely missed a church service in the First Baptist Church, Ede. During the week he occasionally partook of other Christian programmes such as special prayer sessions, and he received Ede clergy of different denominations as visitors to the palace.

But unlike his predecessors Bamigbaye and Lagunju, who set up places of worship linked to their religions in the heart of the town, Laoye did not build a church in either the palace or the market squares of Ede. This may have reflected the greater reliance of Christians in Yorubaland on their denominational churches, which is linked to the fact that Christians are almost never organised at the town level. Even so, many ọbas today build churches in their palaces. One might speculate that *Tìmì* Laoye felt that the religious space in the town's politics had already been taken by Ṣàngó and Islam. How, then, could a Christian be a successful ruler in Ede?

While *Tìmì* Laoye's Christian identity and, predicated on his Western education, his experience as a dispenser in the colonial civil service were useful in enabling him to negotiate with the state in various ways, and in bringing progress in the form of infrastructural development and educational institutions to the town, it also had disadvantages. Christianity did not occupy a large place in Ede's communal history, and it certainly could rival neither Islam nor Ṣàngó. During the early years of Laoye's reign, his distance from these two sources of power weakened him and provided an opening for a Muslim rival, Memudu Lagunju. As a grandson of *Tìmì* Lagunju, Memudu had powerful Muslim credentials and was able to destabilise Laoye's reign for eight years.

After Laoye's installation in 1946, Memudu went to court to challenge an aspect of Laoye's installation as unlawful. Rebuffed at the first instance, he however won on appeal to the West African Court of Appeal (WACA). When Laoye had to leave Ede for Lagos by injunction, Memudu was installed without state consent and held court in his compound, which is not far from the palace. With the help of Lagos leaders such as Adeyemo Alakija, H.O. Davies, Adeleke Adedoyin and especially Bode Thomas, Laoye appealed the decision of the WACA and was eventually able to return to the palace in 1948. His return was celebrated by special services in many churches and among the Ṣàngó worshippers. The Chief Imam also held a special thanksgiving service on the town's Eid prayer ground, suggesting that Laoye was able to count on popular support that crossed all religious boundaries. However, Memudu Lagunju continued to be honoured by his supporters as the 'Muslim *Tìmì*' at least until the final decision on the case – in Laoye's favour – in December 1954.[28]

Faced with this opposition, strengthened by more widespread concerns within the Muslim community about Laoye's Christian bias in educational and land matters as described in the previous chapter, *Tìmì* Laoye asserted his royal authority through multiple religious practice and he frequently attended Friday prayers in the central mosque. However, it was easier for him to emphasise his leadership in the practice of traditional religion. Drawing on his personal knowledge of drumming, acquired during a stay with a maternal uncle as a child,[29] *Tìmì* Laoye assembled in Ede a collection of examples of all drums known in the entire Yoruba-speaking area. He not only sought to master the drums in terms of being able to play them, but he also wanted to understand the spiritual essence of each of those drums.[30]

Through his efforts, Ede became a reference point in the art of the talking drum. Eventually *Tìmì* Laoye was able to showcase the rich and important symbols and messages deriving from various drums in Yorubaland in an international environment. With his group of skilled drummers and poets, *Tìmì* Laoye entertained HRH Queen Elizabeth II of England when she visited Nigeria in 1956. After being awarded the Silver Medal for Chiefs on this occasion, he was later also invited to visit the royal family in England. As both events were seen to increase the town's status, they certainly strengthened his popular support.

Given *Tìmì* Laoye's experiences of being challenged by a Muslim rival, his religious inclusivity may have reflected very practical political considerations. But Laoye also seems to have encouraged the mutual affirmation between different religions out of personal preference, and out of the desire to establish Christianity, like Islam, as a religion that had local roots in Ede. While he emphasised the similarities between Islam and Christianity, he also actively sought to build up a close relationship between *Ṣàngó* and the church, and encouraged *Ṣàngó* worshippers to attend Christian services. The Yoruba scholar Ulli Beier, a close friend of Laoye's, remarked with reference to Ede that:

---

[28] J.A. Laoye, *The Story of My Installation* (Ede: Aafin Timi Ede, 1956), pp. 16–20.
[29] Laoye, *Story of My Installation*, p. 3.
[30] S. Oyeweso, 'Opening speech', *17th Ede day celebration*, Former Baptist High School, Ede (2010).

I know a priestess of Shango who accompanies her Oba every now and then to church. Although she does not believe in Christianity she will yet show respect to the God of her king.[31]

During the 1960s and 1970s, when relations between the different religions in the town no longer reflected the early tensions of Laoye's reign, the *Tìmì* supported the worship of *Ṣàngó* in Ede financially as well as personally, and he invited many of his friends and visitors to witness the annual *Ṣàngó* festival. In 1974, he took his royal support for *Ṣàngó* further than before. Perhaps drawing on the example of the annual celebratory visit to the mosque after the completion of the *Ṣàngó* festival by his Muslim predecessors, *Tìmì* Laoye invited all participants of the festival to a Christian Thanksgiving Service. After the successful final celebration of *Ṣàngó* festival that had been held on Friday 25 October, the *Tìmì*'s entourage joined the congregation of First Baptist Church Ede on 27 October 1974.[32] This group included both Muslim and *Ṣàngó*-worshipping celebrants.

The attendance of Muslims at the church service was not unusual and was generally welcome. However, the participation of a large group of *Ṣàngó* worshippers who were clearly discernible in the Thanksgiving Service was a different matter. *Tìmì* Laoye's entourage included a good number of different worshippers associated with the celebration of *Ṣàngó*, including *Oníbàtá*, *Ẹlẹ́gùn Ṣàngó*, *Àwòrò Ṣàngó* and *Ọlọ́ya*. The *Oníbàtá* are the players of *Ṣàngó*'s sacred double-headed drum. Shaped like an hourglass though with one cone larger than the other, the drum looks very much like the deity's double-headed axe. Since the playing of the drum asserts *Ṣàngó*'s presence, the *Oníbàtá* did not enter the Church for the service.

However, all other *Ṣàngó* worshippers entered the church. The *Ọlọ́ya* are women who worship *Ọya*, the Yoruba deity who was *Ṣàngó*'s third and favourite wife. Because *Ọya* has close affinity with *Ṣàngó*, her followers associate with *Ṣàngó*. During the *Ṣàngó* festival, the *Ọlọ́ya* are involved as dancers to *Ṣàngó*'s drum beats. Also dancers, the *Ẹlẹ́gùn Ṣàngó* are those who are possessed by the deity. Most of them are men, and they are known to be able to invoke *Ṣàngó*'s judicial power and his ability to punish social criminals by throwing thunderbolts at them. On such occasions, they may live for days without food, surviving only on bitter kola. The *Àwòrò Ṣàngó* are predominantly male priests who lead the performance of *Ṣàngó* rituals and propitiation, and who chant *Ṣàngó*'s *oríkì*, the praise poetry that calls to the deity's essence (see next chapter). Both the *Àwòrò* and *Ẹlẹ́gùn* wore their hair braided like women, as

---

[31] U. Beier, 'Festival of the images', *Nigeria Magazine* 45 (1954), 16.
[32] S. Bakare, 'Sango in the Church', *Daily Sketch* (27 October 1974), pp. 1–2.

is required of those who are possessed by the god.[33] They also wore the colour scarlet, which is associated with Ṣàngó, in the church.

Tìmì Laoye's actions were praised in many quarters, and his invitation of Ṣàngó to the church is sometimes referred to as an example of religious 'tolerance' in the town. However, as the visit of the traditionalists to the church was predicated on the Tìmì's royal authority, it was remarkable not because each side accepted the other's practices, but because of its transgressive nature. While it drew on established forms of encounter between Muslims and Ṣàngó worshippers, its symbolic power lay in its disregard for religious boundaries.

The invitation of Ṣàngó to the church differed from the participation of Muslim ọbas in the Jumu'ah prayer after the annual Ṣàngó festival in several ways. The Muslim tradition did not involve bringing men and women into the mosque who were, both through their mode of dressing and appearance and their presence as a group, associated with powers firmly located outside of the mosque. If Ṣàngó worshippers were indeed Muslims – as many are, and as the deity himself is sometimes said to be (chapter 4) – then they moved from the shrine to the mosque as individuals.

Importantly, by separating Muslims and non-Muslims, the traditional Jumu'ah service after the Ṣàngó festival also affirmed the difference between Ṣàngó and Islam. Certainly the participation of Muslims, and especially of a Muslim ọba, in the Ṣàngó festival and thereafter in Muslim prayer, indicated that religious boundaries could be crossed. However, the Jumu'ah service also allowed the Muslims to assert their 'return' to Islam at the end of the festival. Thus while the visit to the mosque at the end of the Ṣàngó festival suggested that the boundaries between different forms of religious practice could be crossed, they did not imply that the boundaries between them were insignificant. As long as each religion was practised in its own place and time, the integrity of individual religions was not challenged, and multiple religious practice was civic rather than transgressive.

In contrast, Laoye's invitation of Ṣàngó worshippers to the First Baptist Church in 1974, while they were still imbued with spiritual power from the festival, challenged the boundaries between Ṣàngó and Christianity. Interestingly, Tìmì Laoye's invitation did not disregard the fact that Ṣàngó worship and Christianity were essentially different forms of religious practice. The fact that the Oníbàtá, who play the drums for Ṣàngó, stayed outside the church, illustrates that concerns over appropriate boundaries – here linked to the aural environment of worship and invocation – were present among all

---

[33] See J.L. Matory, *Sex and the Empire that is no more: Gender and the Politics of Metaphor in Oyo Yoruba Religion* (Minneapolis and London: University of Minnesota Press, 1994), chapters 5 and 6.

participants. It is likely that the reservations about the *Oníbàtá*'s presence in the church was linked to the materiality of the drums associated with *Ṣàngó*, which could neither be abandoned nor find an acceptable place within the church.

But the other *Ṣàngó* worshippers did not come to the church as individuals, as some of them had done in the past. Their bodies, through dress and hairstyles, clearly marked them as devotees of *Ṣàngó* (or *Ọya*). They thus attended the service clearly recognisable as *Ẹlẹ́gùn Ṣàngó, Àwòrò Ṣàngó* and *Ọlọ́ya*, in short, as a group of people linked to – and almost certainly in possession of – a non-Christian power. While they might have been welcome in the church as individuals, their appearance as a group marked by *Ṣàngó* in dress and appearance was a challenge to Christian integrity. Thus, by bringing the *Ṣàngó* worshippers to the church not as individuals but as *Ṣàngó* worshippers, *Tìmì* Laoye drew on his charisma as a transgressor not to validate the worship of both *Ṣàngó* and Christianity in their own contexts but to blur the boundaries that separated them.

For this reason, this visit challenged the integrity of Christianity, and *Ṣàngó*'s visit to the church subsequently raised objections from the Nigerian Baptist Convention, especially outside Ede; the officiating pastor, an Ijesa man from Ilesa, was summoned by the Convention to Ibadan and the headquarters of the Church in order to explain himself. It is likely that a repetition of this visit would not have been well received by the Baptist Church, or by any other church of significance beyond Ede. However, as Laoye's reign came to an end in May 1975, the question was not raised and the 1974 visit to the church over which he presided remained unique. Thus the 1974 visit of the *Ṣàngó* worshippers to the church continues to serve as a reminder both of the power and the limitations of royal authority over religious difference.

While *ọba*s are expected to cross the real or imagined boundaries between different religions by virtue of their spiritual powers, and while individuals may do so in the search for peace or wellbeing, this does not mean that the boundaries are meaningless or arbitrary. By bringing *Ṣàngó* onto Christian territory, *Tìmì* Laoye conflated his role as an *ọba*, charged with 'civic' forms of multiple religious practice, and the transgressive power of *Ṣàngó*. Even if his aim was to raise the status of Christianity with relation to the royal office and traditional practice, in this context *Tìmì* Laoye acted very much like *Ṣàngó*.

Conclusion

As this chapter has illustrated, *Ṣàngó*'s association with contradictory, ambivalent and transgressive positions in Ede has shaped the town's political and symbolic practice and its religious history in a way that has encouraged religious coexistence and engagement, but which is radically different from toleration. While the notion of tolerance is based on the understanding that religious boundaries are solid and impervious to individual agency, Ṣàngó is associated with the production of royal authority through multiple religious practice and the deity's transgression of religious boundaries. As Ṣàngó's authority derives from the ability to challenge religious boundaries, the deity does not 'tolerate' religious difference – it is empowered by it.

Difficult to contain, Ṣàngó is both a primordial deity and a historic civic figure, a civic and a royal deity, and has long played an ambivalent role as both a collaborator with, and a threat to, Islam. The fact that Ṣàngó constitutes the authority of the Tìmì puts the deity at the centre of the town's civil religion, which is predicated on the recognition of all religions as valuable in their own right. However, Ṣàngó's central role in Ede's civil religion is contradictory, because the deity's transgressive nature potentially threatens the social and spiritual boundaries that constitute the social order.

By being closely associated with the Tìmì, Ṣàngó potentially challenges the social and religious harmony implicit in the ruler's 'headship' of all religions. But by investing the Tìmì with personal religious charisma, the potentially transgressive power of Ṣàngó was probably an important reason for the ability of both Tìmì Bamigbaye and Tìmì Lagunju to transform the town's religious identity. Yet, as chapter 2 has illustrated, such projects were successful only until they challenged the understanding that the ọba's practice must remain 'civic' in the sense that it should not disadvantage any section of the community. This tension also shaped the attempts by Ede's only Christian ọba, Tìmì John Adetoyese Laoye, to embed the practice of Christianity more deeply in the town's ritual calendar by inviting the Ṣàngó worshippers to the church.

While the detailed focus on Ede only allows this chapter a limited comparative approach, we suggest that while the practice of transgression may dominate especially in communities shaped by a historical association with Ṣàngó, it may be implicit in other aspects of royal practice. Karin Barber has explained that Yoruba òrìṣà are constituted by an ongoing process of proliferation and merging, which constantly redefines and defies categorical boundaries; the result is that a deity may be 'credited at one moment with one set of characteristics and at another with a different and apparently incompatible set'.[34] As many ọbas are closely associated with òrìṣà, and can be seen as òrìṣà in their own right, we think it is worth exploring to what degree the potential for religious transgression is a more widely shared aspect of ọbaship.

---

[34] Barber, 'Oríkì, women and the proliferation and merging of Òrìṣà', p. 313.

CHAPTER 4

Ṣàngó's Thunder: Poetic Challenges to Islam and Christianity

George Olusola Ajibade

The previous two chapters have explored the relationship between Ṣàngó, Islam and Christianity through the institution of ọbaship and the lives of the Tìmìs of Ede. In this chapter, I look at what Ṣàngó's own words – or, more precisely, the oral texts central to his worship – tell us about the deity, and its relationship to Islam and Christianity. It is through verbal arts that Ṣàngó worshippers invoke the deity, express their personal relationship with Ṣàngó and comment on their roles as Ṣàngó worshippers in the community. Most importantly for the understanding of the texts surrounding Ṣàngó, his worship takes place in a community in which most people identify themselves either as Muslims or Christians. As a result, the texts that surround him form part of a larger web of songs, sermons and other texts in which members of other religions also praise their own god or spread their own faith. The performance of Ṣàngó's oral literature therefore not only asserts his worshippers' position but also comments on the positions of others. Emerging from a competitive landscape of religious performance, Ṣàngó's verbal art is thus part of a collective poetic competition of religions, in which both accommodation and challenge play an important role.

Karin Barber explains that 'Yoruba òrìṣà can scarcely be apprehended without taking into account the specific textuality of the oral genres through which they are created, maintained and communicated with'.[1] An important aspect of the textuality of these oral genres derives from the fact that the òrìṣà exist primarily through the highly personal and emotional bond with individual followers. If we then understand the oral literature surrounding Ṣàngó worship as also reflecting poets' and performers' individual experiences, their spiritual and emotional orientation may determine or colour the perceived religious, social or historical content of the poetry. As the result of highly divergent and

---

[1] K. Barber, 'Oríkì, women and the proliferation and merging of Òrìṣà', Africa 60:3 (1990), 313–37: 313.

personal experiences of Ṣàngó, the oral arts surrounding him cannot offer monolithic articles of faith or understanding. Issuing apparently tolerant appeals for peaceful coexistence even as they appropriate the powers of other religions, they offer glimpses of the ambivalent nature of Ṣàngó's relationship with Christianity and especially Islam.

But despite the openness of many oral texts to potentially conflicting interpretations and meanings, many of them contain similar themes. Almost all of the oral texts surrounding Ṣàngó worship in Ede emphasise his historical importance for the town as well as his powerful nature, masculinity and husbandly authority. As these characteristics play an important role in shaping the relations between Ṣàngó worshippers and practitioners of other religions, it is important to look at the ways in which Ṣàngó lives and is worshipped in Ede today in order to contextualise and understand Ṣàngó worshippers' oral poetry appropriately.

Ṣàngó Worship in Ede

In Ede, Ṣàngó is worshipped daily, weekly (with every fifth day allotted to Ṣàngó as Jàkúta day[2]) and annually, and these periods of worship have not notably changed over time. The daily worship takes place within the house of the devotees. Libations of dry gin are poured at the altar of the deity and bitter kola nuts are placed at the shrine inside the house after prayers. This form of worship is usually confined to the nuclear family members of the devotee. The same applies to the weekly worship, except that it can be slightly more elaborate than the daily worship, and other people from within the compound of the devotee often take part. Those initiated into Ṣàngó worship also have to observe a number of taboos. In Ede these include the smoking of cigarettes, and the eating of àgó (a type of rat), èsúró (red-flanked duiker) and ẹ̀wà sése (cowpeas). The ritual materials for daily and weekly worship depend on the ritual leader, but a chicken must be killed, its blood poured on the altar, and the rest eaten.[3]

The annual Ṣàngó festival in Ede is a much more elaborate event that lasts for nine days. Two days before the start of the public seven-day festival, the Ìyá

---

[2] The Yoruba week consists of four days, each one allocated to a deity (as the first and last day are counted in Yoruba, this is sometimes referred to as a five-day week). Jàkúta is an old Yoruba deity associated with thunder, which is in many ways homonymous to Ṣàngó. In Ede and other Yoruba towns, it has been replaced by Ṣàngó, but retained the name for the day of the week on which Ṣàngó is worshipped.

[3] Interview with Chief Sangodokun, Jagun Ṣàngó of Ede. 3 August 2007. Ṣàngó palace shrine, Ede.

9 The statue of *Tìmì* Agbale with *Ṣàngó* paraphernalia, located behind the royal palace

Ṣàngó, one of the most important priestesses of the deity, fetches water from the Osun river for the ritual cleansing of the *èdùn àrá*, *Ṣàngó*'s thunderstones, and the clothes of *Ṣàngó*. The name of the *Ìyá Ṣàngó* could be taken to suggest that she is the deity's mother, implying her seniority and control over him. However, her name can also be understood as that of a mother pertaining to *Ṣàngó*, and indeed her position is more fluid. This is also illustrated by the fact that she fetches water to wash *Ṣàngó*'s belongings, which marks her as one of the wives of *Ṣàngó*, a position associated with supplication and subjugation.

The transformation of the *Ìyá Ṣàngó* into the deity's wife during this aspect of her worship of him points to *Ṣàngó*'s powers and character. While the gender of Yoruba deities can differ between locations, in Ede and many other Oyo towns *Ṣàngó* is an explicitly masculine deity, and the power he has over his devotees is clearly associated with husbandly authority. However, as suggested by the title of the priestess *Ìyá Ṣàngó*, his explicitly male character also implies an ambivalence to his powers. As Diedre Badejo points out, also with regard to *Ṣàngó*, a widely known Yoruba proverb states: 'Ọkùnrin níí ṣíwájú aya rẹ̀, tí tún tọ̀'yáa rẹ̀ lẹ́yìn' ('A man walks in front of his wife, and [but] he also follows his mother').[4]

---

[4] D.L. Badejo, 'Ṣàngó and the elements: Gender and cultural discourses', *Sango in Africa and African Diaspora*, ed. T.F. Joel and E. Tishken (Bloomington: Indiana University Press, 2009), pp. 111–34: 111.

On the first day of the festival sacrifices are offered at the palace, and prayers for peace, long life, prosperity and protection against natural and man-made dangers are said for the *Tìmì* and the people of Ede.[5] Afterwards the *Tìmì*, the *Ìyá Ṣàngó*, the other *Ṣàngó* priests and priestesses, chiefs and other members of the community go to the *Ṣàngó* shrine at *Odò Ṣàngó* to offer prayers and perform rituals. All walk together, accompanied by drumming and singing in praise of *Ṣàngó*. The *Ìyá Ṣàngó* carries *Ṣàngó*'s calabash and goes ahead of the rest of the people to fetch water from the *Odò Ṣàngó*. Again this ritual points to the ambivalence of *Ṣàngó*'s gendered authority. The fact that the *Ìyá Ṣàngó* walks ahead of the *Tìmì* again suggests her authority – if the *Tìmì* is an incarnation of *Ṣàngó*, as many believe, she might be seen as his mother – while her fetching of water marks her as the deity's wife. Perhaps to avoid a position in which the *Tìmì* himself could be associated with the wifely position adopted by the *Ìyá Ṣàngó*, the *Tìmì* keeps his distance from her when they get to the stream. As she fetches water, the king and his entourage remain on the other side of the Osun river.

After having fetched water from *Odò Ṣàngó*, the *Ìyá Ṣàngó* meets the king and his people on the other side of the river, from where they dance as they return to the town. The water brought from this river is used to wash the *ẹdùn àrá* at around five o' clock that evening. A ram is killed, and its blood is poured on the *ẹdùn àrá*. Plenty of bitter kola nuts are also put at the shrine. Divination is performed by *Bàbá Mọgbà* with bitter kola nuts. Once the divination is positive they begin to praise *Ṣàngó*, singing songs and praying for the prosperity of the community. Around midnight that night a light called *Àtùpà Olójúmẹ́rìndínlógún* (sixteen-points-lamp) is lit, which lights the community's night-time celebration, during which people eat, drink, dance and sing.

On the second day of the festival the *Tìmì* must partake in a sacrifice to *Ṣàngó* by providing the sacrificial ram and cow and eating from them. Other items often associated with sacrifice to *Ṣàngó* include cowries, goats, sheep, oxen, fowls and bitter kola, along with dishes of *àmàlà*[6] served with *gbẹ̀gìrì* or bean soup. The *Agbájere*, one of the *ẹlẹ́gùn Ṣàngó*, carries a ritual fire pot to the four corners of the town. They pray at each corner for the community, the state and the nation at large. It is also believed that the fire and the smoke coming out of the pot are imbued with the power to ward off all evil spirits that might threaten the people in the community. All families that worship *Ṣàngó* dance round the town visiting their in-laws, friends and well-wishers. The

---

[5] A. Adejumo, 'The practice and worship of Ṣàngó in contemporary Yorubaland', *Ṣàngó in Africa and the African Diaspora*, ed. J. Tishken, T. Falola and A. Akinyemi (Bloomington: Indiana University Press, 2009), pp. 44–62: 53–4.

[6] A starchy food made from yam flour.

third to seventh days of the festival are days of feasting, dancing and magical feats.[7]

Like the deity Ṣàngó, the cult members possess àṣẹ, the power to bring things into existence. The various worshippers perform types of magic that demonstrate Ṣàngó's ability to perform extreme physical feats. Some celebrants cut their tongues with razor blades and the tongues grow back together again within seconds. In other cases they remove one of their eyeballs with a sharp knife and it grows back in the socket. As Ṣàngó's eyes and his mouth are closely associated with his swift judgement and his ability to convince people, these magical feats also illustrate the particular powers of the deity. Reminding his followers and their audience of Ṣàngó's command over thunder and lightning and his uncompromising nature, the male chief priest of Ṣàngó in Ede, the Bàbá Mọgbà, is expected to be able to spit fire from his mouth and carry a pot of fire on his head, just like Ṣàngó himself. Through the practical mastery of performance techniques the worshippers manipulate the perceptual world, as it is experienced daily; they play upon, embellish and transform reality. They bring that which is normally inaccessible or imagined into the phenomenal world where it can be observed and contemplated.[8] Certainly the miraculous activities of Ṣàngó's priests instil fear in the hearts of the audience and encourage their admiration and worship of the deity.

During the performance of magical feats, Ṣàngó priests sometimes also put a mortar on their chests and request hefty men to pound raw leaves into powder with pestle. As the Yoruba word for pounding something in a mortar – gún – alludes to the verb gùn, which is used to refer both to the (male) performance of sexual intercourse and to the deity's possession of its followers, this endurance condenses important aspects of Ṣàngó. Matory observes that 'the verb gùn (to "mount") often implies suddenness, violence, and utter loss of self-control – a connotation linking it paradigmatically with Ṣàngó's action upon his possession priests and upon the world'.[9] Certainly, whenever Ṣàngó mounts his devotees they have no will of their own and they are totally subjected to his control.

Reflecting the way in which Ṣàngó can take possession of his followers, those of his followers who are possessed by him are called Ẹlẹ́gùn Ṣàngó (the one mounted by Ṣàngó) or Adóṣù Ṣàngó (the one that fashions his or her hair

---

[7] Adejumo, 'The practice and worship of Ṣàngó', pp. 53–4.
[8] M.T. Drewal, *Yoruba Ritual: Performers, Play, Agency* (Bloomington: Indiana University Press, 1992), p. 90.
[9] J.L. Matory, *Sex and the Empire that is no more: Gender and the Politics of Metaphor in Oyo Yoruba Religion* (Minneapolis and London: University of Minnesota Press, 1994). p. 175.

style after the pattern of *Ṣàngó*), the latter of which refers to the fact that these devotees confirm their structural position vis-à-vis *Ṣàngó* by plaiting their hair like women. These worshippers were chosen by *Ṣàngó* to be filled with his power in order to reveal certain truths and secrets to the world. The initiation ritual creates the deity inside the initiands. Because they are subject to *Ṣàngó*'s physical and spiritual authority, these devotees are always called *Ìyàwó òrìṣà* (the deity's wives), even though they are frequently men. Although male *Adóṣù* can have wives themselves, they join to *Ṣàngó* as wives just as married women join to their husbands. To avoid a gendered constellation that would in turn undermine *Ṣàngó*'s authority, a male and a female *Adóṣù Ṣàngó* must not marry each other.

The non-possession priests of *Ṣàngó* are the *Mọgbà*, who are officially responsible for the initiation of possession priests and priestesses. In the past, the *Mọgbà* was the faithful friend of *Ṣàngó* when he became deified, because he heard the voice of *Ṣàngó* at Koso when he explained how he should be worshipped. That is why up till today the *Mọgbà* are regarded as the close associates of the *Ṣàngó* cult and indeed as the husbands of all *Ṣàngó* worshippers. Apart from the *Baba Mọgbà*, the principal male chiefs in the cult of *Ṣàngó* in Ede are the *Jagun Ṣàngó*, *Ọ̀tún Jagun*, *Òsì Jagun*, *Baálẹ̀ Ṣàngó*, *Àgbàákin*, *Aṣípa*, *Ẹṣinńlá*, *Séríkí* and *Ààrẹ-Àgò*. However, these titles are somewhat flexible, and the worshippers create additional offices as the need arises and as long as there are people to fill them. One of the popular songs sung during the annual worship of *Ṣàngó* in Ede honours the *Mọgbà* and asserts their powerful position in the worship of *Ṣàngó*:

> Baba Mọgbà
> Baba Mọgbà
> Ẹ má fi baba Mọgbà ṣeré,
> Baba Mọgbà.

> Baba Mọgbà
> Baba Mọgbà
> Do not joke with Baba Mọgbà
> Baba Mọgbà.

The female chief of *Ṣàngó* is the *Ìyá Ṣàngó* who is accompanied by *Ọ̀tún Ìyá Ṣàngó* and *Òsì Ìyá Ṣàngó*, her right-hand and left-hand lieutenants. In Ede, as in many traditional communities in Yorubaland, women play crucial roles in entertainment, including during community festivals, religious convocations and the annual festivals of local deities. While men play an important role as drummers, women are also the main performers of *Ṣàngó* religious texts, and the female priests control the singing of songs, recitation and chanting of praise poetry, or *oríkì*, of Ṣàngó. Ṣàngó's verbal art is, like all Yoruba oral art, produced in three distinct but interwoven forms: song, chant or recital.[10] These three forms can be performed together in a single performance, or even completely intermingled. The themes and contents of the three forms are very similar, and may be undertaken by one performer, with only the performance mode differing. Recitation, chanting and songs are all used to praise, worship and adore Ṣàngó. Ordinarily, Ṣàngó is placated with songs, dances, lyrics and sacrifices, and it is this combination of the verbal and visual that forms a complete ritual.

The women's control of the verbal art of the *òrìṣà* means that they control vital passages of communication with Ṣàngó, whose powers they establish and create in this way.[11] As skilful operators, the women operate the 'praising' mechanism through which the flow of spiritual forces is directed and through which, ultimately, multiple aspects of the *òrìṣà*'s personality are constituted.[12] As well as the oral texts that have been handed over to them over the years, they create more oral texts out of their own religious experiences and in response to the prevailing religious situation within the community. It is probably in reflection of different historical as well as personal experiences that the texts surrounding the worship of Ṣàngó offer apparently contradictory views on other religions. While some texts appear accommodating of other forms of worship, others seem to reject it, or even to mock it.

Ṣàngó's Openness to Other Religions

The continued and fervent worship of Ṣàngó in Ede takes place within a community that is predominantly Muslim and has a significant Christian presence. This is not seen as a problem by many people, who believe that different religious groups all have something to contribute to the community, and that their concerted efforts will bring peace and harmony to the town. This belief in the importance of difference may partly be a reflection of the value ascribed to multiplicity and diversity in Yoruba thought and practice.[13] The appreciation

---

[10] A. Babalola, *The Content and Form of Yorùbá Ijala* (Oxford: Clarendon Press, 1966); E. Olukoju, 'The place of chants in Yorùbá traditional oral literature', unpublished PhD thesis (Ibadan: University of Ibadan, 1978); O.O. Olatunji, *Features of Yorùbá Oral Poetry* (Ibadan: University of Ibadan Press, 1984); O.O. Olatunji, 'Classification of Yorùbá oral poetry', *Yorùbá Language and Literature*, ed. A. Afolayan (Ibadan: University of Ibadan Press, 1982), pp. 57–72.

[11] See also Barber, 'Oríkì, women and the proliferation and merging of Òrìṣà', p. 317.

[12] Barber, 'Oríkì, women and the proliferation and merging of Òrìṣà', p. 329.

[13] J. Guyer, 'Traditions of Invention in Equatorial Africa,' *African Studies Review* 3:39 (1996), 1–28.

of difference and multiplicity is expressed in the proverb, 'Ọ̀nà kan kò wọjà' ('It is not a single road that leads to the market').

Of course the widespread preparedness to accept religious difference may also reflect the historical religious landscape. In most pre-colonial Yoruba towns there were various religious cults which coexisted. Significant open confrontation or opposition was very rarely linked to debates about the right (or wrong) of certain beliefs or practices. If people wanted to follow a practice that seemed strange to others, this was considered their business as long as it contributed to the overall good. This belief in the positive communal value of allowing everybody to follow their own form of worship is also expressed in other forms of verbal art, including an *Ifá* divinatory song that is sometimes adapted today to appeal for the coexistence of Islam, Christianity and traditional practices. An older version of the song advocates that,

Ẹ jónífá ó bọfá
Ẹ jónífá ó bọfá
Ẹ jólọ́sun ó bọ̀sun
Ẹ jólọ́sun ó bọ̀sun
Ẹ jólódù ó bodù káyé le gún

Let the *Ifá* worshippers worship *Ifá*
Let the *Ifá* worshippers worship *Ifá*
Let the *Ọ̀ṣun* worshippers worship their *Ọ̀ṣun*
Let the *Ọ̀ṣun* worshippers worship their *Ọ̀ṣun*
Let the *Odù* worshippers worship their *Odù* so that there will be peace on earth.

While this song celebrates the coexistence of different religious practices, it also points to the importance of permitting others to follow these practices. By implying that not allowing others their own form of worship is a potential area of conflict, the song's lyrics suggest that the limitation of others' religious practices is likely to have created conflict even in pre-monotheist communities. Because of the close link between the spiritual and the political in most Yoruba towns, conflict was often associated with attempts to increase the influence of a particular practice that transgressed on the physical, social or aural space reserved for other deities or their worshippers.

As a result, the ability of *Ṣàngó* worshippers to engage with other religions in the public sphere is not noticeably limited by theological considerations. It depends instead on the space given to *Ṣàngó* in the encounter. *Ṣàngó*'s potential openness to the worship of other deities is illustrated during the *Ṣàngó* festival. On the day before the festival begins, *Ṣàngó*'s drummers, the *Oníbàtá*, perform rituals to *Àyàn Àgalú*, the deity of drummers, to ensure their successful playing of the drums during the festival. On the first day of the festival, the use of the sixteen-point-lamp described above illustrates the close relationship of Ṣàngó with Òsanyìn, who is the custodian of this lamp. Among the singers and especially the dancers for Ṣàngó, both during the festival and on other occasions, are the Olóya, worshippers of Ṣàngó's wife Oya, who dance to the drums beaten for Ṣàngó.

In a slightly different way, public Ṣàngó worship in Ede accommodates Christianity and Islam. As illustrated in chapter 3, the Tìmì of Ede, as a representative or incarnation of Ṣàngó, plays an important role in mediating between Ṣàngó, Islam and Christianity. Certainly the celebrations in Ede's mosques and churches after the successful celebration of the Ṣàngó festival illustrate that Ṣàngó worship can coexist peacefully with Islam and Christianity. Although religious irritations and tensions have increased slightly in recent times (partly in reflection of conflicts and debates at the national level) the current Tìmì of Ede, Oba Muniru Adesola Lawal, Laminisa I, continues to emphasise the importance of Ṣàngó for the town and himself in spite of opposition from Muslim and Christian quarters. He notes that,

> We believe Ṣàngó is part of Ede and Ede is part of Tìmì and that is why I have been trying to promote the festival again. People believe once you celebrate this festival that you are no longer a Muslim or a Christian, but I am a Muslim and I know my relationship with God. So, I have tried to raise the standard of the festival so as to attract people from far and wide. The origin of Tìmì itself is Ṣàngó and one should not allow religion to blind fold him as to close his eyes to the traditional worshippers and the culture of the people. I know I am going to give account of my stewardship for all the religious beliefs of my people in Ede before my creator as their burden is on me.[14]

Here Tìmì Lawal asserts that he celebrates Ṣàngó not only because it is his duty towards the community, but also because he knows his personal relationship with God. The assertion of the latter statement is that Tìmì Lawal is such a good Muslim that his relationship with God is not affected by celebration of Ṣàngó, and it could even be taken to suggest that those who are afraid of celebrating Ṣàngó do not have a good personal relationship with God. But beyond the declaration of self-confidence and spiritual power, his statement also emphasises that the oba's celebration of Ṣàngó has a deeply personal dimension. In addition to their reflection on the town's historical association

---

[14] J. Babatunde, 'I never dreamt of being the king – Timi, paramount ruler of Ede', Vanguard (10 March 2013), <http://www.vanguardngr.com/2013/03/i-never-dreamt-of-being-the-king-timi-paramount-ruler-of-Ede>, accessed 19 February 2014.

with Ṣàngó, the verbal arts about the deity's relationship to other religions must also be understood at this personal level.

Ṣàngó's Ambivalence towards Christianity and Islam

One of the songs gathered during the Ṣàngó festival explicitly asserts the belief that one can be a good Muslim or Christian while at the same time worshipping Ṣàngó. As this might be taken to imply Ṣàngó's ability to compromise, or to accept second (or third) place after Islam and Christianity, it is worth looking at the text in more detail:

Méjéèjì la ó máa ṣe
Méjéèjì la ó máa ṣe
Ká ti Ṣọ́ọ̀ṣì dé
Ká tún wádò o Ṣàngó
Méjéèjì la ó máa ṣe
Méjéèjì la ó máa ṣe

Méjéèjì la ó máa ṣe
Méjéèjì la ó máa ṣe
Ká ti Mọ́sáláṣí dé
Ká tún wádò o Ṣàngó
Méjéèjì la ó máa ṣe
Méjéèjì la ó máa ṣe

We shall practise the two
We shall practise the two
When we return from the church
We should also go to Ṣàngó's brook (shrine)
We shall practise the two
We shall practise the two

We shall practise the two
We shall practise the two
When we return from the mosque
We should also go to Ṣàngó's brook (shrine)
We shall practise the two
We shall practise the two

By arguing that Christians and Muslims can be Ṣàngó worshippers, this song asserts the rightfulness of practices that are otherwise denounced as syncretic, and it sets its celebration of two practices against those Muslims and Christians who argue that monotheism implies that Ṣàngó worship should be abandoned. But at the same time, the lyrics leave room for interpretation because they do not state clearly whether the two practices to which the song refers are the same kind of thing. As a result, the apparently accommodating lyrics of this song are more ambivalent than they may seem at first glance.

Thus, some people might hear this song as a patriotic injunction on Ede's Muslims and Christians to keep Ṣàngó alive by visiting his brook after they have gone to the church or mosque. Because the lyrics do not refer to Ṣàngó's spiritual powers in any way, they could even be understood as an exhortation that is entirely independent of religion, and in which listeners are simply asked to maintain the community's heritage by visiting the Ṣàngó shrine. But another way of hearing or singing the song suggests that monotheist and òrìṣà worship are the same kind of practice. If that is the case, then the implication is that none of these religions is exclusive. Given that the monotheist faiths appear as interchangeable while Ṣàngó does not, the song's lyrics could even be taken to imply that Ṣàngó is more important than Christianity or Islam.

Equally open to interpretation are some of the praise-names, or oríkì, for Ṣàngó, some of which clearly describe him as versed in Islam. The chanting of oríkì of Ṣàngó falls into what is called Ṣàngó-pípè (calling of Ṣàngó), which as David Welch has noted, is performed in both 'private worship and cult ceremonies; while in the annual festival (Ọdún), which involves outsiders, the chanting mode is employed in a social context'.[15] In some of his oríkì, Ṣàngó's abilities as a ruler and warrior are closely associated with the command of typically Muslim skills, describing him as a Muslim:

Akéwú-gbẹrú
The one who wins slaves due to his skill in Arabic

Akéwú-gbẹṣin
The one who wins horses due to his skill in Arabic

Aṣàlùwàlá-níbi-ọfà-gbé-ń-rọ̀jò
The one who performs ablutions in the place where arrows rain down

If, as suggested in chapters 2 and 3, the popularity of Ṣàngó was historically linked with the benefits that early Muslims brought to the Oyo Empire in general and Ede in particular, then it is understandable that the deity might also be seen as a Muslim. But what does that mean? Of course it is possible to see this oríkì as a form of camouflage, which was used to take the wind out of the sails of those Muslims who wanted to destroy Ṣàngó: if a deity had converted, then surely it was no longer an idol. But because the assertion that Ṣàngó is a

---

[15] D. Welch, 'Ritual intonation of Yoruba praise-poetry – Oríkì', *Yearbook of the International Folk Music Council* 5 (1973), 156–64: 156.

Muslim presents the deity as capable of agency, it also rejects the view that it is only an idol. If Ṣàngó is so powerful and skilled that he is able to command Muslim skills, this could be taken to mean that he can be a Muslim if he so desires, and especially in order to pursue his war-like aims. It is perhaps the last interpretation to which Karin Barber's comments on the role of oríkì in the communication between òrìṣà and devotee add an interesting twist. She explains that,

> In the propitiation of òrìṣà, as in other ceremonial and ritual activities, oríkì are indispensable [...] oríkì constitute a channel of communication between devotee and òrìṣà through which reciprocal benefits flow. But it is in oríkì that the relationship is most fully realised as a living engagement between a speaker and a hearer. Like all oríkì, the oríkì of òrìṣà are in the vocative case and presuppose a listening subject. The òrìṣà cannot but be there when the speaker exhorts and appeals to it, extols it and insists on its attention in oríkì. The devotee speaks her mind to the òrìṣà, in the process constituting its personality and powers in their fullest form.[16]

If we understand these lines of Ṣàngó's oríkì as the expression of a personal relationship with Ṣàngó, their allusion to his typically Muslim skills may mean different things depending on the individual evoking him, and also for different members of any audience listening to them. Especially for Muslims, the assertion that Ṣàngó was a Muslim may be comforting, and it may allow them to participate in his celebration by simply seeing Ṣàngó as an extraordinary but fellow believer.

For others, and especially for Ṣàngó worshippers themselves, these oríkì verses may assert the reality and agency of the òrìṣà in control of Islam, and for yet others, the chanting of these verses may even be a way of accessing powers associated with Islam. While Islam is not worshipped like an òrìṣà, the allusion to Islamic skills in Ṣàngó's oríkì may thus be a way for devotees to merge Muslim powers with the deity, because 'the exclusive character of the relationship means that each òrìṣà has to be all things to its own devotees'.[17] Through the praise of a Muslim Ṣàngó, his worshippers can therefore appeal to powers normally reserved for Muslims.

Poetic Challenges to Islam and Christianity

In Ede, the appeal to ostensibly different religions, such as Ṣàngó and Islam, is not restricted to traditional worshippers. For example, many Muslims and

---

[16] Barber, 'Oríkì, women and the proliferation and merging of Òrìṣà', p. 316.
[17] Barber, 'Oríkì, women and the proliferation and merging of Òrìṣà', p. 318.

Christians believe that no-one can break an oath covenanted with Ṣàngó. Swearing by Ṣàngó enables citizens of the town to trust relationships or agreements. The spirit of Ṣàngó is also invoked to fish out perpetrators of evil deeds. Indeed, many people believe that the incidences of social misdemeanours such as kidnapping or the forceful seizure of another person's wife are lower in Ede than in other towns because the town's citizens are afraid of incurring the wrath of Ṣàngó. Recently, a highly placed priest in a Catholic church in Ede was seen to rebuke his church member for cursing in the name of Ṣàngó. The interesting point is that the priest did not rebuke his fellow Christian for using the name of a traditional deity and thus potentially incurring God's wrath. His reprimand was based on concern for the parishioner's wellbeing because he knew Ṣàngó as a real force, who would take revenge if his name was falsely taken. He said: 'Ṣàngó kì í ṣoun àmúṣeré, Ṣàngó kì í sini í pa, má danwò mó!' (*Ṣàngó* should not be trifled with, *Ṣàngó* does not kill wrongfully, do not dare it [do not challenge the deity]!')[18]

But while the recognition of Ṣàngó's powers by Muslims and Christians ensures the deity's ongoing importance, it also produces encounters that are perceived as a betrayal of the òrìṣà. For example, many Christians and Muslims privately visit Ṣàngó worshippers in Ede for help, even though this is usually condemned by their religious leaders. However, when such people benefit from the deity's help, they do not always acknowledge it. After a group interview of Ṣàngó worshippers in 2007, I made the following field notes (which I have slightly amended):

> At times, some women who are looking for the fruit of womb [children] visit them [the Ṣàngó priests] to inquire from Ṣàngó what we [they] need to do and he [Ṣàngó] can tell them [the Ṣàngó priests] what they need to do so that such women can have children. In some cases Ṣàngó can tell them to give such women cold water called Àgbo ìdí Ṣàngó [a concoction made at the shrine of Ṣàngó].
>
> But ... after such a woman has 'received her miracle' from Ṣàngó [i.e. after she finds that she is pregnant], she will come to pay her vow [Èjé] secretly and publicly ascribe glory to Christ if she is a Christian and to Allah if a Muslim.

While such behaviour is widely considered hypocritical, it is by no means unusual because many people who have benefited from the òrìṣà in this way fear stigma not only for themselves but also for the children conceived with the deity's help. But for the Ṣàngó priests, the failure to acknowledge the deity

---

[18] Anonymous respondent interviewed by a research assistant for A.S. Ajala in Ede. 22 October 2012.

is seen as a form of betrayal, or even as a form of theft, in which the power of *Ṣàngó* is subsumed under the powers of Christ or God. It is in response to these and other perceived transgressions of Muslims and Christians that other oral texts associated with *Ṣàngó* also assert his difference from Islam and Christianity.

This assertion of difference can even be implied in performances that seem not to engage with Islam and Christianity at all. In the song below, *Ṣàngó* is praised without reference to other religions, and his qualities and powers are showcased by the singers' submission, reverence and unswerving loyalty to *Ṣàngó*. The song talks about the power and the prowess of *Ṣàngó* as a warrior and a fierce, tough and generous person, who is also addressed as the singers' husband:[19]

Lílé:	Atóóbájayé
Ègbè:	Baálé mi ò!
Lílé:	A-bó-sí-gbangba-dámọ-léjọ́
Ègbè:	Baálé mi ò!
Lílé:	Túúláàsí ọkùnrin
	Òjálé-onílé-bọ-tirẹ̀-léyìn
Ègbè:	Baálé mi ò!
Lílé:	Òun ní ń já tirẹ̀ bọlé onílé.
Ègbè:	Baálé mi ò!
Lílé:	Ọkọ mi má mà jálé olódì bọ tèmi
Ègbè:	Baálé mi ò!
Lílé:	Èsù Òdàrà má mà jẹ́ n ríjà Ṣàngó
Ègbè:	Baálé mi ò!
Lílé:	Ọ̀sán gangan níí gbégií wọlú
	A-pani-bí-ọtí
Ègbè:	Baálé mi ò!
Lílé:	A-kọ̀-má-tòṣíká-léyìn
	A-kọ̀-má-gbẹbọ-èké
Ègbè:	Baálé mi ò!
Lílé:	Àlejò kan ò bá ọ léjafùú rí
	A-gbé-sàasùn-tọọrọ-fálágbe
	Aṣàlejò-èèyàn-bẹ́-ẹni-mọ̀-tẹ́lẹ̀.
Ègbè:	Baálé mi ò!

---

[19] The *Baálé* is the senior male of a compound, and as women are expected to marry and spend most of their time in their husband's compound, it is the senior male of their husband's family. Like all in-laws, he would be addressed by a woman married into the compound as her husband.

Lílé:	Arábánbí,
	A-rígba-ọta-ṣẹ́gun,
	A-bọ̀bẹ-gbòòkàn-lákọ̀.
Ègbè:	Baálé mi ò!

Solo:	The one who is worthy to be associated with
Chorus:	My husband!
Solo:	The one that judges the victim in public
Chorus:	My husband!
Solo:	A tough man
	The one that joins somebody else's house to his
Chorus:	My husband!
Solo:	It is he that joins his house to that of somebody
Chorus:	My husband!
Solo:	My husband doesn't join my enemy's house to mine
Chorus:	My husband!
Solo:	Èṣù Ọ̀dàrà prevent me from the wrath of Ṣàngó
Chorus:	My husband!
Solo:	He takes a tree to the town in the noonday,
	The one that makes somebody behave as if he is intoxicated with wine
Chorus:	My husband!
Solo:	The one that refuses to support wicked people,
	The one that refuses to accept sacrifice from a dubious person
Chorus:	My husband!
Solo:	The one that is ever ready for all visitors,
	The one that gave the whole pot of soup to the beggar,
	The one that entertains visitors as if he had been informed
Chorus:	My husband!
Solo:	Arábánbí,
	The one that has plenty of thunderstones to defeat his enemies,
	The one that has hefty knives in his quiver.
Chorus:	My husband!

While this song does not directly refer to monotheism, its praise of Ṣàngó's powers not only confirms his greatness but also serves as an indirect warning to those who might fight with him, i.e. most likely members of other religions. This warning is not only implicit in the song's references to the deity's wrath, his thunderstones and his knives, but also in other lines. For example, by emphasising Ṣàngó's moral integrity, such as his ability to judge people in public, or his refusal to accept sacrifices from, or support, wicked people, the song both questions the integrity of those who are not Ṣàngó worshippers and tries to intimidate them.

The next song, of which I only include two stanzas, reminds us much more forcefully that the texts, and especially the songs, surrounding *Ṣàngó* worship are part of a wider web of texts that argue about the nature of religion and worship. By rejecting the practice of a monotheist religion along with *Ṣàngó* worship, it insists on the equivalence of *Ṣàngó* with the monotheist faiths. Given that the worshippers of the deity are not a homogenous group, it may also be directed against the views of those who assert that they visit the shrine after mosque or the church, as in the song discussed above.

Ṣàngó lá máa bọ ò e e e e e e e
Ṣàngó lá máa bọ ò à á à á à à à
Àwa ò ṣègbàgbó o o o o o o o
Ṣàngó lá máa bọ
Àwa ó kírun o o o o o o o
Ṣàngó lá ó máa bọ

Ṣàngó báramu ò e e e e e e e
Ṣàngó báramu ò à à à à à à
Àwa ò gbàgbọ́ o
Ṣàngó báramu.
Àwa ó kírun o
Ṣàngó báramu.

We shall continue to worship *Ṣàngó*
We shall continue to worship *Ṣàngó*
We are not Christians,
We shall continue to worship *Ṣàngó*
We are not Muslims,
We shall continue to worship *Ṣàngó*
Ṣàngó suits us,

Ṣàngó suits us
We are not Christians,
Ṣàngó suits us
We are not Muslims,
Ṣàngó suits us.

Asking a pertinent question of an imagined Christian proselytiser, the next song takes a step beyond the injunction by monotheists to drop the worship of *Ṣàngó*:

Níbo ló ní n gbé Ṣàngó mi sí o?
Níbo ló ní n gbé Ṣàngó mi sí o?
Bàbá oníkọ́là lọ́rùn

Tó ní kí n gbé Ṣàngó ṣègbàgbọ́,
Níbo ló ní n gbé Ṣàngó mi sí o?

Where does he want me to put my *Ṣàngó*?
Where does he want me to put my *Ṣàngó*?
The man who wears a dress with a collar on his neck
Who said that I should drop *Ṣàngó* to become a Christian,
Where does he want me to put my *Ṣàngó*?

By referring to *Ṣàngó* as a deity owned by the singer rather than something that exists independently of the worshipper, this song celebrates the personal relationship between the singer and *Ṣàngó*. Because the singer exists, it is impossible that *Ṣàngó* does not exist, and thus an exclusive commitment to monotheist practice would mean abandoning a part of herself. But while the song appears at first like a lament over an impossible proposition, it is also funny and rather subversive. The reference to the priest's clerical collar makes fun of pastors and priests by representing them as collared like dogs and thus at least potentially not respectable. Indeed, as slaves were often marked by the wearing of brass collars in the past – and *Ṣàngó* was famous for the number of slaves he captured – the allusion to the priest's collar may even intend to suggest that the priest is subject to *Ṣàngó's* authority, whether he knows it or not.

Finally, the question of where the singer's *Ṣàngó* should be put seems, at the surface, like a simple, and perhaps even forlorn question. However, it can certainly be understood as threatening as well, because it encourages the audience to imagine what might happen in places where *Ṣàngó* was simply left, unguarded by those who normally look after him. What would happen if *Ṣàngó* was left in the church? He might transform or desecrate the space, as was feared by those who opposed the *Ṣàngó* priest's visit to Ede's First Baptist Church in 1974 (see chapter 3). But even this implied threat contains an element of openness to an alternative interpretation: given that *Ṣàngó* has become a Muslim, it is not impossible for him to also convert to Christianity.

In what appears an even more direct mockery and subversion of Islam, other lines of *Ṣàngó's oríkì* confirm his Muslim identity by describing him as a breaker of injunctions:

Nígbà Ṣàngó wà ní Sálúù
Ìmàle níí ṣe
Ẹni tíí forí ajá jiyán,
A-forí-Ẹlẹ́dẹ̀-mùkọ-àwẹ̀.

When *Ṣàngó* was living in Sálúù
He was a practising Muslim
The one who uses a dog's head to eat pounded yam

The one who uses a pig's head to drink pap during Ramadan fasting

In this *oríkì*, Ṣàngó is described as a Muslim, but as one who breaks important Islamic laws. Both dogs and pigs, whose heads Ṣàngó uses to eat and drink, are considered as unclean and thus unsuitable for consumption, and the observance of the Ramadan fast, which Ṣàngó breaks by ingesting pork, is an important command for all Muslims. This *oríkì* can certainly be understood as asserting that Ṣàngó is not really a Muslim: if he had been a good Muslim, he would not have broken the injunctions of his religion. But taken together with the *oríkì* lines discussed in the section above, this section of his *oríkì* can also imply that Ṣàngó is a bad Muslim: someone who reads Arabic and knows how to perform ablutions, someone who knows what can be consumed and when, but who refuses to be bound by this knowledge. As suggested by Farias with reference to Oyo,[20] by describing the *òrìṣà* as someone who refuses to submit to Islam despite intimate knowledge of it, Ṣàngó's *oríkì* mobilises contrasts, and heightens differences, between himself and Islam to assert the independence and boldness of the *òrìṣà*. In such interpretations Ṣàngó remains the ultimate master of Islam.

But despite its audacity, this *oríkì* is ambivalent and open in a way that takes us back to the beginning of our discussion about the relationship of Ṣàngó to other religions. Is it not remarkable that this *oríkì* about Ṣàngó can only be understood by those who already hold some Islamic knowledge? For those who do not know Islam but learn Ṣàngó's *oríkì* to praise Ṣàngó, these lines would even serve to teach them about the animals unfit for Islamic consumption and the importance of the Ramadan fast. Thus, if Ṣàngó's deliberate breaking of Islamic taboos marks him as bold and able to ignore and violate conventions, it nonetheless confirms the existence of these taboos and their importance for other Muslims. Without Islam, how would Ṣàngó demonstrate his powers of transgression? By asserting Ṣàngó's independence from Islamic injunctions, these lines of his *oríkì* nonetheless confirm his close relationship with Islam.

Conclusion

Widely known and enjoyed by Ṣàngó worshippers as well as festival audiences, the verbal arts associated with Ṣàngó illustrate the contradictory and

---

[20] P.F. de Moraes Farias, '"Yoruba origins" revisited by Muslims: An interview with the Arọ́kin of Ọ̀yọ́ and a reading of the Aṣl Qabā'il Yūrubā of Al-Ḥājj Ādam al-Ilūrī', *Self-Assertion and Brokerage: Early Cultural Nationalism in West Africa*, ed. K. Barber and P.F. de Moraes Farias (Birmingham: University of Birmingham African Studies Series, 1990), pp. 109–47: 120.

ambivalent nature of his relationship with Islam and Christianity. Arising from an ongoing engagement with the monotheist religions through verbal arts and especially song, the texts celebrate Ṣàngó both as a deity that coexists with other religions and as an òrìṣà that challenges and surpasses them. This ambivalence is noticeable in the larger body of Ṣàngó's verbal arts, with some texts apparently advocating Ṣàngó's coexistence with the monotheist faiths or asserting a merging of Ṣàngó and Islam, and other texts seemingly rejecting and mocking Islam and Christianity. Depending on the performer or listener, each text in itself is also open towards the opposite interpretation. Where Ṣàngó apparently asserts his ability to coexist with Islam and Christianity, he can also seem to surpass them, and where Ṣàngó rejects and mocks the other religions, he nonetheless exists in relation to them.

The ambivalence and openness of Ṣàngó's verbal art at the personal level clearly reflect the intensely personal nature of òrìṣà worship, which is shaped by different dispositions, experiences and poetic temperaments of performers and audiences. But if the performance of verbal art is bound up with the understanding that everyone's religious experiences are potentially deeply personal, then the ambivalence and openness of these songs can be taken as leaving open the option for others to share in the experience, albeit not in exactly the same way. If we think about the deity's references to Islam and Christianity as producing or imagining shared religious encounters, they equally acknowledge that there are many ways in which such encounters may be experienced, confirming the subtle insight of the proverb that, '"Jọ mí jọ mí", òkúrorò níí ṣoni ín dà' ('"Be identical to me!", such a behest can only be successful if executed by force').

As the meaning of Ṣàngó's verbal arts oscillates depending on the situation and audience, they can be understood as a poetic engagement, or competition, with the other religions. As Ṣàngó emerges both as a collaborator with Islam and Christianity, and as the power that potentially transgresses the boundaries of both, the deity also offers an outside view on the similarities of the monotheist religions that dominate Ede's public life. Like the Tìmì of Ede, Ṣàngó belongs to a community shaped by religious multiplicity and competition and yet also exists, as a potential transgressor of religious boundaries, outside of this multiplicity (see chapter 3). In this, the deity is really different from the world religions. Is it possible that Ede's most important deity contributes to the peaceful relationship between Islam and Christianity by illuminating their similarities?

CHAPTER 5

Compound Life and Religious Control in Ede's Muslim Community

Amusa Saheed Balogun

As described in chapters 2 and 3, the traditions of Ede have it that the introduction of Islam to Ede is due to *Tìmì* Bamigbaye's patronage of Islam, even though he was a powerful Ṣàngó worshipper. The Muslim Buremo Owon-la-a-rogo, or Owonlarogo, came to Ede in order to help *Tìmì* Bamigbaye to defeat his enemies, and he succeeded.[1] After this event, *Tìmì* Bamigbaye allowed him to settle in Ede permanently so that he might continue to support Ede's military might. But even though the collaboration between the *Tìmì* and the Muslim 'prayer warrior' had achieved a shared victory for the town, both maintained their distance from each other.

While *Tìmì* Bamigbaye allowed his subjects to adopt the new faith, he did not embrace the new religion brought by Alfa Buremo. Equally, Alfa Buremo wanted to maintain distance from the town's non-Muslims even as he joined them. He settled in a separate compound near the Ọba's palace, where those he converted several indigenes lived with him and his following increased.[2] By creating a compound, on the basis of religion, Buremo and his followers – and later other Muslims – adapted local forms of organisation normally based on kinship to produce the kernel of the town's Islamic community. The ability of Islam to engender an alternative form of kinship illustrates the ability of Muslims to create Islamic communities that existed independently within a non-Muslim environment. The implications of this practice on the existing debate on Yoruba kinship cannot be explored in this chapter,[3] but as it

---

[1] S.A. Alabi, 'Islam in Ede, 1850–2000', unpublished BA Long Essay (Ile-Ife: Department of History, Obafemi Awolowo University, 2008), p. 31.

[2] Alabi, 'Islam in Ede, 1850–2000', p. 33.

[3] The study of Yoruba kinship has primarily focused on the importance of cognatic descent and on the relationship between kinship and residence. A good overview is provided in J.S. Eades, *The Yoruba Today* (Cambridge: Cambridge University Press, 1980), Chapter 3: 'Kinship and the Yoruba town'.

illustrates the ability of Muslims to separate themselves from non-Muslims, it certainly suggests that the perception of Yoruba Islam as culturally compromised may be misleading (chapter 1).

Irrespective of the determination of the early Muslims, the path of the new religion was not smooth. After the death of *Tìmì* Bamigbaye and the emergence of his younger brother Ojo Arohanran as the new *Tìmì* in the 1840s,[4] the relationship between the *Tìmì* and the Muslim community soured. Although Buremo had been his erstwhile friend, the new *Tìmì* became antagonistic towards the growing Muslim community and began to persecute them. Although Ojo Arohanran is said to have reigned only for three years, his reign was a dark period for Islam in Ede owing to his persecution of the Muslims.[5] The situation was so difficult that Buremo and some of his non-indigenous supporters were forced to leave the town. As a result of the flight of Buremo and his non-native supporters, Owonlarogo's compound fell into disuse.

A new impetus for the spread and expansion of Islam in Ede was provided by the efforts of Prince Abibu (formerly Sangolami) Lagunju and Sheikh Noah, or Nuhu, Adekilekun.[6] Prince Lagunju was a native of Ede who had left the town in his youth and travelled to Ilorin, where he converted to Islam. Among his closest friends and associates in Ilorin was Nuhu Adekilekun, who had also come to study in Ilorin from his hometown, and who followed Prince Lagunju to Ede with his younger brother Musa. When Lagunju was enthroned as the *Tìmì* of Ede, Nuhu Adekilekun emerged as the new head of the nascent Ede Muslim community.[7] As the founders of Ede's second Muslim community, again in the form of an independent compound, Nuhu and Musa established a new settlement near the old Owolarogo Compound. The area under their control was soon called Imole Compound – the compound of the Muslims – as the Ede indigenes who had converted to Islam again came to stay with them (see Map 2).[8]

Tìmì Lagunju and Nuhu and Musa Adekilekun succeeded in converting a large part of the population into the fold of Islam. Throughout the second half of the nineteenth century, they also embarked on a vigorous policy of Islamisation. Islam spread very rapidly because its teachings had a strong

---

[4] See B.R. Isola, 'Islam and society in Ede, 1817–1976', unpublished BA Long Essay (Lagos: Department of History, Lagos State University, 1993), p. 20.

[5] Isola, 'Islam and society in Ede, 1817–1976', p. 20.

[6] Alabi, 'Islam in Ede, 1850–2000', p. 31. See also Siyan Oyeweso, *Eminent Yoruba Muslims of the 19th and Early 20th Centuries* (Ibadan: Rex Charles publication in association with Connel Publications, 1998), pp. 11–33.

[7] Interview with *Alhaji* Ibrahim Dende Adekilekun. 17 May 2012. Ile Imole, Ede.

[8] Isola, 'Islam and society in Ede, 1817–1976', p. 20.

10 The view over Ede from Imole compound

appeal to many people. However, most of the converts at the time had to leave their family compounds and came to live with their teachers. The growth of their compound gave Nuhu and Musa their name Adekilekun, which they had not borne before. The name Adekilekun derives from Ade-ki-ile-okun, i.e. those who increased the population of the compound. Those who came to stay were treated like kin, linking the brotherhood promoted by Islam and the closeness of family relations in many people's minds, even as Muslims and non-Muslims mostly remained separate. Around 1850, *Tìmì* Lagunju turbaned Alfa Noah Adekilekun (c.1850–1903) as the first Chief Imam (*Imamu Jamiu*) of Edeland while Alfa Musa, his younger brother, became Deputy Chief Imam.[9]

Tìmì Abibu Lagunju encouraged people to become Muslims in many ways. One way was through marriage alliances. Significantly, he gave one of his daughters in marriage to the first Chief Imam of Ede, Alfa Nuhu Lagunju. The traditional political support for Islam during the reign of *Tìmì* Habibu Lagunju contributed immensely to the expansion of Islam in Ede. The first Chief Imam and other Islamic clerics from Ilorin used their knowledge of Arabic and

---

[9] Interview with *Alhaji* Abdul Basiru Tijani, Grand Mufti of Imole Compound. 21 November 2012. Imole Compound, 20 Abere Road, Ede. For details on the contributions of Ilorin scholars to the spread of Islam in Yorubaland, see R. Lasisi, 'Oyo-Yoruba and Ilorin relations in the 19th century', *Readings in Nigerian History and Culture*, ed. G.O. Oguntomisin and S.A. Ajayi (Ibadan: Hope Publications, 2002), p. 265.

Islamic doctrine as men of God to convert many people and families to the Islamic faith through open-air *da'wa* (call to the Islamic religion).[10] Trade, intermarriage and the immigration of Islamic scholars from Ilorin and other neighbouring towns also facilitated the growth and development of Islam in Edeland.[11]

With the acceptance of Islam by the ruling elite and the patronage given to Islam and the Muslim leaders, Islamic festivals were celebrated communally, with the *Tìmì* as the town's most distinguished worshipper. Ede also became a place of Islamic learning as Muslim scholars were attracted from Ilorin. As early as 1860, the first Chief Imam of Ede established the first formal centre for Qur'anic and Islamic studies at Imole Compound in Ede. This further contributed to the growth of Ede's Muslim population, and as the children of converts attended the local Islamic centres in order to increase their knowledge about Islam, the community became more educated and sophisticated.

The bulk of the teachers and preachers resided at Imole Compound in Ede, which had become the centre of Islamic education and debate for Ede's Muslims.[12] However, as time passed, converts with powerful positions in their own extended families also transformed their own compounds into Islamic spaces by following the example of Ile Imole. While there are many other Islamic educational institutions and activities within the town, Imole Compound continues to play an important role as an example for the Muslim community at large.

Ede's Traditional Political System and the Organisation of the Muslim Community

In contemporary times, the traditional political administration of Ede is headed by the *Tìmì* who is the paramount ruler of the town. He is assisted by a council of twelve traditional chiefs who are the heads of the major traditional quarters of the town. These include the *Balógun, Babásànyà, Ọ̀tún Balógun, Òsì Balógun, Aṣípa Balógun, Jagun, Àgbàakin, Sérikí, Àyópè* and

---

[10] Interview with *Alhaji* Abdul Basiru Tijani. 21 November 2012.

[11] The factors that are responsible for the spread of Islam in Edeland are the same factors that are responsible for the spread of Islam in other parts of Yorubaland. For details, see O. Lawuyi, 'Islam, economy and political identity: An insight into religious odentifications of the Yoruba', *Annals of the Institute of Cultural Studies* 6 (1995), 4–15: 4.

[12] T. Akinjobi, 'The role of sheikhs and imams in the promotion of Islam in Edeland', *Crowns and Turbans in the Promotion of Islam in Osun State: Essays in Honour of HRM Oba Raufu Olayiwola Olawale, Adedeji II, Akinrun of Ikirun*, ed. S. Oyeweso (Abuja: Mega Press Ltd, 2012), pp. 194–271: 194–6.

Ìkọ̀làbà.[13] The Ìyálóde, head of the women, is the only female member of the Council. The twelfth member of the Council is the traditional deputy of the Tìmì called the Bàbá Kékeré who attends to social, economic political disputes between individuals within Ede Township. The Tìmì, the Bàbá Kékeré and the other eleven traditional chiefs form the Tìmì-in-Council, which is the highest traditional political authority in Edeland.[14] Interpersonal disputes that are considered extremely important and critical, as well as disputes involving groups and societies, compounds, quarters and villages, are attended to by the Tìmì-in-Council. There are also some honorary chiefs who are appointed by the Tìmì-in-Council in recognition of their landmark contributions to the development of the town. Honorary chiefs are drawn from indigenes and non-indigenes of Ede.[15]

The Chief Imam of Ede heads the Ede Muslim Council, which is the umbrella body of all Muslim and all Islamic organisations and mosques in the town.[16] The Chief Imam is based at the Ede Central Mosque, which is in turn located next to the Palace of the Tìmì. The Ede Muslim Council is also headquartered at the Ede Central Mosque. Chief Imam of Ede is deputised by the Naibul Imam (Deputy Chief Imam). Another important chieftain within the Ede Muslim Council is the Mu'aḍḍin (Caller to Prayer) and his assistants. Apart from these three key figures in the Ede Muslim community, there are other officers such as secretary, treasurer, public relations officer and so on, who assist with the smooth running and coordination of the activities of the Council.[17] The present Chief Imam of Ede, Alhaji Mas'ud Husain Akajewole, lists the Àlùfá Àgbà, the Ajánásì, the Balógun Imam, Ẹ̀kẹrin Imam, Ọ̀tún Imam, Ọ̀tún Àlùfá Àgbà, Ọ̀tún Ajánásì, Ọ̀tún Balógun, Ọ̀tún Ẹ̀kerin, Ẹ̀karùǹ and Ẹ̀kẹfà as the most important members of the traditional hierarchy of Muslim leaders under the Chief Imam.[18]

As the ruler of a town noted for its strong Islamic influence, the Tìmì of Ede exercises considerable power over the choice and turbaning of the Chief Imam of Edeland as well as the overall activities of the Ede Muslim Council. This power reflects the historic links between the Tìmì's stool and the advent

---

[13] A. Adegbola, *Ile-Ife: The Source of Yoruba Civilisation* (Lagos: Oduduwa International Communications, 2009), pp. 505–8.

[14] Interview with *Alhaji* Wahab Aminu Ayofe, community leader, Ede. 10 February 2013.

[15] *Ibid.*

[16] These include *Jumu'ah* mosques, where the obligatory weekly Friday prayers are offered on a regular basis, and the smaller compound mosques, sometimes called non-*Jumu'ah* mosques, which are designated for the observation of only the five daily obligatory prayers.

[17] Interview with *Alhaji* Mudathir Adedeji, civil servant. 10 February 2013.

[18] Interview with *Alhaji* Mas'ud Husain Akajewole, the Chief Imam of Ede. 19 April 2012.

of Islam in Ede.[19] Because Ede's Muslim community is aware of its historical roots, and because the power of the *Tìmì* is linked to the coming and entrenchment of Islam, the *Tìmì* has always had some influence on Islamic politics and developments in Ede. However, as pointed out in earlier chapters of this book, the *Tìmì* was also linked, by precedent, to the deity Ṣàngó. Moreover, he faced increasing resistance once he was seen to discriminate against other religions. Finally, he could not be sure that his successors would support Islam as strongly as he did.

Given the expectation of standing above religion that was associated with his office, *Tìmì* Lagunju supported the entrenchment of Islam within the town's existing compound system. Like most Yoruba towns, Ede is constituted into compounds inhabited by the male members of patrilineages, their wives, children and occasionally other members of the family, as well as by tenants. Those descended from the original founders of a compound and the women who are married to them, even though they are originally from other places within and outside Ede, are regarded as indigenes. The oldest male indigenous resident is usually its head, and he is often advised by other senior members. Compounds and the patrilineages that constitute their core form an important corporate identity by virtue of the fact that they control access to land and other resources, such as traditional – or even Islamic – chieftaincy titles. As a result, compounds form an important structure in the economic and political life of the town.

In many ways the compound system in Ede is modelled on the structures of the town itself: compounds have a head, who is in turn advised by representatives of its different sections, who may be the heads of different branches of the extended family. Other advisers to the head of the compound may include elderly representatives, the daughters who have married 'out', and the wives who have married 'in', even though the male descendants of the compound's core patrilineage often have the strongest influence. Like the town itself, Ede's compounds also have their own histories and distinct identities, from which are derived the rules and expectations that guide the behaviour of their inhabitants. Young members of the family, the wives who marry into the family, and especially any tenants who rent rooms or shops within the compound, must follow the rules of the compound leaders.

By encouraging the foundation of explicitly Muslim compounds, *Tìmì* Lagunju naturalised Islam in Ede as a practice that was comparable with existing local practices. By allowing Islamic scholars to become the heads of compounds, Lagunju encouraged the transformation of their Islamic knowledge into a form of authority that also resonated with locally recognised notions of

---

[19] For details, see Oyeweso, *Eminent Yoruba Muslims*, pp. 11–33.

power. As described in previous chapters, the local engagement with Islam was a multi-directional process. While the establishment of Muslim compounds meant that Islam was domesticated within existing structures, the adaptation of the compound system also offered the possibility of religious separation by enabling Muslims to maintain a degree of distance from non-believers.

By being based on shared faith rather than biological descent, Islamic compounds also transformed existing notions of community. While many compounds had one core deity in whose worship everyone was expected to participate, this did not mean that the worship of other deities was disallowed. Indeed, in some compounds, religious innovation was associated with prominent or popular 'outsiders', including wives and slaves. But while kinship and religious practice had always been loosely associated, Islam's ban on the worship of other deities meant that religion played an increasingly important role in the definition of community at the compound level. As this chapter illustrates, the relationship between kinship and descent was redefined in different ways in different compounds. Both Imole and Talafia Imam Compounds were established, albeit in slightly different ways, as Muslim compounds. Especially in Imole Compound, the shared practice of Islam appears more important than biological descent, as those who have converted away from Islam no longer reside in Imole Compound despite their descent. While religious outsiders, for example non-Muslim wives married into the compound, are allowed to practise their religion in line with local Islamic notions of tolerance, they must do so discreetly. Equally, compound members' participation in traditional practices – understood by some as 'tradition' rather than 'religion' – must be confined to spaces outside the compound. Talafia Imam Compound is dominated by a similar commitment to Islam as the compound's defining religion, but the greater presence of Christians and the more accepting attitude of its leaders suggest that its Islamic practices constitute a milder challenge to biological kinship. Clearly, then, the relationship between biological descent and religion is negotiated differently in different compounds and exists along a continuum.

Owing to their association with important Muslim scholars and their strong tradition of Islamic education and scholarship, both Imole and Talafia Imam Compounds are also associated with the line of Ede's Chief Imam. As a result, they are linked with another adaptive replication of existing structures widely associated with Islam in Yorubaland, namely the establishment of the Muslim community both as separate from the town and as imitating its structures.

As in many Muslim towns, Ede's Chief Imam is selected in a manner that resembles the selection of the ọba and that privileges historical achievement. While the ọba is selected from among the descendants of the town's founder or first ruler, the Chief Imam is selected from among the descendants of the early members of the Muslim community, i.e. those whose families are based in an old Muslim compound. After Nuhu Adekilekun from Imole Compound, the town's second Chief Imam was *Alhaji* Aminulah Talafia from Talafia Compound (1903–36).[20] Other compounds from which the town's Chief Imams have come include Akajewole Compound, Lakonu Compound and Jagun Alaro Compound, and together these are often referred to as 'the five compounds'.

Daodu Lagunju Compound, the third compound discussed in this chapter, is a royal compound but became Muslim because of *Tìmì* Lagunju's support for Islam (cf. chapter 2). In this compound, the dominance of Islam is associated with the charismatic leadership of a former ruler of the town, and thus in itself aligned with descent. Certainly, in Daodu Lagunju Compound, non-Muslims must respect the essentially Islamic identity of the compound. However, as the compound maintains its claim to the throne, its members are free to follow all religions because the town's *ọba*ship is associated with the transcendence and even transgression of religious boundaries. Perhaps because of the compound's association with the throne, belonging remains defined primarily by kinship rather than by religion, illustrating the wide continuum along which different Islamic compounds negotiate the tension between descent and religion.

Other historically important Muslim compounds that are linked to important titles in the traditional Islamic hierarchy of the town include Aro, Jejelose, Olujobi, Odunaye, Elekuro, Gbokiki and Ologun compounds. All these compounds, sometimes home to very large extended families and groups of families, understand themselves and each other as exemplary Muslim institutions. Other compounds closely identified with Islam today, either because they were founded as Muslim compounds or because they have Muslim majorities, include Epo, Gbagiimoju, Osun, Igbe Edun Faajo, Olukolo, Esin Nla, Isibo, Oloba, Akaje and Lakonu Compounds.[21] Their sheer number illustrates their power over the sphere of politics shaped by family- and compound-based resources within Ede.

Today, Islam is the dominant religion in most of Ede's old compounds. While the size of Ede's compounds means that even the Muslim compounds are somewhat religiously mixed, the social structures of compounds mean that there is usually a majority or a favoured religion. According to Dokun's survey of religion in ten compounds in Ede in 1973, only one of the compounds surveyed had a Christian majority: in Aridi-Ogo Compound, 225 of the 397 residents were Christians. The remaining compounds had a very clear Muslim

---

[20] Imam Aminullah was however related to Imole Compound through his mother, who was a daughter of Nuhu Adekilekun.

[21] L. Dokun, 'Islam in Ede', unpublished BA Long Essay (Ibadan: Department of Arabic and Islamic Studies, University of Ibadan, 1974), p. 59.

majority, with typically only one or two traditional worshippers to many hundreds of Muslims, and a smaller number of Christians, in each compound.

While immigration has brought more Christians to Ede since the 1970s, and while there are now houses built on independently owned land, most compounds have also seen a significant increase of population. Thus, while many towns have seen a strong shift from Islam to Christianity, it is likely that the overall ratio of Muslims to Christians in Ede has shifted only slightly. As most Muslim-dominated compounds look to the practices in Imole, Talafia and Daodu Lagunju Compounds for inspiration and guidance, a closer study of these corporate bodies is illuminating (Map 2).

Views on Religious Tolerance from Ede's Muslim Compounds

Reflecting the Muslim identity of Imole, Talafia and Daodu Lagunju Compounds, many of their leaders draw on Islamic conceptions of tolerance to structure their relationships with non-Muslims, and especially with any non-Muslim inhabitants of compounds. The leaders of Muslim compounds do not accept that all religions should be considered to have equal claims to validity and truth. Instead, their views on other religions are shaped by the Qur'an. Many of Ede's Muslims would however argue that Islam is inherently tolerant of other religions. Several compound leaders and elders from Ede whom I interviewed about the relationship of Islam to other religions pointed to the importance of Surah 109 (*al-Kāfirūn*, or The Disbelievers) in the Qur'an, which reads:

> Verse 1: Say (O Muhammad) to the disbelievers in Allah
> Verse 2: 'I worship not that which you worship'
> Verse 3: 'Nor will you worship that which I worship'
> Verse 4: 'And I shall not worship that which you are worshipping'
> Verse 5: 'Nor will you worship that which I worship'
> Verse 6: 'To you be your religion, and to me my religion'[22]

This Surah is widely understood as being devoted to the topic of religious tolerance. The early history of Islam, in particular the life of the Prophet Muhammed, is also often used to explain that Muslims should try to live peacefully with non-Muslims. Despite the opposition and even physical torture that his followers suffered in Mecca, the Prophet always approached the unbelievers of Mecca with tolerance. In Medina, Prophet Muhammed did

---

[22] See the Holy Qur'an Chapter 109 in M.M. Khan and M.T. Al-Hilali, *Interpretation of the Meanings of the Noble Qur'an* (Riyadh: Darussalam Publishers and Distributors, 1996), pp. 1125–6.

not attempt to force the city's largely non-Muslim population into the fold of Islam, but he rather made a peace agreement with them and referred to them as *'Ahl al-kitāb* – the People of the Book.[23] The peace agreement guaranteed the physical safety and security of the Jewish community and the freedom to practise their religion as long as that community abided by the terms of the treaty.[24] This understanding of the Prophet's life is reflected in the words of Ede's Chief Imam, *Alhaji* Mas'ud Akajewole, whose Akajewole Compound is also an important Islamic compound even though it is not discussed here (see Figure 6). The Chief Imam explained:

> Whatever the religion of others, we must be tolerant because Prophet Muhammed lived with pagans in Mecca and Medina. He lived with Christians and other believers and he did not harm anybody. Those who converted to Islam, according to the writings, were pleased by the behaviour of the Prophet. No matter where we are, we have to be tolerant. Muslims must show that Islam is a religion of peace. Muslims should not be only Muslims in the mosque but also Muslims everywhere. That is why it is said that Islam is the complete way of Allah. Anywhere a Muslim is, he or she must maintain peace.[25]

To many Yoruba Muslims, the ability to coexist peacefully with members of other religions is a great source of pride, and even a sign of the moral superiority of Islam over Christianity. *Alhaji* Sheikh Ibrahim Dende Adekilekun, a very senior member of Imole Compound and the Chief Imam of Ede's Ansar-ud-Deen society, explained that the Qur'an's religious injunctions clearly state that personal obligations are not annulled by religious difference. Asked about how Muslims should relate to those of other religions, he said,

> The Holy Qur'an says that even if you have a pagan as a parent, you must feed him or her, you will feed them, and you will do everything for them. When he dies, you know he is not a Muslim, you will invite his colleagues [in the religion] that how are we going to bury my father or mother, he is a pagan. If they charge you one million naira, you will have to find money to give them. It is only you will not join them. You will not dance with them, you will not go into the bush with them but you must pay all money that it costs.

---

[23] Although it should be noted that *'Ahl al-kitāb* refers only to Jews and Christians and most of Medina's non-Muslim population were Pagans (*Mushrikūn*) and therefore not part of such a peace agreement.

[24] A. Rahim, *Islamic History* (Delhi: Royal Publishers and Distributors, 2003), pp. 28–31. See also S.M. Rizvi, 'Religious tolerance in Islam', *Ahlul Bayt Digital Islamic Library Project* (n.d.)., <http://www.al-islam.org/articles/religious-tolerance-islam-sayyid-muhammad-rizvi>, accessed 25 September 2014.

[25] Interview with *Alhaji* Mas'ud Husain Akajewole, the Chief Imam of Ede. 19 April 2012.

Islam is so good, no *wahala* [trouble]. It is a religion of tolerance of course. But for you to starve your father or your mother, why? It is not in Islam, no, no, no. That is why I used to tell some Christians, they used to tell their parents that if you do not believe in Jesus, you will not have any right from me, no [meaning: this is wrong].[26]

This understanding of religious tolerance in Islam accords others the right to practise their religion, and one could even argue that it accepts some other religions as having a claim to truth. It does not, however, agree with the notion that all religions have equal claims to the truth.

As this form of tolerance also acknowledges the importance of kinship, it is clear that Islam only partially replaced biological links. Even so, *Alhaji* Adekilekun's description points to the importance of familial obligations across the religious divide, which are however balanced by proscriptions for distance that reflect Islamic values. Thus a Muslim child has to pay for a non-Muslim parent's funeral out of obligation, but he or she must not join them in dancing or going 'into the bush', to avoid having to participate in non-Islamic forms of celebration and thus to compromise her or his faith. In this way, Islam and kinship are closely interwoven in some areas and yet remain distinctly separate in others.

Just as the family lives of Muslims are guided by the need to balance familial and religious obligations, so non-Muslims are guided by the boundaries created by Muslims in line with Islamic injunctions. Importantly, in Islamic compounds, they must agree to behave in a certain way in order not to undermine the supremacy of Islam and Islamic law.[27] Illustrating the many possible ways in which familial, neighbourly and religious obligations can be reconciled, every compound has its own way of achieving peaceful religious coexistence between Muslims and non-Muslims. A closer look at Imole, Talafia and Daodu Lagunju Compounds will illustrate in what way Islamic ideas of tolerance or coexistence are translated into practice.

Imole Compound: The Light House of Islam in Ede

Imole Compound simply means 'Compound of the Muslims' as *Ìmọ̀le* is a Yoruba word for Muslim.[28] As described above, Imole Compound in Ede was

---

[26] Interview with *Alhaji* Ibrahim Dende Adekilekun, Ile Imole. 19 May 2012.
[27] A Muslim community is a place that has a preponderance of Muslim population over people of other religious faiths. An Islamic community refers to a state that is dominated by Muslims and administered according to Islamic law (*al-Sharī'a*).
[28] There are several etymological explanations of the word. To some, it originates from the word 'Mali' because Islam was brought to West Africa and by extension, to Yorubaland,

closely affiliated with Muslims and Islamic scholars from its inception.[29] Over time, the compound has produced many Chief Imams of Ede, and *Alhaji Sheikh Ibrahim Dende Adekilekun*, the incumbent Chief Imam of Ansar-ud-Deen Society, Ede Branch, is an indigene of the compound. Imole Compound is located along Yidi Road in modern Ede. It is surrounded by Olusokun, Alupe and Apena Compounds. According to Dokun, Imole Compound was the first place in Ede where a small neighbourhood mosque, or *Ratibi* mosque, was built, next to a popular well.[30] Today the large compound has many *Ratibi* mosques, which are usually attended by Muslims who live or work close to them or who are in the area during prayer time for the observance of the five daily prayers, particularly Ṣalāt al-zuhr (afternoon prayer) and Ṣalāt al-'aṣr (evening prayer).

11 Salam Basit of Imole compound points to the mosque well

The nearest church to Imole Compound is a small church at Olusokun Compound, which is adjacent to Imole Compound's northern border, but most of the worshippers in the church come from neighbouring Ojoro, Sikako

---

by traders and scholars from Mali. Some people take the word to mean 'a religion of hard people' or 'a religion of hard/strong willed people' from the Yoruba meaning of its sound 'Imo' 'le', i.e. 'hard' 'knowledge', and as this implies, this compound has featured prominently in Islamic history of Ede.

[29] A.A. al-Ilori, *Mujiz Tarikh Nigeria* (Beirut: n.p., 1965), p. 147.
[30] Dokun, 'Islam in Ede', p. 54.

and Abere Compounds.³¹ In the 1970s, all of Imole Compound's 741 inhabitants were reportedly Muslims.³² While the number of people in the compound has certainly increased, it is still almost exclusively Muslim. Although there may be some indigenes of Imole Compound who have embraced Christianity or other religions in new places of residence, there is virtually no home-based indigene of Imole Compound who does not practise Islam. However, the compound has a few Christian inhabitants who moved there as tenants. They are allowed to practise their religion privately, but they must not stage religious activities that call others to Christianity, such as public testimony or healing (usually described locally as 'crusades'), in Imole Compound.³³ In this way, Islam shapes compound identity in two ways: those who belong to the compound but have given up Islam can no longer reside in Imole Compound, and those who reside there but are religious outsiders must practise discreetly.

Among the indigenes of the compound, the most important difference seems to be that between liberal and strict Muslims. There are some Muslim residents in Imole Compound who also participate in the practice of traditional religion. For instance, one of the respondents from Imole Compound explained that he was the custodian of the *Àlùpè Egúngún* masquerade, which is one of the important masquerades in Ede. The *Àlùpè Egúngún* cult is however not based at Imole Compound but in the neighbouring Olusokun Compound. According to this respondent, Islam does not prevent him from participating in Yoruba cultural festivals. Indeed, he prays and fasts regularly as a Muslim. In his words:

> Eégún kò ní kí a má ṣe kírun ń tiwa o. Àwọn baba wa fún wa l'órúkọ Òjé lọ́jọ́ keje tí wọ́n bí wa, wọ́n sì tún fún wa l'órúkọ Ìmọ̀le lọ́jọ́ kejọ. Bí a bá ń ṣe ọdún eégún nínú oṣù kẹfà ọdún, gbogbo wa pátá la jọ́ ń ṣe. Àwọn Alfa gan á máa wá láti ilé Ìmọ̀le wáá jà'akàà eégún.³⁴

> The *Egúngún* cult does not prevent us from praying as Muslims. Our fathers gave us traditional *Egúngún* cult names on the seventh day of our birth and they also gave us Muslim names on the eighth day. When we celebrate the

---

[31] Interview with Mr Ahmed Yakubu, trader. 25 November 2012. Imole Compound, Ede.
[32] Dokun, 'Islam in Ede', pp. 141–50.
[33] Interview with Mr Ahmed Yakubu, trader. 25 November 2012. Imole Compound, Ede. This view was corroborated by a Christian couple, indigenes of Modakeke, who reside in Imole Compound: interview with Mr and Mrs Arinola Jeremiah. 25 November 2012.
[34] Interview with Mr Mufutau Ogunlana, farmer. 25 November 2012. Olusokun Compound, Ede. See also, for similar findings in other parts of Yorubaland: M. Opeloye, 'Evolution of religious culture among the Yoruba', *Culture and Society in Yorubaland*, ed. D.A. Ogunremi (Ibadan: Rex Charles Publication in association with Connel Publications, 1998), pp. 139–48.

> *Egúngún* festival in the sixth month of the year, everybody joins us. Even some Muslim clerics from Imole Compound come to eat from bean cakes provided for the celebrations.

This statement illustrates that for some Muslims, the traditional activities of the town, including the popular *Egúngún* masquerade, are not in direct competition with Islam. However, the participation in *Egúngún* is not as easy for Islamic leaders as the respondent implies. It could not be confirmed who the Muslim clerics mentioned by this respondent might be. Whether or not they were men of influence, they did not celebrate openly with the masqueraders by inviting them to perform in Imole Compound, and they did not bring the bean cakes home. Instead, they went out, possibly secretly, and participated in the *Egúngún* celebrations outside of their compound. Also, even if the leader of *Àlùpè Egúngún* lives in Imole Compound, the shrine itself remains firmly in Olusokun Compound. Thus, the participation of some Muslims from Imole or other Muslim-dominated compounds in Yoruba traditional religious festivals such as *Egúngún* simply reflects the personal discretion of individual Muslims. Explicitly or implicitly, it is agreed that Imole Compound should remain a Muslim space. While individual Muslims from Imole Compound can participate in *Egúngún* and other festivals as individuals, the religious nature of the compound itself is not transformed.

Moreover, not all Muslims in Imole Compound share liberal attitudes towards traditional practice. One highly educated indigene of Imole Compound argued strongly against the participation in non-Muslim (traditional) religious practices:

> Islam requires full and strict compliance with [the] Qur'anic injunction that says that one must enter into the fold of Islam fully and should not follow the footpath of Satan. To me, all other religious activities apart from those of Islam are footpaths of Satan. Therefore, I do not make intimate friends among non-Muslims and I do not see any good in what they do. I cannot eat their festival's food and I cannot even watch them. I consider that sinful.[35]

This respondent was a member of the Ede Branch of the Muslim Students' Society of Nigeria (MSSN), which has played an important role throughout Yorubaland (and Nigeria) in emphasising the importance of practising a 'pure' Islam. This concern with purity means that they have distanced themselves strongly from other religions. The MSSN's emphasis on distance between Islam and other religions arose at least partly out of the experiences of Muslims

---

[35] Interview with Mallam Abass Saliu, schoolteacher. 10 February 2013. Imole Compound, Ede. The Qur'anic verse referred to here is Holy Qur'an Chapter 2, Verse 208.

who entered educational institutions dominated by Christians, and who found themselves subject to Christian moralising and preaching. Perhaps as a result of such experiences, especially those educated Muslim youths represented by the members of the MSSN and other Muslim youth organisations in Imole Compound tend to be more inclined to emphasise the integrity of Islamic practices. They make their views known through frequent open *da'wa* (preaching), religious admonitions at prayer time in the *Ratibi* mosques, and other Islamic religious gatherings such as funeral, naming and marriage ceremonies.

While individual residents of the compound may not agree with the exhortations to maintain the purity of Islamic practice at all costs, the activities of the MSSN members have not led to any form of religious crisis in the compound to date. The liberal Muslims and Christians accept the limitations on their activities because they know that Imole Compound is historically a Muslim compound. Differences of age and status may also play a role in enabling the groups to accommodate each other. As some of the liberal Muslims are older, they believe that some of the more radical younger people may understand the importance of some traditional practices as they grow older. Other liberal Muslims are highly educated and view their participation in traditional religious activities as a mere expression of their culture or patriotism. In turn, the purists believe that they represent a new generation that will bring innovation and improvement to the practice of Islam. Meanwhile, the Islamic leaders from the compound encourage and support the views and activities of the purists, but they see no reason to interfere in the practices of others as long as they do not challenge the fundamentally Islamic nature of Imole Compound.

As a result, Imole Compound remains an example of a Muslim community for the rest of Ede. With virtually no resident Christians, traditionalist activities are limited to the private activities of individuals outside of the compound. As such individuals often nonetheless consider themselves Muslims, traditional practice does not seem like something that might challenge Islam, but more like something that is a contested part of Muslim practice, constantly discussed and debated among Imole indigenes. Unlike the rest of Ede, Imole Compound is thus an almost exclusively Muslim space, where Islam shapes belonging and membership in clear-cut ways.

Talafia Imam: A Muslim-Dominated Compound with Non-Muslim and Non-Indigenous Inhabitants

Talafia Imam Compound is an old compound in Ede that was divided into two sections, or new compounds, at the beginning of the twentieth century. The division of the old compound illustrates yet another way in which religion can delineate boundaries within the extended patrilineages and families that constitute compounds. When one section of Talafia Compound produced the second Chief Imam of Ede, *Alhaji* Aminulah Talafia (who succeeded the town's first Chief Imam Nuhu Adekilekun in 1903),[36] it became an explicitly Muslim compound and was henceforth called Talafia Imam Compound. The new compound became the home of many committed Muslims of Talafia Compound at the time, and today it is the home of the Grand Mufti of Ede, *Alhaji* Sheikh Muhammed Saheed Olanrewaju. Meanwhile, those who did not join the new Talafia Imam Compound eventually came to be called Talafia Baba Abiye, after Samson Oladeji Akande, a much-beloved prophet of the Christ Apostolic Church, who specialised in maternal care and childbirth. Nicknamed Baba Abiye, he built his first church in a part of Talafia Compound where he also resided (see also chapter 7).[37]

Talafia Imam Compound is located along Federal Polytechnic Road, Ede, and its indigenes are predominantly, though not exclusively, Muslim. Because of its proximity to the campus of the Federal Polytechnic Ede, the compound's members let rooms to students and it has many Christian tenants. Talafia Imam is smaller than Imole Compound, and it has only one *Ratibi* mosque in which the Muslim indigenes and tenants observe the five daily prayers. Like Imole Compound, Talafia Imam does not have any church. However, some of the Christian inhabitants of the compound attend churches at nearby Talafia Baba Abiye, while some staff or students of the Federal Polytechnic Ede who reside in the compound engage in Christian fellowship activities within their houses and off-campus hostels.

As in Imole Compound, the fact that Talafia Imam Compound is a Muslim compound means that the religious activities of non-Muslims are permitted but restricted. As the compound contains more Christian tenants than Imole Compound, compound rules are explained clearly to tenants before they move in, in order to avoid misunderstandings. Before moving into the compound all tenants have to agree not to carry out any public Christian activities. This includes not singing any praise song aloud when Muslims are observing the early morning prayer, not walking in front of a Muslim who is praying, and not organising public Christian programmes within the compound.[38] Questioned about the possibility of Christian students organising open religious activities in the compound, one of the respondents had this to say:

---

[36] Akinjobi, 'The role of sheikhs and imams in the promotion of Islam in Edeland', p. 200.
[37] Interview with Mr Michael Ajayi, roadside mechanic. 25 November 2012. Talafia Baba Abiye, Ede.
[38] Interview with Miss Funke Adewumi, HND 1 student of Marketing at the Federal Polytechnic, Ede. 10 February 2013.

Aà lè gbà kí wọ́n ṣe ìsọjí kankan ní bí láéláé. Wọ́n lè máa kọrin wọn kọjá l'ójú títì ìjọba o, ṣùgbọ́n kí wọ́n wáá sọ pé àwọn fẹ́ẹ́ dúró ṣe Ìsọjí àbí Ìsọ́ òru kankan, wọn kò tó bẹ́ẹ̀. Àwọn gan an mọ ibi tí àwọn wà. Àwa ò pé kí wọ́n má ṣe èsìn wọn o, ṣùgbọ́n àdúgbò tiwa rèé, wọn kò gbọdọ̀ dí wa l'ọ́wọ́. Kódà gan bí a bá ń kírun lọ́wọ́, wọn kò gbọdọ́ fa'riwo dí wa lọ́wọ́ bí wọ́n bá ń kọjá lójú títì ìjọba.³⁹

We can never allow them to hold an open crusade here.⁴⁰ They can sing when they pass through major roads, but for them to come to our place and attempt to hold a crusade or a night vigil, they dare not [do it]. They too are aware of where they are. We do not prevent them from practising their religion but this is our neighbourhood and they must not disturb us. In fact, when we are praying, they must not make a noise to disturb us if they are passing by on the streets.

This quotation illustrates the strong sense of ownership that the indigenes of a compound feel about their community and asserts the expectation that the Muslim indigenes of the community should be able to control what happens within its space. The explanation also presents the Christians resident in Talafia Imam Compound as double outsiders: not only does the compound not belong to them because they are only tenants, but it is also a space where they are outsiders by virtue of their religion, because it is owned by Muslims. A non-Muslim tenant of the compound highlighted the difference between everyday interpersonal relations, which are normally friendly, and the sanctions imposed on those who are seen to undermine the corporate identity of the compound: 'The people are nice and accommodating but [they] can be mad with you if you talk ill of Islam in their presence.'⁴¹

The close control of individual behaviour in the space of a compound reflects the double exclusion of Christians from the compound, both as Christians and as tenants. However, given that Talafia Imam Compound has far more non-Muslim residents than Imole Compound, the close policing of Christian behaviour of the compound can also be understood as the reaction to the unease associated with the fact that the many outsiders among the residents of the

---

³⁹ Interview with Alfa Waliyulahi Saheed, son of *Alhaji* Sheikh Saheed Olanrewaju, Grand Mufti of Edeland. 25 November 2012. Talafia Compound, Ede.
⁴⁰ The word *ìsọjí* can be translated as 'revival meeting' or 'spiritual awakening event'. However, following Christian use of the term as 'crusade', local Muslims and Christians describe a large number of mobilising events as 'crusades', including 'anti-corruption crusades'. Some Muslims even refer to Islamic events analogous to Christian 'prayer crusades' with the same term. See the following chapter for an Islamic event locally described (in English) as a 'counter-crusade'.
⁴¹ Interview with Mr Simon Alade, ND II student of Financial Studies at the Federal Polytechnic, Ede. 25 November 2012.

compound could potentially transform the essence of the compound through conversion. The mutual intelligibility of Islam and Christianity, as well as their mutual exclusivity, is aptly described by *Alhaji* Sheikh Saheed Olanrewaju, the Grand Mufti of Edeland and the head of the Muslims in Talafia Imam. He explained:

> Ìyàtọ̀ bíntín ní mbè làárín àwa àti àwọn ẹlẹ́sìn kejì. Àwá gbà pé Ọlọ́hun kannáà ni Mùsùlùmí àti Ìgbàgbó ń sìn. Ìyàtọ̀ tó kàn wà mbẹ̀ nipé bí wọ́n tí mpe Jésù l'Ọlọ́hun, àwa sì gbà pé ọ̀kan nínú àwọn òjíṣẹ́ Ọlọ́hun ni tí à ń pè ní Ànábì Ísá. Àmọ́n ìgbé àlaáfíà là ń gbé pẹ̀lú àwọn ẹlẹ́sìn kejì mbí o, a sì jọ máa ń pàdé ní òde. A máa ń fún àwọn ọmọ ilé-ìwé n'ílé ìgbé bẹ́ẹ̀ni ọmọ mi tó bá fẹ́ làti fẹ́ ẹlẹ́sìn kejì, àyè wà fun, á jẹ́ wípé kádàrá ti ẹ̀ nù un. Àwọn Mùsùlùmí míràn kìí fẹ́ẹ́ gba ẹlẹ́sìn kejì sílé torípé wọ́n á máa dí ènìyàn lọ́wọ́ nígbàtí wọ́n bá ń ṣe àdúà wọn á sì tètè máa ṣọ ilé onílé di ṣọ́ọ̀ṣì wọn. A lèe gba àwọn ẹlẹ́sìn kejì láàyè làti ṣe ìwọ̀de èsìn wọn ṣùgbọ́n wọn kò gbọdọ̀ p'agbo sí àdúgbò yìí.[42]

There is only a slight difference between us [Muslims] and the people of the other faith [Christians]. We acknowledge that Muslims and Christians worship the same God. The only difference is that they call Jesus God while we see him as one of the messengers of God named Isa. That notwithstanding, we live in peace and harmony with one another here and we meet at different occasions. We rent out our vacant rooms to Christian students, and any of my children who chooses to get married to a Christian is allowed because I consider that to be his/her destiny. Some Muslims may not want to rent their houses to Christians because they disturb others when praying and can easily turn houses to churches. We allow Christians to have evangelising events but they cannot hold any crusade in this neighbourhood.

This statement, again, points to the difference between personal religious choices and the rules that apply to the compound as a corporate institution. On a personal level, non-Muslims are made welcome in Talafia Imam Compound, and the Grand Mufti of Edeland even suggests even that he can allow his children to marry Christians. Given that he speaks in a way that refers to both male and female children, who are likely to convert, this suggests that he is less opposed to interfaith marriages than many other parents in Ede (see chapter 10), and by implication very warmly disposed towards his fellow monotheists.

But despite his personal acceptance of Christians, *Alhaji* Olanrewaju also points out that within the compound, their practices can be tolerated only if they avoid challenging the supremacy of Islam and the compound's indigenes.

---

[42] Interview with *Alhaji* Sheikh Saheed Olanrewaju, Grand Mufti of Edeland. 5 December 2013. Talafia Imam Compound, Ede.

This entails a limitation of Christian activities. In practice, Christian spaces in Talafia Imam Compound are limited to a few houses dominated by Christian students and staff of the Federal Polytechnic, Ede and apartments rented by Christians from Muslim landlords. Here, Christian practices are accepted in private spaces and times not marked by Muslim prayer. While the compound's Muslim leaders agree that Christianity is closer to Islam than traditional practice,[43] the fact that Christianity is a religion of religious outsiders means that social and religious boundaries coincide. Reflecting the dominant position of the indigenes vis-à-vis the Christian tenants, the compound's public space appears as clearly Muslim.

However, the different restrictions that apply to the traditionalist activities in which some of the indigenous Muslim compound members participate suggest that the relationship between religion and belonging at the compound level is complex. Like Christian groups, traditionalists are expected to stop singing or noise-making during prayer times, and are not allowed to organise public religious events in any part of the compound. However, the traditionalist residents of Talafia Imam are allowed to walk through the streets of the compound singing and dancing as part of masquerades or other traditional rituals. This means that traditionalists have somewhat greater leeway than the Christians to praise and worship in public because they are members of Talafia Imam Compound. Clearly, while religion plays an important role in shaping the compound's identity, familial belonging also shapes the compound's distinctive religious boundaries.

Daodu Lagunju Compound: A Traditional Royal Compound where Islam Reigns Supreme

Daodu Lagunju Compound is the oldest of the three compounds selected for this study, for it predates the introduction of Islam into Ede.[44] The dominance of Islam within the compound can be traced to *Tìmì* Abibu Lagunju (1847–1900), who helped to establish Islam in Ede in the nineteenth century.[45] Today, the members of the compound remain predominantly Muslim. But because Daodu Lagunju Compound belongs to a section of Ede's ruling family, the religious situation in the compound is different from Imole and Talafia Imam Compounds. As pointed out in chapters 2 and 3, many aspects

---

[43] *Ibid.*

[44] Interview with Prince Imran Oluwasegun Olagunju. 25 November 2012. Daodu Lagunju Compound, Ede.

[45] For details on the role of *Tìmì* Habibu Lagunju in the expansion of Islam in Ede, see Oyeweso, *Eminent Yoruba Muslims*, pp. 11–33.

of Yoruba discourse emphasise that an *ọba* must associate with all religions – Islam, Christianity and Yoruba traditional religions. To honour this obligation, in turn connected to their eligibility for the throne, the people of Daodu Lagunju Compound permit non-Muslims (both Christians and adherents of traditional Yoruba religions) to engage openly in their religious activities.[46] Prince Imran, an indigene of the compound, explained:

> Everybody practises his or her religions freely in this compound. We are very accommodative of people of other faiths and cooperative among ourselves. We also approve of inter-religious marriages among our children and we coexist peacefully. We discourage any form of religious misunderstandings and conflicts. Even though we are predominantly Muslims here, we have a lot of Christian indigenes and non-indigenes living with us here. In fact, most of the shops that are joined with our houses are rented and being used by Christians to earn their livings and we share toilets, bathrooms and other facilities. They fetch water from the mosque's well and they adhere to our conditions that females must cover their heads if they are within the mosque's premises. There have not been any open conflicts between us to the best of my knowledge.[47]

Located along the main road that passes through the centre of the town, Daodu Lagunju Compound has a unique historical position in Ede's religious development. In the pre-Islamic era, the compound was a base for traditional Yoruba religions, including *Ṣàngó* worship. Today many compound members point out that their compound is associated with the coming of both Islam and Christianity to Ede. While *Tìmì* Abibu Lagunju established Islam in Ede, *Tìmì* John Adetoyese Laoye, also of the Lagunju ruling house, was credited with the expansion of Christianity.[48]

This claim to a leading role in the coming of both Islam and Christianity to Ede may seem strange to those who know that during the early years of *Tìmì* Laoye's reign, Daodu Lagunju Compound was the base of his Muslim rival Memudu Lagunju (see chapter 3). It is possible that the rivalry between the two contenders has receded in time; *Tìmì* Laoye is remembered for the achievements he brought to Ede even in his erstwhile opponent's compound. But the claim to *Tìmì* Laoye may also serve to counter the impression that Daodu Lagunju Compound over-emphasises Islam. Associated with a *Tìmì* who had to go into exile for his overbearing pursuit of Islam, and a would-be *Ọba* whose challenge to a reigning Christian *Tìmì* on the basis of religion was

---

[46] Interview with Prince Imran Oluwasegun Olagunju. 25 November 2012. Daodu Lagunju Compound, Ede.
[47] Ibid.
[48] Ibid.

unsuccessful, the compound might be seen by some of Ede's citizens as too Islamic for the production of ọbas. In this context, the claim to Tìmì Laoye and his support for Christianity is also an assertion of the royal nature of the compound.

Even so, practices in Daodu Lagunju Compound do not imply the equality of all religions. Thus, most of the compound's Christian inhabitants are tenants or non-indigenes, which means that they are not expected to have much say in the way the compound is run. While they are free to carry out their activities, these are mainly limited to rented spaces, such as houses and rooms, and the outdoor spaces directly adjacent to such structures. There are no explicitly Christian spaces, such as a church, within the compound. As in Talafia Imam Compound, Christians must engage in their religious activities in ways that do not cause distractions to Muslims during prayers or other religious activities. For instance, no public Christian vigil, 'crusade' or other programme can take place in the compound area near the mosque, particularly during the five daily prayers. Reflecting the interests of majority Muslim indigenes of the compound, attempts by non-Muslims, particularly Christians, to carry out openly religious activities in the compound have been rebuffed in the past.

The relationship between Muslims and adherents of Yoruba traditional religions in Daodu Lagunju Compound is also cordial but not equal. For instance, Ṣàngó, Ògún and Egúngún worshippers and other adherents of Yoruba traditional religions are welcome into the compound during the annual celebrations of their festivals and festivities, and merriments are commonly shared. In fact, most of the members of the Ṣàngó, Ògún and Egúngún cults bear Muslim names and identities. However, there is no traditional religious shrine for the worship of Ògún, Ṣàngó or any other Yoruba deities in Daodu Lagunju Compound because most of these were destroyed during the time of Tìmì Lagunju. But unlike the Christians, many of the traditionalists in the compound – many of whom are also Muslims – are indigenes. As a result, they are able to engage in traditional religious activities openly within the walls of the compound.

As a result, one could understand religious practices in Daodu Lagunju Compound as shaped by contradictory considerations. Because the compound had a charismatic Muslim leader, and today has a Muslim majority, Islam holds a privileged position. As in Imole and Talafia Imam Compounds, there are no non-Muslim places of worship, and the space surrounding the mosque is governed by Muslim interests. However, the compound's important historical role as a royal compound means that its non-Muslim residents enjoy greater relative freedom than in Imole and Talafia Compounds, as some public performances are allowed. But as in Talafia Imam Compound, and possibly for the same reasons, there is a slightly greater acceptance of public performances associated with (traditionalist) indigenes than of those linked to (Christian) non-indigenes in the compound. Thus the boundaries between different religions in this compound are also linked to other forms of social difference, and especially the relationship between indigenes and tenants.

Gender and the Maintenance of Islamic Norms in Muslim-Dominated Compounds

Apart from the control of Christian tenants and traditionalists, all three compounds studied for this chapter also ensure the public dominance of Islam through gendered norms. Some of these norms are implicitly gendered because they refer to activities usually associated with men. Thus the injunction not to defecate, urinate or smoke cigarettes near the *Ratibi* mosques in these compounds is clearly directed at male behaviour because these activities are taboo for women in public. However, other injunctions seem to be aimed at the activities of women. For example, the ban on loud noise in the vicinity of mosques socialises all women resident in the compound into desisting from singing, chanting *oríkì*, or even from scolding their children or squabbling during prayer times. Equally, the fact that they must not throw dirt in the vicinity of a mosque enjoins them to be careful even when sweeping a part of the compound, and thus entrenches respect for Islam in many everyday female activities.

I would like to reflect on the injunctions on women also from the perspective of their collective identities within the compound. As daughters of compound indigenes, women are of course members of the compounds. However, upon marriage, they are expected to move into their husbands' compounds or households where they are no longer under their parents' control. According to local understandings, Islam allows a Muslim man to marry a Christian woman or even a woman of any faith other than Islam, but many Muslim parents would do their utmost to prevent their daughters from marrying a non-Muslim man. Notwithstanding the accepting attitude of *Alhaji* Olanrewaju, cited above, many leaders and fathers in the compounds discussed here would not allow their daughters to marry non-Muslims. This is seen as protecting a compound from an influx of non-Muslim children who can claim to belong to the compound through their mothers.[49]

Rules protecting the Muslim identity of the compound through injunctions upon women's marriage are applied most stringently in Imole Compound,

---

[49] While most Yoruba communities are patrilineal, children's links to their mothers' families are also important.

where any Muslim woman who marries a non-Muslim is instantly disowned by the parents.[50] As chapter 10 illustrates, children disowned by their parents over inter-religious marriages are often forgiven by the parents if the marriage is blessed with a child, but this forgiveness does not always happen. Some Muslim parents, particularly those belonging to high Islamic religious circles, do not forgive those of their children who marry non-Muslims, but instead grieve for them in order to mark their passing out of the family.

Because of the high premium on marriage, the majority of women who live in Ede's traditional compounds are the wives who moved into the compound upon marriage from other houses or compounds. While women are told that their husbands' compounds are their compounds upon marriage, nonetheless as wives they form a separate group from the men or the daughters of the compound (and of course they do occasionally return home to their compounds as daughters). The fact that the group of a compound's indigenes includes its wives, who are not members of the compound by birth, makes the incorporation and socialisation of wives into the compound as important as the control of marriage out of the compound.

Muslim men are allowed to marry non-Muslim women in order to ensure that more souls are won to Islam. This is because it is hoped that a Christian woman who is married to a Muslim man will become a Muslim under his guidance. However, especially in Ede's predominantly Muslim compounds, many Muslims also see a disadvantage in such mixed marriages. This is because the everyday care and upbringing of children and the care of the home are the primary duties of women, making it a disadvantage if the wives of Muslims are not able to train the children in Islamic ways. Some people also fear that the Christian mothers of nominally Muslim children might attract them to Christianity (cf. chapter 10).

An even greater concern is the fact that there are examples of Christian women in Ede who have succeeded in converting their Muslim husbands. In order to avoid such a reversal of Yoruba and Islamic notions of gendered authority, many compound leaders exert strong pressure on would-be wives to convert or at least to promise that their children will be Muslims. In Imole Compound, one of the respondents stated that his second wife was a Christian and even a pastor's daughter. However, she had converted to Islam after the marriage.[51] Another respondent from Imole Compound had a second wife who was a Christian. While she has remained a Christian, her children bear Muslim

---

[50] Interview with Ustaz Mikail Hamzat Adekilekun, Missioner of Al-Fatihu Qareeb Islamic Society, Ede Branch. 21 November 2012. Imole Compound, Ede.
[51] *Ibid.*

names. Such practices aim to ensure the ongoing overlap between religious and social boundaries that defines Ede's Muslim compounds.

In the Muslim compounds discussed here, even the Christian women who are tenants are expected to take on board some forms of behaviour, such as respect in all everyday activities for prayer times and the space of the mosque. Also, when non-Muslim women are invited to events and gatherings in the compounds, they are expected to dress like Muslim women by using small veils to cover their hair as Muslim women do. This practice is widely discernible during wedding, naming and funeral ceremonies throughout Ede. One reason for this is that within the social space of the compound, women can form close friendships among each other, irrespective of their status as wives or tenants. The subjection of all women to certain rules prevents wives married into the compound, possibly from non-Muslim backgrounds, from following the examples of tenants and resisting the expectations of their husbands and their marital families.

Both Imole and Daodu Lagunju Compounds have popular wells, but the location of Daodu Lagunju Compound means both that there are few local sources of water and that many neighbours are non-Muslims. Non-Muslims are explicitly permitted to fetch water from the mosque well. However, non-Muslim women are, like Muslim women, told to cover their heads when they go to the mosque to fetch water, because a woman is not expected to reveal her hair within the mosque's premises.[52] While unintended violations of this rule (owing to ignorance) are overlooked, deliberate actions may result in admonishment and eventually frictions between the concerned parties. A Christian trader who does her trade in Lagunju Compound confirms this thus:

> Àwá á máa bá ara wa ṣe nìhín dáadáa. Kò sí ìyàtọ̀ kankan láàrín wa. Kódà, mọ́sáásí láti n pọnmi ń gbogbo ìgbà. Sùgbọ́n a máa borí bí a bá ti fée wọlé o. Báabá sì ti ṣe tán, àá sí orí wa padà. Kódà lásìkò ẹ̀ẹ̀rùn tí omi máa ń wọ́n tí wọ́n á sì máa ti kànga kí wọ́n lè rí omi sàlùwàlá, a máa rèé gba kọ́kọ́rọ́ lọ́wọ́ dàdánì páa fẹ́ẹ́ pọnmi.[53]

> We relate with one another mutually here. There is no difference between us [Muslims and Christians]. In fact, we fetch water from the mosque regularly. But we cover our heads before we enter the mosque and we uncover it when we are done. Even during the dry season when water is scarce and the well is

---

[52] Interview with Prince Imran Oluwasegun Olagunju. 25 November 2012. Daodu Lagunju Compound, Ede.
[53] Interview with Mrs Janet Akanbi, petty trader. 10 February 2013. Lagunju Compound, Ede.

locked to enable worshippers to get water for ablutions, we will go to collect the keys from the person that calls prayers when we need to fetch water.

The fact that the caller to prayer gives the women access to water, presumably to fulfil their duties as wives and mothers, instead of reserving it for ablutions, reflects the importance accorded to women, both as wives and mothers, as well as the humanity of Islam as it is practised in Ede. At the same time, the privileging of wives' and mothers' needs affirms the importance of these roles, which are in turn associated with compliance with the rules that govern their husband's, and his family's, collective life. Rewarding obedience, such rules help to socialise both wives and female tenants into the practices or rules of the compound. As a compound's core lineage is defined by patrilineal descent, the general expectation that all women behave in particular ways in the compound helps to maintain its religious integrity.

Conclusion

At first glance the study of Ede's three most historically important Muslim compounds illustrates that compounds are strongly shaped by their different histories, which gave rise to subtly different rules and practices in every compound. But underlying the differences between the compounds are also important similarities, which reflect both their shared engagement with Islam and their shared understanding of compound life. Importantly, in all the Muslim compounds discussed here, behaviour is governed by rules that assert the dominance of Islam and the compound's indigenes. In many cases, the privileging of Islam within the compound also affirms kinship and the social boundaries of the compound.

However, the relationship between Islam and kinship is negotiated with subtle differences between these compounds: while Imole remains the compound where descent is most clearly subsumed under religious identity, the relationship between Islam and descent is more complex in Daodu Lagunju Compound, where the Islamic identity of the compound is based on descent from *Tìmì* Laoye, and yet the very importance of descent from the town's royal line also means that non-Muslims are accepted, as long as they recognise the pre-eminence of Islam. The practices of these three compounds suggest that while the introduction of Islam into Ede was capable of transforming kinship, it did so in different ways in different compounds. In this way, religion, kinship and compound identity continue to shape each other: while religion plays a crucial role in maintaining the corporate identity of many compounds, it is at the same time subject to the social logic of kinship obligations.

In all Muslim compounds, belonging also produces forms of religious coexistence. Thus, even in Imole Compound, the participation of compound members by birth in traditionalist activities is considered more tolerable than conversion to Christianity. For those who do not consider traditional practice as a rival religion to Islam, but simply as a form of custom or culture that has its benefits quite separately from religion, traditional practice is not a threat to Islam at all. While this view is not widely shared by Muslim leaders and intellectuals, many feel that as traditional practice does not require individuals to convert away from Islam, it simply produces 'bad' Muslims who may still find their way back to a more satisfying practice of Islam. We may speculate, then, that the non-exclusive nature of traditional worship, which reduces the risk of apostasy and leaves open the possibility for reform, contributes to its tolerance by Islamic leaders.[54]

Many of Ede's learned Muslims acknowledge Christianity as being much more similar to Islam than traditional practice because of its shared monotheism, which is reflected in Islamic prescriptions of tolerance towards Christians. However, often greater restrictions are placed upon the practice of Christianity because, unlike traditional practice, it requires practitioners to abandon their Muslim identities and is thus is very clearly a rival religion to Islam. Another probable reason is that Christianity in Ede is overwhelmingly associated with tenants, i.e. outsiders who do not really belong to the compound.

As the relationship between kinship, everyday sociality and Islamic practices continues to be negotiated in different ways across compounds, many aspects of religious-cum-social control are explicitly and implicitly addressed to women. The insistence that all women follow the compound rules predates Islam and is designed to maintain the overall culture of the compound in order to pass on its values to the next generation. However, the very fact that female behaviour is subject to so much regulation also suggests that women who join the compound from the outside as wives are recognised both as crucial, and as potential threats, to its continuing religious and social existence. While the concern over disobedient women is not limited to Muslims, it is possible that the relatively strong emphasis on the control female behaviour reflects the close link between familial and religious ties in Islamic compounds.

The fact that the tolerance of religious others is shaped by rules that reflect the interests of Muslim indigenes makes it almost impossible for Christians to assert themselves at the heart of the town, where most public spaces belong to land owned by Ede's old compounds and families. While traditional practices

---

[54] Participation in traditional practices is rarely understood by Yoruba Muslims as worshipping other gods beside God, i.e. *shirk*. Traditional practices such as òrìṣà worship are often considered as practices involving other (lesser) spirits.

are occasionally accepted, Christians are constantly reminded of being outsiders both by virtue of their religion and their belonging. As most land and buildings belong to old compounds, and as Christians can only express themselves in a limited way, they cannot set up prayer houses or churches in existing buildings (not to speak of building churches). Most land in the heart of the town has been fully developed. Even so, most Muslim land owners would not sell or lease land within the centre of Ede to non-Muslims, irrespective of whether they plan to build residential, commercial or religious buildings.

In this way, the Islamic character of the old town is closely linked to the history of the town's compounds, and to local practices of land and compound ownership and indigeneity. As chapter 7 shows, matters are different in the newer areas of the town, where Muslims and Christians live in houses and occupy spaces that do not usually have an established religious identity. Here those who are able to create new spaces for living and interaction are able to stamp these institutions with their own religious or spiritual rules. But both in the centre of Ede and beyond, the social dominance of Islam is not based on a uniform policy or practice. The differences between the three compounds studied in this chapter demonstrate that Ede's Muslims do not subscribe to one culturally or locally mediated understanding of Islam, and nor do they envision kinship and the toleration of Christianity and traditional practice in only one form. As the relationship between descent, belonging and religion is negotiated along a continuum in different compounds, the Islamic character of Ede is based on a multiplicity of Islamic practices and interpretations.

CHAPTER 6

Challenges and Affirmations of Islamic Practice: The Tablighi Jamaat

Adeyemi Balogun

While Ede is a predominantly Muslim town, Islam is practised in many different ways. A study of the Tablighi Jamaat, one of several reformist Islamic groups in the town with a small but significant following, contributes to an understanding of the diversity and difference within Yoruba Muslim life. As different and contradictory debates and practices exist within Ede's Muslim community, any reflection on their religious interaction in everyday life must explore how this is experienced in the relationships between Muslims of different backgrounds and convictions. Relationships between different Muslim groups take place not only in the form of abstract theological debates but also in the negotiation of social relations, material interests and political ambition. Exploring the Tablighis' relationships with other Muslims in Ede not only by looking at their theological arguments but also by exploring their everyday relations and practices, this chapter discusses the local meaning of the Tablighi insistence on travelling tours for *da'wa* or proselytisation, as well as their rejection of traditional everyday Yoruba practices such as prostrating and kneeling on greeting. Also looking at non-Muslim views on the Tablighi Jamaat, this chapter emphasises the ways in which the interaction between different religious groups 'is conceived and experienced indigenously within specific African societies'.[1]

The Tablighi movement has expanded very successfully over the past decades and is known to have millions of followers in about 150 countries around the world, including West Africa. But despite the group's growing presence in Nigeria, recent studies on Islamic organisations in Nigeria, and particularly in the south-west of Nigeria where the group has been particularly successful, are silent on its activities. Perhaps because the Tablighi Jamaat has been studied primarily as a transnational movement, with relatively little attention to the

[1] A.E. Akinade, 'The precarious agenda: Christian–Muslim relations in contemporary Nigeria', *Journal of Islam and Christian-Muslim Relations* (2002).

way in which this movement is appropriated by different groups in the local context, its activities in Nigeria are associated with rumours and misconceptions. Often, the Tablighi Jamaat's membership, its activities and relationships with other religious groups in Nigeria are automatically considered to be politically radical without any close examination of the context in which they operate.[2] Following a recent study of the Tablighi Jamaat by Marloes Janson, which highlights the important role played by the organisation in the re-imagination of social roles and ambitions of young people in the Gambia,[3] this chapter explores in which way members of the Tablighi Jamaat challenge and confirm the local practice of Islam in Ede.

Discussing Tablighi and non-Tablighi views, this chapter argues that the Tablighi Jamaat plays a contradictory role within the Muslim community of Ede. Challenging practices and institutions that are closely associated with the importance of Islam in the town, the practices of the Tablighi Jamaat illustrate the diversity of Islamic debates. The group's insistence on a personal relationship with God appeals to many Muslims and demonstrates the enduring and powerful appeal of Islam beyond its established social institutions. However, the group's vision of a better and more equal society on the basis of an equality based on Islam, and by implication excluding non-Muslims, means that they are perceived as uncompromising both by the town's Muslims and non-Muslims. As a result, the Tablighi Jamaat has been less successful in Ede than other reformist Muslim groups.

The Establishment of the Tablighi Jamaat in Nigeria

The Tablighi Jamaat was founded in 1926 by Mawlana Muhammed Ilyas (1885–1944) in northern India. Descended from a line of Sufi scholars, Ilyas drew on Sufi principles of leadership emphasising correct ritual practice to spread a reformist message. His movement originally emerged to counter Christian and Hindu proselytisation that targeted local Muslims.[4] But Ilyas also felt that as the *'ulamā'* (Islamic scholars) concentrated on teaching in the mosques and other educational institutions, many Muslims in India had abandoned the true teachings of Islam. Owing to the gap of knowledge between the

---

[2] F.A. Burton, 'Tablighi Jamaat: an indirect line to terrorism', *STRATFOR* (23 January 2008), <http://www.stratfor.com/weekly/tablighi_jamaat_indirect_line_terrorism>, accessed 30 August 2012.

[3] M. Janson, *Islam, Youth, and Modernity in the Gambia: The Tablighi Jama'at* (Cambridge: Cambridge University Press for the International African Institute, 2014).

[4] J.A. Ali, 'Islamic revivalism: A study of the Tablighi Jamaat in Sydney', unpublished PhD thesis (Sydney: University of New South Wales, 2006), pp. 140–1.

'*ulamā*' and the Muslim laymen, many Muslims began to question the validity of various Qur'anic injunctions. In response, Ilyas argued that the responsibility of teaching and propagating the message of Islam was not limited to the '*ulamā*' alone but was obligatory for every Muslim.[5]

Before he established the Tablighi Jamaat, Ilyas was a member of the Deobandi movement, which also emphasises aspects of the Sufi tradition and in particular the spiritual journey towards God.[6] As pointed out by Metcalf, both movements place 'emphasis on encouraging a range of ritual and personal behavioural practices linked to worship, dress, and everyday behaviour'.[7] However, they do so by reference to Islam's pristine texts, the Qur'an and the Hadith, which they see as sources of cultural pride and a guide to the rebirth of Muslims in a world where they are powerless. As a result, their message is clearly Reformist, and they also abhor Sufi and customary practices such as the worship of saints, or the elaborate life cycle celebrations popular in sections of the Muslim community.

Both the Deobandi and the Tablighi Jamaat challenge clear distinctions between traditional or Sufi Islam on the one hand and Reformist Islam on the other. Metcalf and Roy both argue that they are distinguishable from 'Islamist' Islamic movements. But while Roy refers to the Deobandi and Tablighi movements as 'neo-fundamentalist', Metcalf prefers the word 'traditionalist' because they represent continuity with earlier Islamic institutions, especially those who teach in the mosques. But unlike groups such as the Muslim Brothers in Egypt and the thinkers of the Iranian revolution, the Tablighi Jamaat has no explicit political agenda.[8] Rather, its leaders teach their members to emulate Prophet Muhammed in attitude, behaviour and dress. This is why they also call themselves the *ahlu-sunnah* (those who follow the deeds of Prophet Muhammed).

Mawlana Muhammed Ilyas was of the opinion that in order to emulate the Prophet, every Muslim should withdraw from mundane activities and go out to propagate the message of Islam.[9] This became the primary activity of its

---

[5] Janson, *Islam, Youth, and Modernity in the Gambia*, pp. 72–3.

[6] M.A. Rana, *Tablighi Jama'at: Discourse and Challenges* (Islamabad: Pak Institute for Peace Studies, 2009), p. 1; and A. Godlas, 'Sufism – Sufis – Sufi Orders', *Islam and Islamic Studies Resources* (n.d.), <http://islam.uga.edu/Sufism.html>, accessed 25 September 2014.

[7] B.D. Metcalf, '"Traditionalist" Islamic activism: Deoband, Tablighis, and Talibs', *Social Science Research Council* (n.d.), <http://essays.ssrc.org/sept11/essays/metcalf.htm>, accessed 25 January 2013.

[8] Metcalf, '"Traditionalist" Islamic activism'.

[9] Rana, *Tablighi Jama'at: Discourse and Challenges*; Godlas, 'Sufism -- Sufis – Sufi Orders', pp. 1–2.

members, who embarked on *khurūj* (missionary tours) for the *jawla* (mobilisation) of Muslims in all contexts.[10] These tours or outings, which are also the Tablighi Jamaat's most distinctive activity, are to be undertaken ideally for one year but at least four months in a volunteer's lifetime, forty days in a year, three days in a month, and two and half hours in a day. Members often go on missionary tours (*tablīgh*), to convey the message of Islam, *da'wa*, in travelling parties or *jamā'āt* of several men, sometimes accompanied by their wives. It is from this activity that the Tablighi Jamaat derives its name.

Today, the Tablighi Jamaat can be regarded as a transnational organisation. The internationalisation of the movement began after Ilyas's death in 1944. After that his son, Mawlana Muhammad Yusuf (1917–65) took up the leadership of the movement, and he sent missions overseas. His successor, Mawlana In'amul Hasan, died in 1995 and today the Tablighi Jamaat no longer has a single leader but is led by a consultative committee (*Shūrā*), under which the movement continues to expand. Currently the movement has members in more than 150 countries across South East Asia, the Middle East, North America and the South Pacific.[11] Members gather annually at Raiwind, Lahore, in Pakistan for the *ijtimā'*, which is a special teaching session. Here, prayers are offered and reports are collected from various branches of the movement across the world.[12] This gathering attracts up to a million people, making it the second biggest annual Muslim meeting after the *hajj* (pilgrimage) in Saudi Arabia.[13]

As few of my Tablighi respondents in Nigeria knew about the history of the movement, the date of the arrival of the movement in Nigeria could not be firmly established. But although the knowledge of my respondents was mostly vague, there seemed to be a general sense that the movement's arrival in Nigeria dated back to the 1950s.[14] The literature confirms the 1950s as the relevant decade.[15] Generally, these sources trace the emergence of the Tablighi

---

[10] L.F. Oladimeji, 'The role of the Jama'tut-Tablighi in the promotion of adult and non-formal education among Muslims in Nigeria', *Education Crises in Nigeria: Arabic and Islamic Studies Perspectives*, ed. M.A. Muhbbu-Din (Jos: NATAIS Publication, 2007), pp. 16–28: 18.

[11] Ali, 'Islamic revivalism: A study of the Tablighi Jamaat in Sydney'.

[12] L.F. Oladimeji, 'A sociological analysis of experiences of selected Jama'atut Tabligh in the Nigerian society', *Science and Religion in the Service of Humanity*, ed. A.P. Dopamu (Ilorin: LSI and NASTRENS, 2006), pp. 390–400: 391.

[13] M.K. Masud, *Travellers in Faith: Studies of the Tablīghī Jamā'at as a Transnational Islamic Movement for Faith Renewal* (Leiden: Brill, 2000).

[14] Interview with Alfa Muhammed Idris, Arabic teacher/tailor. 24 January 2013. Odeyinka Road, Ikire.

[15] Lateef Oladimeji dates the coming of the group to the late 1950s, whereas Abdullahi Muhammed puts the date at 1956. See L.F. Oladimeji, 'Roaming about for God's sake:

Jamaat in Nigeria to a group of Pakistani visitors, possibly under the leadership of a man called Hassan Badawi.[16] It was recounted by some of my informants that the Tablighis trekked from the south-west to the north of Nigeria and stopped over in mosques in Yoruba towns and villages.[17]

According to one of my respondents, the party's initial preference for the north of Nigeria was due to their belief that the region had a large population of Muslims whom they could educate. It was also believed that after proselytising Muslims in the north, the Tablighi message would trickle down to the south. When the party got to the north, they were said to have been received by political and religious dignitaries such as Sir Abubakar Tafawa Balewa and Sir Ahmadu Bello, one of whom embarked on a forty-day *khurūj* with the Pakistani party.[18] However, the Pakistanis were said to have discovered that local Muslims did not appreciate the movement's message, and they returned to Lagos Island in the south.[19]

One respondent suggested that those who received the Pakistani party in Lagos also misunderstood them and thought that they were just being introduced to another Muslim *ẹgbẹ́* or society, a form of social gathering that was common among the elite in this period.[20] Therefore, according to this respondent, those who accepted the Tablighi path did not fully appreciate the objectives of the movement until some of them were invited to Pakistan to participate in the annual *ijtimā'*. Those who came back from Pakistan later made it known to other Muslims that the Tablighi movement was not a social gathering but a genuine sacrifice towards promoting the cause of Islam.

One of the Lagos Muslims who accepted the path of the Tabligh Jamaat volunteered his residence at Ita Balogun Street in Lagos Island for the meetings of the movement. This became the first Tablighi headquarters in Nigeria. It was from this location that other Muslims from places such as Ikeja and

---

The upsurge of the Jama'atut Tablighi in Nigeria', *Degel: the Journal of FAIS* 7:52 (2007), 52–73: 52; and A. Muhammed, 'The Tabligh Jammaat influence in the midst of controversy', *Islam Online* (n.d.), <http://islamonline.net/en/529>, accessed 15 August 2012.

[16] Muhammed, 'The Tabligh Jammaat influence'.
[17] Interview with Alfa Muhammed Idris, Arabic teacher/tailor. 24 January 2013. Odeyinka Road, Ikire.
[18] Interview with Dr M. Adam, Tabligh and academic. 13 April 2013. Department of Electrical Engineering, Obafemi Awolowo University, Ile-Ife.
[19] Interviews with Alfa Mutiullah Abubakre, Tabligh. 1 November 2012. Ansar-Ud-Deen Central Mosque, Station Road, Ede; and Alfa Muhammed Idris, Arabic teacher/tailor. 24 January 2013. Odeyinka Road, Ikire.
[20] Interview with Dr M. Adam, Tabligh and academic. 13 April 2013. Department of Electrical Engineering, Obafemi Awolowo University, Ile-Ife.

Ibadan were said to have joined the Tablighi movement.[21] After some years at Ita Balogun, the headquarters of the movement was moved to Surulere, and later to Adaranijo Street, Oluti, Badagry Expressway, before moving its permanent headquarters to Masjid Noor in Araromi, Eiye-nkorin, Ilorin, Kwara State. After the Tablighi Jamaat had established a firm presence in Yorubaland it spread to other parts of the country, including Northern Nigeria, though it presently remains most popular in the south-west. Today, the Jama'at has more than 300 Tablighi centres across Nigeria, and the annual *ijtimā'* in Araromi attracts over 150,000 participants.[22] However, as this chapter illustrates, the relationship between the Tablighi Jamaat and other Muslim groups is often complicated and requires forms of toleration that are not dissimilar to inter-religious tolerance.

The Tablighi Jamaat in Ede

The rise of the Tablighi Jamaat in Ede was part of a more general process of diversification within the town's Muslim community. Since the 1930s, which saw the arrival of the Sufi order of the Tijaniyya in the town from Kano, the hitherto fairly homogenous Muslim community in Ede began to experience lively internal debate. By the 1960s, non-mainstream Muslim groups in Ede included the Qadiriyya, at the time a strong rival to the Tijaniyya in northern Nigerian politics, and which was also introduced from northern Nigeria. The liberal reformist Ansar-Ud-Deen society and the Ahmadiyya reached Ede from Lagos, but while both of these groups were positively disposed towards Western education, the Ahmadiyyas' claim that there were prophets following Muhammed meant that it was far less popular than the Ansar-Ud-Deen. Other non-mainstream groups included the conservative Fakafaka movement based in Offa, which criticised all things Western and whose members wore beards and turbans.[23] Later the reformist Muslim Students' Society of Nigeria (MSSN) and the Muslim Congress (TMC) formed branches in Ede, which attracted Western-educated Muslims who sought to address the imbalances in Nigeria's Christian-dominated tertiary university system.

As different Muslim groups competed for acceptance and influence, debates about Islamic reform and innovation began to take an important place among Ede's Muslims. As a result of this development, large mosques were

---

[21] Interview with Alfa Muhammed Idris, Arabic teacher/tailor. 24 January 2013. Odeyinka Road, Ikire.

[22] Janson, *Islam, Youth, and Modernity in the Gambia*, p. 75.

[23] L. Dokun, 'Islam in Ede', unpublished BA Long Essay (Ibadan: Department of Arabic and Islamic Studies, University of Ibadan, 1974), pp. 99–117.

built by the new groups, usually outside of the old city centre, and new Islamic leaders and hierarchies developed under the overall remit of the Chief Imam. Chapter 11 suggests that the majority of Muslims in the town are affiliated to the Tijaniyyah Movement, the Ansar-Ud-Deen Society and the Nasrul-Lahi-Fatih Society (NASFAT), a charismatic reformist movement that has become popular especially among Yoruba Muslims since the 1990s. In the context of intra-Muslim competition, the Tablighi Jamaat can be regarded as one of the less popular religious groups in Ede. However, owing to their distinctive practices and clothing, as well as their personal commitment to financially, physically and emotionally exhausting mission work, they are the focus of much debate both among Muslims and Christians about the nature of Islam. As a result, study of the Tablighi Jamaat offers interesting insights into both the debates that shape Ede's Muslim community and the wider engagements between Muslims, Christians and practitioners of traditional religions.

While the exact date of the arrival of the movement in the town cannot be firmly established, it is likely that Tablighis had made their presence known in the town before they established a permanent *markaz* (branch building). One of my Tabligh respondents, Imam Adeyemo Hassan, said he joined the movement in Ibadan more than twenty years ago, even though Tablighis were then meeting at Ede.[24] Although he was not sure about the date, Imam Muhammed Fatih of the Ansar-Ud-Deen Society observed that the Tablighis had been making use of the Ansar-Ud-Deen Central Mosque as their Ede branch for more than fifteen years.[25] It therefore seems plausible to suggest the 1990s as the date of formal establishment of the movement in Ede. The permanent *markaz* of the movement is now located along Muslim Grammar School/Yidi Road.[26]

However, the movement itself has been present in Ede for longer. Some Tablighis in Ede are said to have been involved in the movement's activities for about forty years.[27] Some of those between the ages of 50 and 70 joined the

---

[24] Interviews with Imam Adeyemo Hassan, Imam. 12 October 2012. Allahu Lateef Central Mosque, Ede; Alfa Mutiullah Abubakre, Tabligh. 1 November 2012. Ansar-Ud-Deen Central Mosque, Station Road, Ede.

[25] Interview with Imam Muhammed Fatih, Imam Ratibi, Ansar-Ud-Deen Central Mosque, Station Road. 1 November 2012.

[26] In November 2012 when I attended the meeting of the movement, the Ansar-Ud-Deen Central Mosque located on Station Road, Oke Gada was the branch of the movement. When I attended the meeting on 24 January 2013, I was told that this meeting was the fifth since they had moved to their new location. This puts the date of their relocation at 31 December 2012.

[27] Interview with Imam Adeyemo Hassan, Imam. 12 October 2012. Allahu Lateef Central Mosque, Ede.

movement in other towns like Ibadan and Ilorin. These early Tablighis had to face opposition from clerics in many parts of Yorubaland, who saw their reformist agenda as a distortion of Islam. However, while many non-Tablighis remain critical of some of their activities, they are widely accepted as Muslims.[28] In addition to the senior members, the movement has also attracted young people, mostly from the age of 20 to 40. Some of the younger members work as farmers, tailors, carpenters and auto-mechanics. But as Janson reports for the Gambia,[29] many of the young Tablighis in Ede are Western-educated and employed in tertiary institutions, banks, hospitals and public corporations.

Women play an important role in Tablighi activities. However, owing to my own gender, I was not able to speak to many Tablighi women and therefore cannot discuss their practices in detail here. I was told that most women are introduced into the movement by their husbands, who are meant to teach them about the Tablighi path. My observation of Tablighi women was that many of them were trying to stay in their homes even if they could not afford seclusion, engaging in petty trades such as plaiting hair and selling pap, groundnuts and biscuits in their places of residence. However, women also hold regular meetings where they teach one another lessons based on the reading texts of the movement, including the Qur'an and Hadith. Perhaps most importantly, they are allowed to embark on three, fifteen and forty days of *khurūj*, usually with their husbands.[30] This means that they play an important role as missionaries among other women in their own right.

Members of Tablighi Jamaat in Ede are not organised along a bureaucratic structure like the Ansar-Ud-Deen Society.[31] While they primarily attempt to reach out to fellow Muslims, membership of the movement is also kept open to non-Muslims. As people are allowed to join and leave the movement's events as they wish, many Tablighis do not see themselves as belonging to a religious society. Owing to some similarity in dress and practice, some people may be members of the Tablighi Jamaat at one time and members of other Muslim groups in Ede, such as the Al-Haramani Society and the Muslim Students' Society of Nigeria (MSSN), at other times. In common with Tablighis in other parts of the world, the Tablighis in Ede meet every Thursday at their *markaz* from about 5:30pm until Friday morning, during which time they have

---

[28] Interview with Muhammed Abdul-Salam, Tabligh. 6 March 2013. Odeyinka Road, Ikire.
[29] Janson, *Islam, Youth, and Modernity in the Gambia*, pp. 225–54.
[30] Interviews with Dr M. Adam, Tabligh and academic. 13 April 2013. Department of Electrical Engineering, Obafemi Awolowo University, Ile-Ife; and Muhammed Abdul-Salam, Tabligh. 6 March 2013. Odeyinka Road, Ikire.
[31] Interviews with Imam Adeyemo Hassan, Imam. 12 October 2012. Allahu Lateef Central Mosque, Ede; and Alfa Mutiullah Abubakre, Tabligh. 1 November 2012. Ansar-Ud-Deen Central Mosque, Station Road, Ede.

lectures on subjects such as faith, good deeds and the fear of God. Tablighis take advantage of the presence of Muslims of other Islamic groups during these weekly meetings to seek volunteers for the *khurūj* for three-day, forty-day or four-month periods, during which they stay at various mosques inside and outside the town.

In many contexts, Tabilighis therefore appear simply as fellow Muslims with a strong emphasis on correct practice as derived from an (often literal) interpretation of the Qur'an and especially the Hadith, and the reports of sayings and deeds of the Prophet Muhammed. Both Tablighis and some other Muslim groups in Ede believe that all Muslims are in fact 'tablighi', since the term 'tablighi' refers to those who are propagating the message of Islam in various forms – such as doing good to fellow human beings, taking care of one's family, observing the five pillars of Islam (faith, prayer, fasting, alms giving and pilgrimage), reciting the Qur'an, telling the truth, and other injunctions in the Qur'an and the Hadith.[32] However in a different interpretation, a 'tablighi' refers to someone who completes his or her Islamic faith.[33] This interpretation has given rise to some disagreements because it implies that the majority of the town's Muslims, who do not follow the Tablighi Jamaat's interpretation of the Islamic texts, are not 'completing' their faith. It is the Tablighi Jamaat's implicit and explicit criticism of the practices of other Muslims in Ede that illuminates the diversity of the town's Muslim community.

Missionary Travel, Equality and Personal Morality in the Tablighi Jamaat

From its inception, the Tablighi Jamaat has imagined itself as a missionary movement. Based on the belief that every Muslim has a responsibility to leave the comfort of their house and invite people into Islam, members are continually encouraged to go on *khurūj* and to speak or preach to other Muslims about how to live their lives in a godly way. For the Tablighis, going out to talk to people is the practice of Prophet Muhammed that he enjoined upon his followers. As such, it is part of the observance of the *Sunna* (the practices of Prophet Muhammed). One of my respondents said, 'the rank and file of the Muslims is

---

[32] Interviews with Abdul-Salam Olawole, Imam, Ansar-Ud-Deen, Div IV. 2 October 2012. Sawmill Area, Ede; Kozeem Abdul-Hamid, trader. 7 November 2012. Sawmill Area, Ede; and Muhammed Abdul-Salam, Tabligh. 6 March 2013. Odeyinka Road, Ikire.

[33] Interviews with Abdul-Salam Olawole, Imam, Ansar-Ud-Deen, Div IV. 2 October 2012. Sawmill Area, Ede; Kozeem Abdul-Hamid, trader. 7 November 2012. Sawmill Area, Ede; Alfa Mutiullah Abubakre, Tabligh. 1 November 2012. Ansar-Ud-Deen Central Mosque, Station Road, Ede; and Muhammed Abdul-Salam, Tabligh. 6 March 2013. Odeyinka Road, Ikire.

predicated basically on an assumption [sic] by Prophet Muhammed that you have to invite everybody into Islam'.[34]

Indeed, some members of the Tablighi Jamaat believe that by going out to preach about Islam they personally follow the example of the Prophet. Another of my respondents argued, 'Prophet Muhammed himself started his prophethood by talking to people... there is evidence for going out for *da'wa* [invitation to Islam].'[35]

However, other Muslim groups do not believe that the observance of all aspects of the *Sunna* is obligatory, and are of the opinion that the *Sunna* must be interpreted and practised in the light of prevailing societal realities and cultures.[36] While most Muslims in Ede believe that the propagation of the message of Islam (*da'wa*) is compulsory for all Muslims, they are opposed to the Tablighi outings or *khurūj*, which involve leaving one's house and sleeping in mosques for many days and months.[37] The position of many Muslims is that God enjoins every Muslim to start the work of propagation from their immediate family, including teaching them the proper way of worship, providing for their needs, and other responsibilities set out by the Qur'an and the Hadith.[38] For them, the Tablighi Jamaat's emphasis on leaving one's family for extended periods in order to propagate the religion among strangers is a misinterpretation of Islamic requirements.

But the *khurūj* is so central to Tablighi practice that it fulfils more than just one function. While its practitioners believe that their outings are necessary to propagate the message of Islam, they also see them as a way of renewing their own faith, of seeking forgiveness of their sins and of being closer to God. As Tablighis devote themselves to worship, learning and mysticism while on tour, it is an opportunity for self-development and spiritual growth.[39] A Tablighi respondent explained:

---

[34] Interview with Imam Adeyemo Hassan, Imam. 12 October 2012. Allahu Lateef Central Mosque, Ede.

[35] Interview with Brother Mikhail Abu Muslim, civil servant and Tabligh. 8 November 2012. Ansar-Ud-Deen Central Mosque, Station Road, Ede.

[36] Interview with *Alhaji* Nureni Lawal, civil servant. 28 October 2012. Siyan Oyeweso Street, Sawmill Area, Ede.

[37] L.F. Oladimeji, 'Tablighi movement in Nigeria: Conceptions and misconceptions', *Journal of the Faculty of Islamic Studies and Arabic* 5:81 (1999–2000), 73–79.

[38] Interviews with *Alhaji* Nureni Lawal, civil servant. 28 October 2012. Siyan Oyeweso Street, Sawmill Area, Ede; and Ismail Ishola, Ahlu-Sunnah and teacher. 2 October 2012. Sawmill Area, Ede.

[39] Interview with Imam Adeyemo Hassan, Imam. 12 October 2012. Allahu Lateef Central Mosque, Ede.

People usually ask why we are so insistent on going out to propagate the message of Islam. What they do not know is that the outing is not only to preach and call other Muslims to Islam. It is also meant to renew our individual faith. This is because this world is full of sins and the only avenue to renew our faith is to isolate ourselves from it and be closer to God. ... when you point one finger [at] another person, the remaining four [are] directed at you.[40]

This emphasis on self-improvement is linked to an experience of sharing and communality during the *khurūj*, which is often very strong. Janson argues that especially the outings in which men and women participate are liminal, i.e. that they emphasise a shared experience of equality outside of the social hierarchy.[41] This is also true in Nigeria, where Tablighis enjoy the rotation of duties and responsibilities among members during the programme. Indeed, irrespective of their degree of Islamic knowledge, all members are welcome to give lectures about Islam. Interestingly the Tablighi Jamaat's emphasis on spiritual equality illustrates that it also shares aspects of practice with modern Muslim organisations that are on the other end of the political spectrum, such as the Nasrul-Lahi-Fatih Society (NASFAT).[42] Like the Tablighi Jamaat, NASFAT is organised along a flat hierarchy and affirms the sincerity of commitment and faith over formal training. Its weekly prayer meetings and wakes also give space to all members to share their experiences and their faith.

The centrality of the *khurūj* for the Tablighi Jamaat is confirmed by the fact that they usually convert new members by enjoining them to follow them on *khurūj* for three-day, forty-day or four-month periods. In this way the Tablighis believe they will renew their personal relationship with God and thus become better Muslims. Many Tablighis also believe that going on tour imbues them with protection against the ordeals of life, and gives them the power to confront Satanic forces. The powers inherent in the experience of the *khurūj* are recognised by other Muslims. A non-Tablighi confirmed to me that miracles happen to Tablighis during this period of engagement:

That outing is good. When the TJ [Tablighi Jamaat] go out for propagation, miracles do happen. Their families are also blessed. I give you an example of a Tablighi who went out with no provision for his family. But before he came

---

[40] This quotation is taken from my field notes. 24 January 2013. Tablighi Markaz, Ede Muslim Grammar School/Yidi Road.
[41] Janson, *Islam, Youth, and Modernity in the Gambia*.
[42] B.F. Soares, 'An Islamic social movement in contemporary West Africa: NASFAT of Nigeria', *Movers and Shakers: Social Movements in Africa*, ed. S. Ellis and I. Kessel (Leiden: Brill, 2009), pp. 178–96.

back, a stranger came to his house to give his wife some foodstuffs. That is the kind of miracles I am talking about.[43]

The Tablighi Jamaat's emphasis on individual spiritual closeness to God also finds expression in their concern with personal piety and goodness. Mutiullah Abubakre, a member of the Tablighi Jamaat, explained the group's constant striving to observe the true teachings of Islam as an ongoing struggle: 'People say we are Tablighis, but we are not the best of Muslims. [But] we are also making attempt[s] to be the best. That is why we are calling on other Muslims to follow this path.'[44]

As part of this struggle, the members of the Tablighi Jamaat continue to build on their spirituality throughout their lives. In that, they see themselves as different from other spiritual Muslim groups. As one member of the Tablighi Jamaat pointed out, many Tablighis believe that other Muslims might not be able to build on their spirituality once they have graduated under their teachers.[45]

However, observation in the Muslim community of Ede suggests that this argument may apply to only a few Muslims who are interested in learning only the basics of the Qur'an and other Islamic texts. In fact, many Muslims in Ede continue to build on their spirituality, and in particular Tijaniyyah members are known to observe their mystic practice every day, after the early morning, afternoon and evening prayers. Indeed, there are many Muslims, especially the clerics, who continue their learning process in the religion in a manner that includes spiritual knowledge. For that reason I would like to suggest that it is the shared knowledge of the spiritual struggle that helps to create some respect and admiration for Tablighis among other Muslims. For those Muslims in Ede who believe that Tablighis really are the best Muslims, their observation is premised on the plain and pious behaviour of its members:

> the TJ... are the best. They don't tell lies, but other Muslims lie. The TJ does not engage in *Zinā'* (adultery), but other Muslims do. The TJ does not collect money from anyone. They don't court before wedding. They have no girlfriends. ... Also, when they are talking to you, they go straight to the point, and as dictated by the Qur'an.[46]

---

[43] Interview with Abdul-Afeez, electronic engineer. 8 November 2012. Elerin Area, Ede.
[44] Interview with Alfa Mutiullah Abubakre, Tabligh. 1 November 2012. Ansar-Ud-Deen Central Mosque, Station Road, Ede.
[45] Interview with Imam Adeyemo Hassan, Imam. 12 October 2012. Allahu Lateef Central Mosque, Ede.
[46] Interviews with Ayinde Sikiru, trader. 4 November 2012. Sawmill Area, Ede; and Olapade Wasiu, trader. 4 November 2012. Sawmill Area, Ede.

The perception that members of the Tablighi Jamaat are special because they aspire to be 'the best Muslims' in their personal lives is especially shared by some of the younger members of the group.⁴⁷ One of my Tabligh respondents believed that God loves Tablighis because they always talk about Him to other people everywhere they go and praise them. Clearly this understanding is closely linked to the expectation that Tablighis attract miracles. According to my informant, it is especially Tablighis' *da'wa* efforts that established their special bond with God:

> As a person, how would you feel if someone goes about saying good things about you to people, telling them that you are great, that you are merciful, and encouraging them to like you, among others? You will realise that the person you are talking about will continue to like you more and more.⁴⁸

The debate focusing on the Tablighi Jamaat's call to *da'wa* and travel illustrates the potential transformative power of Islam as a religion of individual empowerment and self-perfection outside of established institutions. While other groups share the group's emphasis on personal spiritual growth and a personal relationship with God, the Tablighi Jamaat's implicit disregard of family life and obligations is a direct challenge to those who see Islam as primarily as a form of social order. Clearly the association's radical commitment to personal spiritual achievements at the expense of social conventions also applies to those who occupy low positions within extended family networks, and especially the young. But the (partial) acceptance of the Tablighi Jamaat's message by Muslims of different ages and backgrounds suggests that there is a wider sense of unease among many Muslims about the mutual implication between Islam and familial institutions (see previous chapter). By emphasising piety and achievement outside of family and compound structures, the Tablighi Jamaat's offers an alternative vision of Muslim success.

Tablighi Debates about 'Authentic' Islam

Mawlana Muhammed Ilyas's concern over the 'authenticity' of Islam practised by the Tablighi Jamaat meant that he warned them against many temptations that might distract them from the right path. In line with the implicit asceticism of travel and *da'wa* among strangers, members are encouraged to shun

---

⁴⁷ Interviews with Brother Yusuf Daud, student. 8 November 2012. Ansar-Ud-Deen Central Mosque, Station Road, Ede; and Abdul-Ganiyyu Mubarak, student. 8 November 2012. Ansar-Ud-Deen Central Mosque, Station Road, Ede.

⁴⁸ Interview with Dr M. Adam, Tabligh and academic. 13 April 2013. Department of Electrical Engineering, Obafemi Awolowo University, Ile-Ife.

worldly desires and consume little in order not to be distracted from their duty to Islam. While the Tablighi Jamaat does not reject modernity in all its ramifications, its members believe that by avoiding worldly wealth, they will have an abundance of it in *janna* (paradise).[49] As a result, the Tablighis refrain from collecting money on many occasions, including important life-cycle ceremonies such as weddings or the naming of a newborn baby.[50]

Like the Muslim Students' Society of Nigeria (MSSN) and the Muslim Congress (TMC), the Tablighi Jamaat also criticises clerics for collecting money when they lead such rituals. Most especially, they blame these clerics for encouraging *bid'a*, or unlawful innovation, in the practice of Islam. Practices they consider innovative and therefore inauthentic include the celebration of *Mawlid al-Nabī* (the birthday of Prophet Muhammed), *Walimatul-Qur'an* (the celebration of a student's completion of the Qur'an), and *Walimatul-Sahadah* (the graduation ceremony when one has achieved the status of a cleric). They also oppose the collection of money on occasions such as naming ceremonies and eating during funerals, all of which are seen to be responsible for moral decadence in the Muslim community.[51] As one Tablighi respondent noted:

> There are many differences between us and other religious groups. Other Muslim groups, particularly the *alfas*, are engaged in *bid'a* [innovation]. They go to burial ceremonies and eat, when they know that God forbids Muslims from eating or celebrating the dead. Some of them also participate and eat during Ṣàngó festivals in the palace of the king. This is why we are different from them. The TJ is here to uphold the *Sunna* of Prophet Muhammed.[52]

Criticisms such as this generate resentment and hot debate in the mosques and during public occasions. Some of the clerics interviewed during my field survey clearly demonstrated their resentment of the members of the Tablighi Jamaat, which usually centres on the Tablighis' lack of training in Arabic and the Islamic disciplines. Many Muslims are also critical of the *Fazail-il-Amal*, the main reference book of the movement, which is read by the Tablighis in English. Critics are of the opinion that the texts contained therein are not substantiated by the Qur'an or the Hadith, nor by the major schools of thought in Islam.[53]

---

[49] Metcalf, '"Traditionalist" Islamic activism'.
[50] Interview with Imam Adeyemo Hassan, Imam. 12 October 2012. Allahu Lateef Central Mosque, Ede.
[51] *Ibid.*
[52] Interview with Brother Yusuf Daud, student. 8 November 2012. Ansar-Ud-Deen Central Mosque, Station Road, Ede.
[53] Interview with Ismail Ishola, Ahlu-Sunnah and teacher. 2 October 2012. Sawmill Area, Ede. See also Y. Sikand, 'The Tablighi Jama'at's contested claims to Islamicity', *Indian Muslim Observer* (24 June 2010).

Indeed, many Tablighis rely on a few lessons taught in their meetings or outings for their own preaching. Because the movement emphasises the need for every one of them to embark on propagation, the urge is always there for them to demonstrate their knowledge, even if it is flawed. But the Tablighis do not believe that knowledge of Islam should be the exclusive preserve of the Imams or Sheikhs, to whom the Muslim community usually defers on matters of religion.

Such differences are exacerbated by the fact that Tablighis disagree with other Muslim groups over important aspects of behaviour. Male Tablighis do not shake hands with women and avoid all close contact with them. They also squat during urination, both in public and in private, which not all Muslims do. But perhaps most importantly, a Tablighi male does not bow his head or prostrate when greeting an elder, and neither does a female kneel when greeting, as is common in Yoruba towns. Rather, they greet others while remaining standing. For the Tablighi, prostration and kneeling are not signs of respect, because, they argue, they are not required by God. Why then should they be required by human beings? But for many Muslims in Ede, this is a clear case of rebellion against society. They argue that Islam teaches deference to parents and the elderly, and they see the Tablighi practice as going against what their tradition requires and their religion permits.[54] One opponent of Tablighi practice argued:

> ... if you look at the attitude of the Tablighi Jamaat, they don't bow to anybody. They greet you, but they don't bow. They don't bow or prostrate to their parents. They only say *As-salamu Alaykum*. Is this what we are taught in school or in our culture? And God told us to respect our culture. ... If these people cannot respect their parents, then we cannot call them Tablighis, because their behaviour is abnormal. If you go contrary to what your religion says, then you are abnormal.[55]

Some Muslims also criticise the Tablighi Jamaat for raising the *Sunna* practices that are less mandatory or less important above those that are mandatory and important,[56] or for distorting and misunderstanding the *Sunna*.[57] The example commonly referred to by many Muslims is the dress of the Tablighis.

---

[54] Interviews with Ustaz Oyewale, Arabic teacher. 8 November 2012. Elerin Area, Ede; Mr Mufutau, electronic engineer. 8 November 2012. Elerin Area, Ede; and Abdul-Afeez, electronic engineer. 8 November 2012. Elerin Area, Ede.

[55] Interview with Imam Qozeem Abdul-Azeez, Imam. 1 November 2012. Daodu Folarin Mosque, Timi Street, Ede.

[56] Interview with *Alhaji* Nureni Lawal, civil servant. 28 October 2012. Siyan Oyeweso Street, Sawmill Area, Ede.

[57] *Ibid.* and interview with Ismail Ishola, Ahlu-Sunnah and teacher. 2 October 2012. Sawmill Area, Ede.

Male members of the Tablighi Jamaat usually keep beards and wear three-quarter trousers (sometimes with Pakistani kaftan), while the females cover their body from head to toe, sometimes with their eyes or face open.[58] Many Muslims agree that Prophet Muhammed enjoined them to keep their trousers to the ankle in order to ensure that they are kept clean from dirt. However, the Tablighis are notorious for keeping their trousers far above the ankle. What is particularly offensive to some is the manner of dress of female Tablighis, whose long black dresses sweep the street. This is said to be contradictory to the teachings of Prophet Muhammed on cleanliness.[59] Rejecting such criticisms, Tablighis often see those who argue this way as lazy people who are not willing to practise the religion the way they are supposed to.

The Tablighi Jamaat's asceticism and its rejection of social, personal and aesthetic standards that are otherwise widely accepted further illustrate the group's potential challenge to the social role of Islam in Ede. By challenging material hierarchies within the Muslim community, the celebration of achievements, and even hierarchies of age and Islamic learning as 'innovation', the Tablighis suggest that such practices currently exist outside of a real Islam that is measured in personal morality and devotion. But if the Tablighis' rhetoric and practice offers a radical criticism of existing social relations and material hierarchies, it is also partly utopian. By asserting their own radical equality with others, Tablighis also suggest that a different kind of community – both more egalitarian and more beloved by God – is possible.

Relations with Other Muslim and Non-Muslim Groups

While many Muslims participate in the debates surrounding the Tablighi Jamaat, not many believe that these forms of disagreement within the Muslim society create a dividing line. It is widely believed that Islam consists of following the teachings in the Qur'an and Hadith and upholding the six articles of faith of Islam, which include belief in the oneness of God, angels and the day of judgement.[60] As the Tablighis subscribe to this version of Islam, they do enjoy good relationships with various Muslim organisations in Ede, including

---

[58] Interview with Mr Wahabi Fadesere, civil servant. 8 November 2012. Agbeni Street, Ede.

[59] Interviews with *Alhaji* Nureni Lawal, civil servant. 28 October 2012. Siyan Oyeweso Street, Sawmill Area, Ede; and Abdullahi Shuaib, Tijaniyyah. 7 November 2012. Station Road, Ede.

[60] Interviews with Abdul-Salam Olawole, Imam, Ansar-Ud-Deen, Div IV. 2 October 2012. Sawmill Area, Ede; and *Alhaji* Abdul-Lateef Alade, deputy Imam. 8 November 2012. Oloungbebe Mosque, Asawo Street, Ede.

the Ansar-Ud-Deen, Nawair-Ud-Deen, Tijaniyyah, Qureeb, Ansarul-Il-Islam, Hababudeen, Tajudeen and the Nasrul-Lahi-Fatih Society (NASFAT).[61]

Thanks to these relationships, the Tablighis have been allowed to stay in many mosques across the town for their weekly meetings, tours and other programmes. For instance, before the establishment of their own branch in December 2012, the Tablighis used the Ansar-Ud-Deen Central Mosque for their Thursday weekly meetings. According to the Imam of the mosque, the Tablighis requested to use the mosque for the propagation of the message of Islam, and as that is also the aim of the Ansar-Ud-Deen, they opened their mosque to them even though they disagree with some aspects of Tablighi practice and belief. But not all mosques in Ede have been receptive to the Tablighi Jamaat. In some cases they were tolerated only after appeals from the congregation. A Tablighi who was a former secondary school principal told me,

> We went to one outing, near Poly Ede Mosque. Before we came to that mosque, the *jamā'āt* of that mosque had vowed not to allow us in their mosque. When we got there, the *jamā'āt* told us that they do not entertain the TJ [Tablighi Jamaat] in their mosque. But we told them that we are also Muslims like them and that we have come to remind them of what God had told us to do as Muslims. As God would have, about five percent of the *jamā'āt* were youths and were my former students in the secondary school. These youths pleaded with their parents on the need to allow us in the mosque, which they did.[62]

However, even where mosques welcome Tablighi activities, disagreements between Tablighis and non-Tablighis can lead to conflict – and ultimately require toleration. In Ede, this happened in the mosque of the Ansar-Ud-Deen Society, where a disagreement between a cleric and some Tablighis over religious matters spiralled into a dispute in which the cleric was publicly challenged. According to the cleric,

> they [the Tablighis] wanted to provoke me on certain issues. That day was tough, but I made it known to them that they lack the knowledge of Islam. Although they were ready to get me down with their questions ... I proved to them that they don't know anything about Islam. ... [Eventually] somebody had to go and report to the Chief Imam at Imole Compound [to settle the dispute].[63]

---

[61] Interview with Abdul-Salam Olawole, Imam, Ansar-Ud-Deen, Div IV. 2 October 2012. Sawmill Area, Ede.

[62] Interview with Imam Adeyemo Hassan, Imam. 12 October 2012. Allahu Lateef Central Mosque, Ede.

[63] Interview with Imam Muhammed Fatih, Imam Ratibi. 1 November 2012. Ansar-Ud-Deen Central Mosque, Station Road, Ede.

These incidents and reflections illustrate both the tension and the overall cohesion, and commitment to tolerance of those whose practices one disagrees with, within the Muslim community. But disagreements between Tablighis and other reformist groups such as the Muslim Students' Society of Nigeria (MSSN) on the one hand, and the majority of Muslims in Ede on the other hand, have also centred on how Muslims should relate with members of other religions. The opinion of most people in Ede is that members of different religious groups should relate well with one another on a personal level, and it is permissible in Islam for Muslims to maintain good neighbourliness with others as long as they keep to their religion. Non-Tablighi Muslims in Ede therefore attend the Eid celebrations of their Muslim friends, even if they are members of other Muslim groups.[64] As illustrated in chapter 11, many of them also visit the homes of their Christian tenants or friends to greet them on Christmas, and visit the market place or the palace of the *Tìmì* to celebrate traditional festivals.

However, members of the Tablighi Jamaat, the MSSN and other smaller groups do not participate in celebrations held by non-Muslims.[65] Although they relate with Christians and traditionalists as fellow human beings in markets, workplaces and in the community, they do not associate with their non-Muslim religious practices.[66] This practice emphasises that the alternative community they imagine really is founded in one religious practice, and therefore has no space for outsiders. The limitation of their social interaction to bare toleration in turn makes the Tablighis outsiders in Ede. As a result, they are often accused of being the cause of religious squabbles in the town.[67] Indeed, both Muslims and non-Muslims see the Tablighis as confrontational and not forgiving if offended.[68]

An incident often referred to by my non-Tablighi interlocutors to support this view was the Dag Heward Mills Healing Jesus Crusade, which took place

---

[64] Interviews with Mr S. A. Agunloye, tailor. 8 November 2012. Timi Street, Ede; Ustaz Oyewale, Arabic teacher. 8 November 2012. Elerin Area, Ede; and Abdul-Afeez, electronic engineer. 8 November 2012. Elerin Area, Ede.

[65] Interviews with Brother Yusuf Daud, student. 8 November 2012. Ansar-Ud-Deen Central Mosque, Station Road, Ede; Abdul-Ganiyyu Mubarak, student. 8 November 2012. Ansar-Ud-Deen Central Mosque, Station Road, Ede; and Imam Adeyemo Hassan, Imam. 12 October 2012. Allahu Lateef Central Mosque, Ede.

[66] Interview with Imam Adeyemo Hassan, Imam. 12 October 2012. Allahu Lateef Central Mosque, Ede.

[67] Interview with Imam Qozeem Abdul-Azeez, Imam. 1 November 2012. Daodu Folarin Mosque, Timi Street, Ede. See also interview with *Alhaji* Yisa Oyelade. 27 March 2012. Poly Road, Ede. Interview conducted by Segun Adewusi and Tosin Akinjobi.

[68] Interview with Wunmi Eyitayo, student. 2 October 2012. Tantalizers, Iwo Road, Ibadan.

in Ede in 2011. Radio and television publicity programmes were used to invite the public to the Christian crusade. The organisers of the crusade, most of whom were outsiders to the town, also put up posters, banners, billboards and other paraphernalia in several parts of the town. Moreover, they painted houses and other structures in orange with the words: 'Healing Jesus Crusade – Dag Heward Mills'. However, as they did this without the permission of the indigenes and owners of the compounds and properties affected, many Muslims were offended by the behaviour of the crusade organisers. According to a prominent Muslim cleric in the town,

> the Christians [were] the ones overstepping their boundary. How can you be painting someone else's house because of crusade? They even tried to put a banner in front of my house, but I protested. ... I can say all Muslims in the town protested, but not against the crusade itself but against the method of publicity.[69]

12 'Healing Jesus Crusade' propaganda in Ede

Not all Muslims were as measured in their response, as many of them felt that the casual disrespect of the crusade organisers implied their general insolence vis-à-vis the community. Given the crusade organisers' audacity, some people began to suspect that they wanted to dupe or bully the population into

---

[69] Interview with *Alhaji* Olagunju, Ekerin Imam Ede. 1 November 2012. Station Road, Ede.

conversion through their activities. Some Muslim groups were so upset that they threatened violent action. However, after intervention by the *Tìmì* of Ede, his chiefs and other community and religious leaders, it was suggested that those who felt passionately about the matter should organise a competing or Islamic 'crusade' on the days of the missionary activity instead. Some Muslims then printed flyers urging fellow believers not to be carried away by miracles and displayed banners and mobilised clerics, urging Muslims to continue to believe in God. The Tablighi Jamaat, as well as other reformist groups such as the MSSN, played an important role both in the original protest and the mobilisation for what they described as the 'counter-crusade'.

13 Islamic counterpropaganda to 'Healing Jesus Crusade' in Ede

The threat of violence and the sometimes terse sermons of the 'counter-crusade' were perceived by many Muslims as an overreaction to the (real) offence caused by the Christian crusaders. But such views were countered with different visions of the community by members of the Tablighi Jamaat, several of whom confirmed to me their personal involvement in the protest.[70] Rather than seeing their threats and campaign as an intolerant reaction, they explained it as part of their collective responsibility as Muslims. They also emphasised that despite some threats of violence, the protest against the

---

[70] Interviews with Brother Yusuf Daud, student. 8 November 2012. Ansar-Ud-Deen Central Mosque, Station Road, Ede; and Abdul-Ganiyyu Mubarak, student. 8 November 2012. Ansar-Ud-Deen Central Mosque, Station Road, Ede.

crusade never actually became violent. In this way, a Tablighi who narrated his view of the events of 2011 to me subtly implied that the Tablighi Jamaat even played an important role in preventing local anger and protest from escalating:

> All Muslims are one family. Anything a Muslim does is also done by the whole community. The protest against the crusade was the collective effort of Ede Muslim community. We the TJ are not violent. Islam forbids Muslims from engaging in violent act[s]. However, there are Muslims who engage in violent act[s]. If we see such a person, our duty is to call that person and tell him to stop what he is doing.[71]

The association of the MSSN and Tablighi Jamaat with the counter-activities has created the impression among some Christians that the Tablighis are aggressive and intolerant of other religious groups.[72] Some Christians expressed their discomfort with Tablighis, even though they might be living together in the same rented compound or house.[73] Clearly this discomfort expresses the understanding by Christians that they are not part of the community envisaged by the Tablighi Jamaat. But the mutual unease of Christians and members of the Tablighi Jamaat may also reflect the fact that the degree of personal interaction between these two groups simply is much more limited than that between others. This suggests that the experiences and encounters of individuals influence more abstract views of the community just as much as theological arguments.

The Economy of Religious Reform

Establishing the Tablighi Jamaat as an ostensibly unpolitical movement, Mawlana Muhammed Ilyas insisted that Tablighis should stay away from frivolous discussions and unrewarding activities, including socio-political issues.[74] However, as Ruth Marshall has pointed out, while religion is not simply a form of politics, it cannot easily be divested of political import because it is 'a site of *action*, invested in and appropriated by believers'.[75] Perhaps it should

---

[71] Interview with Brother Mikhail Abu Muslim, civil servant and Tabligh. 8 November 2012. Ansar-Ud-Deen Central Mosque, Station Road, Ede.
[72] Interview with Wunmi Eyitayo, student. 2 October 2012. Tantalizers, Iwo Road, Ibadan; and Mr A. Adetayo, civil servant. 2 October 2012. Alajue Area, Ede.
[73] Interview with Mrs Felicia Ojo, trader. 1 November 2012. Orita Abangudu, Ede.
[74] L.F. Oladimeji, 'The Tabligh movement and Jehovah's Witnesses in Nigeria: A comparative analysis of their propagation strategies', *Fluorescence of Arabic and Islamic Studies in Nigeria*, ed. I.Z. Oseni (Ibadan: HEBN, 2008), pp. 90–9: 96–7.
[75] R. Marshall, *Political Spiritualities: The Pentecostal Revolution in Nigeria* (Chicago and London: University of Chicago Press, 2009), p. 22.

be added that in any multi-religious society like Yorubaland, the activities of every religious group are also interpreted and understood by its outsiders. The social role played by a religious group is defined in the tension between the self-perception of one's actions and the understandings of others.

One important site of action for any religion is the relationship between the material and the spiritual. In the context of overall economic pressure, Tablighis see their religion as directed against an overly materialistic approach to life. Emphasising the spiritual primacy of their practices, they see concern with worldly matters as an obstacle to their mission. As one of my Tablighi respondents pointed out,

> What we have realised is that many Muslims do not want to practise the religion of Islam the way Allah enjoins. Many of them are interested in chasing money and other worldly things for survival. But Prophet Muhammed wants complete religion from us. He also wants complete devotion. God did not tell other Prophets about the need to complete their religion, but He told Muhammed that He wanted complete religion from Muslims. That is why He told Prophet Muhammed, 'O ye Muhammed, We have completed your religion for you.' But when the Prophet died, some people [said] they cannot practise the religion the same way the Prophet practised the religion.[76]

Their view is confirmed by some respondents who believe that following the Tablighis will not guarantee their economic and social desires. According to one of them, 'it is not possible to live by their ideals in this society. Everybody wants to survive and make it in life. If you go by the way of the Tablighi Jamaat, you might not be able to survive in this life.'[77]

However, not all Muslims accept that the Tablighi Jamaat is an idealistic and non-materialistic organisation. The popular perception in the town is that like other religious groups in Ede, the Tablighi Jamaat is a competitor for material benefits and power. This view derives from historical reflection on Ede's religious landscape, in which both churches and Islamic organisations are perceived to have broken away from their former group because of their leader's desire to have control over a group of their own. Within the Muslim community, the La Jamah group and the Al-Haramani Society are believed to illustrate this process. Many people believe that the leaders of new religious groups promote alternative theologies and practices in order to create a gap

---

[76] Interview with Alfa Mutiullah Abubakre, Tabligh. 1 November 2012. Ansar-Ud-Deen Central Mosque, Station Road, Ede.
[77] Interviews with Ayinde Sikiru, trader. 4 November 2012. Sawmill Area, Ede; and Olapade Wasiu, trader. 4 November 2012. Sawmill Area, Ede.

between them and other groups that will enable them to establish close control over a clearly defined group of followers.[78]

As a result, many people in Ede see religious difference as motivated by personal or economic factors such as greed and the desire for control rather than by spiritual concerns.[79] Some respondents believe that religious leaders point out what they consider as faults in each other's practices simply in order to gain recognition and financial support. In this process, they distort established religious facts and give new meanings to suit their objectives.[80] Other respondents even suggested that some leaders turn to radical religious doctrines in order to be able to afford affluent lifestyles through the donations from their followers.[81]

In this regard, one respondent pointed to the example of the Muslim Fakafaka group, which he considered similar to the Tablighi Jamaat in terms of dress and behaviour. The group originally condemned many innovations such as the use of radio and television. However, leaders of the group now have cars, and this was seen by the respondent both as a result of their exploitation of their followers and of their insincerity in the condemnation of innovation.[82] In such cases, reflections about tolerance should probably reflect the fact that intolerance can form part of a social and economic strategy that is only partly directed at reducing normatively 'bad' practices. In the case described here, intolerance can also simply reflect a form of social competition.

While not all Muslims ascribe such cynical motives to the leaders of the Tablighi Jamaat, many observe that despite their emphasis on the spiritual, they are seeking for power and relevance of their own.[83] In a society dominated by the Muslim clerics from the town's old Islamic compounds and with many years' training in Arabic and Islamic sciences, this desire for social relevance has some political implications. One respondent, a cleric, narrated what happened when he contested for the leadership of a mosque: 'when I wanted to

---

[78] Interview with Adeyombo Adewumi. 6 October 2012.
[79] Interviews with *Alhaji* Rahmoni Oladiran, trader. 4 November 2012. Sawmill Area, Ede; and *Alhaji* Olagunju, Ekerin Imam Ede. 1 November 2012. Station Road, Ede. See also S. Oyeweso, 'The state and religion in a plural society: The Nigerian experience', *Islamic Culture* 63:4 (1989), 65–80: 72.
[80] Interview with *Alhaji* Rahmoni Oladiran, trader. 4 November 2012. Sawmill Area, Ede.
[81] Interview with Mr Bintinlaye, electronic engineer. 7 November 2012. Siyanbola Road, Ede.
[82] Interview with *Alhaji* Olagunju, Ekerin Imam Ede. 1 November 2012. Station Road, Ede.
[83] Interviews with *Alhaji* Rahmoni Oladiran, trader. 4 November 2012. Sawmill Area, Ede; *Alhaji* Olagunju, Ekerin Imam Ede. 1 November 2012. Station Road, Ede; Imam Qozeem Abdul-Azeez, Imam. 1 November 2012. Daodu Folarin Mosque, Timi Street, Ede; and Adeyombo Adewumi. 6 October 2012.

become the Imam, one of the Tablighis also wanted to become the Imam. This Tablighi tried all his efforts, including blackmailing to become the Imam, but they all came to naught.'[84] He later contended that the reason why Tablighis behave this way was to gain followers over whom they could assert their own authority:

> Let us look closely and ask ourselves, why are they doing this? We can say they want to gain converts or followers. They want to become leaders. If they can gain more followers, they would be able to assert their authority. But Prophet Muhammed has told us that no Muslims should fight to become an Imam, except the *Ladhani* [the one who calls to prayer].[85]

However, members of the Tablighi Jamaat would argue that one should not confuse the motives of the Tablighi Jamaat as an organisation with those of its members. Many members are still only trying to adjust to the teachings of the movement, and are therefore imperfect in attitude and behaviour. As illustrated above, this is a point that is readily admitted by Tablighis, who say they are not perfect but are only making efforts to practise their faith in ways that are closer to those of Prophet Muhammed and his companions.[86] One Tablighi I spoke to discussed the problem of imperfection as a serious challenge and mentioned the case of a boy who had followed them on *da'wa* with Indian hemp on him.[87]

Irrespective of personal failings, in the context of Ede the objectives of the Tablighi Jamaat are clearly political. By assuming a position of authority in the Muslim community, telling Muslims what is wrong and right about their religion, the Tablighis criticise and discredit the existing clerics. Sikand argues that when the Tablighis criticise the immoralities of Muslims and discourage their members from engaging in and discussing political issues outside of religion, they work towards establishing a more Islamic society.[88] Following that line of argument, the Tablighis' refusal to accommodate the practices of

---

[84] Interview with Imam Qozeem Abdul-Azeez, Imam. 1 November 2012. Daodu Folarin Mosque, Timi Street, Ede.

[85] *Ibid.*

[86] Interviews with Imam Adeyemo Hassan, Imam. 12 October 2012. Allahu Lateef Central Mosque, Ede; and Alfa Mutiullah Abubakre, Tabligh. 1 November 2012. Ansar-Ud-Deen Central Mosque, Station Road, Ede.

[87] Interview with Imam Adeyemo Hassan, Imam. 12 October 2012. Allahu Lateef Central Mosque, Ede.

[88] Y. Sikand, 'The Tablighi Jama'at and politics: A critical re-appraisal', *ISIM Newsletter* 1:13 (2003), 42–3. Cited in S. Turner, '"These Young Men Show No Respect for Local Custom" – Globalization and Islamic revival in Zanzibar', *Journal of Religion in Africa* 39 (2009), 237–61: 248–9.

non-Muslims and their involvement in the protest against the 2011 crusade suggest that they might also be critical of the political hierarchy of the town.

But at the same time, Tablighis are taught that everything that happens to them in life, including political oppression, is an act of God, and therefore they should not question why this happens or lament over it. While some of the more radical Muslims think that this discourages activism against socio-political injustices,[89] or absolves Muslims of their duty to react against oppression and injustice,[90] it has been instrumental in promoting peace in Ede.

Conclusion

While the Tablighi Jamaat in Ede is part of a global Islamic reform movement, its role in Ede is shaped by the constellation of other groups within the community. In several crucial areas, the Tablighi Jamaat was closely identified by respondents with other conservative reformist groups such as the Muslim Students' Society of Nigeria (MSSN), which also attracts younger, Western-educated Muslims. Janson explains the attraction of the Tablighi Jamaat to Western-educated youth in the Gambia by suggesting that the movement's relatively low emphasis on knowledge of Arabic and other Islamic disciplines allows Muslims who have received little Islamic education to take on positions of religious authority. This is probably true for Nigeria too, but unlike the Gambian context, there are also several explicitly liberal Yoruba Muslim organisations that attract similarly educated young people, including the Nasrul-Lahi-Fatih Society (NASFAT),[91] an important part of Ede's 'mainstream' Muslim community. It therefore seems as if education and the emphasis on personal faith are not necessarily associated with a doctrinal position in Ede (and Yorubaland), but simply form part of the way in which a younger generation of Muslims wishes to explore its religion.

Given the greater popularity of NASFAT, the Tablighi Jamaat cannot be said to represent the aspirations of the younger generation of Western-educated Muslims, but perhaps those of a conservative section of that generation. While NASFAT's emphasis on spiritual development in a context of shared humanity (and tolerance for both Muslims and non-Muslims) appeals to a majority of young people who understand Islam as an inclusive religion, the Tablighi Jamaat attracts those who believe that spiritual development

---

[89] Muslims in South Africa are said to have expressed similar views of the Tablighi Jamaat during the Apartheid regime there. See E. Moosa, 'Worlds "Apart": The Tabligh Jamat under Apartheid, 1963–1993', *Journal for Islamic Studies* 17 (1997), 28–48: 46–7.
[90] Sikand, 'The Tablighi Jama'at's contested claims to Islamicity', p. 7.
[91] Soares, 'An Islamic social movement in contemporary West Africa'.

must be anchored by the strict observance of Islamic practice. Nonetheless, both movements share an emphasis on equality and personal development that points to interesting similarities between experiences and expectations of Western education and popular imaginations of authentic Islam.

While I was, as explained, unable to speak to many Tablighi women, I think that their missionary activity is important in this context. Given the fact that many people – and especially older Muslims – still assume that the religion of women is determined by their fathers and husbands (see also chapter 10), the fact that the Tablighi Jamaat takes female religiosity seriously resonates with the practices of other modern Muslim groups. While women in most Muslim associations can join regular prayer groups, the MSSN has a dedicated sisters' circle, and women are very active in the Nasrul-Lahi-Fatih Society. Thus the more recent Yoruba Islamic movements place high importance on female religious activity and provide spaces where women can increase their spirituality as well as express themselves. Marking the Tablighi Jamaat as a modern Muslim association in the Yoruba context, its emphasis on female activity illustrates another generational shift in Yoruba Islam.

The Tablighi Jamaat's focus on personal growth, morality and spirituality as well as a personal relationship with God points to further similarities with other modern Muslim Yoruba groups, including both the (conservative) MSSN and the (explicitly liberal) NASFAT. It is regrettable that there is not much literature comparing different modern Muslim movements in Yorubaland. However, the spiritual focus on the personal has been discussed for the Born-Again or Pentecostal Christian movement. Indeed, some authors have discussed the notion of a 'Pentecostal Islam', which, like Pentecostal Christianity, offers new ways of engaging with aspects of local culture and the pressures and temptations of modernity.[92]

While the association with Pentecost is not appropriate for any form of Islam, it seems that there are currently important shared practices among some Muslim and Christian believers. The fact that most of Ede's Muslims, and many of the members of the MSSN and Tablighi Jamaat, accepted the Christian practice and terminology of the 'crusade' as a legitimate form of seeking religious followers, and even organised a 'counter-crusade' shows that even in apparently radical groups like the Tablighi Jamaat, many members are prepared to use strongly symbolic Christian language to describe Islamic activities. Even though the term 'crusade' is used widely in apparently non-religious contexts – for example, shortly after coming to office in 1999, former President Obasanjo launched an 'anti-corruption crusade' – the concept of the 'crusade' has been criticised by *Alhaji* Adam al-Ilori, one of the most influential

---

[92] See the discussion in Janson, *Islam, Youth, and Modernity in the Gambia*, pp. 260–5.

Islamic scholars in Yorubaland.[93] Its adoption, at least in English discussions of Muslim responses to the 2011 Dag Heward Mills Healing Jesus Crusade, suggests that most of Ede's Muslims are remarkably open to Christian terms of religious engagement. But even if members of the Tablighi Jamaat are prepared to engage with Christian terms and practices, these are obscured by their social and theological distance from Christians in everyday life, and by their practical opposition to their Christian content.

Drawing on a wide range of religious debates and practices, the practices of the Tablighi Jamaat highlight the importance of personal piety and the equality of all Muslims, and thus emphasise the importance of Islam as a religion capable of both personal and social transformation. By challenging attitudes and dispositions associated with family and compound life as well as existing social, economic and even spiritual hierarchies, the Tablighi Jamaat offers a very critical view of the town's institutions and, by implication, important pillars of the Muslim community. But at the same time, the preparedness of many of its members, and of other members of the Muslim community, to overlook what they consider 'minor' theological disagreements, means that the Tablighi Jamaat's challenges are at least partly accommodated within the Muslim community. Thus while the group offers an alternative vision to the practice of Islam in Ede, it remains an integral part of the local Muslim community.

But within the wider range of religious practices and dispositions in Ede, members of the Tablighi Jamaat seem to be at the very end of the spectrum. While they have admirers and collaborators in the Muslim community, the fact that their practices challenge institutions and notions of community that make space for non-Muslims means that many Muslims also disagree with their practices, as do the majority of non-Muslims. Given the similarities of the group's personal practices with those propagated by the liberal and highly popular NASFAT, and its additional appeal of being part of an international movement, it is likely that the Tablighi Jamaat's attempt to redraw the boundary of social communality so as only to include Muslims is the reason for its relative lack of appeal. Irrespective of the potential advantages of a narrower interpretation of religious tolerance, it appears that only very few Muslims in Ede wish to assert a vision of community in which non-Muslims do not feature.

---

[93] See P.F. de Moraes Farias, '"Yoruba Origins" Revisited by Muslims: An interview with the Arọ́kin of Ọ̀yọ́ and a reading of the Aṣl Qabā'il Yūrubā of Al-Ḥājj Ādam al-Ilūrī', *Self-Assertion and Brokerage. Early Cultural Nationalism in West Africa*, ed. K. Barber and P.F de Moraes Farias (Birmingham: Birmingham University African Studies Series, 1990), pp. 109–47: 129.

CHAPTER 7

The Baptist Church in Ede: Christian Struggles over Education and Land

Olukoya Ogen and Amusa Saheed Balogun

As the earlier chapters of this book have illustrated, Islam was established in Ede at the town and compound level by individuals committed to contributing to the town, dramatically so in the figure of Buremo, the town's first Muslim, who helped the *Tìmì* save Ede by miraculously defeating the Ibadan army (see chapters 2 and 3). While the conversion to Islam of individuals created difficulties in many families and compounds, the creation of new and explicitly Muslim compounds helped to resolve these. And although the reign of the town's first Muslim *Tìmì* met with resistance, it nonetheless contributed to the acceptance of Islam as the dominant religion. While the later emergence of competing Muslim groups illustrates the tensions internal to the town's Muslim community, it is fair to say that by the early twentieth century Islam was firmly rooted in Ede both at the town and compound level.

In contrast, Christianity arrived in Ede through missionaries whose primary aim was to convert individuals, whom they offered often exclusive access to educational and spiritual resources. These resources were usually linked to the wider networks of their particular church, which provided the initial funds required to set them up. Understanding individual change as the basis for communal progress rather than vice versa, the overall wellbeing of the town, or even the formation of an ecumenical Christian community at town level, was a secondary concern for many Christian missionaries. But if the low degree of inclusion into local structures disadvantaged the development of a Christian community, it did not always disadvantage Christian individuals, who were drawn into networks beyond the town through their educational achievements. As a result, the early Christian groups in Ede experienced a strong tension between loyalty to the individual churches, which often provided the resources that made Christianity attractive, and the need to be embedded in the town's relevant forms of social and political organisation.

In towns like Ede, this perceived Christian emphasis on individual success rather than the public good thus challenged notions of town politics in which all sections contributed to communal progress. Churches that were not embedded in local institutions, and which therefore did not have to engage with such local views, consequently remained limited in their ability to participate in the social and political life of the town, even if they could draw on significant resources for the growth of the community. In contrast, churches that catered strongly to the expectation of communal contribution found strong local acceptance. But while such organisations were often recognised as making an important contribution to town life, their reliance on charisma and local particularity could also mean that they were not fully able to access the extra-local resources, such as education, which were also crucial to the town.

Exploring the role of Christianity in Ede through a focus on the Baptist Church, this chapter examines how the success of the Baptist Church illustrates the importance of *both* wider religious networks and rootedness in local social structures for the establishment of Christianity in predominantly Muslim towns. As one of the earliest Christian bodies to make contact with the people of Ede, the Baptist Church has remained a prominent Christian denomination in the town despite the growth of many new-generation Pentecostal movements.[1] As a result, the Baptist Church offers an interesting study of a religious minority in a Muslim-dominated town. Muslim–Christian struggles have historically centred on Christians' use of education for conversion as well as the limited access to land especially of churches with few local converts. More recent areas of disagreement include differences over religious education and dress codes in Ede's schools and the refusal of some Muslims to rent their rooms or houses to immigrant Christians.

While Muslims and Christians relate closely in many other areas of everyday life, struggles over land, schooling or residence are strongly shaped by the fact that Islam is widely seen as the religion of the town's indigenes and of Christianity as the religion of the town's strangers or outsiders. Practising the religion of the town's strangers or outsiders, Christians thus rely on the tolerance of others. However, recognising that tolerance is not solely a reflection of normative values but also a competitive practice in the struggle over believers, they often adopt the opposite approach in order to assert moral (and spiritual) superiority.

---

[1] The major sources of data for this chapter are: written responses to questionnaires administered to selected Baptists in Ede; qualitative interviews with Baptists, other Christians, Muslims and traditional religious practitioners; archival records; and information from the extant secondary literature on the Baptist movement in Ede and other parts of Yorubaland.

The Early Baptist Mission in Ede

Successful Christian missionary activities took place in Yorubaland from the mid-nineteenth century onwards. This was due partly to the efforts of freed slaves of Yoruba origin who returned from Sierra Leone to cities such as Badagry, Lagos and Abeokuta. These people had been exposed not only to Christianity but also to missionary training in Sierra Leone and they helped propagate the Christian faith in Yorubaland.[2] Led by Henry Townsend and freed slaves like Samuel Ajayi Crowther, the Anglican Church Missionary Society (CMS) arrived in Badagry in 1842. CMS churches were subsequently built in towns including Abeokuta (1846), Lagos (1851), Ibadan (1853) and Oyo (1856). Wesleyan Methodist missionaries arrived in Badagry in 1842 and built a missionary station there under the leadership of Thomas Birch Freeman, and Methodist mission stations were also opened throughout Yorubaland, including Abeokuta, Ibadan, Ilesa and Lagos.[3] Other prominent European missionary bodies in Yorubaland in the nineteenth/twentieth century were the Roman Catholic Church, the Presbyterian Church and the Foreign Mission Committee of the United Presbyterian Church of Scotland.[4]

The Baptist Church came to what is now Nigeria in 1850, when the Southern American Baptist Convention sent Thomas Jefferson Bowen to West Africa as a missionary. After preaching in Badagry, Abeokuta, Ketu and Iseyin, Bowen built his first mission station in Ijaye, then a thriving warrior town, in 1852. His first African convert was a woman, Oyindaola of Biolorunpelu community (near Abeokuta), but it was at Ijaye that Bowen first baptised an African convert by the name of Tella on 23 July 1854.[5] Also in 1854, Bowen succeeded

---

[2] T. Tamuno, *The Police in Modern Nigeria, 1861–1965: Origins, Development and Role* (Ibadan: University of Ibadan Press, 1970), p. 1.

[3] J.F.A. Ajayi, *Christian Missions in Nigeria, 1841–1891: The Making of a New Elite* (London: Longmans 1965), pp. 31–9.

[4] Ajayi, *Christian Missions in Nigeria, 1841–1891*, pp. xiii–xiv.

[5] For some useful materials on early Baptist history in Nigeria, see the following: Bowen's Diary, entry for 16 July 1854 as collected and compiled in C.F. Roberson, 'The Bowen Papers: A Compilation of Private and Business Papers of Rev. Thomas Jefferson and his wife Laurenna Henrietta (Davis) Bowen', Private Collections available at J.C. Pool Memorial Library, The Nigerian Baptist Theological Seminary, Ogbomoso, Oyo State, Nigeria (n.d.); S. Pinnock, *The Romance of Missions in Nigeria* (Richmond VA: Educational Department of Foreign Mission Board of Southern Baptist Convention, 1917); L.M. Duval, *Baptist Missions in Nigeria* (Richmond VA: Educational Department of Foreign Mission Board of Southern Baptist Convention, 1928); C.S. Green, *New Nigeria: Southern Baptists at Work in Africa* (Richmond VA: Educational Department of Foreign Mission Board of Southern Baptist Convention, 1936); R.I. Rotberg, *Missionary Researches and Travels* (London: Frank Cass and Company Ltd, 1968); J. Atanda, ed., *Baptist Churches in Nigeria, 1850–1950: Accounts of their Foundation and Growth*

in building the first Baptist Chapel in Ijaye.[6] He was assisted in nurturing the nascent Baptist Church by fellow missionary W.H. Clarke, who arrived in September 1854. As Ijaye lost importance and population after it suffered a major defeat by Ibadan in the 1860s, this church is known as Ijaye-Orile Baptist Church today.

As the original Baptist community spread out, Baptist communities were founded in different parts of Yorubaland. From the late 1850s onwards, Baptist churches were established in Oyo towns including Ogbomoso, Ilorin, Ibadan, Iwo, Igboho, Saki and Oyo, as well as in Lagos, Abeokuta and Ijebu.[7] Unlike other mission churches, the Baptist Church thus had a very strong presence and influence in the central part of Yorubaland.[8] Its strongholds were in Yoruba towns and cities which were shaped both by the legacy of the Oyo Empire and by the early presence, and often dominance, of Islam. Like other early Christian missionaries in Oyo,[9] the early Baptists in Ede thus had to contend with opposition from adherents of Yoruba traditional religions as well as from established Muslim communities.[10] It is possible that this encouraged a strategy that relied at least partly on missionaries with established roots in their respective communities.

(Ibadan: University of Ibadan Press, 1988). See also T. Collins, *The Baptist Mission of Nigeria, 1850–1993: A History of the Southern Baptist Convention Missionary Work in Nigeria* (Ibadan: Associated Book-Makers Nigeria Ltd, 1993); J. Okedara and S.A. Ajayi, *Thomas Jefferson Bowen: Pioneer Baptist Missionary to Nigeria, 1850–1856* (Ibadan: John Archers, 2004); I. Adedoyin, *J.T. Ayorinde, A Study in the Growth of the Nigerian Baptist Convention and Moses Oladejo Stone and the Beginning of Baptist Work in Nigeria* (Ibadan: Nigerian Baptist Book Store, 1998); and S.A. Ajayi, *Baptist Work in Nigeria, 1850–2005: A Comprehensive History* (Ibadan: Book Wright Publishers, 2010).

[6] Samuel Johnson alludes to the fact that Reverend Bowen of the American Baptist and other CMS missionaries played positive roles in mitigating the impact of Ibadan–Ijaye war of 1859–65 on the people of Ijaye. See S. Johnson, *The History of the Yorubas: from the earliest times to the beginning of the British Protectorate* (Lagos: CMS Bookshops, 1921), p.345.

[7] See among others: J. Atanda, ed., *W.H. Clarke's Travels and Explorations in Yorubaland, 1854–1858* (Ibadan: University of Ibadan Press, 1972); Atanda, *Baptist Churches in Nigeria*; and I. Adedoyin, *The Place of Ogbomoso in the History of Nigerian Baptists* (Ibadan: Penthouse Publications, 2005).

[8] See the growth of Baptist Churches in Nigeria in Atanda, *Baptist Churches in Nigeria*. A major pointer to this fact is the siting of Bowen University (named after J.T. Bowen, the pioneer of Baptist Mission in Nigeria and owned by the Baptist Convention of Nigeria, the umbrella body of all Baptist Churches in Nigeria) at Iwo, another Muslim-dominated town in Oyo-speaking areas of Osun State.

[9] Atanda, *W.H. Clarke's Travels*, pp. 92–187.

[10] See Ajayi, *Baptist Work in Nigeria*, pp. 171–85.

Baptist work in Ede started in 1900 by Jacob Oyeboade Akerele, an indigene of Ede who had spent his formative years in Ogbomoso and converted to Christianity there (see chapter 2).[11] Baptist records suggest that as a native of the town, Akerele was purposely sent to Ede because it was believed that he would find it easier to win converts.[12] Akerele's church started under a tree in front of his family house, and between 1902 and 1910, he succeeded in leading thirty of his converts, including several converts from Islam, to Ogbomoso for Baptism.[13] Impressed by Akerele's accomplishment, Tìmì Adelekan, the then monarch of Ede, offered him a portion of land at Babasanya compound to build a place of worship for the nascent Christian community in Ede. Many Christian leaders came from Ogbomoso to supervise the building of the church, which became the first place of worship for all Ede Christians and was named 1900 Pioneer Christian Memorial Hall.

However, the 1900 Pioneer Christian Memorial Hall was short-lived as conflicts broke out among some of the leading pioneer members of the church, illustrating the tensions around belonging that Christianity faced from the beginning. Jacob Akerele, a native of the town, tolerated polygamy while many of the Christian immigrants to the town, under the leadership of L.O. Fadipe, opposed this. Jacob Akerele and the indigenous people of the town who supported him broke away to establish the First Baptist Church at Oke Apaso. In the meantime, Reverend L.O. Fadipe's faction remained at Babasanya until the church building collapsed. But without access to local land or the resources to rebuild their church, the members of this faction of the church then rotated Sunday services to their various houses. As the town's first Christian community collapsed, some members of the church reverted to Islam and traditional religious practices.[14]

---

[11] Atanda, *Baptist Churches in Nigeria*, pp. 156–8.

[12] C. Roberson, *A History of Baptists in Nigeria, West Africa, 1849–1935 (with Appropriate Projections into Later Years)*, released in 1986 as Roberson Papers and kept as Private Collections at J.C. Pool Memorial Library of the Nigerian Baptist Theological Seminary Ogbomoso, Oyo State, Nigeria (n.d.).

[13] J. Atanda, *First Baptist Church, Oke-Apaso, Ede, Osun State: A Century of Practical and Expansive Evangelism in Edeland, 1900–2000* (Osogbo: A Centenary Celebration Souvenir printed for the Church by Ademola Printing Press, 2000), p. 4.

[14] See Atanda, *Baptist Churches in Nigeria*, pp. 156–8 and *First Baptist Church, Oke-Apaso, Ede*. In his own assessment of the crisis that faced the Baptist Mission in Ede in the last years of the nineteenth century, Prof. (Revd) Joseph Abiodun Ilori, former President of the Nigerian Baptist Theological Seminary, Ogbomoso, held that it was part of the great racial schism between blacks and whites that affected Baptist family worldwide during this period. The Ede crisis, according to him, was a spillover of this crisis in other Baptist churches in Nigeria, particularly those of Lagos. He was interviewed at Ilori International Group of Schools, Ede, on 5 December 2013.

In order to unite and revitalise the Baptist Christian mission in Ede, Reverend Benjamin Laniyi and Scott Patterson, an expatriate, were seconded to Ede from Ogbomoso in 1914. The two men succeeded in reconciling the different factions of the Baptist Church by 1917, when Reverend Laniyi was also succeeded by Pastor E.D. Ladipo. It was under Pastor Ladipo that the Church succeeded in recruiting more converts. As the community grew, additional preaching stations were established at the Laala and Okesasa areas of Ede. Succeeding Pastor Ladipo, Pastor J.A. Ajani assumed duties as the head of Baptist Mission in Ede in 1934. His major achievement was the expansion of the Apaso Baptist Church.[15]

Other pioneers of the Baptist Mission in Ede included Mr Samuel Foyeke, Mr David Taiwo, Mr Sam Laniran, Mr Oyewale, Mr Ephraim Adeomi, Mr Benjamin Akintola, Mr John Ilori, Jeremiah Pelu, T. Akinkunmi, Eman Adewusi, Jacob Egbe, Elijah Amusan, Daniel Ojo, J.A. Ajani, Daniel Adeagbo, J. Akanbi, Sam Alabi, Nathaniel Oyerinde, Reverend T.A. Taiwo (1936–46), Pastor P.O. Adebanwi (1946–7), Reverend A. Ajani (1949–53), Reverend D.T.T. Afolayan (1954–82) among many others.[16] Significantly, from 1934 onwards, the Baptist Mission in Ede succeeded in establishing churches in Ede town and its suburbs.[17] Today, Baptist churches across Edeland include First Baptist Church Apaso, Oore Ofe Baptist Church Oke-Gada, Mercyland Baptist Church Sabo-Elerin, Iroyin Ayo Baptist Church Akala-Iseki, Obada Baptist Church Adetoto and many others.[18]

Education, Conversion and Belonging

As the Baptist community expanded, it followed general missionary practice at that time and established schools. In 1921, the community opened an elementary school known as First Baptist Primary School Oke-Apaso, which

---

[15] *Ibid.*

[16] Some of the names of pioneer Baptists in Ede mentioned here are taken from Atanda, *First Baptist Church, Oke-Apaso, Ede* and the list of delegates from First Baptist Church, Oke-Apaso, Ede, who attended the Annual Baptist Associational Conference from inception in 1915, available in the minutes of the conferences kept at the J.C. Pool Memorial Library of the Nigerian Baptist Theological Seminary, Ogbomoso, Oyo State, Nigeria. We thank the Librarian and other staffers of the Library, particularly Mr A. Adeniran, the Library Officer, for their warm reception and making the Minutes available to us during our data-gathering visit to the Library between 21 and 23 November 2013.

[17] These include Alajue, Elerin, Iseki-Oloro, Obadan, Oloki, Olodan, Adogbe, Sekona, Ido-Osun, Ofatedo, Sabo, Agbinpa, Araromilogun, Gbendelen, Kusi and Ogobi.

[18] For a list of all Baptist churches and preaching stations in Ede up to the year 2000, see *First Baptist Church, Oke-Apaso, Ede*, pp. 53–4.

was followed by a second Baptist Primary School in Oke-Agudu (a different quarter of Ede) in 1945, Iseki Oloro Baptist Day School in 1955, and Obada Baptist Day School in 1976. After a Baptist Teachers' Training School (now defunct) was established in Ede in 1949, a Baptist Day Secondary School was established at Sekona-Ede, and in 1961 a Baptist High School was opened.

These educational institutions played a prominent role in Baptist evangelism. Certainly in its first decades, First Baptist Day School Ede was used to convert many Muslim and traditionalist pupils to Christianity. Some of the converted ex-Muslims are now leading Baptists in their own right, although their Muslim origin is still reflected in Muslim names, such as Deacon Seidu A. Alabi, Mr Aderinko Asani, Mr Suarau Oyerinko, Mrs Wosilatu M. Lasubulu, Mr Buraimo B. Odunaye, Mr Bakare O. Amoo, Mr Mudasiru O. Arowolo and Mr Wahabi Iyiola Oyetunji.[19] But while the conversion of pupils was successful in the sense that it helped entrench Christianity among the indigenous families of Ede, it also irritated and even offended members of the town's Muslim community, who perceived it as unpatriotic or selfish because they felt that valuable knowledge should be shared freely among all of Ede's citizens without exception.

As the Baptist schools belonged to a Christian community that had ties to the established families of the town, its leaders were aware of these objections from the Muslim community. It is probably for this reason that unlike in many other mission schools at the time, conversion was not compulsory, even though it was strongly encouraged by staff. As a result, many Muslim pupils who attended Baptist schools remained Muslims. Some of these include men who are prominent Islamic leaders today. *Alhaji* Sheikh Salahudeen Olayiwola, the Chairman of the Osun State Muslim Ummah, went to Baptist Primary School in Oke Agudu. Today he is the Proprietor of the Arabic and Islamic Institute in Ede, which attracts scholars and students from Yorubaland and beyond. *Alhaji* Sheikh Saheed Olanrewaju, the Grand Mufti of Edeland, attended Baptist Primary School in Talafia Baba Abiye. Partly based on his personal knowledge of Christianity, *Alhaji* Olanrewaju acknowledges not only the distinctions but also the similarities between Islam and Christianity (see chapter 5).[20]

The importance of the Baptist Church's local entrenchment in Ede is illustrated especially by comparison with other Christian missions. Another early

---

[19] Atanda, *First Baptist Church, Oke-Apaso, Ede,* p. 10. The original Muslim names of these converts should be noticed: Seidu, Asani, Suarau, Wosilatu, Buraimo, Bakare, Mudasiru and Wahabi respectively.

[20] Interview with *Alhaji* Sheikh Saheed Olanrewaju, Grand Mufti of Edeland. 5 December 2013. Talafia Imam Compound, Ede.

Christian mission to Ede was the Church Missionary Society, which arrived in 1911.[21] The Anglican community was built up from the house of one Mr Akeju, an immigrant to Ede from Ipetumodu, who resided in Alajue compound. When the community expanded, the first Anglican Church in Ede was built in 1920 in Oke Egan,[22] and like other churches, the Anglicans also established branches in different Ede villages.[23] As a means of proselytisation, the first Anglican school was opened in Ede in 1929, with a first set of students including several Muslim children from Imole compound.[24] But despite some local successes, most of the Anglican converts were migrants to Ede, and despite its long presence in the town, it has not achieved the local influence of the Baptist Church. Locally referred to as a church 'for strangers', the Anglican Church plays a much smaller role in town politics than the Baptist Church.

Like the Anglican Church, the African Church came to Ede through an immigrant to the town. Its pioneer was one Mr Coker, a cocoa trader who came to Ede for produce business.[25] Ebenezer African Church was built at Apoaro's compound Ede in 1926. After the destruction of the Church by rain in 1940, a new African Church was established in Oke Egan in 1940, from which it has spread to many parts of Ede.[26] An African Church primary school was

---

[21] The Anglican Mission was one of the five oldest European Christian missions that came to Nigeria under Henry Townsend in the 1840s. Cf. Ajayi, *Christian Missions in Nigeria*, p. 1.

[22] The Anglican Church was assisted for a while by a European school master-catechist, Dr K. Scott Patterson, who came to Ede from Osogbo. Interview with Reverend Canon O.A. Fabuluje, presiding Pastor, St Peter's Anglican Church. 2 April 2013. Oke-Egan, Ede; Chief Rufus Oluwole Ojeniran, Baba Ijo, St Peter's Anglican Church. 30 April 2013. Oke-Egan, Ede; and Reverend S.T. Adeyemi, Chairman, Ede Parish, Ife-Osogbo Diocese of the Anglican Communion. 29 May 2013.

[23] Early Anglican churches include St Peter's Anglican Church, Sekona, St John Church Oke Gada, St James Church Awo, Adetola Ayeni Memorial Church Owode, St John's Church Alajue, St Paul's Church Ara, Anglican Church Ioye, Anglican Church, Apata, Anglican Church, Akoda, Anglican Church Iso Isu, Ede and a host of others.

[24] See Anglican Diocese of Osun, *Outline History of Churches in the Diocese of Osun Anglican Communion* (Osogbo: Safesight Publishers, 2007), pp. 78–94.

[25] He was not a clergyman or missionary but a businessman whose attitudes to life inspired many people to embrace Christianity through him.

[26] A third African Church was opened in Ede at Agbongbe in 1944 by a faction of members who broke away from the Ebenezer Church at Oke Egan. Today, the African Church Ede is a force to reckon with in the Ife-Osogbo Diocese. The African Church now has branches including Bethlehem African Church Agbongbe, Ebenezer African Church Oke Egan, St Stephen's African Church Alajue and Christ African Church, Sasa, Ede. Interview with Chief S.O. Fadara, Otun Baba Ijo, Bethlehem African Church. 10 May 2013. Agbongbe, Ede.

established in 1945 near Ebenezer African Church, Oke Egan.[27] However, as in the early Baptist Church, a doctrinal split divided the Ebenezer African Church into a faction of indigenes and another one of non-indigenes. Unlike in the early Baptist church, this rift has not entirely healed and therefore continues to limit the local influence of the African Church.

The Christ Apostolic Church illustrates the success that could be achieved by churches that were led by Ede's townspeople. The founder of the local Christ Apostolic Church, the late Prophet Samson Oladeji Akande of Kusi compound, was a native of Ede. He was a Muslim by upbringing and had attended Islamic school. He became blind in 1935 and had series of problems including poverty, childlessness and unemployment, and eventually even attempted suicide. Originally called Salami, he changed his name to Samson when he converted to Christianity in 1938. He joined the Christ Apostolic Church just eight years after it was founded by Late Apostle J.A. Babalola.[28] In 1939, he established the first Christ Apostolic Church in Ede on a portion of land in the Talafia area given to him by *Tìmì* Sanusi Akangbe. Because of his wonderful and miraculous activities, and particularly his successful ministration for barren women, he was nicknamed Baba Abiye by his teeming followers. Talafia was once a single compound, which was divided along religious lines in the early twentieth century (see chapter 5). The part of Talafia where Akande's church was established is known today as Talafia Baba Abiye.[29]

Under Akande, the Christ Apostolic Church grew from strength to strength and its community in Ede became one of the strongholds of CAC in Yorubaland.[30] One reason why Akande became so popular and influential in the CAC worldwide was that its founder, Apostle Joseph Ayo Babalola, died while visiting Prophet Akande (or Baba Abiye) in Ede in 1959.[31] This was widely taken to confirm Akande's own spiritual powers, and the regard

---

[27] S.A. Ojo, *History of African Church in Ede, Osun State* (Ede: Monec Printers, n.d.), pp. 1–7.

[28] L. Dokun, 'Islam in Ede' (Ibadan: Department of Arabic and Islamic Studies, University of Ibadan, 1974), p. 37; F. Adelegan, *Nigeria's Leading Lights of the Gospel: Revolutionaries in Worldwide Christianity* (Bloomington IN: Westbrow Press, 2013), p. 395.

[29] See F. Akande, *'Baba Abiye', The Making of the Prophet: The Testimony of Prophet Samson Oladeji Akande* (Ede: Gospel Promotion Outreach, 2002).

[30] Baba Abiye organised crusades and revivals in Ede and other neighbouring villages. In 1956, he hosted the annual national convention of the Christ Apostolic Church in Ede, and it was a huge success. The first CAC primary school was established in 1945 and a CAC Bible Training School was opened in the town in 1952. This was in addition to the establishments of CAC Churches in Ede and other neighbouring towns and villages. See Akande, *'Baba Abiye'*.

[31] Interview with Pastor Timothy Funso Akande, Pastor Gospel Promotion Outreach, CAC Ori-Oke Baba Abiye. 21 March 2013. Iwo-Ibadan Road, Ede.

of other CAC members certainly increased Akande's status in Ede. But more importantly for the role of the CAC in Ede, Akande established a prayer mountain, locally known as Ori-Oke Baba Abiye, between Awo and Iwoye in 1944 (Map 2). The mountain has a church and hostels for visitors who come to pray and seek solutions for their socio-economic and spiritual problems, including barrenness. Although the mountain was established by a Christian cleric, its healing powers have never been linked to pressure to convert. As a result, many of those who come to this mountain and benefit from its wondrous healing powers are members of other religious faiths in and outside Ede.

This example illustrates that the association with Prophet Akande, or Baba Abiye, entrenched the Christ Apostolic Church in Ede not simply because its leader was a popular member of an established local family with access to the *Tìmì* (although this undoubtedly helped). As a member of an old Ede family, Akande was not only able to acquire land for meaningful religious activities, but he also understood that giving goods associated with religion – whether education or healing – in strict exchange for conversion was considered as a selfish form of behaviour that disregarded the wider interests of the community of the town. Today many of Ede's Muslims continue to appreciate Akande's spiritual leadership, hard work and sheer determination.

Steering a middle way between the charismatic local entrenchment of the Christ Apostolic Church and the detached professional activities of the Anglican Church, the early Baptist Church also faced some opposition in Ede, both from the Muslim community and from adherents of traditional religions. As pointed out above, most criticism was directed at activities perceived to involve forceful proselytisation. As the leaders of the older and more central compounds of the town, such as Imole, Talafia Imam and Daodu Lagunju (dominated by Muslims), Olosun (dominated by *Ọ̀sun* worshippers) and Ologun (dominated by *Ògún* worshippers), were either Muslims or adherents of traditional religions,[32] they limited the access of Christians to land deliberately to prevent the conversion of Muslims and traditional worshippers to Christianity.[33] As a result, the sites upon which the early Baptist and other churches were built in Ede in the first half of the twentieth century were located on the outskirts of the town. However, many of the places considered as outskirts in the early twentieth century now form the part of the most developed parts of contemporary Ede township that surround the old centre of the town.

---

[32] Oral information from our local guide in Ede, Mr Yusuf Sikiru Abiona, indigene of Ede and Part IV student of History at Obafemi Awolowo University. 15 July 2013.

[33] Questionnaire responses from Mr Ogunwale Sunday Olufunsho, clergy, Mercyland Baptist Church. July 2013. Elerin, Sabo Road, Ede.

In 1946 the coronation of John Adetoyese Laoye (1946–75) as the first Christian *Tìmì* of Ede contributed immensely to the expansion of the Baptist community.[34] As set out in chapters 2 and 3, *Tìmì* Laoye was one of Ede's early Baptist converts. Just as *Tìmì* Abibu Lagunju (c.1847–1900) had used his position to aid the cause of Islamic expansion in Ede during his reign, *Tìmì* Laoye openly identified with the Baptists and supported their cause in a number of ways. As a result, his reign witnessed an increase of Christians also among the indigenous families of Ede. This is partly illustrated by the phenomenal increase in the number of Christians in Edeland during his 29-year reign, but also by the fact that the Baptist Church did not find it difficult to obtain land for new churches and institutions during this period. The construction of a new church building at the historical site of First Baptist Church, Apaso, Ede was also begun during his reign but completed a year after his demise in 1976.[35]

14 First Baptist Church Ede

Despite his personal allegiance to the Baptist Church, *Tìmì* Laoye identified with all Christian denominations in Ede. Eventually he also encouraged mutual and peaceful inter-religious interactions in the town during his reign and related well with both traditionalists and Muslims. Since the end of *Tìmì*

---

[34] See Oba Adetoyese Laoye, The 7th Timi of Ede, *An Address of Welcome delivered to the Islamic Congress held at Ede on the 3rd & 4th August, 1963* (n.p., n.d.). We are grateful to late Omo-Oba Elkanah Laoye for making this invaluable document available.

[35] Atanda, *Baptist Churches in Nigeria*, pp. 156–8.

Laoye's reign, the Baptist Church – and the Christian community in general – has not had a champion of similar prominence, and it had to readjust to being a minority community in a town with a predominantly Muslim elite. While there is no indication that the Christian community has declined, it seems that Muslim–Christian relations, while continuing to be peaceful and cooperative on the surface, have also slightly deteriorated again, certainly from what pertained during the late 1960s and 1970s. Areas of disagreement and resentment seem to exist especially in the areas of land ownership, education, and the renting out of living space.

Churches, Christian Structures and Struggles over Land Ownership

While there are many Christian churches of different denominations in contemporary Ede, the historical success of the Baptist Church is confirmed by the fact that it has more churches and schools than any other single Christian denomination in the town today.[36] As indicated earlier, most Baptist churches and schools are located in areas previously regarded as outskirts, far from the compounds of Muslims and traditional religious worshippers. When they were given out, the plots of land now holding churches (including Apaso where the oldest Baptist Church in Ede is located) were considered unimportant because they were not part of the old town. Today, these areas are seen as newly developed areas where Christians and Muslims have equal rights to use spaces for religious purposes. Churches around these areas are relatively big, and there are also a number of smaller mosques for Muslim landlords and tenants.

In these new areas where churches and Christian schools are located, the influence of Muslims is not as strong as in the heart of the town. In spite of this, Baptist leaders still allude to the fact that Christians in these areas encounter some forms of antagonism from Muslims.[37] This can be explained as the result of two perceptions that have shaped Muslim–Christian relations in Ede throughout the twentieth and the early twenty-first century: namely local notions of land ownership and the importance of indigeneity vis-à-vis tenancy. Both are closely entwined and mutually reinforcing, and linked to the compound system that dominates Ede. Together they play an important role in limiting the expansion of Christianity in the town.

While the churches in newer areas of Ede are built on privately owned land, some Muslims still feel that they retain a degree of ownership over this land.

---

[36] It is estimated that there are about nineteen Baptist churches and five Baptists schools in Ede today. Questionnaire responses from Deacon Z.A. Oke, retired teacher and clergy at First Baptist Church. July 2013. Oke-Apaso, Ede.

[37] Questionnaire responses from Deacon Z.A. Oke, retired teacher and clergy at First Baptist Church. July 2013. Oke-Apaso, Ede.

This is because originally all the lands surrounding the old centre of the town were owned by family groups from the older Ede compounds, most of who were, and remain, Muslims (see chapter 5). But even where the land was sold to the present landlords with the full agreement of all members of the family, many citizens of Ede believe that the present landlords remain in the debt of the original owners of the land for their willingness to part with it. This belief is widely spread in Yorubaland, and former landowners and their descendants in Ede and elsewhere often expect to be treated with special consideration, or at least to be acknowledged, by those who have acquired the land that originally belonged to their families.

As a result of this widespread privileging of historical and especially communal land ownership, new landlords experience problems of various kinds. Thus, members of branches of the compound's core lineage who were not part of the original land sale often harass the new owners by claiming that the land still belongs to them, forcing new owners to pay out substantial sums for land they have already bought. Moreover, the former owners of land often also expect to have a say in the way their land is used. But while this problem affects Nigerians in many parts of south-west Nigeria and beyond, in Ede this often affects land formerly owned by Muslims that is now built up with churches and other Christian structures.[38] Especially the degree of noise produced by Christians by drumming during Muslim prayer times or night vigils is contested. Again, it appears selfish of those who owe their land to local families to use structures built on this land to inconvenience their former benefactors.

Finally, the members of families or compounds that previously owned the land on which Christian structures have been built also expect a degree of recognition from the new owners, expressed simply through interpersonal relationships, visits and consultations. But where the leaders and elders of a church are drawn from outside of the town, as is of course the case in many of Ede's churches that are part of a wider denomination, they are often unaware of these historical obligations. Christian leaders and elders often suffer for their perceived ignorance of the social duties associated with their positions and possessions, and over time resentment leads to friction and disputes concerning the use of the land.

However, while the complex nature of land ownership continues to shape Muslim–Christian relations, it would be wrong to attribute this practice solely to religious rivalry. Similar practices occur in the development of new areas in most Yoruba towns, where they are often far less explicitly linked to religion than in Ede. An important underlying motive for the reappropriation of

---

[38] See also questionnaire responses from Reverend (Dr) M.A. Alabi, clergy, First Baptist Church. July 2013. Oke-Apaso, Ede.

land that has been sold by the original owners is greed, and often encroachment practices simply force landowners to give up possession or to pay for land twice (or thrice, or even more frequently).[39] However, given Ede's widely accepted self-perception as a Muslim town, albeit one with a widely accepted pre-Islamic history, these practices appear, in their local context, as religiously discriminatory. As the following sections illustrate, local struggles over land may be particularly encouraged by a sense of threat experienced by some Muslims in the face of apparent Christian expansion.

Living Space for Christians

Throughout Ede, Christians struggle to rent living space. Using the example of three important Muslim compounds, chapter 5 has illustrated that where such compounds let rooms or houses to Christians, the tenants must abide by strict laws that ensure that the overall Muslim nature of the compound is not undermined. Similar practices are used by many Muslim landlords even in individual houses in the newer areas of the town. For Christians, it can become extremely difficult to find a place to live where they are allowed to practice their religion openly.

As a respondent noted,

> Some sects among the Muslims treat Christians with suspicion while some treat Christians with respect. It is difficult for Christians to secure rooms to rent. Where [it is possible to secure rooms for rent], there are laws guiding Christian tenants.[40]

While this statement illustrates that many Christians are aware of the significant internal differences within the Muslim community, it also points to the fact that the practices adopted by the town's old Muslim compounds serve as an example for parts of the Muslim community. Clearly some Muslims use their positions of power within their compounds to avoid engagement with Christians and Christianity. Indeed, the non-compliance of Christians with such rules can lead to harsh reactions by their landlords, and thus entail bitter experiences for the offenders. As a member of the Baptist Church pointed out, Muslim reactions to unsanctioned Christian activities in their houses or compounds can be severe:

---

[39] Such practices are described for Lagos in S. Barnes, *Patrons and Power: Creating a Political Community in Metropolitan Lagos* (London: Manchester University Press, 1986).

[40] Questionnaire responses from Reverend (Dr) M.A. Alabi, clergy, First Baptist Church. July 2013. Oke-Apaso, Ede.

[Some Muslim landlords] may force them [the Christians] to pack out [leave their rooms/ houses]. In some houses, landlords may put signposts to their houses that there is no vacancy for Christians.[41]

Asked why many Muslims refuse to rent their houses to Christians in Ede, a Muslim respondent argued that Christians often abuse the trust placed in them, for example by turning rented residential apartments or commercial shops into mini-churches or worship centres.[42] Another Muslim respondent referred to the example of some Muslim women who were denied the opportunity of selling food items on Sundays at an undisclosed church in Ede early in 2013.[43] He took this example to imply that Christians also discriminate against Muslims in the town, and he therefore felt justified in discriminating against them in turn. This comment illustrates that even by renting out space, many Muslim indigenes feel that they are doing Christian strangers a favour by allowing them to carve out a space for themselves in the compound and wider community. From this perspective, it is up to the Christians to show that they are worthy of such privilege.

Beyond the question of reciprocity, the harsh reactions of some Muslims to Christian activity and transgression also arise from the Muslim impression that Christians do not abide by all rules that constitute the community. This in turn is explained by the fact that they are not indigenes and therefore not as committed to the community as the historical 'owners' of the town. This comment points to the importance of perceptions of indigeneity in almost all areas of Muslim–Christian relations in Ede. But it is important to note that indigeneity is perceived, and put to work, in different ways: while some Muslims generally perceive Christians as immigrants, the local roots of the Baptist Church also mean that other Muslims consider (some) Christian communities, and their members, as indigenes of the town. As a member of the Baptist Church noted, 'some Muslims treat Christians fairly because some of the co-founders of Baptist Churches are from either Muslims or traditional religionists [sic, meaning: from established compounds in the town]'.[44]

As a church that has a strong claim to indigeneity in Ede, leaders of the Baptist Church understand the importance of the landlord–tenant relationship for positive relations between Muslims and Christians. All the Baptist

---

[41] Questionnaire responses from Reverend G.J. Oladele, clergy, Oore Ofe Baptist Church. July 2013. Oke-Gada, Ede.

[42] Interview with Ustaz Mikail Hamzat Adekilekun, Missioner of Al-Fatihu Quareeb Islamic Society, Ede Branch. 6 July 2013. Imole Compound, Ede.

[43] Interview with Mrs Rafatu A. Amoo. 28 November 2013. Total Market area, Ede.

[44] Questionnaire responses from Mr Ogunwale Sunday Olufunsho, clergy, Mercyland Baptist Church. July 2013. Elerin, Sabo Road, Ede.

members of the clergy who responded to our questions explained that the Christian property owners in Ede with whom they relate do not discriminate on the basis of religion in renting their residential or commercial property out to people.[45] In order to counter charges of selfishness, Baptist clergy in Ede encourage their property-owning members to rent rooms and other spaces to Muslims.

Professor J.A. Ilori, an indigene of Ede as well as a former President of the Baptist Seminary at Ogbomoso, admits that some Christian tenants disturb their Muslim landlords during prayers and other religious activities. He referred to the example of one of his Muslim friends who used to complain to him about the unacceptable activities of his Christian tenants.[46] One suspects that it is partly because he is a committed indigene of the town that Professor Ilori is able to offer such a measured response. As an indigene, he is privy to the expectations and experiences of his religious others. Perhaps unlike some immigrant Christians who have few personal ties to the community and simply wish to transform it, he remains aware of the town's deep Muslim roots. However, he suggested also that the growing competition between Muslims and Christians in Ede was also linked to a shift in the numerical relationship between Muslims and Christians:

> There is stiff competition between Muslims and Christians in this town. They compete for limited available resources among themselves. They also desire to dominate each other. This is complemented by the fact that [the] majority of our people, particularly the elderly ones are illiterate and uninformed. This leads to rivalry and bitterness among the majority Muslims and the fast growing Christian population.[47]

If indeed the Christian population of Ede is growing, then the Muslim opposition to Christian public activity is also linked to a sense of encroachment. Given the Christian dominance of the education sector in Ede, the Muslim fear of Christian infringement on their own community is also clearly noticeable in debates about schools and education.

---

[45] This claim is however refuted by some Muslims in Ede who accuse Christians of refusing to rent their properties (houses or shops) to Muslims in some parts of new areas in Ede. These include Mr Raimi Fasasi, trader. 27 November 2013. Timi Market, Ede; Mrs Rafatu A. Amoo. 28 November 2013. Total Market area, Ede; and *Alhaji* R.O. Gbadamosi, retired teacher. 28 November 2013. Akoda compound, Ede.

[46] Interview with Professor (Revd) Joseph Abiodun Ilori, former President of Nigerian Baptist Theological Seminary, Ogbomoso and Proprietor of Ilori International Group of Schools. 5 December 2013. Ilori International Group of Schools, Ede.

[47] *Ibid.*

Schools, Religious Education and the *Hijab*

European Christian missionaries were the first agents of Western education in Nigeria when they established the first primary and post-primary schools in Nigeria in the 1840s and 1850s, often to aid proselytisation.[48] It was only in 1899 that, in response to allegations by the Muslim community in Lagos that the missionaries were using their schools to convert Muslim children to Christianity, the colonial government established the first secular (government) primary school in Lagos.[49] However, the colonial takeover and regulation of schools in the twentieth century did not fundamentally alter the Christian dominance of the education sector in Nigeria, which persisted throughout the colonial period.

Following the end of the civil war in 1967–70, the Federal Military Government under General Yakubu Gowon enabled the takeover of schools from missionary bodies in Nigeria in order to reduce tension between different Nigerian constituencies.[50] Gowon's policy was implemented differently in different states, but most Yoruba-speaking states in Nigeria officially introduced Islamic Religious Knowledge (IRK) alongside Christian Religious Knowledge (CRK), as subjects for Muslim and Christian pupils respectively, in the curricula of government schools. Since this period, organised Muslim communities in most Yoruba towns have demanded the incorporation of Islamic studies in school curricula for Muslim children.

Today, all government-owned (former) Baptist schools in Ede retain a predominantly Baptist and Christian teaching staff, but they also have at least one teacher of Islamic Religious Knowledge responsible for instructing Muslim children at least once a week. Conversely, the government-owned (former) Muslim schools in the town, such as Ede Muslim Grammar School and Bamigbaye Memorial Grammar School, employ a teacher of CRK for their Christian students.[51] It is important to add that even some of the privately owned Christian schools in Ede employ the services of teachers of Islamic Religious Knowledge to instruct Muslim children in their schools to retain

---

[48] See S. Osoba and A. Fajana, 'Educational and social development during the twentieth century', *Groundwork of Nigeria History*, ed. O. Ikime (Ibadan: Heinemann Educational Books, 1980), pp. 570–600: 571.

[49] A.B. Fafunwa, *History of Education in Nigeria* (Ibadan: NPS Educational, 1977), pp. 91–5.

[50] See for instance, C. Akomolafe, 'A comparative study of principals' administrative effectiveness in public and private secondary schools in Ekiti State, Nigeria', *Journal of Education and Practice* 3 (2012), 39–45: 39; and N.A. Nwagwu, 'The state take-over of schools in Nigeria: A controversy', *Journal of Educational Administration* 17 (1979), 75–86.

[51] Interview with Mr Raimi Fasasi, trader. 27 November 2013. Timi Market, Ede.

and attract Muslim pupils from a town with a preponderant population of Muslims.[52]

But despite the general compliance with the government directives and widespread popular expectations, the teaching of IRK in Ede's Christian schools is resented by some members of staff. Especially in schools where the church contributes significantly to the running of the school, staff continue to be employed in line with the former religious identity of the school. As a result, many staff members see themselves as defined by their religious commitment rather than their employment at a government-owned school. This is the case in many of Ede's Baptist schools. Outlining the point of view held by many Baptist, and indeed Christian, teachers, a respondent explained,

> the imposition of the teaching of Islamic Religious Knowledge on Baptist Schools is a major challenge. Imposition of *hijab* on students at Baptist schools is also a problem. Similarly, there is also the refusal to teach Christian Religious Knowledge in Muslim schools in Ede.[53]

This comment illuminates some of the reasons for Christian resentment in greater detail. As in Christian schools, staff at Muslim schools can be reluctant to offer religious education in the other monotheist religion. The respondent's complaint about the Muslim refusal to offer Christian education refers to an expectation of reciprocity in the accommodation of the religious other that is perceived to be unmet. As several Christian private schools offer Islamic Religious Education, this respondent clearly understands reciprocity between Islam and Christianity as consisting of the same level of commitment from Muslim and Christian private schools. However, not all Muslims would agree with this particular view of reciprocity. Indeed, many Muslims would argue that as Christians still dominate the education sector, they also still have a relative advantage. According to them, full reciprocity, i.e. the teaching of Christian Religious Knowledge by Muslim private schools, should only be expected once the overall playing field is level. Thus, different perceptions of what constitutes reciprocity mean that both Muslims and Christians can feel that the other side's educational expectations and practices leave them at a disadvantage.

Equally importantly, the response above raises the issue of dress codes in schools. It should perhaps be added that in the past, Muslim girls at Christian schools were not allowed to wear a *hijab*. However, many Ede Muslims have

---

[52] Oral information from our local guide in Ede, Mr Yusuf Sikiru Abiona, indigene of Ede and Part IV student of History at Obafemi Awolowo University. 15 July 2013.
[53] Questionnaire responses from Deacon Z.A. Oke, retired teacher and clergy at First Baptist Church, Oke-Apaso, Ede. July 2013. First Baptist Church, Oke-Apaso, Ede.

become increasingly convinced of the benefit of following an explicitly Islamic dress code, and in particular many parents insist that their daughters should wear a *hijab*. At least in principle, *hijabs* can now be worn by female students in government-owned schools. But like the former owners of the town's land, the old owners and leaders of modern institutions like Christian schools feel that they should still be able to play a role in their use, especially if they continue to contribute to them financially. Thus many Christian staff at government-owned Christian and Baptist schools in Ede consider the wearing of the *hijab* in their school an infringement on the collective identity of their institution.

Following this logic, many private Christian schools insist that *hijab*-wearing Muslim girls take off their headscarves at the school gates and attend school without an open display of their religious otherness. Aware of the dissatisfaction with the limited provisions for wearing *hijab* at Christian private schools, Muslim educational entrepreneurs have established private Muslim nurseries, and primary and secondary schools in Ede. Examples of these include An-Nuur Nursery and Primary School, Islamic Comprehensive College, and Al-Fareed International College, among others.[54] The establishment of these new Islamic schools has partly addressed the problems emanating from the controversy surrounding of the wearing of *hijab* by female Muslim students.

However, in 2013 a reclassification and merger of schools by the administration of Osun State under Governor Aregbesola once again resuscitated the argument over school dress codes in many towns and villages across the state. In Ede, most schools affected by this reorganisation are not schools previously established by missionary or religious bodies but community schools which have both Muslim and Christian pupils in their enrolments.[55] However, perceiving a reorganisation of educational provision as a threat to the integrity of Christian schools, the Baptist Church in Osun State is taking steps to ensure that the legacies of the founding fathers of the churches and schools are not eclipsed through the new education policy of the state government.[56]

Overall, the level of disagreement and debate about religious education and appropriate school dress codes illustrates that formal education remains an important issue for Muslim–Christian relations. As many schools remain open to students irrespective of religion, they remain important places of Muslim–Christian encounter and engagement. However, as a place of encounter, the

---

[54] *Ibid.*
[55] Interview with *Alhaji* R.O. Gbadamosi, retired teacher. 28 November 2013. Akoda compound, Ede.
[56] Interview with Professor (Revd) Joseph Abiodun Ilori, former President of Nigerian Baptist Theological Seminary, Ogbomoso and Proprietor of Ilori International Group of Schools. 5 December 2013. Ilori International Group of Schools, Ede.

educational landscape is still shaped by the dominance of Christians, which is understood by many Christians as conveying ownership over the practices surrounding education. This can be seen as threatening by many Muslims who consider schools the main space of contestation over the religious identity of the next generation.

Conclusion and Outlook: Everyday Encounters between Christians, Muslims and Traditionalists

Despite the underlying tensions between Muslims and Christians over land ownership, tenancy and education, most Christians in Ede have personal and everyday relationships with religious others, especially Muslims. Citizens of Ede normally participate in social activities like naming ceremonies, funeral outings, housewarmings and birthday celebrations of members of other religions. People simply share the joys of childbirth, building of new houses, funeral ceremonies, birthday celebrations and other social festivities irrespective of their different religious affiliations. While some Islamic and Christian groups, such as the Tablighi Jamaat and Muslim Students Society (MSSN) discussed in chapter 6, or the Deeper Life Bible Church, discourage the participation of their members in these events, this is not the case for the Baptist Church. In the Baptist Church, the general practice is that individual discretion is upheld in attending events organised by Muslims and people of other religious faiths. This would normally depend on the kind of relationship between them and the celebrants, i.e. depending on whether the relationship is based on filial or kinship duties, residential or work and business obligations, friendship, etc.[57]

Religious festivals are another means of inter-religious interactions in Ede between Christians, Muslims and adherents of traditional religions. The Baptist Mission in Ede does not prevent its members from visiting Muslims during festivals like *Eid al-Adha* (*Iléyá*, or the celebration of Ibrahim's willingness to sacrifice Ishmael) and *Eid al-Fitr* (the celebration of completion of Ramadan), and it encourages and welcomes Muslim friends, family members and acquaintances to celebrate with their Baptist hosts during Christmas, Easter or other Christian celebrations. But although the Baptist community in Ede maintains cordial relationships with people of all faiths, including traditional religious worshippers in the town,[58] it officially forbids any form of

---

[57] Questionnaire responses from Mr Philip Adebayo Jolaoye, retired media practitioner. July 2013. First Baptist Church, Oke-Apaso, Ede.
[58] Questionnaire responses from Reverend G.J. Oladele, clergy, Oore Ofe Baptist Church. July 2013. Oke-Gada, Ede.

intimate involvement in traditional religious practices associated with deities such as Ògún, Ṣàngó and Òsun.[59]

Just as many Muslims permit their sons to get married to females of other faiths provided the woman is ready to embrace Islam, Baptists also approve of Christian males getting married to non-Christian women. The expectation is that in such marriages, the women would eventually become Christians. However, the general feeling in Ede is that more converts are won from Islam to Christianity through inter-faith marriages. While this has been a major concern for Ede Muslims over the years, it means that members of the Baptist Church are in practice often quite accepting when their female members marry Muslims. Some Baptists however hold that it is better to get married to people of the same faith to avoid family frictions and religious differences (see also chapter 11).[60]

Other methods of preaching Christianity by the Baptists in Ede include regular revivals and outreach programmes as well as 'crusades' in strategic places within Ede and the outlying villages as well as radio and television programmes. Night vigils, monthly public evangelism, and annual general open-air services are other means through which the Baptists in Ede preach the gospel to both Christians and non-Christians in Ede.[61] However, in contrast to the crusade of Dag Heward Mills in 2011, which, as discussed in the previous chapter, led to strong disagreement in the town, a respondent noted that in the Baptist Church, 'the gospel is preached with moderation and much caution to avoid violence and confrontation'.[62]

Religious competition and rivalry between Muslims and Christians in Ede also surrounded the establishment of two Christian universities on Ede's outskirts in the past decade. However, none of these conflicts has turned violent

---

[59] Questionnaire responses from Deacon Z.A. Oke, retired teacher and clergy at First Baptist Church. July 2013. Oke-Apaso, Ede; and Reverend (Dr) M.A. Alabi, clergy, First Baptist Church. July 2013. Oke-Apaso, Ede.

[60] Professor (Revd) Joseph Abiodun Ilori belongs to this category of people. His position is that interfaith marriage is not encouraged and that it is better to remain unmarried than to be married to a partner of other faith, since it is not compulsory to get married biblically.

[61] A collection of questionnaire responses from the five Baptist clergies in Ede namely: Mr Ogunwale Sunday Olufunsho, clergy, Mercyland Baptist Church. July 2013. Elerin, Sabo Road, Ede; Mr Philip Adebayo Jolaoye, retired media practitioner. July 2013. First Baptist Church, Oke-Apaso, Ede; Deacon Z.A. Oke, retired teacher and clergy at First Baptist Church. July 2013. Oke-Apaso, Ede; Reverend G.J. Oladele, clergy, Oore Ofe Baptist Church. July 2013. Oke-Gada, Ede; and Reverend (Dr) M.A. Alabi, clergy, First Baptist Church. July 2013. Oke-Apaso, Ede.

[62] Responses from Mr Philip Adebayo Jolaoye, retired media practitioner. July 2013. First Baptist Church, Oke-Apaso, Ede.

thanks to the intervention of the *Tìmì* and the traditional and religious elites of Ede. On a positive note, the religious competition between Muslim and Christian groups in Ede has even resulted in developmental progress in the town. To check the Christian dominance of educational and healthcare institutions, Muslim groups have established Islamic schools, hospitals, libraries and other social facilities in Ede. Moreover, after the Christian Adeleke University and the Redeemer's University came to Ede, a proposed Islamic University known as Hijrah University has now been sited in the town (Map 2).

In the context of religious competition, people of different religions also advertise their religion through everyday activities. However, reflecting the different histories and local roots of their religions, Muslims and Christians seem to follow slightly different strategies. While Muslims often assert the importance of Islam though local notions concerning the control of land, compounds, houses and public spaces, Christians often rely on individual generosity. Some Christians, for example, see their willingness to rent out rooms to Muslim tenants (as discussed above) as a form of missionary activity because they believe that the favour of renting out their room to Muslims may show them the beauty of Christianity. They also believe that the daily encounter with Christianity will eventually win the tenants' souls for Christ. A respondent noted that, 'Christian landlords do give Muslim tenants freedom and relate well with them so that they can be wooed to Christ.'[63]

As in Muslim–Christian marriages, these practices reflect the belief of many Christians that in a direct encounter between Islam and Christianity, Christianity will be the more attractive religion. However, the association of tolerance with religious competition also implies that tolerance itself can be used competitively. In Ede, and indeed most Yoruba towns, toleration itself has its own appeal: while Ede's Christians rely on the tolerance of the predominantly Muslim townspeople, they assert their moral and spiritual superiority by exceeding their hosts in tolerance.

While it is difficult to confirm the putative growth of Christianity conclusively for Ede, the agreement of both Muslims and Christians in Ede on the fact that the number of Christians in the town is growing, as well as the findings discussed in chapter 11, suggest that this perception is correct. If this is indeed the case, it will be interesting to see what such demographic change will mean not only for Muslim–Christian relations but also for the relationship between Christianity and the structures that shape the social and political life of the town.

---

[63] Questionnaire responses from Mr Ogunwale Sunday Olufunsho, clergy, Mercyland Baptist Church. July 2013. Elerin, Sabo Road, Ede.

CHAPTER 8

Freedom and Control: Islam and Christianity at the Federal Polytechnic

Akin Iwilade and Oladipo Fadayomi

Like many ostensibly secular institutions in Nigeria, the Federal Polytechnic of Ede is a space that is in reality highly contested between two religions: Islam and Christianity. The institution operates within a predominantly Muslim town, but a large proportion of its staff and students are Christian. In the educational space of the Federal Polytechnic, religious contestation is often expressed through truth-claiming rhetoric from different sides. However, there is a strong commitment within the institution to ensure that such claims do not lead to conflict. A senior member of staff in the institution explained that, 'a Christian will tell you that [...] what I believe is supreme, a Muslim will also say [...] what I believe is supreme, but what is important is how you pursue these claims'.[1]

The role of religious rhetoric in shaping the construction of the other in educational contexts has been given some attention in the literature.[2] Aware of the potential problems associated with intense competition, the leadership of the Federal Polytechnic has taken an active approach towards preventing conflict by controlling both Muslim and Christian activities through integration into the institutional hierarchy. This chapter explores the forms of religious coexistence and tolerance produced by this institutionalised incorporation of Islam and Christianity at the Federal Polytechnic.

Reflecting local ideas of authority in relation to the ownership of social and physical space, the leadership of the Federal Polytechnic has established clear

---

[1] Interview with O. Adeleke, Deputy Registrar, Academics. 19 January 2013. Federal Polytechnic, Ede.
[2] See for instance P. Omoluabi, 'The psychosocial bases of violence, cultism and religious fanaticism in Nigerian tertiary institutions', *Citadels of Violence: A CDHR Publication on the State of the Campuses of Nigerian Tertiary Institutions*, ed. J. Ogunye, S. Jegede and J. Akinsola (Lagos: CDHR, 1999); E. Obadare, 'White-collar fundamentalism: Interrogating youth religiosity on Nigerian university campuses', *Journal of Modern African Studies* 45:4 (2007), 517–37.

rules for the management of the mutually exclusive claims of Muslims and Christians on campus. In line with more generally held ideas about religious neutrality as equal treatment or at least a lack of disadvantage (see chapters 2 and 3), the institution conceives of Muslims and Christians as equal counterparts linked into the university hierarchy in parallel ways. All Muslim and Christian groups and individuals are automatically part of a community associated with their respective religion and led by university staff. Thus the institution both creates cohesive Muslim and Christian communities and maintains control over their activities. In this context, good relations, and indeed tolerance, between Muslims and Christians are based on the premise that Islam and Christianity are equivalent religions with internally cohesive practices and clearly circumscribed boundaries. The absence of Muslim–Christian conflict from the campus of the Federal Polytechnic suggests that the treatment of Islam and Christianity as religious equals has had a positive impact on inter-religious relations. Institutionalised tolerance was achieved by turning both Islam and Christianity into primary instruments for maintaining order on campus.

In addition to confirming Muslim and Christian groups as equal, their incorporation into the Federal Polytechnic's hierarchy also enforces their cohesion. This internal cohesion, however, contributes to intra-religious pressures, especially in the case of Islam, where doctrinal differences between some groups are significant. The establishment of a single hierarchical Islamic community within the Federal Polytechnic led to the only religious conflict that has affected the Federal Polytechnic of Ede, between members of the Ahmadiyya and the Muslim Students' Society of Nigeria (MSSN). While conflict may have been encouraged by student links to religious institutions beyond the Federal Polytechnic, it also led to an even closer collaboration between educational authorities and religious leaders as the conflict was resolved, largely confirming existing practices of the institutionalisation of religion on the campus. The way this conflict was resolved illustrates that the competing claims of different religious communities operating on the campus of Ede's Federal Polytechnic are only validated insofar as they conform to a particular model of authority, in which knowledge claims based on interpretations of the Bible or Qur'an conform to the categories of religion defined within the Federal Polytechnic and the surrounding community. Individual claims are continually modified to ensure mutual (and intra-religious) solidarity and tolerance.

While the institutional control and management of Muslim and Christian activity prevents excessive competition and feelings of marginalisation among religious groups and individuals, it also means that the vast majority of students are primarily identified by their religion. As a result, extra-curricular forms of activity and mobilisation that are not primarily associated with religion are accorded only secondary importance, and students for whom religion is not a primary interest feel excluded from the forms of mutual recognition and validation associated with religious organisation. While students are not actively prevented from holding non-religious values and mobilising along secular lines, the nature of the Federal Polytechnic's investment into the management of religious competition means that the universalising ethic that underpins higher education – understood here to mean the ideas of freedom, liberty and openness that ideally govern the intellectual and physical space of institutions of higher learning – is both challenged and upheld. The Federal Polytechnic's processes of religious control thus emphasise the importance and equity of Islam and Christianity, but also marginalise those students with interests that are largely unrelated to religion. Therefore, the production of tolerance on the basis of religious equality within the Federal Polytechnic gradually blurs the distinction between religion and secular intellectualism.

Religion in the Public Sphere: The Power of Unity

As Ibrahim notes, religion today is a product of modernity as well as a response to it.[3] Rather than withering away under a secular modernity, the expansion of the religious sphere in Nigeria has largely been driven by global processes of modernisation, including migration, the globalised media, urbanisation and education. Religion is, in this context, a response to the economic marginalisation and social exclusion that have been a consequence of neoliberal economic policies in Africa. Recognising the importance of religion in making sense of social change, Habermas notes that, 'religious movements process the radical changes in social structure and cultural dissynchronies, which under conditions of an accelerated or failing modernisation, the individual may experience as a sense of being uprooted'.[4]

In Nigeria, the impact of economic hardship and the emergence of new forms of associational life in the 1980s are closely linked,[5] and the rise of self-help groups in urban centres was a direct implication of the imposition of structural

---

[3] J. Ibrahim, 'Civil society, religion and democracy in contemporary Africa', *Civil Society and Authoritarianism in the Third World*, ed. B. Beckman, E. Hanson and A. Sjorgen (Stockholm: Stockholm University, PODSU, 2001), pp. 183–95: 185.
[4] J. Habermas, 'Religion in the public sphere', *European Journal of Philosophy* 14:1 (2006), 1–25: 1.
[5] A. Olukoshi, 'Associational life', *Transition Without End: Nigerian Politics and Civil Society under Babangida*, ed. L. Diamond, A. Kirk-Green and O. Oyediran (Ibadan: Vintage Press, 1996), pp. 450–76.

adjustment.[6] Subsidy-cutting initiatives forced ordinary people to seek help in informal associations designed to help them make sense of the bewildering economic and social challenges they faced. Many charismatic religious movements began to expand around this time, offering their members spiritual as well as worldly techniques to prepare for an increasingly insecure future. This process was especially noticeable in institutions of higher education.

Since the colonial period, there has been a tension between the modernising ethos and the expression of religious fervour and fundamentalism in Nigeria.[7] As most schools were linked to missionary churches, education and religion were often closely entwined. While there are a larger number of ostensibly secular state schools and Islamic schools today, religious fervour frequently gives meaning to the social anomie, uncertainties and frustrations that underpin institutions that have been long underfunded. Faith helps young people make sense of unpredictable term dates, poor facilities, sometimes unqualified faculty, endemic sexual harassment and arbitrary and unjust institutional decisions. It also helps them to prepare – in a way – for a very uncertain post-university life where good grades do not necessarily guarantee jobs, and much is dependent on patronage and, sometimes, sheer luck.

It is therefore not surprising that the decay in university infrastructure during the 1980s coincided with the rise of religious (particularly Christian) charismatic and fundamentalist movements in these institutions. These charismatic movements within higher education institutions fed into the later emergence of Pentecostal and revivalist churches within the wider society. Marshall traces the emergence of Pentecostalism to the 'interdenominational student groups of the newly formed Nigerian universities'.[8] Similar evidence

---

[6] This argument resonates with many other analysts of civil society and/or the private sphere in Nigeria, e.g. U. Ohachenu, 'Learning from below: Indigenous non governmental grass root organizations in governance and democratization', *Governance and Democratization in Nigeria*, ed. O. Dele, K. Soremekun and A. Williams (Lagos: Spectrum, 1995), pp. 111–29; A Ninalowo, 'Specifications on trade unionism: Democratization and contradictory realities', *Governance and Democratization in Nigeria*, ed. O. Dele, K. Soremekun and A. Williams (Lagos: Spectrum, 1995), pp. 147–65; E. Osaghae, 'The role of civil society in consolidating democracy: An African comparative perspective', *Africa Insight* 27:1 (1997), 15–23.

[7] We are conceptualising fundamentalism here not in the pejorative sense used by the security and political establishment, but to refer to what Obadare describes as 'a combative defence of the literal "truth" of a religious text': Obadare, 'White-collar fundamentalism', p. 520. This, according to Giddens, is 'the use of ritual truth to deny dialogue actively': A. Giddens and C. Pierson, *Conversations with Anthony Giddens: Making Sense of Modernity* (Cambridge: Polity Press, 1998), p. 330.

[8] R. Marshall, 'Power in the name of Jesus', *Review of African Political Economy* 52 (1991), 21–37: 22.

has been provided for the emergence of violent fundamentalist Islamist movements such as El ZakZaky's Shiite movement in the 1980s and 1990s in northern Nigeria, which grew out of Muslim students' societies in the Ahmadu Bello University, Zaria.[9] The current Boko Haram insurgency also appears to have been partly inspired by a number of young students in northern Nigerian institutions.[10] In south-west Nigeria, Muslim groups that were increasingly active on university campuses include the Muslim Students Society of Nigeria (MSSN), and more recently charismatic Muslim groups like NASFAT that operate under the MSSN's umbrella.

But in addition to providing meaning, religion is also a means by which Nigerians access, challenge and retain power in educational institutions. In societies like Nigeria, where political institutions struggle to claim legitimacy, and where economic hardship alienates large swathes of the population from the formal economy and politics, recourse to the sacred is a critical part of navigating the geographies of exclusion. As noted by Ellis and ter Haar, in many African countries 'religious discourse can be seen as an attempted remedy [of institutional breakdown] by means of a reordering of power'.[11] Deeply embedded in the discourses about power and dominance, religion has become an important tool in higher education institutions in Nigeria and the Federal Polytechnic Ede.

The appropriation of religion for shaping power relationships has also involved the framing of specific social spaces of inclusion and exclusion in south-west Nigeria. Given the Christian missionary roots of the Nigerian education system, religion's role in constructing insider and outsider identities within post-colonial education is part of a long and complex historical process that can only be explored in part here. From its beginnings, Christian-cum-Western education had an exclusionary character in which many outsiders were forced to become insiders (by converting) if they wanted to improve their life chances through education.[12] But the apparent contingency of Christianity and modernity in colonial education also affirmed the value of Muslim communal organisation, as this has enabled a competing investment into educa-

---

[9] A. Adesoji, 'The Boko Haram uprising and Islamic revivalism in Nigeria', *Africa Spectrum* 45:2 (2010), 95–108.

[10] R. Loimeier, 'Boko Haram: The development of a militant religious movement in Nigeria', *Africa Spectrum* 47:2–3 (2012), 137–55.

[11] S. Ellis and G. ter Haar, 'Religion and politics in Sub-Saharan Africa', *The Journal of Modern African Studies* 36:2 (1998), 175–201: 176.

[12] See also T. Biedelman, *Colonial Evangelism: A Socio-Historical Study of an East African Mission at the Grassroots* (Bloomington: Indiana University Press, 1982); K. Lord, 'Implicit religion: A contemporary theory for the relationships between religion, state and society', *Journal of Contemporary Religion* 23:1 (2008), 33–46.

tional catch-up in many localities. Given the close association of education with either one or the other world religions, the context of higher education today provides interesting insights into the tensions between religion and the apparently secular nature of state-funded educational institutions.

'Even though there is Freedom of Religion, there has to be Control': Faith, Order and Identity in the Federal Polytechnic, Ede

Even though indigenous religious practices remain important for some sections of the population, most citizens of Ede publicly consider themselves either Muslim or Christian. Islam is more intricately connected to Ede's pre-colonial history than Christianity and has been the religion of power since then.[13] However, Christianity has also maintained a large and growing presence, especially since the 1980s, a period roughly coinciding with the Pentecostal boom in Nigeria.

Ede's Polytechnic, established by the Federal Government in 1992, was a key entry point of Pentecostal Christianity into the town. One reason for this is that it quickly became one of the core drivers of migration into the town. Along with the Nigerian army barracks and Adeleke University, the polytechnic is one of the most obvious sources of non-indigene migration – among both staff and students – to the town. In studies of the impact of the presence of federal establishments on towns like Ede, it has been show that migration is often driven by the tendency of federal establishments to seek to be representative of the general national population.[14]

This desire for representativeness means that an institution like the Federal Polytechnic Ede draws its students and staff from a wide geographical area covering much of south-western Nigeria, and has a large and growing population from other regions of the country. As a result, religious debates and practices – including those of charismatic Christian groups – from larger urban centres are easily shared and adopted. Thus the Federal Polytechnic, including the areas of the town that house its staff and students, draws to the town of Ede patterns of religious activity associated with the regional centres of population, such as Lagos and Ibadan.

Reflecting national as well as regional competition between Muslims and Christians, space on campus is contested between the two dominant religions of Islam and Christianity. Faced with a political economy in which formal

---

[13] S. Oyeweso, *Ede in Yoruba History* (Lagos: Multi Vision Publishing House, 2002), pp. 77–107.
[14] See for example F. Egwaikhide, V. Isumonah and O. Ayodele, *Federal Presence in Nigeria: The 'Sung' and 'Unsung' Basis for Ethnic Grievance* (Dakar: CODESRIA, 2009).

education apparently has little value, revivalist versions of Christianity, and to a lesser degree, reformist Islam, appeal to both staff and students of the polytechnic. For many groups and individuals, heightened forms of religious practice and self-fashioning provide an alternative form of existence to that seemingly offered by a state that is increasingly perceived as corrupt.

However, competition also exists between denominations and sects within the world religions. While denominations of one religion may profess similar central ideas, they nonetheless congregate and interact within sometimes mutually exclusive social structures. A good example of this would be Pentecostal Christian groups of the Deeper Life Bible Church and the Mountain of Fire and Miracles. Both denominations discourage their members from social interactions outside the group, even with fellow Christians who do not accept the strict interpretations of the scripture that such groups believe is essential to making the claim to being 'Born Again'. As will be described in more detail below, such attempts at distance from other groups also exist among the polytechnic's Muslim groups. As a result, the polytechnic is, like most institutions in southwest Nigeria, shaped by a complex landscape of religious competition.

While in other parts of Nigeria this religious competition has led to increasing religious conflict, eventually spilling from university environments to wider politics, this has not been the case in the Yoruba-speaking states and institutions. This lack of conflict reflects many different aspects of the Yoruba historical experience, including the nature of the local encounter with Islam and Christianity. But one important aspect of this degree of local tolerance is the relationship of both world religions to the social order. As in many locations, both Islam and Christianity are deliberately associated with communities and, in this form, included in the organisation of the Ede Polytechnic. Religious tolerance is thus institutionalised through shared inclusion, on largely equal conditions, into campus life.

One reason for this is that both Christianity and Islam are understood as affirming important local values that predate the arrival of the world religions. This notion creates and affirms mutual respect between the religions, and it also constitutes religious practice as always implicitly authoritative. Very few Yoruba-speakers would challenge the understanding that both Islam and Christianity affirm the importance of deference to elders. It is generally understood that students who are religious and active within a religious social framework are far more likely to respect institutional authority. It is the recognition of this fact that explains the importance assigned to religion within the Ede polytechnic. As Ayo Adebesin, the polytechnic's Chaplain, puts it:

> If an academic institution doesn't create an environment to further the cause of religious activities, you will find out that some students might be left drifting

and they could begin to get into groups that are unethical; so the religious act [sic] help to maintain some level of decorum.[15]

The understanding that religiosity is linked to respect for authority is shared by the Muslim staff of the polytechnic. Creating institutional structures to monitor and organise religion is seen by staff to be critical to the maintenance of peace and harmony on the campus.[16] The Deputy Imam of the institution, who is also a member of academic staff in the Department of Environmental Studies, pointed out that 'even though there is freedom of religion, there has to be control'. He explained that he saw it as part of his community's job to 'X-ray the performance of our students'. In this context, performance was seen not only as an academic issue but as the general behaviour and attitude towards authority of the students.[17]

The widespread belief that both world religions are associated with the maintenance of societal values and institutional order justifies their inclusion into the institutional hierarchy. Understood as inextricably linked to the ethos of higher education, Islam and Christianity are not only associated with the personal spirituality of individual students, but they also form the focal points for collective organisation, inclusion and, ultimately, social control. Given the institutionalised nature of Muslim–Christian relations, mutual tolerance too could be understood as reflecting the institution's authority.

Religion and Institutional Order in the Federal Polytechnic Ede

Religion influences the downward flow of power and authority both directly (through formal processes) and in subtle and ideological ways. These structures of power are key to the way in which religion guarantees, or at least influences, the peaceful coexistence of different groups within the institution. At the same time religious structures of authority also constitute familiar patterns of control that appear embedded in broader generational relations.

Within the polytechnic, both Muslims and Christians are represented centrally as a group, even though many staff members maintain primary links to outside religious sects and denominations. Given that almost all members of the polytechnic belong to one or the other group, this ensures an inclusive form of representation (which, in the case of university staff, exists independently from union politics). But the inclusive arrangement also prevents the

---

[15] Interview with Ayo Adebesin, Polytechnic Chaplain. 4 February 2013. Federal Polytechnic, Ede.
[16] *Ibid.*
[17] Interview with I. Yusuff Adeyemi, Deputy Imam and staff, Department of Environmental Studies. 4 February 2013. Federal Polytechnic, Ede.

emergence of breakaway factions that might challenge the status quo of the institution through radical reinterpretations of sacred texts or practices. In this way, individual disagreements linked to religion are subject to corporate control, both within and between religions.

On campus, a Chaplain and a Chief Imam have the authority to represent the interests of the two world religions, and to ensure order within the communities by mediating disputes and promoting cohesion.[18] As noted by the Deputy Registrar of Student Affairs, these central authorities are responsible for all the sub-groups within the broad religion. This broadens the reach of the central polytechnic authorities, and while it allows all (monotheist) groups and sects to 'gain more recognition', the sub-groups remain firmly within the broader umbrella of Islam or Christianity. Of course this arrangement does not prevent inter-religious connections between Muslim and Christian groups, or disagreement within them, but it represents a conscious effort to subsume disagreement to broader 'religious' interests and thus to ensure representation by religion.[19]

The Chief Imam and Chaplain are members of staff of the polytechnic. They are employed primarily in secular positions as either academics or administrators. Nonetheless, they often adjudicate in disputes and provide general spiritual and organisational leadership. However, according to virtually all respondents, one of their key roles is to keep an eye on students. For instance, all groups have to route their applications for registration on campus through either the Polytechnic Chaplain or Chief Imam as appropriate.[20] These authorities then recommend the student religious organisations to the Division of Student Affairs for registration. Without this recommendation (and registration), faith-based student organisations are not allowed to operate on the campus, and neither can they use the institution's facilities. Initial registration is later followed by annual registration exercises in which the authorities audit financial accounts and are able to refuse registration to any group deemed to have overtly challenged the authorities or created threats to peace on campus.[21] In this way, students' religious groups are, from the beginning, subjected to the guidance of a religious authority rather than a secular institutional framework.

---

[18] Interview with Adeniyi Adenusi, Deputy Registrar, Student Affairs. 4 February 2013. Federal Polytechnic, Ede.

[19] *Ibid.*

[20] Interview with Ayo Adebesin, Polytechnic Chaplain. 19 December 2012. Federal Polytechnic, Ede.

[21] Interview with Ayo Adebesin, Polytechnic Chaplain. 4 February 2013. Federal Polytechnic, Ede.

Neither the Imam nor the Chaplain has used their power assertively to exclude groups from operation on campus. Exclusion is usually only temporary, and only with regard to administrative lapses such as the failure to submit audited accounts. Indeed, the authorities have never banned a faith-based student organisation or denied registration for reasons other than minor administrative lapses. The lack of conflict in this area suggests a high degree of compliance from the students' religious organisations, who – in line with the religiously imbued values of respect for authority and elders – consider themselves an important and even constitutive part of the polytechnic and its community. But equally importantly, it reflects the fact that the institution's policy really aims for the prevention of breakaway groups that might draw on religious rhetoric to become a focal point of critique and resistance.

This form of organisation confirms and legitimises the existing hierarchies within the institution, which are also reflected within the Muslim and the Christian communities, headed by the Chief Imam and Chaplain respectively. In either group, students are not allowed to hold leadership positions beyond a certain level. Indeed, they are obliged to respect as well as have periodic consultations with senior members of staff who also double as religious leaders. By embedding religious rhetoric within broader generational relations that promote respect for elders as well as within the more formal institutional ethos of respect for the constituted authority of polytechnic administration and faculty, the organisation of the religious communities at the polytechnic also legitimises everyday non-religious relations of power on campus, whether they are intellectual challenges or those associated with inadequate facilities and services. In this way, the world religions play an important role in the legitimisation of differences between staff and students.

However, within the different religious communities, different forms of hierarchy reflect the different historical experiences of Islam and Christianity. While the Christian community is organised following a representative system, all Muslims groups at the polytechnic are part of the umbrella organisation of the Muslim Students' Society of Nigeria (MSSN). This particular role of the MSSN, usually associated with a reformist interpretation of Islam, also draws other Muslim groups into particular forms of control. The implications of the enforced internal cohesion, especially of the institution's Muslims, are illuminated by a closer look at the 2002 conflict between the MSSN and the Ahmadiyya at Ede Polytechnic.

A Religious Conflict and its Resolution

During the year 2002, mutual irritations between the MSSN and the Ahmadiyya centred on the way in which members of these groups responded to ideological or theological differences – an issue that had caused division in Ede in the past (see chapter 5). Several Muslim groups were exercised by what they perceived as the Ahmadiyya's lack of orthodoxy, and responded to the perceived threat of a division within the Muslim community by highlighting what they saw as the flawed beliefs and practices of the group in public speeches and sermons. In response to the public embarrassment doled out by those Muslim preachers critical of the Ahmadiyya, Ahmadi students sought greater distance from their fellow Muslims, and many Muslims allegedly observed that the Ahmadis did not pray behind a non-Ahmadi, an implicit insult.

Following these tensions, the leaders of the Ahmadiyya group on campus lobbied for a registration independent of the Muslim Students' Society of Nigeria (the umbrella organisation of all Muslim student organisations registered at the polytechnic). When members of the MSSN discovered that the Ahmadi students had approached the school management over the launch an association of a separate Ahmadiyyah Muslim Student Association (AMSA), some of them forcibly interrupted an Ahmadiyya meeting and violent conflict ensued.[22]

But rather than deal with the conflict through the institution's established disciplinary process, the authorities opted to allow the religious leadership to handle the crisis.[23] Investigating a violent conflict on the campus of the – ostensibly secular – polytechnic, the committee set up to mediate in this crisis was made up solely of Muslims, including of course the polytechnic's Chief Imam as well as other leaders from the polytechnic and beyond. The involvement of a large number of Muslim leaders from the town of Ede, most of whom did however have a link to the institution, helped settle matters among the two groups. The assumption underlying this decision was that students were more likely to obey their religious leaders, and that any recommendations or measures adopted by staff but not legitimised by their Islamic leadership would lead to resistance. [24]

The Muslim leaders involved in settling the case included Mr Adeniyi Adenusi, a leading Ahmadi in Ede and currently a Deputy Registrar in the Division of Student Affairs at the polytechnic. Mr Adenusi is a former president of the Ahmadiyya Group in Osun State, a member of the Elders Council of the Ahmadiyya in Osun State and one of the leading Islamic figures in Ede town. As a member of staff at the polytechnic, he was also a patron of the student-led

---

[22] Interview with *Alhaji* Daud Olukayode Akindele, Senior Accountant, Osun State Local Government Service Commission. 10 July 2014. Federal Polytechnic, Ede.
[23] *Ibid.*
[24] Interview with Ayo Adebesin, Polytechnic Chaplain. 4 February 2013. Federal Polytechnic, Ede.

Ahmadiyya Group on campus. While Mr Adenusi's prominent position in the polytechnic may have encouraged the leaders of the student Ahmadiyya group to demand greater independence from the mainstream Muslim community,[25] he was now able to play a crucial role in the reconciliation of the two groups. His presence ensured that the resolution of the conflict between the MSSN and the Ahmadiyya was considered acceptable by the Ahmadi students.

As a first step, the committee members provided medical treatment for the injured and ensured that no lives were lost. After deliberations on the issue at hand, the committee insisted that each group respect each other's autonomy and freedom. No punitive measures were adopted but the group considered to have been the aggressor, the MSSN, had to tender apologies to the Ahmadiyya. In turn the Ahmadi students were asked to remain within the fold of the MSSN.

It is unclear if the institution would have been able to limit the violence so quickly if it had not relied on the influence of religious figures on the campus. Given the preponderance of Christians among the staff, a secular engagement with the conflict may have created more resistance among the groups concerned. Moreover, it is likely that the institution would have decided on some punishment of the aggressor, in which case bitterness and resentment might have contributed to future conflicts. Given the religious bias among the staff of the polytechnic, most of whom are Christians, such bitterness might possibly even have led to disagreements between Muslims and Christians.

As it were, the resolution of the 2002 conflict was successful because almost all those involved accepted the authority of those involved in its mediation to restore the institutional order. But the fact that a violent intra-Muslim conflict was resolved only by Muslim religious leaders, and not by the secular authorities or necessarily following the guidelines of the federal institution, also indicates the precariousness of secular institutional authority in this setting. Moreover, both the nature of the conflict and its resolution point to the importance of the polytechnic's internal religious structures for the creation of religious communities. As in the town of Ede, the polytechnic and its Chief Imam are strongly invested both in maintaining the unity of the Muslim community despite significant ideological differences. Incidentally, the post-conflict agreement that there was to be only one Muslim community has been used as a precedent in debates by other Muslim groups striving for independence from the MSSN. It is on the basis of this consensus between the town's and the polytechnic's Islamic leaders that the Muslim community's relationship with non-Muslims is then facilitated.

---

[25] Interview with *Alhaji* Daud Olukayode Akindele, Senior Accountant, Osun State Local Government Service Commission. 10 July 2014. Federal Polytechnic, Ede.

Student Views on Religion and Social Control

The importance of religion for the sustenance of institutional order is further illustrated by the fact that when tensions of a non-religious nature emerged, such as student protests over the high level of fees and the lack of basic infrastructure in November 2001, the polytechnic relied on its religious leaders to call for calm. In this situation, the leaders issued general statements appealing for calm and understanding, but they also made direct overtures to students known to them in the hope that they would exert a calming influence on student opinion.

But as the processes and procedures in place at the Federal Polytechnic Ede affirm values about respect and authority that are legitimised by both world religions, they also exclude those members of staff and those students whose identification with religion is less intense or direct.[26] While such individuals are rather unlikely to be directly involved in religious conflicts, they are however more distant from the existing structures of authority, because these are so strongly shaped by the agency of religious leaders and religiously justified processes of social control. Especially for students who do not identify intensely with religion, this means a greater degree of alienation from the polytechnic overall.

A survey we carried out among a small number of randomly selected students of the polytechnic found that students who do not hold strong religious convictions, or who do not consider religious participation as part of their routine activities on campus, were less content with the institution than more religious students.[27] Not only were they less satisfied than their more intensely religious peers with way the institution was run, but they were also less happy with the kind of infrastructure provided by the authorities. Irrespective of gender and religion, less intensely religious students were also found to be more likely than others to challenge authority and disregard rules.

Interestingly, these students also appeared to be aware of the way in which the politics of the institution affected their experience of higher education. Thus they were more likely than their peers to have participated in student protests, and also more likely to be members of explicitly political student groups like the Committee for the Defense of Human Rights (CDHR). There are no easy answers as to what the causative relationship could be in this regard, but there was a strong correlation between a religious identity of low intensity and

---

[26] As very few people in Nigeria identify as non-religious, this is not a useful category for the purpose of this argument.

[27] The survey was of 30 randomly selected students of the polytechnic, 16 of whom were Christian and 14 Muslim.

distrust for authority. The findings therefore suggest that religious participation plays an important role both in shaping students' perceptions of authority in the institution, as well as their engagement with this authority.

Indeed, one respondent pointed out that one of the reasons there has been peace on campus is that many members of staff are 'either pastors or alfas'. He suggested that because of this high level of faith and leadership, polytechnic staff is able to meet students within social structures that predispose them to deference.[28] This is not to suggest that students interact with staff in their religious capacity at all times, but rather that religious channels have become important complements to formal ways of interaction and that they have been appropriated by the authorities for the purpose of maintaining public order. As illustrated by a quote from a student not routinely active in religious activities on campus, this leaves many students who are unhappy with the status quo feeling further disenfranchised:

> The religious leaders in Ede Poly are not different from the people causing all our problems. They just use Jesus to blackmail us into submission. Those student 'Born Agains' [sic] are so docile. They think all our problems can be solved through prayer. I'm a Christian but I don't like the way these fellowships follow the authority like sheep. They are a part of the problem.[29]

It is unlikely that the tendency of students outside routine religious activities to distrust or challenge authority is simply a coincidence. The more critical attitudes of less intensely religious students may of course be a response to a specific experience or feature of power within the polytechnic. However, this was not indicated in our survey. It therefore seems more likely that it is a general critical engagement with the declared intention of the institution's religious authorities to maintain control over students, and thus the way in which religion is bound up with the social order of the institution. Of course the critical attitude of the less intensely religious students is also likely to reflect the fact that in a society increasingly shaped by religious discourse and debate, it does take some rebelliousness to refrain from the intense and routine engagement with religious activities. This may have reduced the psychological barriers to challenging authority within the institution.

---

[28] Interview with Ayo Adebesin. Ayo Adebesin, Polytechnic Chaplain. 19 January 2013. Federal Polytechnic, Ede.

[29] Interview with anonymous students of the Federal Polytechnic, Ede. 16 January 2013. Federal Polytechnic, Ede.

Conclusion

By discussing the integration of religious structures of control into the functioning of the ostensibly secular Ede polytechnic, this chapter has explored the role of religion in Nigerian institutions of higher learning. We argued that the contemporary importance of both Islam and Christianity reflects the decline of secular notions of postmodernity, and especially the Nigerian crisis heralded by structural adjustment and political decline from the 1980s onwards. For many people in and engaged with education, faith – and hope – bridged the growing gap between educational attainment and expected life chances.

In Yoruba society, with its traditionally high regard for education, these issues were perceived as relevant by both Muslims and Christians, and both Islam and Christianity were understood as effective and legitimate forces in the personal struggle for meaning and success. Adopting the community model of religious organisation historically established by Yoruba Muslims for both religions, the Ede polytechnic also rooted itself in the wider community. While the polytechnic's Chief Imam mirrors the activities of the town's Chief Imam in providing leadership to a community made up of very diverse groups, the Chaplain provides cohesion to the mostly non-indigenous interests of the institution's Christians. In this way, the religious communities of the polytechnic are linked both to the acceptance of the institution in the host community, and to the success of the institution more generally.

But by producing a set-up that manages religious difference through channels of formal and informal control, the religious politics of the polytechnic emphasise the unifying nature of compliance with the existing structures of authority. Of course the institutionalisation of religious tolerance and intra-religious unity cannot prevent all conflict, but even when existing structures have been challenged, mediation along representative lines has always been successful in preventing the emergence of stand-alone groups that might provide a basis for more general challenges to the institution.

As religion has become a significant factor in shaping power and relations of dominance and control, intense religious engagement tends to indicate consent to the existing relations of power – and vice versa. As even apparently non-religious conflicts are also resolved through recourse to religion, less intensely religious students are less invested into the institution's structures of power, pointing to an implicit but important tension between the institution's existence as an apparently secular centre of knowledge production, and its reliance on religion as a means of social control.

CHAPTER 9

Religious Accommodation in Two Generations of the Adeleke Family

Ibikunle H. Tijani

In the context of Ede's religiously plural society, religious identification is both a producer and a product of distinct corporate and social identities. But religion is not reduced to its social function: it offers a wide range of visions of personal and community success. While some visions focus on exclusive religious practice, the general emphasis on good relations between members of different religions confirms that at the personal level, religious difference is not necessarily understood as a problem. This chapter explores the way in which the embrace of both Islam and Christianity has shaped the life of one of Ede's prominent families. It illustrates in what way religious plurality – rather than a privileging of one or the other religion – also contains the possibility for the creation of successful institutions, and by implication offers a vision of the town as religiously diverse rather than explicitly Muslim.

While the study of Yoruba kinship and family relations has a long history, it has traditionally focused on the lineage system, the relative importance of the paternal lineage and the importance of shared residence in compounds for the making of family ties.[1] Though a close study of politics in any Yoruba town illustrates that family ties are often fluid and dependent on context,[2] Karin Barber has emphasised the importance of human agency, and creativity, in

---

[1] See P. Lloyd, 'The Yoruba lineage', *Africa* 25 (1955), 235–51; W.B. Schwab, 'Kinship and lineage among the Yoruba', *Africa* 25:4 (1955), 352–74; and D.R. Bender, 'Agnatic or cognatic? A re-evaluation of Ondo descent', *MAN* 1:5 (1970), 71–87 for a discussion of descent groups. See J.S. Eades, *The Yoruba Today* (Cambridge: Cambridge University Press, 1980), pp. 37–64 on the importance of compounds in structuring family life.

[2] See, for example, J.D.Y. Peel, *Ijeshas and Nigerians: The Incorporation of a Yoruba Kingdom 1890s–1970s* (Cambridge: Cambridge University Press, 1983); I. Nolte, *Obafemi Awolowo and the Making of Remo: The Local Politics of a Nigerian Nationalist* (Edinburgh: Edinburgh University Press for the International Africa Institute, 2009).

the drawing and redrawing of family boundaries.[3] Equally, the importance of Islam in confirming and mediating kinship has been discussed in chapter 5. And while several authors note that many Yoruba extended families have both Muslim and Christian members (as well as often some traditionalists), the way in which family relationships may be structured in order to transcend religious difference has not been investigated in detail.

Most extended families in Ede are shaped by the control of family elders and leaders over practices within the house and, especially in the old or indigenous Ede families, the control of practices in the compound. House or compound rules apply to direct descendants of the family, wives married into it and tenants on family land, although they may do so in different degrees. As described in chapter 5, most of Ede's families and compounds have a strong religious identity, and the elders' control of compound and family affairs includes the limitation of religious activities that challenge their religion. However, even in the predominantly Muslim setting of Ede, there are also families where acceptance and mutual agreement between practitioners of different religions are strongly emphasised. But while close relationships between members of different religions often rely on tolerance, they can also encourage forms of multiple practice and participation that transcend religious boundaries.

This is the case in Ede's prominent Adeleke family, which is the subject of this chapter. The origin of the Adeleke family's mixed Muslim–Christian identity is linked to the education and travel beyond Ede of one of its members, Raji Ayoola Adeleke, who eventually married a Christian Igbo-speaker, Esther Nnena Adeleke. In their married life, and their relationships with other family and community members, they have emphasised the productive collaboration of Muslims and Christians for the greater good. Retaining close family ties as well as good links with the town of Ede, their descendants have taken on both Muslim and Christian identities. While some family members only tolerate difference, others welcome and celebrate it, including through the practice of the other religion.

While exploring the way in which family relationships can tolerate or transcend Muslim–Christian differences in everyday life, the chapter reflects on the personal and religious journeys of individual family members. Exploring the interplay between religious identification and different forms of contribution to the community of Ede (and beyond), this chapter also suggests that the unity displayed by the Adeleke family offers an interesting political vision. This vision does not challenge the town's predominantly Muslim identity, but

---

[3] K. Barber, *I Could Speak until Tomorrow: Oriki, Women and the Past in a Yoruba Town* (Edinburgh: Edinburgh University Press, 1991).

its emphasis on belonging irrespective of religion also offers a view of the town in which religion appears as secondary to other forms of solidarity.

A Colonial Marriage: Raji Ayoola Adeleke and Esther Nnena Adeleke (née Akpara)

Born into a Muslim family indigenous to Ede, Raji Ayoola Adeleke's official birthday was 27 December 1923. However, some believe that Raji was at least eighty years old when he died in 1993, hence he might have been born in any year between 1900 and 1913.[4] He was the first child of Adeleke, the son of Onigbinde from the Oluronbi family, a prominent family then considered to belong to the town's elite. Ayoka, the biological mother of Raji, died upon giving birth to the infant boy. She had been a member of the highly respected Jagun family and a daughter of Iyalode Anke whose father Ogunran was reputed to be one of the first leaders and settlers in Ede. Iyalode Anke was also a rich trader and merchant of dyed cloth, kola nut, palm oil and other goods. Iyalode Anke is reputed to have owned slaves and servants during her time, and it is said that during the nineteenth century, her influence stretched to political relations between Ede, Ibadan and the rebuilt capital of Oyo.[5]

After his mother's death, Raji was raised by Iyalode Anke and his father Adeleke. Adeleke later had six children from other wives, but by all accounts he considered his first-born, Raji, an outstanding son.[6] Like many Muslim children, Raji first attended to his Qur'anic education. He was tutored by Alfa Muyibi, a migrant from Nupe, at Gege Qur'anic School, where he completed his training in or before 1930. Raji then married his first wife Muniratu who bore him three children: Sidikatu, Mulikat and Rasheed.

But because Raji's father cherished Western education, he encouraged his son to enrol at St. Peter's Primary School, Ede in addition to his Qur'anic education. Raji was therefore a young adult when he began school, but he spent only three years there (1935–8) before studying at Ibadan Grammar School (1939–43). Raji then earned a registered nurse certificate from the Nursing School of the University College of Ibadan in 1947.[7] As a popular student in

---

[4] Such disagreements about age reflect the patchiness of the colonial state at the beginning of the twentieth century. However, as the registration of births and deaths in Nigeria remains inconsistent, many Nigerians still have an official birth date that does not necessarily correspond with local or family knowledge.
[5] A study of Iyalode Anke's life and times would be an interesting contribution to the study of women in nineteenth-century Yorubaland.
[6] Interviews with Hon. Sunday Ogundiji. 9 December 2013. Adeleke University, Ede; and Coach Alao Adediran. 9 December 2013. Adeleke University, Ede.
[7] Interview with Sidikatu Adeleke. 29 May 2012. Ede.

Ibadan, Raji courted friendship from Muslims and Christians alike. Upon graduation, Raji was employed as a clerk in the Medical Service Unit of the colonial government and began practical training as a nurse.

Owing to the scarcity of schools in northern Nigeria, the majority of employees during this period were southern Nigerians from the Eastern and Western Provinces. Moreover, the predominance of mission schools in the south meant that Nigerians in the colonial medical service were largely Christians.[8] It was during his training as a nurse that Raji met Esther Nnena Akpara, a Christian and an Igbo, who later became his wife. When Raji completed his nursing education in 1944 he was posted to the colonial Government Hospital, Abakaliki in the Eastern Province. Esther, who was also employed by the colonial state, followed him.

Esther Nnena Akpara began life in 1925 as the only child of her parents, who were indigenes of Akwete in Abia State. Both her parents were successful traders who wanted their child to enjoy the benefits of Western education. After her primary school education, Esther enrolled at Mary Haney Memorial Girls' School, Oron in January 1940. She completed her secondary education in 1944 and proceeded to the Saint Louis Teaching Hospital, Aba, where she became a nurse and midwife in 1947. Esther was a devout Christian who, for most of her adult life, was a member of the Cherubim and Seraphim Church, a church founded by Moses Orimolade Tunolase in 1925 and which emphasises prayer and healing.

The bond between Raji and Esther, across ethnic and religious divides, seems to have been one of respect and love for humanity, liberalism and the family. For those who knew Raji, his marriage to Esther, a religious and ethnic outsider to his own family and community, was not really that remarkable. As well as having an accommodating nature, Raji was primarily concerned with how well people were living, and not what their differences might be. While working as a nurse, Raji became an early member of the Union of Nurses (later the Nigerian Union of Nurses, NUN), which was founded in 1948. His active engagement as a unionist helped Raji participate in the protest against the state of African employees in the colonial medical service. He was a successful and popular union leader and was eventually elected vice chairman of the United Labour Congress.[9]

---

[8] See H.I. Tijani, 'Dr. Abubakar Ibiyinka Olorun-Nimbe: Islam, Western modernity and the making of a twentieth century elite', *Actors and Institutions in the Development of Islam in Lagos State*, ed. S. Oyeweso and M. Raheemson (Ibadan: Matrixcy Books, 2013), pp. 536–62.

[9] H.I. Tijani, *Union Education in Nigeria: Labor, Empire, and Decolonization since 1945* (Basingstoke: Palgrave Macmillan, 2012), pp. 99–102.

Raji's concern for the welfare of others was shared by Esther, although in slightly different form. According to her children at least, her life was shaped by 'her unwavering devotion to the wellbeing of others and [her] unquestionable love for Christ'.[10] Both Raji and Esther believed that differences in religious affiliation should not limit the human capacity to interact with one another in society. Perhaps in reflection of the optimism of the decade leading up to independence, Raji and Esther set out to build a society that was more just and equitable than in the past.

Esther's concern for Raji's wellbeing was shaped by her own wifely responsibilities. Esther was unwavering in her Christian faith and she introduced her children and stepchildren (all of whom were nominally Muslims in reflection of their father's religion) to Christianity. But despite her strong commitment to Christianity, she fully accepted the responsibilities that fell to her as the wife of a Muslim. This included the preparation of meals before sunrise and after sunset during the month of Ramadan, the Muslim fasting period. According to Modupe Adeleke-Sanni, Esther and Raji's daughter, 'for thirty days and nights [during Ramadan], [Esther] dutifully cooked and woke up, even before sunrise, to ensure that [her husband's] meals and other needs [were] met'.[11]

Esther's support of her husband's Islamic fasting reflected a widely held ideal, according to which a wife's duties include spiritual as well as emotional and physical support. While this expectation often means that women convert upon marriage, the conversion of Christian wives is not strictly required in Islam and marriages between Muslim men and Christian women are possible. However, such marriages do not reduce the duty of Muslim men to fulfil their religious obligations, such as fasting during Ramadan. Esther's preparedness to fulfil Islamic duties in addition to her own Christian practice illustrates the importance of female religious agency for all interfaith marriages (see chapter 10). It also illustrates that the transcendence or mediation of religious boundaries, often by women, plays an important role in enabling interfaith relations at the personal level.

A Political Career and its Social Commitments

As a government employee and prominent union leader in the late colonial and early postcolonial period, Raji had returned to Ede and he had become one of its most distinguished sons by the early 1970s. In the preparations for the return to civilian government in 1979, Esther and Raji supported the Unity

---

[10] M. Adeleke-Sanni, 'Tribute', *Celebration of Life, Funeral and Outing Services* (n.p., 2009), p. 29.

[11] Interview with Mrs Modupe Adeleke-Sanni. October 2012. Ede.

Party of Nigeria (UPN). This party was led by the Yoruba politician Obafemi Awolowo, who had dominated politics in the Western Region and the Yoruba-speaking states (and beyond) since the early 1950s.[12]

There was a lot of grassroots support for Raji, who eventually stood as a senator on the UPN platform. Part of his popularity derived from the fact that Raji had a natural disposition that many people associated with ọbaship and chieftaincy. He courted the friendship of people with different religious backgrounds, and although he was a Muslim, Raji was not averse to participating in either Christian or traditional religious ceremonies. In this way, he showed his respect for Islam and Christianity, as well as the traditional religion in the town.[13] Unlike some parents in families shaped by a dominant religion, Raji also encouraged his children to marry the men and women they chose, irrespective of their faith.[14] This form of sociability convinced many people that, given greater responsibilities, Raji would not discriminate against any groups on the basis of religion or other forms of social difference.

When the National Electoral Commission (NEC) announced the results of Osun II Senatorial District in 1979, people were not surprised that he won the Senatorial seat.[15] As a senator, Raji strongly supported the UPN's programmes and principles, such as free education, free medical service, social security plans for the elderly and a sound economy based on exploring other resources beyond oil. However, after the military takeover in 1983, he was disillusioned with politics and retired to assume the role of chairman of his own company, Pacific Farms, in Ede. Both Christians and Muslims were employed by Pacific Farms, and Raji encouraged religious harmony and respect for Islam and Christianity, as well as the traditional religion, in all his political and business endeavours.

As a highly successful son of Ede, Raji was offered several chieftaincy titles. In recognition of his role and status within the Muslim Nawar-Ud-Deen Society, to which he belonged, and the Muslim community in general, Raji was made the *Balógun Àdínnì* of Edeland, which is a powerful title given to a non-clerical leader of the Muslim community. However, Raji was also offered traditional chieftaincy titles. Despite the great honour they confer, such titles are sometimes refused by Muslims because of their association

---

[12] Nolte, *Obafemi Awolowo and the Making of Remo*.
[13] Interviews with Hon. Sunday Ogundiji. 9 December 2013. Adeleke University, Ede; and Coach Alao Adediran. 9 December 2013. Adeleke University, Ede.
[14] *Ibid.*
[15] According to NEC report, Raji Ayoola Adeleke, UPN had a total vote of 115,368, while candidates of other parties had the following votes: A. Durosomi, NPN – 19,559; O. Fabode GNPP – 2,001; and E. Oyebola NPP – 453.

with the pre-Islamic past. However, as a patriot of his hometown, Raji proudly accepted the titles offered to him. Raji Adeleke first became the *Aṣípa* of Ede, a traditional title usually given to a man very close to the *Tìmì* of Ede, and later he was even made the *Balógun* of Edeland. Because of Ede's history and prowess in warfare, the *Balógun* is the second-in-command to the *Tìmì* in the traditional governance of the town.

As both the *Aṣípa* and the *Balógun* titles carry some traditional responsibilities, they illustrate Raji's achievements and his contribution to his hometown, but also his willingness to assert his chiefly authority in a manner similar to the *ọba*: by transcending religious difference. As a Muslim man married to a Christian woman and holding traditional titles, Raji projected authority and power through his ability to 'stand above' religious division.

Following her husband to Ede, Esther had to adjust to living in a Muslim Yoruba town. She took her move as a challenge to share her faith with its citizens. Drawing on her husband's good relationship with *Tìmì* Tijani Oladokun Oyewusi (1976–2007), she persuaded the *Tìmì* to facilitate the purchase of a piece of land for the building of a Cherubim and Seraphim Church in Ede. While the Cherubim and Seraphim in the town had fewer than 20 members in its early days, Esther was able to draw on the deep local roots of her in-laws to attract both indigenes and strangers living in Ede into her church.[16] Eventually her service to the Cherubim and Seraphim Church would earn her the title 'Senior Mother-in-Israel', which is the highest-ranking title for a female in the order.

At the same time, Esther was expected to fulfil her obligations to her husband's community. As a wife of the *Balógun* of Edeland and a top-level member of the Muslim community, Esther had a responsibility to meet the needs of other members of the town, and this included her in-laws, the Chief Imam and the local Muslim community, and the members of the *ummah* more generally. As a result, she regularly cooked food and provided Ramadan gifts for large numbers of people. In addition, she contributed rams in order to ensure that their distribution to Muslim faithful across Ede town and beyond during the annual Muslim festival of *Iléyá* (also called Eid al-Adha or Eid al-Kabir) could proceed without any rancour.

Esther continued to contribute gifts and time to the Muslim community even after her husband's death in 1993 and only ceased to offer support during Ramadan and *Iléyá* when, at the age of 86 years, she slept in the Lord as a devout Christian on 29 November 2009. The fact that this was widely interpreted as a sign of love and respect for her husband illustrates the unequal expectations of men and women in interfaith marriages more generally: while

---

[16] Interview with Senior Apostle A. Adeleke. October 2012. Ede.

he was admired for his ability to 'accept' his wife's religion, she had to combine, or perhaps straddle, Islamic and Christian practices for the rest of her life in order to be accepted as a 'good' wife in Raji's extended family, and in Ede as a whole.

But if her role as the Christian wife of a Muslim leader was demanding, Esther's engagement with both Islam and Christianity also enabled her to become highly popular, and to lay the foundations of a family that was open towards both Islam and Christianity. While she had joined the Adelekes as a religious outsider, her practice of supporting both religions enabled her both to continue to practise Christianity and to present the virtues of Christianity to Muslims both within and outside of her family.

Community above Religion: Commitment to Community Development in the Second Generation

Raji Adeleke encouraged his wives to have a close relationship, with this stance reflecting both traditional Yoruba values and Raji's general commitment to improving the human condition through solidarity and mutual support. More importantly, he encouraged close bonds between the offspring of both his wives, and both wives cooked for and looked after each other's children. As a result, Esther's children had close knowledge of Islam not only through their father but also through their mother's co-wife. At the same time, Muniratu's children were also brought up by Esther, and thus had a first-hand experience of a lived Christianity that was respectful of Islam, and that reflected widely admired wifely qualities.

Having grown up with a Muslim father and Muslim and Christian mothers, all of Raji Adeleke's children are either Muslims or Christians, though the extended family includes some traditional worshippers. While Muniratu Adeleke's late son Rasheed remained a Muslim, her two daughters became Christians even though both their parents were Muslims. While the conversions to Christianity of these two daughters (Mrs Sidikatu Alao, also known as 'Mama Liberia', and Mrs Mulikatu Akani) also stemmed from deeply personal reasons, it is likely that their childhood knowledge of Christianity, and the particular appeal of Esther's religious practice, made the decision to convert much easier.

Like the late Rasheed Adeleke, Esther's first son *Alhaji* Isiaka Adeleke remained a Muslim. A Senator in 2007–11, Isiaka embarked on a highly successful and ongoing political career, discussed in more detail below. Isiaka's five younger siblings, however, are all Christians. They include Dr Adedeji Tajudeen Adeleke, the founder of the privately owned Adeleke University at Ede's outskirts, as well as Anne Bisi Ojeogwu, Sister Iyabo, Chief (Mrs)

Modupe Adeleke-Sanni and Dr Ademola Nurudeen Adeleke. Thus all of Raji's female children became Christians.

A closer look at the achievements of two of Esther's other children illustrates the different ways in which their religiously mixed upbringing has shaped the lives of the second generation of Adelekes. Raji and Esther's son Adedeji learned from his parents that education is an important aspect of development. When Adedeji was a student at Adventist High School, Ede in 1971–5, his father Raji was delighted when the school principal, Mr Enoch Dare, allowed him to pay Adedeji's tuition at the Adventist High School in instalments.[17] This, perhaps, remained memorable to Adedeji, and education has remained the most significant area of his contribution to society.

Adedeji's enterprises have reflected the Seventh-Day Adventist Church's emphasis on serving both God and humanity, and in his speeches he often stresses the importance of living a humble life.[18] In 1996, Adedeji set up the Springtime Development Foundation (SDF) as a non-profit Non-Governmental Organisation (NGO). The SDF is part of his commitment to the less privileged in the society, and it provides financial support towards educating men and women as well as distributing welfare and relief services.[19] But while Adedeji provides furniture, books and sponsorships for students from Ede, his services to education are not limited to the local community; he has also funded a number of other educational projects in Ile-Ife in Osun State, Ilisan Remo in Ogun State, and in Edo State.

To immortalise the name of his father, Dr Adedeji Tajudeen Adeleke decided in 2011 to provide local access to tertiary education by setting up a private university rooted in the Adventist ethos. Instead of locating the institution in Lagos or any major city in Nigeria, he chose the family hometown, Ede.[20] As the founder of Ede's Adeleke University, he established an explicitly Seventh-Day Adventist institution that nonetheless seeks to contribute to the personal and spiritual development of people of all religious backgrounds. Adedeji explicitly noted that the aim of the university is to 'encourage students to prepare for dynamic and spiritually inspired life of service for humanity within whatever secular occupation they plan to pursue'.[21]

---

[17] Interview with Mrs S. Dare. 22 November 2012. Ede.
[18] Interview with Hon. Sunday Ogundiji. 9 December 2013. Adeleke University, Ede.
[19] Interview with Dr Z. A. Babarinde, chief executive officer, Springtime Development Foundation. October 2012. Ede.
[20] Interview with Professor Dayo Alao, Babcock Consulting. July 2011. Babcock University.
[21] D. Adeleke, 'A speech by Dr Deji Adeleke-Adeleke University, Ede, Osun State, on the inauguration of the Board of Trustees of Adeleke University', *Adeleke University* (n.d.), <http://www.adelekeuniversity.edu.ng/news/?id=1e12f77a-0d13–49ce-a85d-21d9bee97d3f>, accessed 11 December 2013.

Adeleke University is a clearly Christian institution whose staff are expected to attend daily and weekly Christian devotions, which are facilitated by the Seventh-Day Adventist chaplaincy. However, the composition of staff includes Christians of various denominations as well as Muslims, and the university campus includes, unusually for a Christian Higher Education Institution, a mosque for Muslim students. Perhaps inspired by the example of his mother, it seems as if Adedeji Adeleke has embraced the practice of a form of Christianity that validates and acknowledges Islam, even though his university is primarily constituted as a Christian space.

Beyond his Adventist service to humanity, Adedeji also cultivates relationships with people of other religious faiths, both in Ede and beyond. Unlike most Christian universities in Nigeria, Adeleke University makes a mosque available for its Muslim students and staff. In Ede itself, Adedeji interacts freely with prestigious traditional institutions and he enjoys speaking to Muslim clerics. Indeed, his sympathies for Ede's Muslim community are so strong that he donated a significant sum of money towards the completion of the new Ede Central Mosque.[22]

Another of the second generation of Adelekes, Chief Modupe Adeleke-Sanni, has taken on her mother's role as the community's most important Christian supporter of the Muslim community. In the name of the Adeleke family, she distributes an average of five hundred rams during such festivals as *Iléyá* (Eid al-Adha), and she also contributes generously to the successful celebration of Ramadan. Modupe also negotiates religious diversity in a way that is unprecedented by anyone within the family. In addition to her generosity to Ede's Muslims, Modupe fasts during both the Muslim and the Christian fasting periods, thus suggesting that it is possible to bridge the gap between Islam and Christianity through great piety.

Modupe's contributions to the town have been recognised by the *Tìmì* of Ede, who has rewarded her care and love of the community with the title of the *Yèyé* of Edeland, which recognises Modupe as the symbolic mother of all of Ede's citizens. But while the traditional title ostensibly refers to her (stereotypically) female ability to mediate between different groups, Modupe's support of the Muslim community does not reflect marital pressure – it is freely chosen. It is therefore also recognised as a demonstration of strength, and Modupe is sometimes admiringly referred to as the 'Thatcher' of the Adeleke family.

Overall, the second generation of the family – especially Isiaka, Adedeji and Modupe – have continued the philanthropic work of their parents by

---

[22] Interviews with Coach Alao Adediran. 9 December 2013. Adeleke University, Ede; and *Alhaji* Nureni Lawal. 15 December 2013. Oyeweso Street, Ede.

establishing industries and institutions that employ family members, relations and fellow citizens of Ede and Nigeria or train them in skills that empower them to be self-employed.[23] Through these activities, the family provides funding, welfare and job placements for those in need. Following their parents' example, they engage with the Ede community on the basis of its perceived needs, rather than because of religious affiliations.

Like their father, most members of the family engage with religions other than their own in a manner reminiscent of the *ọba*'s role as the head of all religions. This illustrates that the participation in a wide range of religious practices can be part of a more general habitus of power, which is also adopted by leaders and chiefs under the *Tìmì*. It is widely understood not as contradictory or inconsistent, but as a form of morality and generosity of spirit that maps onto the humanitarian activities for which the Adeleke family is known. It is also widely perceived as contributing to the mutual goodwill and understanding between Ede's Muslims and Christians, and as helping – even if just by example – to resolve and prevent religious rifts within the community.

But while the openness of all Adeleke children to members of the other religion is clearly part of the family's political appeal, it also reflects different gendered expectations. Modupe's participation in both Muslim and Christian fasts transforms markers of religious difference into complementary indications of personal piety that resonate with social harmony. Her apparent yielding to different demands resembles practices adopted by women in interfaith marriages (see next chapter), and it subtly contrasts with the approaches of her brothers that highlight their personal autonomy.

Isiaka Adeleke: Political and Religious Flexibility for Ede's Benefit

The political career of *Alhaji* Isiaka Adeleke (Esther and Raji Adeleke's first son) suggests that the ability to accommodate and transcend religious division may also have contributed to Ede's prominent place in local party politics. Isiaka spent his youth in Eastern Nigeria and, having been brought up in a cosmopolitan household, became fluent in Yoruba, Igbo and English. He received his primary and secondary education at Christian schools in Enugu and proceeded to further education at Alafia Institute, Ibadan, before leaving for undergraduate and postgraduate study in the United States. Upon his return from the US, Isiaka invested into local businesses, worked in his

---

[23] Provision of such opportunities is not devoid of contesting issues and 'prebendalism', as in the case of the establishment of Adeleke University in 2011. This aspect of the family history is not covered in this study, neither is the author contemplating researching it. Perhaps younger scholars can research into this in the future.

father's company, Pacific Farms, and began a career as a civil servant at the local government level.

Despite his exposure to Christian educational institutions and his time spent in the United States, Isiaka retained his Muslim identity, while emulating his father's genial and open attitude towards religious others. Like his siblings, he sees beyond religious affiliation in order to relate with everybody in the community,[24] and he employs the services of both Christians and Muslims in his business establishments.

As a leading Muslim of Ede and indeed Osun State, Isiaka Adeleke has sponsored the pilgrimage of many Muslims to Mecca, and he regularly felicitates with the *'ulamā'* (Muslim scholars) during the *Iléyá* festival through such gifts as rams. But he has also demonstrated his willingness to support religious others by regularly contributing to the festivals and activities of traditional worshippers, and by donating goods and money to many of Ede's churches during festivals and harvest ceremonies. Most importantly, Isiaka hosts a monthly Christian prayer meeting of members of the Christian Association of Nigeria (CAN) in his house.[25] Given that CAN is one of the Christian groups that tends to be very vocal in its criticism of Muslims, this illustrates not only Isiaka's ability to bridge religious boundaries but also his active contribution to the ongoing communication between Muslims and Christians in Ede.

Like his sister Modupe, Isiaka has been rewarded for his contribution to the development of the town with traditional titles from the community, which he has proudly accepted. Today, Isiaka is the *Aṣíwájú*, or leader, of Edeland.[26] In this role, Isiaka maintains strong communal ties and emphasises both the role of morality and the importance of the shared cultural heritage in order to transcend religious differences.[27] This is possible at least in part because like many family members, he is able to make friends with a wide range of people,

---

[24] O. Lawal, 'Isiaka Adeleke: The central Issue in Osun politics', *The Sun* (3 July 2013), <http://www.sunnewsonline.com/news/politics/isiaka-adeleke-the-central-issue-in-osun-politics>, accessed 12 December 2013.

[25] Interview with *Alhaji* Adio. 15 December 2013. Oyeweso Street, Ede.

[26] Other communities have also awarded him important titles: he is the *Ọ̀túnba* of Ejigboland, the *Ògánlá* of Ikirunland, the *Jàgùnnà* of Ireeland, *Bàbá Ọba* of Joga Orile, *Aṣípa Atayeṣe* of Ibadan and *Ààrẹ Akáyéjọ* of Erin-Osun.

[27] A description of the Yoruba home is contained in A. Mabogunje, 'The Yoruba home', *ODU* 5 (1985), 28–36. Similarly, early scholars such as Bascom, Lloyd and Schwab have written about the Yoruba people. See W. Bascom 'The principle of seniority in the social structure of the Yoruba', *American Anthropologist* 44 (1942), 37–46; Lloyd, 'The Yoruba lineage'; W. Schwab, 'Continuity and change in the Yoruba lineage System', *New York Academic Science* 96 (1962), 590–605.

including kings, chiefs and professionals as well as artisans, market women and students, both old and young.[28]

However, Isiaka's ability to relate to different religious groups has also been linked to the broad base of political support he enjoys in Ede and Osun state.[29] Drawing on this support, Isiaka Adeleke was elected as the first Executive Governor of Osun State, which had been created out of Oyo State in 1991. Despite the annulment of the 1993 presidential election and the return to military rule later that year, Isiaka – who was not yet 40 at the time – maintained his involvement in politics. During the return to civilian rule in 1999, he joined the People's Democratic Party (PDP), which controlled the central government until its defeat in 2015. On the platform of the PDP, he was elected Senator for the Osun West Senatorial District in 2007–11. As a governor, Isiaka kept an open-door policy, and was seen to be stretching himself both financially and in terms of his time in an effort to attend to the requests emanating from the palace, mosques, churches, schools, factories and offices.[30] Isiaka lost his senatorial seat to the opposition in 2011, reflecting the return of Yoruba opposition politics to south-western Nigeria following the 2007 elections. However, even though he could not return to the Senate he did not lose his influence over Ede politics. The presidential election of that year certainly suggests that he won Ede's votes for the PDP.[31]

In the light of his father's close association with Yoruba opposition politics, there has been some debate about Isiaka Adeleke's decision to join the PDP rather than the opposition. However, his ability to draw on grassroots support has meant that Isiaka has had powerful defenders even among his political opponents. In a speech at the inauguration ceremony of Ede's Adeleke University in February 2012, Rauf Aregbesola, the Governor of Osun State and a member of the then opposition party All Progressives' Congress (APC), argued that Isiaka's commitment to communal development made him an important political leader. Given this appreciation, it is perhaps not surprising that Isiaka Adeleke joined the APC in May 2014, partly in the hope of bringing further development to Ede and Osun State after a confirmation of the APC in the August 2014 elections in the state.[32]

While Isiaka Adeleke's political star is still rising, his successes so far suggest that religious accommodation has served him well in the political arena.

---

[28] O. Oladipo, *The History of Osun State: From Zero to Hero*, Vol. III (Ibadan: Simlad Nigeria Ltd, 2010), p. 231.
[29] Interview with *Alhaji* Nureni Lawal. 15 December 2013. Oyeweso Street, Ede.
[30] *Ibid.*
[31] Lawal, 'Isiaka Adeleke'.
[32] 'Adeleke finally defects to APC', *Nigerian Tribune* (Ibadan, 1 June 2014).

Clearly his refusal to be tied down by religious boundaries has enabled him to build the strong grassroots support on which his career is based. But it is also likely that his strong commitment to subsuming religious difference to the overall development and progress of Ede has enabled Isiaka to approach his political career more flexibly, and to ensure the successful representation of his town by eventually following his father's footsteps in leading Yoruba opposition politics. In this sense, Isiaka's religious openness has been politically productive, suggesting that like traditional leadership, party politics in Yorubaland remains an arena shaped by the importance of multiple religious practice, religious accommodation and mutual recognition.

Everyday Relationships in the Adeleke Family

As the trajectories of Isiaka, Adedeji and Modupe Adeleke suggest, all children of Raji Adeleke have stayed close to each other. Perhaps as a result of their shared experiences in a multi-religious and multilingual home, the descendants of Raji Adeleke, as well as their more distant relations, consider family membership to be more important than other forms of division. Siblings and half-siblings, as well as their mature children, meet regularly to discuss family concerns. As in many Nigerian families, this can involve a redistribution of money or other resources between family members, and is therefore based on the preparedness of wealthier family members to assist their kin. In addition, the Adelekes ensure that all family members have some knowledge of both Christianity and Islam. Thus they meet to celebrate *Iléyá* and the end of Ramadan at the mansion of *Alhaji* Isiaka Adetunji Adeleke, and they also meet to celebrate Christmas Day at the mansion of Dr Adedeji Tajudeen Adeleke.[33]

The Adeleke family is also remarkable for its members' ability and willingness to support one another, irrespective of their differences. The rich in the family habitually come to the aid of the less privileged family members in whatever capacity they can, to help them make ends meet or achieve their pursuits in life.[34] This attitude, which has helped further cement family ties, is not common in many extended families, where the less privileged often only derive a marginal benefit from the wealth of a rich family member. The reluctance to assist others in such families may be linked to religious difference, but more often it reflects strained relationships between the children of different

---

[33] An oral account from Mrs S. Dare notes: the late Pa. Raji required one thing from his children – celebrate Muslim festivals with me. This they did without any reservation whatsoever during his lifetime. There is evidence of continuity since the death of the patriarch. Interview with Mrs S. Dare. 22 November 2012. Ede.

[34] Interview with *Alhaji* Adio. 15 December 2013. Oyeweso Street, Ede.

mothers. Clearly Raji did not encourage such competition and, together with Muniratu and Esther, successfully fostered warm relations between all his children. As Alao Adediran, one of Raji's grandsons through his first wife Muniratu, explains,

> in spite of our religious differences, there is mutual understanding in the family. There is no discrimination. We see ourselves as one. We ate from the same pot. We see ourselves as having only one mother, and we can enter each other's house any time.[35]

Given Raji's political belief in mutual support towards progress, it appears as if the first generation of Adelekes successfully instilled its political values within their family. But if the family was shaped by these political values, it was also bounded by them. Family disagreements are not an unusual occurrence in the extended family system, but to date no conflict in the Adeleke family has involved members of the wider community, not to speak of friends. While this chapter cannot discuss any conflicts within the family, it is known that like other extended families, members of the Adeleke family sometimes disagree with each other. Commonly during such occurrences, people afflicted by grievances invite family friends or community leaders to mediate and resolve their differences. However, the Adeleke family has consistently managed to deal with such disagreements within the family, ensuring that family disagreements stay out of the public domain.[36] A grandson of the family explained that,

> When people look at us in the family, they think we don't have issues against one another. That is not true. We have issues that cause disagreement among us, and we express them in the family. But, the public will hardly know this because we continue to relate with one another like family even when we are fighting. And, we are conscious not to allow outsiders to interfere in our family dispute, and anybody that interferes will not be happy at the end of the day. This is because we have a way of resolving our dispute in a way that would render … intervention useless.[37]

The ability to contain grievances has been helped by the family's adherence to a clear model of leadership, in which authority and respect are accorded the eldest family member in decision-making. In many families there are members who respect the decision of the richest individual in their midst, and existing rifts can deepen when those who agree with the eldest feel increasingly

---

[35] Interview with Coach Alao Adediran. 9 December 2013. Adeleke University, Ede.
[36] Interviews with Hon. Sunday Ogundiji. 9 December 2013. Adeleke University, Ede; and *Alhaji* Nureni Lawal. 15 December 2013. Oyeweso Street, Ede.
[37] Interview with Hon. Sunday Ogundiji. 9 December 2013. Adeleke University, Ede.

estranged from those who believe that wealth bestows the ability to lead a family. Of course within the Adeleke family, Isiaka's prominent status means that relative seniority and the greatest wealth are in the same hands.[38] In the face of disagreements, the existence of clear structures of authority may sometimes make it easier to find a lasting solution.

Beyond Isiaka's clear leadership of the family, however, it is likely that the strong commitment to resolving problems internally has also contributed to the family's prominent position. While Ede is a predominantly Muslim town, most Adeleke family members in the second generation – with the obvious exception of *Alhaji* Isiaka Adeleke – are at least nominally Christians. Moreover, the Adeleke family plays an important political role in Ede's traditional politics even though at least Esther's children could also be considered outsiders on their mother's side. Since much of the popular respect and admiration for the Adeleke family is based on its members' reputed ability to accommodate differences, a public family disagreement – irrespective of the cause – would likely undermine the family's social standing and could even undermine the political influence enjoyed by the family in Ede.

As long as the family is united, family members' solidarity with each other serves both as a template for the community's perception of the family and as an example for the community at large. Yet the silence surrounding the Adelekes' current arrangements makes it more difficult to explore the gendered nature of religious accommodation, especially in the context of marriage and immediate family. But understood both against the clearly formulated concerns about the subversion of Islamic compounds by non-Muslim women (chapter 5) and parental reservations about the interfaith marriages of their daughters (chapter 10), the silence surrounding the religious views of younger women in the Adeleke family illustrates the crucial role of women's agency for the success of marriages and the public life of families and extended families.

In the public realm, the combination of the Adeleke family's social and political success, linked to its members' preparedness to engage positively with individuals from a range of different (religious) backgrounds, presents to others a vision of success through solidarity and unity vis-à-vis the outside. By facilitating close relationships and mutual understanding between people of different religions in Ede, the Adelekes do not challenge the widespread notion of Ede as a Muslim town, and their Muslim members can indeed be seen as validating Islam as the religion of peace. But at the same time, the success of the Adeleke family, clearly linked to its unity and solidarity, implies that beyond tolerance, the willingness to act across religious boundaries that

---

[38] Interview with *Alhaji* Nureni Lawal. 15 December 2013. Oyeweso Street, Ede.

has contributed to making the family great will contribute to the future progress of the town.

This certainly complicates a narrow interpretation of the discussion in chapter 5, which focused on the way in which the family and compound system in Ede helped to entrench Islam. While the present dominance of Islam within local families and compounds and the ongoing association of Christianity with immigrants tends to promote the interest of Muslims over those of Christians, this is clearly not inevitable. Where family ties and compound politics can draw on other forms of solidarity and rely on the support of women, they may also accommodate, or even support, an encounter of Islam and Christianity on more equal terms.

CHAPTER 10

Marrying Out: Gender and Religious Mediation in Interfaith Marriages

Insa Nolte and Tosin Akinjobi[1]

As the example of the Adeleke family illustrates (chapter 9), there are many contexts in Ede where individuals from a variety of backgrounds live and work close to each other, from shared houses, compounds and neighbourhoods to mutual invitations to celebrations and joint business interests. As a result of such everyday interactions, many people have friends from a different religious background, and sometimes such friendship develops into marriage. These religiously mixed marriages – and the challenges associated with their implicit challenge to corporate identities shaped by religion – are the subject of this chapter. Exploring the complex network of religious, gendered and social attitudes and practices that shape interfaith marriages, the chapter illustrates that interfaith marriages are often initially associated with conflict, which appears to give way to mutual tolerance. However, the achievement of this tolerance tends to rely on women's multiple religious practice and mediation of religious difference.

There is no general agreement in the literature on interfaith marriage about what constitutes a difference in religion or faith,[2] but in this chapter we use the

---

[1] The authors wish to acknowledge an unpublished literature review on inter-religious marriage by Nicola Jolly, which provided useful references and contextual data. See N. Jolly, 'Inter-religious marriage: Literature review', unpublished literature review for the 'Knowing Each Other' project (2012). Comments and published references drawing on this review will be clearly marked below.

[2] For some studies a Catholic–Protestant or Shi'a–Sunni marriage may be considered interfaith, whereas others refer to the crossing between religions such as Christian–Muslim or Hindu–Sikh. James Davidson and Tracy Widman use 'interfaith' to refer to any marriage with a non-Catholic, for instance marriage between Catholic and Lutheran Christians: J. Davidson and T. Widman, 'The effect of group size on interfaith marriage among Catholics', *Journal for the Scientific Study of Religion* 41:3 (2002), 397–404. Somnur Vardar includes Sunni–Alevi marriages as inter-religious. See S. Vardar, 'Inter-religious marriage in the Greater Istanbul municipality, Turkey', *Inter-Religious Marriages among Muslims: Negotiating Religious and Social Identity in Family and*

terms 'inter-religious' and 'interfaith' to describe marriages crossing two religions. We include both marriages in which husband and wife have different religions and those in which one partner used to belong to a different religion but has since converted.[3] While statistics in this area are difficult to obtain or non-existent, there seems to be a higher number of interfaith marriages in Ede, and probably in other parts of Yorubaland, than in most parts of Africa[4] or Europe.[5] The survey data discussed in more detail in chapter 11 suggests that between 14 and 20 per cent of marriages in Ede are inter-religious marriages. But despite their high incidence, interfaith marriages are often more difficult than others.

In Ede, an interfaith marriage could mean, for example, a marriage between a Muslim woman and a Christian man, or marriage between a Christian woman and a man who is an adherent of the deity Ṣàngó or another òrìṣà. It is important to note that many people also marry across denominational boundaries, and that proposed marriages between some Muslim or Christian groups or denominations can create as much opposition as marriages between the religions. However, for the purposes of this chapter we will concentrate on marriages between individuals who belong, or belonged, to different religions. Today, most inter-religious marriages are between Muslims and Christians. Very often, plans for marriage between individuals of different religions create consternation or criticism. The role of inter-religious marriage remains hotly debated in Ede's religious communities. As both Muslims and Christians are, these days, divided into competing groups and diverse denominations, conservative sections of both world religions preach against inter-religious marriage. The Tablighi Jamaat Islamic group discussed in chapter 6 and some

---

Community, ed. A. An-na'im (New Delhi: Global Media Publications, 2005), pp. 217–91. See Jolly, 'Inter-religious marriage', p. 1.

[3] We also include one couple where both husband and wife converted, albeit several years apart from each other.

[4] In Senegal, where an increasing number of marriages have been registered since 1988, only 138 registered inter-religious marriages took place in Greater Dakar between 1974 and 2001. C. Bop, 'Inter-religious barriages in Dakar, Thies, and Ziguinchor, Senegal', *Inter-religious Marriages among Muslims: Negotiating Religious and Social Identity in Family and Community*, ed. A. An-na'im (New Delhi: Global Media Publications, 2005), p. 190, cf. Jolly, 'Inter-religious marriage', p. 8.

[5] Voas suggests that while up to 10 per cent of marriages in the UK are religiously mixed, most of these are between a Christian and person with 'no religion/non-stated'. Less than one per cent of the UK Christian population have a spouse from 'other religious groups', including Judaism, Buddhism and Islam. D. Voas, 'The maintenance and transformation of ethnicity: Evidence on mixed partnerships in Britain', *Journal of Ethnic and Migration Studies* 35:9 (2009), 1497–1513: 1501. See Jolly, 'Inter-religious marriage', p. 7.

of the less well-integrated churches in Ede mentioned in chapter 7 strongly discourage interfaith marriage, based on scriptural exegesis and theological reasoning. Other groups, however, are more accepting of the practice.

But in a society shaped by lineage and compound life, marriages are not simply the private affairs of two individuals. For the perception and experience of inter-religious marriage, considerations rooted in everyday expectations about marriage and gender are at least as important as religious injunctions. Drawing both on Qur'anic prescriptions and on local notions that consider men the guardians of women, many of Ede's Muslim families are more reluctant to allow their daughters to marry Christians than vice versa. As a result, many – but by no means all – religiously mixed marriages are unions between Muslim husbands and Christian wives.

Local views about wifely attitudes towards their husbands' religion are expressed in the proverb *èsìn ọkọ ni èsìn iyàwó*, i.e. the husband's religion is the wife's religion. This implies that a woman should adopt, or at least support, the religious practices of her husband, and that she must allow her children to be trained in his religion. As this means that women are more likely to convert in inter-religious marriages, and that their children are likely to have a different faith from the woman's parents, intermarriage is often especially painful for the parents of a woman who fear to 'lose' her to another religion. But equally, a man's parents may fear that his wife will create religious division in the house or compound, because she might use her influence over her children to attract them to her own religion, thus dividing the family in the next generation.

While such fears and objections break up some couples, others overcome the initial opposition of their extended families to achieve stable and happy marriages that are tolerated by both sides of in-laws. For this, the agency of women is crucial. Because a daughter's marriage to a man with another religion is widely seen as challenging the religious authority of her own family, and especially of her father, a woman usually experiences greater rejection than a man when she announces plans for a union across religious boundaries. Reconciliation is often only achieved when a child is expected or born, meaning that in addition to marshalling the psychological and material resources for a separation from her family, a woman must achieve pregnancy in order to pursue her marriage against familial pressure.

Once an inter-religious marriage is confirmed by childbirth and parental recognition, women's roles as links, or mediators, between two different families are extended to include the conciliation of different religions. Even when a woman does not convert, she usually supports the religious activities of her husband and his family, thus acquiring knowledge about important practices and celebrations of his religion. At the same time, certainly during visits to their father's houses and compounds, even women who have converted to their husband's religion participate in the religious activities of their natal families. As a result, the success of interfaith marriages often reflects the willingness and ability of women to participate in different religious practices, and to mediate between different religious attitudes and practices.

The role of women as religious mediators between their natal and their marital families often also shapes religious practice elsewhere. In times of need, and especially when ensuring her own wellbeing or that of her husband and children, a woman may draw on practices from both religions to ask for divine mercy or favour. Therefore familiarity with more than one religion contributes in important ways to the female experience of religion and spiritual power.

Muslim and Christian Views on Inter-Religious Marriage

While a wide range of views exist on inter-religious marriage in Ede, there are both Muslims and Christians who frown at interfaith marriages. Christians often draw on St Paul's message in 2 Corinthians 6:14 to justify their objection to the practice.[6] This objection is founded on the difficulty inherent in the joining of people with divergent core beliefs and values. However, other Christians believe that anyone has the freedom to choose her or his partner for life. This attitude is found most often among those who may be identified as liberal Christians and is based on 1 Corinthians 7:14.[7]

In some of Ede's older churches, missionary practices of the early twentieth century are retained; in particular, men married outside the faith are not permitted to take communion. However, today most mission churches simply discourage those in mixed marriages from taking an active part in the activities and development of the institutions beyond attending. In a perhaps more realistic departure from these forms of social control, many Pentecostal churches allow members married outside the faith to register as workers and even to take part in the other related activities of the church, such as evangelism. This could be seen as a way of motivating believers in mixed marriages to win the souls of their partners.

---

[6] 'Be ye not unequally yoked together with unbelievers: for what fellowship hath righteousness with unrighteousness? and what communion hath light with darkness?' Translation from the King James Authorised Version of the Bible.

[7] 'For the unbelieving husband is sanctified by the wife, and the unbelieving wife is sanctified by the husband: else were your children unclean; but now are they holy.' Translation from the King James Authorised Version of the Bible.

In the Islamic community, the rules for marriage to non-Muslims resonate with local ideas, in the sense that it is more acceptable for a man to marry outside his religion than for a woman. Based on Qur'anic verses dealing with inter-religious marriage, including Surah 60:10[8] and Surah 2:221,[9] it is expected that both men and women marry Muslims, but men may also marry women of other monotheist religions, such as Christianity. It is generally accepted that no specific authorisation is given in the Qur'an for women to marry outside the faith, and it is assumed that a Muslim woman married to a non-Muslim would have to take on the religion of her husband.

Couples in interfaith marriages often experience pressure from their respective faith communities to ensure that these are the dominant religion in the family. All religious communities believe that parents are accountable for their children and that it is better for the family if the children share one religion. Religious leaders in the husband's community may attempt to discourage him from allowing his wife to practise a different religion, while the community of the wife may look for means and ways of cajoling the man into following his wife to the church (or, less frequently, the mosque) in the attempt to win his soul, and by implication those of the children. In this way they try to hold both mother and father to account for the children's religious future. As a result, the decision to enter into an inter-religious marriage is rarely easy.

---

[8] 'O you who believe! When believing women come to you as emigrants, examine them, Allah knows best as to their Faith, then if you ascertain that they are true believers, send them not back to the disbelievers, they are not lawful (wives) for the disbelievers nor are the disbelievers lawful (husbands) for them. But give the disbelievers that (amount of money) which they have spent [as their Mahr] to them. And there will be no sin on you to marry them if you have paid their Mahr to them. Likewise hold not the disbelieving women as wives, and ask for (the return of) that which you have spent (as Mahr) and let them (the disbelievers, etc.) ask back for that which they have spent. That is the Judgement of Allah. He judges between you. And Allah is All-Knowing, All-Wise.' Translation by Muhammad Taqi-ud-Din Al-Hilali and Muhammad Muhsin Khan, *Noble Quran* (n.d.), <http://www.noblequran.com/translation/>, accessed 15 June 2014.

[9] 'And do not marry Al-Mushrikat (idolatresses, etc.) till they believe (worship Allah Alone). And indeed a slave woman who believes is better than a (free) Mushrikah (idolatress, etc.), even though she pleases you. And give not (your daughters) in marriage to Al-Mushrikun till they believe (in Allah Alone) and verily, a believing slave is better than a (free) Mushrik (idolater, etc.), even though he pleases you. Those (Al-Mushrikun) invite you to the Fire, but Allah invites (you) to Paradise and Forgiveness by His Leave, and makes His *Ayat* (proofs, evidences, verses, lessons, signs, revelations, etc.) clear to mankind that they may remember.' Translation by Muhammad Taqi-ud-Din Al-Hilali and Muhammad Muhsin Khan, *Noble Quran* (n.d.), <http://www.noblequran.com/translation/>, accessed 15 June 2014.

Kinship and Marriage

Apart from pressure by their religious communities, most inter-religious couples also have to confront the objections of friends and families. Because of the expectation of wifely support for their husbands' practices, parental interventions are most frequently directed at women. For some women, the thought of this degree of confrontation with elders and parents is unbearable. A female Muslim interviewee explained to us that she received a marriage proposal from a Christian man but rejected it because her parents would not have allowed her to proceed with the marriage.[10] But families also intervene if they fear that their male children are contemplating a marriage outside the bounds of their own religion. In the case of Mr Ahmed, an electrician who had wanted to marry a Christian girl he met in Lagos in the 1970s, it was the intervention of an aunt by marriage that ended a relationship that crossed both religious and sub-ethnic boundaries. He remembered:

> My uncle's wife whom I stayed with sent a message to my people at home that if care is not taken, the way I'm going in Lagos I will eventually marry a Christian, in fact the girl is an Ijebu girl.[11] They [the family in Ede] said that will not be possible. So I married a Muslim woman [to] which they all gave their consent.[12]

In some cases of inter-religious friendship, considerations about the future of a mixed-religious family were paramount. Alfa Mikail Hamzat Adekilekun works as a missioner for a prominent Islamic group in Ede, and he is a member of the historically Muslim Imole compound discussed earlier in this book. However, as a popular and easy-going person, he also enjoys the friendship of non-Muslims, and at one time in his life he developed a close friendship with a Christian girl. He explained,

> It is not as if I had no Christian girlfriend, I had them. In fact, there was a particular one... [But] I said that cannot be possible because that can cause enmity, because one of the gains of our marriage are children. And when these children start coming, are we going to divide the family, that one child will follow the mother's religion, and the other should follow that of the father? I will not be able to unite the family as I want. It will be as if I want to destroy what I used my hand to build![13]

---

[10] Interview with *Alhaja* Monsurat Abiola. 1 June 2012. Alapa Street, Ede
[11] The Ijebu are a mixed Muslim–Christian sub-group of the Yoruba whose relationship with Oyo was occasionally difficult.
[12] Interview with Mr Rafiu Debo Yusuf (Baba Adekilekun). 31 May 2012. Poly Road, Ede.
[13] Interview with Alfa Mikail Hamzat Adekilekun. 17 May 2012. Imole Compound, Ede.

In Alfa Adekilekun's case, is likely that his membership of a compound that emphasises a distinctly Islamic identity influenced his decision not to consider marriage to a Christian girlfriend. As illustrated in chapter 5, in explicitly Muslim compounds like Imole the congruence between social and religious boundaries is close, and those who leave the fold of Islam often lose their *de facto* membership of the compound and extended family. In such a compound, the children of a Christian mother, should they choose to follow her religion, might find themselves without the many benefits of membership that would otherwise have been their birthright.

However, while the concern with avoiding interfaith marriage reflects strong religious commitment, it also exposes a fault line within Ede's Muslim community. Alluding to Qur'anic injunctions, several of the survey respondents pointed out that inter-religious marriage is not unIslamic per se, saying that 'Islam allows us to marry someone of another religion',[14] or, more precisely, 'Islam allows [inter-religious marriage] if she were a Christian only. Also, the lady should be very knowledgeable in her religion and knows what my religion teaches.'[15] The conflict between the demands of kinship and the Qur'anic provision for intermarriage between Muslim men and Christian women was summed up – in a somewhat nostalgic reference to a better past in which women were less assertive – by Ede's Chief Imam, *Alhaji* Mas'ud Akajewole:

> It is not advisable at all, as far as Islam is concerned, that Muslim should marry a Christian. According to the Qur'an, in the olden days, Muslims were allowed to marry from Christianity because Christians have their own holy book but in this generation, it is not advisable at all and I have reasons for it. ... The training given to the Christian girl is that she should try to convert her husband to Christianity. If she fails, she would convert the children but she would first start with the husband. ... It is dangerous for such a man because according to the Muslim tradition, we must account [for] the way we lived in life.[16]

As this quotation illustrates, the rejection and acceptance of interfaith marriage also revolves around a negotiation of appropriate gendered behaviour within the marriage. Imam Akajewole's concern over marriage to Christian women by Muslim men refers to the tension between the rules and expectations guiding Islamic family and married life and individual behaviour that

---

[14] EDEOLU088: 'Islam fi aye gba pe ki fe elesin miran'. This and similarly marked quotes (below) are taken from anonymous 'Knowing Each Other' survey responses collected in Ede and discussed in more detail in the following chapter.
[15] EDEADE122.
[16] Interview with *Alhaji* Mas'ud Akajewole, the Chief Imam of Edeland. 19 April 2012.

shapes Ede's religious life. But his reservations also acknowledge the fact that the individual dispositions to challenge such structures themselves reflect religious dispositions. The greater Christian emphasis on individual faith makes interfaith marriage slightly easier for Christian than for Muslim women. But it also gives greater legitimacy to Christian women to challenge their Muslim husbands and in-laws' expectations, thus complicating their responsibility to guide the lives of their families in an Islamic way.

Debates about Marital Love

In debates about marriage and especially inter-religious marriage, competing ideas of love – and its role in past and present – are mobilised by both opponents and supporters of mixed marriages. Like Imam Akajewole, some respondents suggested that religious intermarriage was easier in the past, when women's love implied greater submission. In this understanding of love, women would, irrespective of individual faith, happily adopt the religion of their husband in order to be at one with him. However, such love was threatened today by demands for gender equality. In this vein, Alfa Adekilekun explained that

> My mother was born into a Christian family [and converted to Islam upon marriage]. Those days, love was the determinant factor. ... But these days of gender equality, women will tell you, you have your own certificate [of belonging to a religious community], [and] I have my own.[17]

This somewhat nostalgic view of marital love emphasises the importance of wifely submission, and it was echoed by some of the responses to the survey discussed in the next chapter. So, one respondent commented that 'Compatibility is very necessary for a peaceful home',[18] while another noted that in a mixed marriage 'there could be no love between us and there would not be understanding'.[19] In this conceptualisation of love, the paramount links between husband and wife are understood to be authority, understanding and compatibility. While this nostalgic understanding of love is not romantic in the sense that it reflects passionate sexual and emotional attraction,[20] it nonetheless emphasises the importance of love as a bridge between the different lives and experiences of men and women.

---

[17] Interview with Alfa Mikail Hamzat Adekilekun. 17 May 2012. Imole Compound, Ede.
[18] EDESDA120.
[19] EDETAL007: 'Toripe ife ko le wa laarin wa ati pe ko nii si igboaraeniye'.
[20] This definition of romantic love draws on J. Cole and L.M. Thomas, eds., *Love in Africa* (Chicago and London: University of Chicago Press, 2009).

The suggestion that inter-faith marriage would affect marital love also implies that religion and marriage sometimes have competitive claims to women's emotional lives. Most women indeed draw on both marriage and religion in the search for a fulfilled life. The status and sense of self-worth of most women in Ede is inextricably linked to their marital status, and especially their ability to bear and raise children. As male provision is the counterpart to female submission, many women rely on support from their husbands and marital and extended families to fulfil their duties as wives and mothers.[21]

However, to protect those they love, many women also draw on access to spiritual power that is shaped by intensely individual experience.[22] Thus, while a man can usually expect the support of his wife in his own religious activities, his control over her is limited by the high social value placed on motherhood. It would be morally and emotionally difficult for any man to prevent his wife from accessing spiritual powers with which he is not familiar if she is desperate to protect their child. Especially in polygamous marriages, where women are expected to draw emotional satisfaction primarily from the close relationship to their children, a failure to become pregnant or a child's suffering may encourage a woman to turn to prayers and practices that are not normally used in her husband's house, thus suspending wifely obedience in the name of maternal duty and self-realisation.

It is perhaps not surprising that the notion of love mobilised by those who are in successful inter-religious marriages sometimes downplays the importance of religion. *Alhaja* Layonu, a Christian-to-Muslim convert after her marriage, explained that after a disappointing experience with a Christian suitor she reconsidered the weight she would give to a man's faith, which in turn changed the course of her romantic life. She said, 'it is the individual that matters. ... I decided that any man that comes my way and I see that he is my type of man, I will go for him irrespective of religion.'[23] Such sentiments were also echoed by several respondents from the survey. One respondent remarked that 'love is different from religion',[24] while another declared, 'the only thing I

---

[21] Many women also receive material support from their natal families; this is often less acknowledged because it implies a criticism of the husband and his family to provide for her and his children.

[22] A similar point is made in J.D.Y. Peel, 'Gender in Yoruba religious change', *Journal of Religion in Africa* 32:2 (2002), 136–66. Peel suggests that the particulars of female self-realisation shaped Yoruba gendered conversion to Christianity in the nineteenth century.

[23] Interview with *Alhaja* Layonu (anonymised). May 2012. Ede.

[24] EDEFPE125: 'Toripe ife yato si esin'.

believe much is love, once I have a true love for her and she also have a genial love to me there is nothing that can stop me from marry[ing] her'.[25]

The emphasis on the importance of this kind of true love in marriage often focused on the partner's individual qualities as well as the couple's desire to be happy with each other. Clearly pointing to more modern forms of love than that associated with female submission, these descriptions implied both more equitable and more intimate relationships within the marriage than those centred on wifely submission.[26] At the same time, references to true love were often explicitly romantic. When challenged by parents and siblings about his decision to marry a Christian, Mr Lawal not only emphasised that this was his one chance at love and happiness, but even evoked fate, saying

> I have tried all I could to settle with another person, it did not work for me, do you want me to remain single? Let me accept this one as my fate. If you don't want to come near us just leave her like that, I believe this is my wife.[27]

As the notion of romantic love emphasises the importance and uniqueness of the individual, its successful mobilisation is partly linked to the ability to make decisions independently of kin's religious concerns. This is relatively easy in families where religion does not play an important role in establishing belonging, such as the Adeleke family discussed in chapter 9. Familial opposition against inter-religious marriage tends to be lower in more traditional families where the notion of wifely submission and conversion resonates with what we have called the nostalgic view of marital love above.

But in other contexts, those who insist on their love in order to embark on successful inter-religious marriages are frequently those who are ready to challenge, if only over this point, the authority of their kin and elders. Cole and Thomas indicate that the willingness and ability to defy the wishes of parents and family is often an important aspect of modern love, reflecting – and perhaps also promising – greater independence from parents and kin both during courtship and marriage.[28] Many individuals who assert their marital choices against the wishes of their family members draw on important resources, including material, educational and other forms of social capital as well as self-confidence.

As especially the interfaith marriages of women are often initially perceived as a form of defiance by their kin, they also tend to be linked to social groups in which women are emotionally and financially secure enough to embark on

---

[25] EDETAL031.
[26] Cole and Thomas, *Love in Africa*, p. 26.
[27] Interview with Mr Lawal (anonymised). May 2012. Ede.
[28] Cole and Thomas, *Love in Africa*, p. 25.

marriage without the initial consent of their parents or fathers. While there are many individual reasons for the decision to go ahead with marriage to someone from another religion, this factor points to the growing importance of female education and higher education, which enable women to attain greater independence at the age of marriage. As the educational achievements of Christian women remain relatively higher than those of Muslims, this suggests another reason for the predominance of Christian women in interfaith marriages.

Also, while some inter-religious marriages take place as a result of neighbourhood friendships, many interfaith couples are the result of encounters at university or in a professional context. By this time of their lives, both men and women have met individuals from various ethnic and religious groups, and reflected on their compatibility with them. Thanks to their education and life experience they are also often in a position where their qualifications and prospects for the future are good, and their self-confidence is high.

Even so, the possibility of an inter-religious marriage forces couples to examine their relationships with others, especially their parents and close kin. Especially for women, the process of embarking on an inter-religious marriage involves careful consideration and preparation. For many couples, then, the process of considering a union across the religious boundary involves a process that includes 'challenging their own stereotypes, empathy for the other community, and a critical perspective towards their own community'.[29] But again, this is a process for which men and women with education at secondary level and beyond are often better equipped than others.

Social Reciprocity and Parental Authority

Given the good relationships between religions in Ede and south-west Nigeria more generally, people in interfaith marriages often experience the initial displeasure of their families and friends primarily as 'the response of others to their mixedness'.[30] Tension and difficulty surround the fact that inter-religious marriages challenge the stability of social boundaries shaped by religion either

---

[29] R. Chopra and J. Punwani, 'Discovering the other, discovering the self: Inter-religious marriage among Muslims in the Greater Bombay area, India', *Inter-Religious Marriages among Muslims: Negotiating Religious and Social Identity in Family and Community*, ed. A. An-na'im (New Delhi: Global Media Publications, 2005), pp. 45–162: 140.

[30] C. Caballero, R. Edwards and S. Puthussery, *Parenting 'Mixed' Children: Negotiating Difference and Belonging in Mixed Race and Faith Families* (York: The Joseph Rowntree Foundation, 2008), p. 55. See Jolly, 'Inter-religious marriage', p. 39.

directly (through the inclusion of religious others in the family) or indirectly (though the threat of religious difference in the next generation).

Where marital partners retain different religions, mixed marriages also challenge general norms of social reciprocity in various ways. As the important rites of passage associated with family life are usually facilitated by the world religions, mixed marriages exist in an in-between space where social agency is limited. This is clearly illustrated by the possibilities associated with the formalisation of an inter-religious marriage. While most weddings are important social affairs, inter-religious marriage ceremonies tend to be short and rather bland. They are usually conducted at the marriage registry offices located at local government secretariats, where each member of the couple swears on the holy book of her or his professed religion.

This is in stark contrast to the marriages performed in churches and mosques, where the parents are celebrated and praised for their success of raising responsible adults, and where lavish parties can be arranged that establish the social worth of the family and extended family. These large social occasions serve as 'social payments' of the couples' parents and family, which reciprocate for the goodwill of others, and moreover are widely taken to illustrate good character, loyalty and consistency.[31] Thus a child who refuses the parents a prominent involvement in her or his wedding not only prevents them from celebrating their achievement (of seeing a child reach this stage of social adulthood) as expected, but indirectly insults them.

Weddings have become so significant as social payments that their ostentatious celebration by Christians has transformed Islamic practice in Ede. In the past, Islamic wedding ceremonies were performed in the living room of the bride's parents with only a short prayer. However, by the 1950s it was felt that the grandeur of Christian marriage ceremonies could attract Muslim women to marry a Christian, and most Muslim organisations in Ede now accept both English and native dresses for marriage; this includes a white wedding gown as long as it is modest. Muslim organisations such as the Ansar-ud-Deen society in Ede have established public wedding ceremonies. They also issue wedding certificates, which are vital for bridal changes of name and for visa applications at the embassies.[32] In this context, the disincentive and social disadvantage of the small marriage ceremony available to interfaith couples should not be underestimated.

---

[31] T. Lawuyi and T. Falola, 'The instability of the naira and social payment among the Yoruba', *Journal of African and Asian Studies* 27:3 (1992), 216–28: 223. See Jolly, 'Inter-religious marriage', p. 39.

[32] Interview with *Alhaji* Ibraheem Tijani Dende Adekilekun, Chief Imam of Ansar-Ud-Deen Society. 19 April 2012. Ede.

In addition, parents are concerned about two potential outcomes of interreligious marriage: the possibility of their child's conversion to their partner's religion, and insecurity about the religion of the grandchildren. Both might be perceived as personal disappointments or even as failings. As it is widely believed that parents should be able to guide the behaviour of their children, the actions of a child who is seen to digress openly from his or her expected path may be taken to imply that her or his parents have not exercised their authority wisely. For example, if a Christian couple was visited by their Muslim grandchildren who could not recite the Lord's Prayer, they might feel that they had failed as Christian parents.

Moreover, given the importance of paternal descent and authority in the compounds and families in Ede, the decision of a child, especially a daughter, to marry a member of another religion appears to be a challenge to paternal authority, and by implication a social embarrassment. Thus if an elderly Muslim based in an explicitly Muslim compound was visited by children or grandchildren unable to recite the Qur'an, he or she might, irrespective of their personal feelings, be considered unsuitable for taking on a position of authority in the compound. Irrespective of religion, parental reactions often reflected both personal disappointment and fear of social embarrassment.

The most dramatic experiences of rejection were narrated to us by women. *Alhaja* Layonu, brought up as a Christian, told us that when she announced her decision to marry a Muslim, her father exclaimed, 'he said over his dead body, that don't I know his position in the church? ... He declared that do I want put him to shame and he said he would rather die, that I should allow him to die before I go ahead.'[33] Mrs Oluwaseun, a Muslim convert to Christianity whose professional success had allowed her to make a regular financial contribution to her parents' wellbeing, told us that upon the announcement of her conversion, her father's reaction was 'terrible and violent, it got to a stage he said he would not receive a dime from [her] again'.[34]

Clearly addressing the fact the intermarriage can be understood as undermining the integrity of a lineage or of paternal authority, some fathers punish children (especially daughters) who convert or marry out of their religion by no longer considering them as kin. The exclusion of a disobedient daughter from her natal family can even extend to the far future, when the father in question would turn into an ancestor. One of our Muslim respondents openly stated that his daughter who married a non-Muslim would not only be disowned but would also be barred from his funeral.[35]

---

[33] Interview with *Alhaja* Layonu (anonymised). May 2012. Ede.
[34] Interview with Mrs Oluwaseun (anonymised). May 2012. Ede.
[35] Interview with Mr Ajagbe (anonymised). June 2012. Ede.

Social Reproduction and Familial Reconciliation

In many cases, familial reconciliation takes place when a grandchild is expected or born. In turn, failure to conceive in good time can undermine a couple, and may undermine a religiously mixed marriage more quickly than a marriage sanctioned by both sets of parents. By the time a couple expect a child, the immediate familial anger over the couple's failure to get married in an impressive and enjoyable ceremony may have abated, and the unhappiness or embarrassment over a hypothetical grandchild who might not be able to recite a prayer or text in the grandparents' religion may seem less relevant given the imminent arrival of a real grandchild. For those who were worried about the divine support for a mixed religious union, the arrival of a grandchild also proves that the union is not devoid of blessing.

Equally importantly, by the time a man and a woman who have challenged or disregarded the importance of kinship ties become parents, they have, by producing children themselves, reaffirmed the importance of kinship. By extending family ties into the future, young men and women who offended their parents by making their own marital choices have at least potentially taken on the same burden of responsibility as their parents, and of course they have also exposed themselves to the possibility that their children may defy them.

Often other women, especially grandmothers or elderly relatives, assume the responsibility of being the peacemaker between parents and children in this situation. A female respondent told us that her mother and her aunty mediated between her and her father after she had been abandoned by her family for three years, after which time she had finally become pregnant.[36] In another case, a (formerly Muslim) Christian female respondent explained that,

> Papa was a Muslim, so he was not happy about it, but later my grandmother intervened and she told him the truth that if he wants to enjoy his child he had better forget about it ... he later agreed and we became very good friends before he died.[37]

But although the estrangement from kin is usually stronger between the wife and her family, the reconciliation between the mixed-religious couple and her kin often explicitly focuses on the husband. Reflecting the general understanding that the role of a husband is to determine most aspects of his wife's life, marriage transforms the rift between parents and daughter into a

---

[36] Interview with *Alhaja* Layonu (anonymised). May 2012. Ede.
[37] Interview with Mrs Idris (anonymised). May 2012. Ede.

disagreement between parents and husband. As a result, fathers and husbands often take on the roles of (former) opponents during reconciliation. *Alhaja* Layonu explained how the differences with her father were settled when she was six months pregnant:

> The day we decided to go and visit my father, we first of all stopped at my elder sister's house at Iseyin ... I stayed there, I didn't follow my husband to our house. He went to see my father ... I don't know what they discussed over there but I know that was when we were accepted and they later brought my father to where I was staying in my sister's house. So, since that time, he [my father] accepted us as his children.[38]

The focus on reconciliation between a woman's father and her husband appears at first glance simply to reflect the widespread understanding that men are considered the heads of nuclear family groups. However, since most people consider it more shocking for a daughter to disobey her family than for a son, the casting of the son-in-law as the offender also conceals the gendered nature of this transgression, and the fact that such a marriage would have been impossible without the active and ultimately successful defiance of male authority by the woman involved. In that sense, the privileging of male agency during reconciliation also restores social norms of male agency and female submission and mediation.

Women and men in interfaith marriages must contend not only with displeasure from their own immediate families, but also with pressure from their spouses' families.[39] Even after a formal reconciliation, a woman is more likely to be at the receiving end of such pressures, because she is expected to become a supportive member of the husband's family. There are some traditional roles, such as participating in the family chores and religious ceremonies, which are expected from the *ìyàwó ilé*, literally meaning 'the wife married into the house'.

Like all wives, women in inter-religious marriages must therefore devise means of meeting the needs of their natal as well as their marital families. Where two religions are involved, a good wife must become at least superficially acquainted with the demands of both. As a result, the distinction between mixed-faith and conversionary marriages that is sometimes adopted in the literature is not helpful for the discussion of women's experience of interfaith

---

[38] Interview with *Alhaja* Layonu (anonymised). May 2012. Ede.
[39] The greater social pressure on women to 'adapt' in interfaith marriages is also highlighted in research on many other parts of the world, albeit with some exceptions (e.g. Jewish women in mixed marriages); cf. Jolly, 'Inter-religious marriage', pp. 32–8.

marriage in Ede.[40] As wives, they are obliged to participate regularly in the religion of their husbands even if they have not converted.

For instance, during *Iléyá* (Eid al-Adha) festival, all women married to Muslims are expected to visit the extended family of their husbands to help with the preparation of the ram traditionally slaughtered on that day and other household chores. If a Christian wife were to shy away from her responsibilities during Muslim events in the name of her religion, she would defy what is expected of her by virtue of having married into her husband's family, and she would likely be admonished by the other wives in the husband's patrilineage (and, if she persisted, by its male elders). Mrs Idris, a Christian woman married to a Muslim explained that,

> Because my mother-in-law is still alive, during *Iléyá*, I will have to travel down to Lamonrin Compound [where the mother-in-law lives] to prepare ram and everything. Then people from my own family will come and felicitate with my mother-in-law.[41]

The organisation of social functions such as naming ceremonies is another area that can potentially put a strain on relations between parents, in-laws and the new couple. In order to maintain good relations with all sides of the family, a child of such a marriage is usually given two religious names by the extended families. In most cases, the husband's extended family takes the morning session in which his religious leaders are invited to give names to the child. Later in the afternoon, the religious leaders of the wife come for theirs. Mrs Yusuf, another female Christian respondent married to a Muslim explained,

> If we are to do naming ceremony, my mother-in-law will bring [an] Alfa from Ede, they would give the child a Muslim name and later in the evening, members of my church would come and we would do the naming ceremony.[42]

The doubling of such ceremonies, albeit in a way that privileges the father's religion, restores or reaffirms the sense of familial order that has been challenged by the contrasting demands of two different religions. Even if two celebrations take place, wives are expected to organise and support both their natal and their marital families during these events. Apart from the cost

---

[40] For a detailed discussion of terminology, see J.A. Romain, *Till Faith Do Us Part: Couples who Fall in Love across the Religious Divide* (London: Fount Paperbacks, 1996), pp. 1–4; N.E. Zemmel, 'Intermarriage, variations on a theme: Examining the reality of mixed and conversionary marriage in contemporary Anglo-Jewry', unpublished PhD thesis (Birmingham: University of Birmingham, 1999), pp. 12–15. See Jolly, 'Inter-religious marriage', p. 1.

[41] Interview with Mrs Idris (anonymised). May 2012. Ede.

[42] Interview with Mrs Yusuf (anonymised). April 2012. Ede.

implications, the fact that wives' duties are doubled in this context points to an important principle in the management of inter-religious marriages. While both husbands and wives may be subject to criticism for marrying outside their religion, women bear the main responsibility for ensuring that their nuclear families, and especially their children, straddle the competing demands of two religious traditions (see also chapter 9).

Everyday Married Life with Two Religions

In marriages between Muslims and Christians, there are many areas in which agreement must be negotiated and discussed. Given the power accorded in compound and family life to the husband, his family and its elders, this negotiation is especially important for women, who are expected to obey the decisions about religion made by their husbands. Important wifely duties include the preparation of the husband's food and the satisfaction of his sexual desires. In an interfaith marriage whereby the woman is a Christian and the man is a Muslim, the woman will have to prepare her husband's food in accordance with Islamic requirements during the Ramadan fast. In addition, when the woman is fasting during Lent, she may wish to avoid sexual intercourse, as celibacy is considered by many Christians to be an important aspect of fasting. Similar difficulties arise when the religions of the spouses are reversed. As these examples illustrate, inter-religious marriages may require more patience from both partners than those where both partners follow the same faith.

Also, and despite the widely accepted notion that children should have their father's religion, the religious experiences of children from inter-religious marriages are often complex. Children in a marriage between a Muslim man and a Christian woman, formally under their father's authority, would normally attend Qur'anic school and receive religious instructions in their father's religion. However, owing to the emotional proximity to their mothers that most children enjoy, many children would also be closely acquainted with Christianity. Since children normally share a bedroom with their mother, they might observe their mother reading the Bible, praying and pursuing other religious activities in her room. Children might also see their mother getting ready for church and might even follow her there occasionally. Thus reflecting the complementary roles of fathers and mothers, many children in mixed-religious marriages experience their father's religion as associated with his authority within the family, while the religion of their mother would be an integral aspect of childhood intimacies.

Expectations of women's subservience are limited by a widespread dislike of pressure in the area of religion. As the example of Esther Adeleke illustrates, as long as a wife fulfils her duties to her husband and his family, she usually remains free to practise at least some aspects of her religion for herself (chapter 9). Also, while men can and do expect wifely support for their own religious activities while their wives live with them, they cannot really interfere in their wives' activities during visits to her parents, especially as many men are reluctant to spend considerable time with their in-laws.[43] More importantly, if a mother was prevented by her husband from praying and caring for herself or for a sick child in the way of her own religion, he would be considered responsible – and indeed selfish or wicked – if the woman became unwell or if a sick child failed to recover.

Given the general reluctance to enforce conversion, many spouses who made the decision to convert to the other's religion only did so after some time, and because they found it appealing to do so. Thus *Alhaja* Layonu affirmed that she began to admire her husband's way of worship after marriage, and she eventually requested to be taught how to become a Muslim. She said of her husband that,

> He prayed every day at night, between 1am and 3am he is up [sic]. Every blessed day. If there is any problem, he will overlook it, pray and fast. During the month of Ramadan he will complete the fasting. He trained me to be fasting. So that altitude [sic] of worship was what I cherished because in my family too, worship was the main thing. ... Then he taught me how to pray and since then, no going back.[44]

In some cases, the husband converted to the religion of the wife. However, such conversions contravene societal expectations of good wifely behaviour and imply that the wife has more power, or is somehow spiritually stronger, than the husband. As a result, such conversions are often represented in a manner that de-emphasises any agency the wife may have had in this process. Mrs Lagbaja explained her husband's conversion thus:

> I didn't do it, it was another lady, God used another lady to do it, according to what [my husband] told me, he actually wanted to befriend the lady, so the lady invited him to a programme in her church. Then he said, if I attend this programme, would you come and visit me? And the lady said yes so, on attending the programme then he decided to change, and that was all. We both attended the wedding ceremony of the lady, it was a big testimony.[45]

---

[43] There is no formal avoidance taboo between men and their in-laws, but many people consider a man's extended enjoyment of his in-laws' hospitality as emasculating.
[44] Interview with *Alhaja* Layonu (anonymised). May 2012. Ede.
[45] Interview with Mrs Lagbaja (anonymised). May 2012. Ede.

The fact that Mr Lagbaja's wife highlights her husband's desire for the friendship of another woman to explain his conversion is interesting. While ostensibly affirming that she had nothing to do with his decision to become a Christian, her narrative nonetheless confirms the importance of emotional closeness and companionship for conversion. But by referring openly to the husband's freedom to seek female friendship outside marriage, Mrs Lagbaja also emphasised her husband's dominance within the marriage.

This apparent confession was slightly surprising given both the relative formality of the interview situation and the degree of composure and self-control displayed by Mrs Lagbaja in other interactions. But Mrs Lagbaja's story is perhaps explained by its implication that if Mr Lagbaja sought out female friendship outside his marriage, he was not a man under his wife's thumb. As a husband with authority over his wife, Mr Lagbaja's conversion must have been his very own choice. By equating her husband's control over his religious life with his marital autonomy, Mrs Lagbaja illustrates the pressures that shape male religiosity and further confirms the gendered nature of religious mediation and conversion.

Conclusion

As illustrated in this chapter, the decision to embark on an interfaith marriage is often difficult. It is also, from the beginning, strongly gendered because it challenges the authority especially of women's families and fathers. The potential conflict between natal and marital families has greater consequences for women, who may find that their natal families disown them. But as long as the union produces children, initial resentment usually turns into acceptance, especially if the women in such marriages are able to mediate social and religious relationships between their natal and their marital family carefully, usually through at least occasional participation in both religions.

In the kind of Muslim–Christian marriage that was discussed in this chapter, religious relationships are strongly shaped by gender. The everyday religious lives of men and fathers are primarily shaped by their engagement with their own religion. In contrast, a woman's mediating role usually involves attaining a degree of knowledge and expertise in the practices expected of women during both Muslim and Christian festivals. Some knowledge of both parental religions is also often expected of the children of such unions. Overall, it appears that the success of inter-religious marriages largely depends on female agency, which relies on both the woman's preparedness to make a marital choice independently of her family, and her ability to mediate between families after reconciliation.

Even so, the reconciliation processes that often follow the initial estrangement between a woman and her family focus on men. Thus a daughter's defiance of her natal family is generally resolved by the establishment of proper in-law relationships between her father and her husband. In contrast, the role played by a woman in producing good relationships between her natal and marital families, mainly by ensuring that her children have some knowledge and understanding of both religions, is simply considered an extension of normal wifely activity.

While the emphasis on male agency can be understood as a result of the patriarchal structures that shape Yoruba social life, it also illustrates the nature of women's social power. Exposed to more than one religion on a much more regular basis than men, women in inter-religious marriages are not only social but also religious mediators, familiar with a range of theologies, debates and discourses that may not be known to their husbands. This knowledge is rarely acknowledged openly, but it is instrumental to women's ability to care for themselves and others, most importantly their children. For that reason, inter-religious marriage is a social formation that contributes significantly to the lived experience of female religiosity, and by extension to the ongoing negotiation and overall effervescence that characterises religious life in Ede and beyond.

CHAPTER 11

Everyday Inter-Religious Encounters and Attitudes

Rebecca Jones and Insa Nolte

Expanding on the theme of personal relationships across religious boundaries, this chapter offers an overview of attitudes and experiences that reflect and shape relations between Muslims, Christians and traditionalists in Ede. Its main source is an ethnographic survey carried out in Ede between April and June 2012, which focused on the role of religion and religious difference in the private and professional lives of our respondents, and which explored their attitudes towards religious difference.[1] The survey included both qualitative and quantitative questions, and it was accompanied by the production of field notes and diaries in order to allow for later questioning. The aim of this survey was to offer an insight into the relative importance of a range of features of Yoruba life that have been associated with the peaceful coexistence of religions, and survey work was also accompanied by a significant number of qualitative interviews focusing on people's everyday experience and engagement with religious difference.

Based on an evaluation of just under 300 survey responses, this chapter offers an overview of Ede's religious landscape. Confirming Ede's strong Muslim majority, the chapter also points to the different social bases associated with Islam and Christianity. As we discuss, our survey data shows that Muslims in Ede are more likely than Christians to be indigenes of the town, and they tend to have a lower degree of education than Christians. This confirms the widely held impression, discussed in several previous chapters, that while Islam is the town's established majority religion, it is subject to challenges associated with immigration and the dominance of Christianity in the education sector. Exploring the incidence and direction of conversion in Ede, we also look at the fact that our survey indicated a higher number of converts to Christianity than to Islam. We explore converts' reasons for changing

---

[1] The survey also served as a pilot for the larger study carried out for the 'Knowing Each Other' project (see chapter 1).

15 Team member Kehinde Akinduro discussing the survey with potential respondents

their religion as well as their thoughts on the conversion of others. However, despite the recent growth of Christianity in Ede associated with immigration and educational expansion, the town nonetheless maintains its very large Muslim majority.

This chapter also expands on the arguments of previous chapters by exploring attitudes to, and experiences of, inter-religious encounters across a large cross-section of citizens of Ede, both Christians and Muslims. As such, it draws together this book's focus on the ways that religious difference shapes life in Ede through its institutions – ranging from kingship and the worship of Ṣàngó to families and compounds and educational and religious institutions – and the everyday encounters of its citizens. The chapter explores our survey respondents' views on the practice of traditional customs and religion (bearing in mind that all but one of our respondents identified as Muslim or Christian), and looks at distinctions our respondents made between 'culture' and 'religion'.

As our survey also examines Muslim and Christian views about each other, the chapter suggests that respondents often focus on points of convergence between the two religions (such as their mutual faith in 'one God') or admire similar aspects of each other's practice (such as the perceived good character of people of the other religion). But they also admiringly describe aspects of the other's religion that they feel are lacking in their own, indicating a positive appreciation for religious difference. As the vast majority of our respondents had friends of the other religion, these overwhelmingly affirmative, and often insightful, forms of knowledge about the other religion were clearly linked to high levels of inter-religious sociality and friendship.

In the conclusion we explore what these findings might imply for our understanding of religious tolerance, encounter and coexistence in Ede. We suggest that inter-religious relations are related in complex ways to shared belonging, especially because the importance of indigeneity contributes to different experiences and attitudes among Muslims and Christians. At the same time, everyday forms of encounter drawing on shared Yoruba-ness, as well as on friendship and family bonds, emphasise the compatibility of Muslims and Christians. It therefore seems that both tolerance and the different forms of coexistence 'beyond tolerance' within Ede are closely linked to other forms of multi-religious community, both above and below the town level.

The Survey

The survey consisted of a variety of questions designed to help us understand how people in Ede interact with people of other religions in everyday life. As well as asking respondents for their views on other religions – focusing on Christianity, Islam, and 'traditional religion' – we asked respondents about inter-religious interactions in their daily lives, such as whether they attended weddings, funerals and naming ceremonies of people of other religions, and whether they or anyone in their family had changed their religion or married someone of a different religion. We also explored how social categories such as gender, age and education level affected people's responses and their attitudes towards inter-religious interaction.

Under the leadership of Olukoya Ogen, a team consisting of Bayo Adewusi, Charles Omotayo, Kehinde Akinduro and Tosin Akinjobi, as well as our local gate-keepers *Alhaji* Rasheed Adio and *Alhaji* Nureni Lawal, administered the questionnaire to 291 respondents. A total of 191 of the respondents were selected in a randomised door-to-door approach. We selected three major streets in Ede – Oluobinu Street, Talafia Street and Poly(technic) Road – for the door-to-door approach. These roads start at the royal palace and market place and lead outside the town, meaning that they offer access to older as well as newer sections of the town. The team members went from door to door handing out questionnaires to the inhabitants or to people they met there.

In addition, to compare the responses from the door-to-door survey with responses from more professional environments, team members also went to several schools, hospitals, universities, professional associations and local government offices to ask for responses from a sample of the people working there. They were successful in eliciting 100 responses in total, from the

Ede South Painters' Association (ESPA), Adeleke University, Ede Federal Polytechnic, Ede Muslim Grammar School, Ansar-ud-Deen School, the Baptist Junior and Senior High School, the Seventh-Day Adventist Senior School, and Ede North and Ede South Local Government Secretariats.

We produced versions of the survey in English and Yoruba, and respondents could request whichever version they were more comfortable with. Field researchers left the surveys with the respondents to fill in, and returned to pick them up several days later. They then went over the surveys with the respondents so they could clarify any question of which they were unsure. This was important especially in the case of respondents who were unable to write at the level required by the survey. Eventually, 108 questionnaires were answered in English, and 183 in Yoruba. The survey reflects a mostly even spread of respondents across all ages from 18 and over, though we ended up with slightly more respondents in the 20–35 year-old category than in other categories. While we aimed for a 50–50 split between men and women, only 37 per cent of our respondents were women. The main reason for this preponderance of male responses was that several women refused to take part in the survey without the explicit permission of their husbands, which could not always be obtained.

The wider context of Nigerian politics meant that the survey work was often challenged. Despite having obtained the permission of the *Tìmì* of Ede for the survey work, team members found that many potential respondents were reluctant to participate in the survey. Disillusioned with the governmental institutions that are normally associated with survey work, several respondents suspected the team of working for ulterior political motives in which they wanted no part. The experience of terrorism in northern Nigeria also shaped responses, and in one case team members were openly asked whether they were checking on Muslims' everyday practices in order to report these to the violent Boko Haram group. It was in such contexts that the ability of our local gatekeepers, *Alhaji* Adio and *Alhaji* Lawal, to explain that the survey was part of a research project based in Nigeria and the UK, was extremely important.

After the completion of the survey, questionnaires were taken to the UK, where the survey responses were entered into an electronic database by Rebecca Jones. Yoruba responses were translated into English by Rebecca Jones, Olusola Ajibade and Oluwakemi Olabode. Responses were subjected to a primary analysis in Dedoose (mixed methods analysis software) and, where relevant, later explored using SPSS. A draft report, in some ways a precursor to this chapter, was produced for the academic and community workshop at Adeleke University, Ede, in December 2012, where the idea for this volume was first mooted. During the event, traditional and religious leaders as well as other interested citizens of Ede discussed the findings and suggested further ways of exploring and thinking about the data, some of which have found their way into this chapter.

In interpreting the survey we are aware that responses to this survey (as in any survey) may represent what people *say* they do rather than necessarily what they actually do. Respondents are free to lie, make mistakes, hedge their answers or present themselves in a particular light, should they so wish. In order to exclude surveys filled in imprecisely, our field researchers took care to question inconsistent responses. In places in this chapter we read the survey responses alongside our researchers' field notes in order to produce a fuller picture. But, in fact, our respondents' presentation of a public self in this way is the very subject that interests us in this chapter, as we explore how respondents publicly discuss their attitudes to religious encounters and difference. Furthermore, we consider the demographic information we have gathered in the course of this survey to be of significant value, since quantitative data on religion in south-western Nigeria is scarce.

Ede's Religious Landscape: Religion, Education and Indigeneity

As expected, Islam was the dominant religion among our respondents: 74 per cent were Muslims, 26 per cent were Christians, and only one person said they were a traditional worshipper. It should be noted that our field notes and other survey responses refer to traditional practice among respondents more frequently, suggesting that a good number of respondents practise a monotheist religion alongside traditional worship. The under-representation of traditional practice therefore arises out of its *de facto* compatibility with the world religions for some respondents, whose participation in such practices does not prevent them from considering themselves Christians or Muslims. While traditional practices are sometimes not mentioned out of embarrassment or the notion that such practices should not be the subject of a questionnaire, their silencing probably also reflects the fact that traditional practice does not offer a clearly bounded position of faith, as is widely associated with the term 'religion'.[2] It is therefore usually only those who abstain from monotheist religion who assert that they follow the 'traditional religion'.

Ede's citizens align themselves with a number of religious institutions. Most of our Muslim respondents were members of the widely popular Nasrul-Lahi-Fatih Society (NASFAT, 45 per cent), which encourages an intensely personal and emotional engagement with Islam also described in chapter 6.

---

[2] It may be nonsensical, for instance, to talk about the secular in relation to Yoruba traditional religion, which does not admit of a dichotomy between 'worldly' and 'religious', the two being fused together in everyday life.

The next most popular groups among Muslims were the Ansar-ud-Deen (6 per cent) and Tijaniyya (5 per cent) groups, and those who said they did not have any particular denomination (5 per cent). There were a wide variety of smaller groups named by Muslims, numbering 34 in total. It is important to note that because of its current popularity, the Nasrul-Lahi-Fatih Society often also serves as a social meeting space, and that the membership in this group (or indeed most other Muslim groups) does not normally preclude individuals from attending neighbourhood mosques or mosques and events organised by other Muslim groups.

Among the Christians, the most popular denomination was the Baptist Church, described in more detail in chapter 7. As one of the town's oldest and best-established churches, it was home to 21 per cent of the Christian respondents. In our sample the Baptist Church was followed by the Seventh-Day Adventists (15 per cent of Christian respondents), though these mainly came from Adeleke University, and the Anglican Church (12 per cent). However, there were also many who identified with modern 'Pentecostal' churches, including the Redeemed Christian Church of God, Winners Chapel, Mountain of Fire and Miracles Ministries, Deeper Life Bible Church, and Victory Life Ministries, as well as respondents who described their church as 'gospel' or 'Bible-based'. If we consider all of these churches to be Pentecostal or neo-Pentecostal, their members constitute 25 per cent of Christians in Ede. This number rises to 36 per cent if the Christ Apostolic Church, an older church usually described as an Aladura or 'prayer' church, but which has strong Pentecostal features, is included.[3]

Islam and Christianity in Ede have different profiles with regard to education and indigeneity. There is a strong association between religion and migration to the town. Among the door-to-door respondents from Oluobinu, Talafia and Polytechnic Roads, many of whom were residents of the town's old compounds, 90 per cent were Muslims. Meanwhile, in the sample drawing on Ede's professional and mostly educational institutions, only 44 per cent of respondents were Muslims, with the remainder Christians. But the educational institutions were home to a high proportion of the town's non-indigenes; overall, 17 per cent of our respondents were non-indigenes of Ede, but in the institutions we sampled this rose to 36 per cent of respondents. This was particularly the case at Adeleke University. Also, Christians were more likely than Muslims to be non-indigenes of the town; only 51 per cent of

---

[3] It is difficult to classify the Christ Apostolic Church (CAC) because it is an older church of Aladura origin, which nonetheless shares important features with contemporary Pentecostal churches.

Christian respondents were indigenes, but 91 per cent of Muslim respondents were indigenous to Ede.

Christians also tended to have a higher level of education than Muslims, both among Ede's indigenes and the town's immigrants. On the basis of a close reading of some questionnaires as well as field observations, we suspect that some of our respondents have answered questions about their educational attainment by referring to institutions they attended (but did not necessarily complete) rather than the completion of particular levels of education. But even with a very careful reading of the responses, the differences in educational attainment seem dramatic, with 33 per cent of Christians in our survey claiming to be educated at undergraduate level, compared to 11 per cent of Muslims. The size of this gap was somewhat affected by the administration of our questionnaire to a large number of predominantly Christian staff at Adeleke University, nearly all of whom had undergraduate degrees. However, there was still a difference within the door-to-door sites in Oluobinu, Talafia and Polytechnic Roads, where 11 per cent of Christians were educated at undergraduate level, compared to 2 per cent of Muslims, and 32 per cent of Christians were educated to diploma level, compared to 18 per cent of Muslims.[4]

Overall, then, these findings confirm the widely held impression that the immigration from other Yoruba towns (or, in a few cases, farther afield), and especially the immigration of highly qualified individuals in the field of education, plays an important role in the growth of Christianity in Ede. However, Christianity also remains strongly associated with conversion.

Education and Conversion

Suggesting a higher degree of religious fluidity than we could have deduced from qualitative research, 7 per cent of our respondents from Ede said they had changed their religion at some point in their lives. However, the direction of these conversions did not reflect the influence of the Muslim majority within Ede. Instead, it confirmed Muslim concerns about the attractions of Christianity and the refusal of Christian wives to submit to Muslim husbandly authority. Thus, of our overall number of converts, only 25 per cent had converted to Islam (from Christianity or traditional religions), and 75 per cent had converted from Islam to Christianity.

---

[4] Most Muslims in these roads were educated to secondary level (42 per cent), while diploma level (including HND and NCE as well as those respondents who simply stated 'diploma') was the most common level for Christians (32 per cent).

Importantly, conversion was clearly associated with the town's educational and local government institutions. Among the respondents from Oluobinu, Talafia and Polytechnic Roads, only 3 per cent had changed religion. In contrast, 15 per cent of the respondents from the institutional sample had converted. Conversion was also linked to education, with 30 per cent of those who had changed their religion asserting that they had post-secondary education, while there were no primary school leavers who had changed their religion.[5] More non-indigenes had changed their religion than indigenes of Ede: 5 per cent of indigenes and 18 per cent of non-indigenes had converted (not necessarily while living in Ede).

While these findings confirm that the growth of Christianity in Ede is taking place through immigration, they also point to the importance of higher education for conversion to Christianity. The fact that the number of converts is also higher among non-indigenes again points to the greater ease with which individuals can withdraw from pressure to maintain the religion of their families or compounds if they move away from their hometowns. Even so, it is likely that this trend also reflects the relative dominance of Christianity especially within the secondary and tertiary education sector, where young people often come into contact with often Christian role models and mentors.

Indeed, the uneven direction of conversion among our respondents is also reflected in the reasons they give for their conversion. The small number of converts to Islam gave only two types of reasons for changing their religion: two formerly Christian women had converted owing to marriage to a Muslim, and two formerly Christian men had converted after coming into contact with Muslim associations or preaching.

The much larger number of converts from Islam to Christianity gave a wider variety of reasons for becoming Christians. Three women said they had converted to Christianity for marriage.[6] A male respondent pointed out that as a member of the Royal Family of Ede, he has 'freedom of religion'.[7] Another group of respondents talked about coming into close contact with Christians. However, among this group, reasons or conversion were more differentiated than among converts to Islam. Two respondents mentioned staying with

---

[5] There was no obvious correlation with age; a range of respondents from the age of 26 (at the time of answering the survey) to older than 76 had changed their religion, though it was not always clear from their answers at what age they had done so.

[6] Given that most religiously mixed marriages in Ede are between Muslim husbands and Christian wives, the fact that there are more female converts to Christianity than to Islam because of marriage suggests that not as many Christian women convert in marriage as might be expected.

[7] EDEADE112. This and subsequent references in this format refer to unique identifiers for each survey respondent.

Christian family members (both sisters), and three respondents had attended Christian educational institutions where, as one respondent put it, 'I became convinced about Christianity doctrines/morals.'[8] Another respondent, perhaps less resilient than Ede's Muslim leaders *Alhaji* Olayiwola and *Alhaji* Olanrewaju, both of whom attended Baptist schools (see chapter 7), explained, 'I went to Baptist school and everybody must be Christian, there is no chance for Muslim religion there.'[9]

The remaining eight Muslim-to-Christian converts, making up the majority of those who changed from Islam to Christianity, described their reasons for favouring Christianity in personal or theological terms, such as 'I am convinced that Christ is real',[10] or 'I believed I've found the right path'.[11] Illustrating what is often perceived as a disadvantage of Islam, namely its reliance on Arabic, one respondent said that he converted to Christianity because he felt 'inadequate being a Muslim and with little understanding of the religion'.[12] It is possible that confident and explicitly religious reasons given by other converts also reflect the generally greater accessibility of Christianity, especially to those fluent in English.

Changes of denomination or sect within a religion were even more common than changes of religion, with 23 per cent of Muslims and 29 per cent of Christians who had not changed their religion reporting that they had changed their religious denomination or sect. Of the Muslims who had changed their denomination, 54 per cent (both men and women) had changed to NASFAT, clearly the most successful contemporary Muslim group (see chapter 6). The rest had turned to a very wide variety of other denominations. Again, their reasons for doing so included both pragmatic considerations and personal and spiritual concerns. Several women explained that they had changed for reasons of marriage, e.g. 'it [the original mosque attended] is far from my husband's house'.[13] Other responses emphasised personal conviction, such as 'Amadiyya is true practising of Islam',[14] 'I prefer Nasfat'[15] and 'for more spiritual upliftment'.[16]

Of the 21 Christians who had changed denomination, the most common denominations they had changed to were the Redeemed Christian Church of

---

[8] EDEADE116
[9] EDEADE131
[10] EDEBHS116
[11] EDEADE129.
[12] EDEADE128.
[13] EDEOLU038: 'Nitoripe o jinna si ile ọkọ mi'.
[14] EDESDA122.
[15] EDEPOL060: 'Nasfat jẹ ẹsin (ijọ) to wu mi'.
[16] EDEADE126.

God (RCCG) (19 per cent), the Anglican Church (10 per cent) and 'Pentecostal' (14 per cent). Four had changed for reasons of marriage, another had changed because of a 'family issue',[17] and another because her parents had changed denomination when she was a child. Of the remainder, several cited preferences for the style and theology of their new denomination: one man who had changed from the Anglican to the RCCG said he preferred its Bible teaching,[18] while a former Baptist who had also changed to RCCG cited its 'more interesting programme'.[19] A formerly Anglican woman who had changed to the Christ Apostolic Church said she did so because 'it is a spiritual and prayerful church'.[20] Another group referred to 'fervency', 'spiritual upliftment and growth',[21] or finding 'more truths in the Bible in the latter denomination',[22] all of which suggest the importance of practices associated with Pentecostalism.[23]

But while the high incidence of conversion and change of denomination might suggest that it is a generally accepted practice, respondents' answers to the question of why other people changed religion stand in marked contrast to converts' descriptions of their own changes of religion. Respondents' own conversions were sometimes described as a response to marriage or the close engagement with another religion. But by far the most common reason given for the conversion of others was 'problems' (a category including illness, spiritual problems, poverty, infertility and a desire for miracles) followed by lack of conviction in one's former religion. Several respondents argued that conversion was the result of greed or insatiability (*ojúkòkòrò*), 'laziness' or 'intolerance'.

The difference between the explanations for one's own conversion and that of others suggests that conversion is widely perceived as ambivalent. While turning to a new religion may be positive and empowering on an individual level, it also undermines forms of belonging partly associated with religion, such as family and compound life. Also, those who convert are also suspected by others of not striving hard enough in the religion they were brought up in, or of having an unseemly desire for the benefits offered by other religions. Unable to draw on the forces offered within their own religion, converts are perceived to turn to a religion that appears to offer easier access to what is desired. In this reckoning, conversion can be seen as illuminating the gulf

---

[17] EDEADE117.
[18] EDEESL137.
[19] EDEAUD155.
[20] EDEPOL079: 'Nitori to je ijo emi ti o si je ijo aladura'.
[21] EDEBHS115.
[22] EDEADE113.
[23] Such practices have also been adopted by the older mission and independent churches.

between a person's social position and their ambitions, and it may be perceived as reflecting a lack of moral fibre.

Given the relatively high number of converts to Christianity and the strong link between this form of conversion and exposure to higher education in Ede, it is likely that the widespread ambivalence about conversion also reflects complex attitudes towards social mobility, and especially towards social mobility through education. It is possible that the idealisation of steadfastness and constancy in the debate about conversion also implicitly asserts the value of indigeneity vis-à-vis non-indigenes. After all, non-indigenes not only boast a higher number of converts than the indigenes but also left their hometowns to seek better luck in Ede. In conversation, however, a focus on the inconstancy of (abstract) others usually appears primarily as an indirect assertion of the speaker's ability to control her or his life. And while resentment about conversion may exist at an abstract level, it is rarely aimed at individuals and is certainly balanced by general admiration for personal success.

'There is Religion and there is Culture': Views on Yoruba Traditional Practice

While all but one of our respondents aligned themselves with Christianity and Islam – religions embedded in the town through its institutions, both religious and non-religious – our survey suggests they also participate in Yoruba customs and 'traditional' life in a range of different ways, often at the level of the family or lineage and other social institutions.

When we asked respondents which Yoruba customs they had in their family, the highest proportion of respondents (19 per cent) claimed they did not have any Yoruba customs in their family. It is likely that these respondents hail from families or lineages that abolished such customs upon conversion to Islam or Christianity (as for example in the Muslim compounds described in chapter 5), although it is also possible that some respondents did not wish to share this information. After this, the most common customs reported were *Egúngún*, *Ṣàngó* and *Ògún* worship. There were a large number of other *òrìṣàs* named (particularly *Ifá*, *Ọ̀sun*, *Èṣù*, *Ọya*, *Ọbàtálá*, *Ìpedì* and *Agbájere*), but also ostensibly less religious customs such as blacksmithing, hunting, drumming, weddings, facial markings, naming ceremonies and respect for elders.[24]

In order to elaborate further on respondents' attitudes towards traditional practice, whether or not they officially lay claim to it within their lineage or

---

[24] When asked to name 'customs and traditions' in Ede more generally, respondents gave a similar list, but this time only 1 per cent of respondents said there were no such customs. *Ṣàngó* and *Egúngún* were by far the most frequently mentioned customs, followed by *Ògún*, *Ìpedì*, *Ifá* and *Ọ̀sun* worship.

family, we asked respondents whether they appreciated Yoruba customs.[25] By not giving any explicit definition of 'Yoruba customs' we were able not only to gauge general dispositions but also to gain an insight into how respondents themselves defined 'Yoruba customs', and moreover into how ideas about religion, culture and duty are debated by Muslims and Christians in Ede.

A clear majority of 81 per cent of respondents said they did appreciate Yoruba customs, while 5 per cent said no, and 9 per cent said it depends, with little difference between Muslims and Christians. Both Christians and Muslims who said they did not appreciate Yoruba customs said it was because of their religious beliefs, often referring to the importance of monotheism.[26] For instance, one Muslim gestured to the concept of *shirk*[27]: 'Yoruba customs and traditions lead [one] to associate bad things to Allah (God).'[28]

The group of respondents that was circumspect about its relationship with Yoruba customs was also acutely aware of its religious potentiality. Eleven respondents, both Christians and Muslims, explained that they appreciated those aspects of Yoruba customs that were not against their beliefs: 'I only appreciate Yoruba customs and traditions that does not [go] against the tenet[s] of Islam,'[29] and 'I appreciate any culture that does not go against my Christianity believe [sic].'[30]

The aspects of Yoruba customs named by certain respondents as being against their religious beliefs – sacrifice, idol worship, ritual activity and 'fetish' – again confirm that a critical attitude towards Yoruba customs is strongly driven by respondents' association of such practices with a religious repertoire or position of faith. For the majority of respondents, meanwhile, who said they liked or respected Yoruba customs, the aspects they most frequently appreciated were respect (particularly for elders), Yoruba ways of dressing, and what they saw as 'traditional' Yoruba behaviour or character, such as honesty and integrity. If we follow the distinction between 'cultural' and 'religious' aspects of Yoruba 'customs' made by some of our respondents, these and most of the

---

[25] The question asked was 'Do you appreciate Yoruba customs and traditions?' or in Yoruba, 'Nje e mo riri asa ati ise Yoruba?' Respondents were asked to answer yes, no, or it depends, and were asked to explain their answer.

[26] Some respondents claimed that they simply did not know anything about Yoruba customs, whether through choice or circumstance, for example: 'Because I was not trained in Yoruba customs' (EDEADE109).

[27] Arabic: the sin of idolatry, polytheism or associating others with God.

[28] EDEFPE129.

[29] EDEEMG146.

[30] EDEADE130.

other answers on this subject referred to 'cultural' aspects of Yoruba customs such as food, greetings, language, songs and marriage.[31]

We also wanted to gauge how people think about 'Yoruba customs' in the less abstract forms in which they are practised – for example, to maintain the wellbeing of a family – in order to explore the contemporary embedding of such practices in institutions of kinship. The survey asked respondents for their views on a Yoruba song that asserted that adherence to Islam or Christianity did not prevent a person from participating in their family's or lineage's rites.[32] A very large number of responses to this song were neutral, arguing that such decisions were up to the individual or simply explaining the ideas expressed by the song. Only 22 per cent of respondents explicitly agreed with the notion that family rites and monotheism could be combined, while 35 per cent said their religion did not allow it.

While critical responses to the song again strongly emphasised religious discourse,[33] appreciative responses made reference to the importance of tolerance, religious freedom and heritage. Some respondents described how traditional rites are embedded in social institutions such as their family or their everyday work activities (for instance, hunting). Other responses, which

---

[31] There were, however, also a number of Christian and Muslim respondents who described their admiration for aspects of the culture in ways we could characterise as religious, including the òrìṣà, the work of babaláwo and traditional healers, festivals, and the religious fervour of adherents of traditional religion. It was not always clear from their answers whether they saw this as 'religion' or 'culture', and, indeed, whether this was a distinction these particular respondents would find useful.

[32] Respondents were asked for their views on the following song:
Àwa ó ṣorò ilé wa o
Àwa ó ṣorò ilé wa o,
ẹ̀sìn kan kò pé – ò ye
ẹ̀sìn kan kò pé – ò ye
ká wa ma ṣorò.
Àwa ó ṣorò ilé wa o.

We will perform the rites of our ilé [family, lineage, compound]
We will perform the rites of our ilé
there is no religion that says – it is not right
there is no religion that says – it is not right
that we should perform the rites.
We will perform the rites of our ilé.

[33] Some 65 per cent of those, both Christians and Muslims, who opposed the practising of lineage rites referred to it being against their religion to do so. For instance: 'This song is against our religion; Christians should no longer sing this kind of song, because it does not fit with our religion' (EDEOLU004: 'Orin yi tako esin wa onigbagbo ko gbodo mon ko iru orin bayi tori wipe ko ba esin wa mun'), or: 'This song is against the Islamic doctrine because in Islam there nothing like the rites of family' (EDEAUD150).

focused less on everyday life but rather on an intellectual appreciation of traditional customs, emphasised the importance of Yoruba culture, traditions and heritage, and of these 17 respondents discussed the moral obligation of not forgetting the beliefs and practices of their forefathers in the modern world or in the face of foreign religions. Other explanations centred on the importance of fostering cooperation, harmony or good relations within society, and suggestions that not all lineage rites were contrary to world religions.[34]

A group of respondents conceptualised family rites as somewhat different from Islam and Christianity, mainly because they predated the arrival of the world religions, but also because they were historically important or a matter of personal choice. By suggesting that such rites are a matter of heritage or personal choice, or that they might be reformed in order to take on a Muslim or Christian face, these answers often affirm, directly or indirectly, that the practice of family rites occupies a very different social space from that occupied by the world religions.[35] One Muslim respondent gave a particularly nuanced explanation of the difference between religion and tradition or customs (àṣà) as he saw it, suggesting that Islam and traditional religion were parallel to each other but therefore implicitly distinct, with both having their own 'customs':

> As a Muslim who understands his religion, [I believe] religion and culture are different from each other, moreover all religions have their customs, Islam has its own customs and so too traditional religion has its own customs. Islam has principles such as prayer, *zakat*, fasting, *Hajj*, Islam has customs of naming, weddings, worship practices and so on. And similarly the customs of traditional religion have similar worship practices, naming ceremonies, weddings and rules of behaviour.[36]

---

[34] These more positive views on the practice of lineage rites by monotheists covered a range of views emphasising the recent arrival of the world religions, individual choice and areas of compatibility between the world religions and lineage rites, e.g. 'The Yoruba culture tolerate customs and tradition irrespective whether you a Muslim/Christian. Their belief is that individual are converted either Muslim/Xtian' (EDEESL145), and 'It depends on such rite. There are rites that are even allowed or encouraged in religions like Islam or Christianity. Male circumcision is an example' (EDEADE122).

[35] In fact, 11 respondents argued explicitly that religion and culture were separate spheres, and that culture, traditions or customs therefore did not impinge on Christian or Islamic religious practices. For instance, respondents affirmed that: 'This song is unice [unique] 'cos we don't normally forget our tradition. And it doesn't disturb [sic] our religion Christian or Muslim or *Ifá*' (EDEPOL036); 'The song is just trying to demarcate between religion and tradition. Emphasising the fact being a Christian does not prevent me from imbibing our culture' (EDESDA120); 'The modern religion is quite different from culture' (EDEBHS134).

[36] EDETAL028: Gẹgẹbi ọmọ elesin Islam ti ẹsin rẹ ye, ẹsin ati asa yato si ara wọn.

More succinctly, another Muslim respondent simply stated: 'There is no way [to] put culture apart [aside]. There is religion and there is culture.'[37]

These two positions epitomise the main ways in which respondents negotiated an accommodating relationship between world religions and traditional religions: the first asserts the separate but equal nature of Islamic and traditional custom, while the second proposes a difference between religion and (implicitly traditional) culture. However, in contrast to those who rejected traditional practices because of their religious nature, the more accommodating views tended to emphasise their cultural meaning.

But while the acceptance of traditional practice was loosely linked to a distinction between a cultural and a religious interpretation of traditional practice, it was also associated with religious difference. Thus, Christians were much less likely than Muslims to say they participated in traditional customs, with only 13 per cent of Christians (compared to 22 per cent of Muslims) saying they would actively participate in traditional customs. Given that many Christians in Ede are non-indigenes, it is likely that this difference reflects the impact of family ties on religious practice as discussed, for example, in chapter 5. The social expectation of participation in family and lineage rites or the town's traditional festivals is much stronger for those who 'belong'. It is therefore possible that an understanding of local practices as custom – rather than religion – is more intuitive for those with family, and family concerns, in the town.

However, it is possible that this difference also reflects, at least to some degree, the rise of Pentecostalism, since it appears to respond to the strong warnings about family rites that are often part of Pentecostal theologies. Clearly Pentecostal concerns about family customs help migrants to maintain greater distance from their kin at home, should they so wish, and thus a remaking of both self and community.[38] But migration also often puts migrants at a disadvantage vis-à-vis the indigenes of their new town, who have greater access to local resources through the town's traditional and, in Muslim towns like Ede, Islamic institutions. Thus Pentecostal warnings about the potentially corrupting influence of traditional practice also explain the experience of a particular form of disempowerment, or even turn it into a moral triumph.

> Bakannaa gbogbo esin loni asa wọn, esin Islam ni asa tirẹ beni esin abalaye ni asa tire, Islam ni awon ilana bi irun kiki, saka yiyo, awẹ gbigba, Hajj sise, Islam ni asa isọmọ lorukọ, igbeyawo, ilana ijosin ati be be lọ. Bẹ si ni asa esin abalaye ni ilana ijosin ti ọrọ naa si jọ ara wọn, isọmọ lorukọ, igbeyawo, ati iwa ilana idari awọn eniyan.

[37] EDEESL147.
[38] R. Marshall, *Political Spiritualities: The Pentecostal Revolution in Nigeria* (Chicago and London: University of Chicago Press, 2009).

Muslim Views of Christianity, Christian Views of Islam

In contrast to our respondents' views about traditional practices as not always 'religious', Muslim and Christian respondents firmly acknowledged the status of both Christianity and Islam as religions. Our survey asked respondents what they liked or respected about Islam and about Christianity, and the answers revealed the extent to which encounters with religious others are embedded in everyday life in Ede.

Most of the Christian respondents who described what they liked about Islam focused on explicitly religious aspects of Islam that were related through observations of what Muslims do. The largest proportion of respondents, 16 Christians, commented on the way Muslims pray, particularly their dedication to the five daily prayers: 'I respect their strong faith and the way they take their prayers seriously,'[39] explained one Christian respondent, while another Christian linked Muslim prayer with his ideal of Christian prayer: 'If you see a true Muslim, you will be attracted to the religion because of their commitment to praying five times a day and the holy book tells us to pray without ceasing.'[40] Similarly, 11 Christians commended the dedication or sincerity that they felt Muslims showed towards their religion. Other aspects of Islam that Christian respondents particularly liked included Muslims' belief in God (implicitly shared with Christians), the way Muslim women dress, and the way Muslims conduct burials and weddings. Drawing examples mainly from daily Muslim life and discipline, these comments highlight the everyday nature of many Muslim–Christian encounters.

Similarly referring to lived experiences involving Muslims, 12 Christian respondents described their admiration for Muslims in terms that focused less on the explicitly religious aspects of Islam and more on the perceived character of Muslims, often focusing on honesty and openness: Muslims were praised for being 'straightforward',[41] 'Very reliable, trustable and promising keeper',[42] 'caring even to the time of tribulation',[43] 'naturally good',[44] and for

---

[39] EDEADE135.
[40] EDEADE138: 'Bi e ba ri Musulumi gidi esin wọn yio wu yin se nitori wakati marun wọn yo ma lo dede ati pe iwe mimo so fun wa pe ki ama gbadura laisimi'.
[41] EDEEMG170; EDEFPE102.
[42] EDEBHS136.
[43] EDESDA120.
[44] EDEADE130.

their 'patience',[45] their love towards each other, and for relating 'positively'[46] with others without making trouble.[47]

A smaller number of Christian respondents mentioned aspects of Islam that are more abstract and theological. These included the Qur'an, ritual cleanliness, fasting during Ramadan, belief in life after death and destiny, Islam's nature as a 'religion of peace', *Sharia* law, and the fact that the way they practise their religion 'is the same way all over the world'.[48] Especially the last two points also highlight two aspects of Christianity that are sometimes perceived as shortcomings that Christians should seek to overcome, namely the fact that contemporary Nigerian Christianity has no equivalent to Islam's legal tradition, and that the denominational divisions within Christianity can appear deeper than those within Islam.

Many of the aspects of Christianity that Muslim respondents liked were similar to those that Christians liked about Islam, and they similarly often focused on observable behaviour, including belief in one God or in the same God as Muslims, the perceived unity of Christians, their good character and behaviour, their sincerity and devotion to their religion, and their steadfastness in prayer. Twenty-one respondents described their respect for Jesus or for Christians' belief in Jesus: for example, 'I praise the prophet Yissa, child of Mariam.'[49] This response is indicative of a strategy also used more broadly in Christian and Muslim inter-faith relations: 11 respondents to our survey refer to Jesus as a (Muslim) prophet, describing him using terms such as '*Ànábì*' ('prophet') or '*Òjíṣẹ́*' ('messenger'). Other explicitly religious aspects of Christianity our Muslim respondents admired included prayer,[50] worship, the Bible, commitment to churchgoing, festivals, moral teachings and religious instruction. Two respondents described how Christians 'preach peace',[51] echoing the Christians' approval of Islam as a religion of peace.

Another significant proportion of answers focused on the perceived characteristics of Christians, such as being 'honest, friendly and always ready to assist',[52] being of 'good character',[53] 'patience',[54] and their '[a]cceptance of

---

[45] EDEPOL075: 'suuru'.
[46] EDEESL148.
[47] EDEFPE125: 'Toripe awon Musulumi ti mo mo ki se jangbon'.
[48] EDETAL034.
[49] EDETAL008: 'Mo fi iyin mi fun anabi Yissa ọmọ Mariam'.
[50] Prayer was mentioned as a positive aspect of Christianity by seven Muslims, while it was mentioned by 15 Christians as something they liked about Islam.
[51] EDEENL158; EDEESL145.
[52] EDEAUD154.
[53] EDEAUD150.
[54] EDEPOL080: 'suuru'.

everybody and love for other'.[55] Eighteen Muslims also commented on unity among Christians, particularly noting that they help each other (rather than remarking on strictly religious unity, as many respondents did about Muslims). Statements such as 'United they stand and work toward helping themselves,'[56] and 'They behave like biological brothers'[57] may reflect the comparatively greater preparedness of some churches and Christian communities to accept and support poor members.

Emphasising again the everyday nature of Muslim–Christian relations, a further eight respondents commented on the perceived tolerance of Christians for Muslims (which was not something Christians described about Muslims). For instance, one Muslim remarked: 'Most of them respect me and my religion. They allow me to do things the way my religion permits me. Aside from worship, we do things in common and there is trust.'[58]

Indeed, a proportion of the answers from Muslims to this question aimed to draw out the links between Christianity and Islam rather than describe Christianity's distinctiveness. Thus one Muslim remarked that 'A Muslim who does not believe in the Bible and Jesus does not practise his/her religion completely,'[59] while another pointed out that 'the same things as are in the Quran are in the Bible'.[60] Other respondents noted that 'Their religion resembles Islam,'[61] or that 'There is no difference in Islam and Christianity.'[62]

However, nine Muslims said they liked the principle of 'one man, one wife' in Christianity (with some adding approvingly that they perceived Christians to have fewer children than Muslims). In this reference to monogamy they were presumably indicating something they saw as distinctively Christian, even though some older Nigerian-initiated churches permit polygamy. It should be noted that anecdotal evidence suggests that the number of polygamous marriages in Yorubaland has steadily declined over the past two decades or more. It is not clear what exact factors are contributing to this development, but it is likely that urbanisation and the growing costs of childcare and education play a role in this development. As polygamy is declining among Muslims as well as among Christians, monogamy may well appear as a more general form of progress to some sections of the population.

---

[55] EDEEMG142.
[56] EDEBHS134.
[57] EDEESL149.
[58] EDEADE122.
[59] EDETAL020: 'Musulumi ti ko ba gba bibeli ati Jesu gbọ, esin rẹ ko i pe'.
[60] EDEOLU021: 'Nitoripe okanna niwon oun towa ninu Quran ni o wa ninu Bibeli na'.
[61] EDEOLU089: 'Esin won dabi esin Musulumi'.
[62] EDEOLU018.

Overall, then, both Muslim and Christian views on the other religion often focused on points of congruity between the two religions, even if the religions were not conceptualised as identical (though some Muslims felt that Christianity was 'included' in Islam). Where there were perceived differences between the religions, respondents often focused on aspects of religious practice that they recognised in their own religion but which they felt were in fact better practised by the other religious community (such as the Muslim commitment to prayer or Muslim unity, versus the Christian commitment to churchgoing and greater mutual support among individual Christians). While some respondents offered general and theological reflections on the other religion, most examples used to illustrate similarities or shared dispositions between the religions were drawn from everyday encounters and observations.

While we did not ask respondents to describe aspects of the other monotheistic religion they disliked, nonetheless not all respondents were positive about the other religion. Nine Muslim respondents could not describe anything they liked about Christianity (just as some Christians could not mention anything they liked about Islam). Those who could not say anything positive about the 'other' religion often referred to lack of knowledge about it.[63] While it is clearly possible that those predisposed to avoid the 'other' religion also seek to avoid close friendships with those of other religions – indeed, this is a practice encouraged by several Pentecostal churches and groups like the Tablighi Jamaat – these responses also point to the importance of regular personal encounters and relationships across the religious divide for the coexistence of Islam and Christianity in Ede.

Religious Sociality and Friendship

The intersection between social institutions such as kinship and everyday interactions between people of different religions became especially apparent in our investigation of inter-religious sociality at social occasions in Ede. The majority of our respondents (76 per cent) said they regularly attended social occasions hosted by people of the other monotheist religion, and a similar percentage of people (80 per cent) said they would allow people of different religions to attend a family member's funeral. This high level of approval for religious interaction at such events suggests that despite Ede's strong Muslim majority, participation in the celebrations of both Muslims and Christians is the normal experience for its citizens.

---

[63] Very occasionally, however, respondents described a dislike of specific perceived characteristics of Christians, such as favouring Christians over others.

However, there was some disagreement among our respondents as to how they would handle active involvement in the religious aspect of a ceremony. Only 46 per cent of respondents would allow people of a different religion to say a public prayer at a funeral. Responses for other life events were slightly more liberal; 51 per cent of respondents were happy to have public blessings from people from other religions at a naming ceremony for their new child, and 56 per cent of respondents would allow people from other religions to give a public blessing at a family member's wedding. The staggered liberality suggests the differential importance of these life events, with funerals the event most in need of close management. Even so, the fact that roughly half of our respondents would be happy to hear prayers of the other monotheist religion at such an event illustrates a high degree of acceptance by Muslims and Christians of each other's religions.

Our respondents were far less welcoming of the active participation of traditionalists. This confirms the impression that Islam and Christianity are perceived as more congruent (as 'religions'). Nonetheless, tolerance of traditional practices was still relatively high, with 36 per cent saying they would allow people from other religions or traditional groups to contribute to the entertainment at a funeral,[64] and 36 per cent of respondents agreeing to people representing the parents' family traditions being involved or giving public blessings at a child's naming ceremony.

Respondents provided three main arguments against allowing people from their family traditions to provide entertainment at a funeral: that *celebrating* at a funeral – particularly with songs and dancing – was against their religion (in the case of Islam especially); that they did not want traditional worshippers there; and that it was against their religion in general. One respondent made a distinction between traditional worshippers being present at a funeral and actively participating in it: 'They can come but they can't participate, because Islam does not teach us to do so.'[65] Another pointed to the importance of different degrees of participation by saying that 'I would agree, but they are only allowed to eat'[66] [i.e. to spectate rather than have more active involvement]. Thirteen respondents referred to particular things they would be worried

---

[64] In explaining their answers to this question, some respondents were concerned that there should be no performances by traditional worshippers, while others categorically stated that there should be no entertainment at a funeral.

[65] EDEPOL107: 'Won le wa sugbon won ko le kopa nitori Islam ko ko wa be'.

[66] EDEOLU079: 'Ma gba ounje nikan ni won le je'.

about: *shirk*, sin, singing, alcohol, 'division and chaos',[67] 'unwanted things'[68] and 'problems'.[69]

As in the discussion of continued practice of family rites, those who were open to the idea of traditional entertainment at a funeral often tried to demarcate a space for 'tradition' that was non-religious, either by conceptualising it as entertainment rather than religious ritual – 'entertainment is just like fun for me',[70] 'they will add to the colour of the occasion'[71] or 'it is merry making'[72] – or by returning to the idea of a separation between religion and tradition or culture: 'culture and traditions must be respected',[73] or 'religion is different from culture in the Yoruba community'.[74] However, fewer people argued that there was a separation between religion and culture than in response to other questions, perhaps implying that a funeral is viewed as an explicitly religious event.[75]

There were only some small differences between religions in response to questions about the participation of religious others in major celebrations.[76] Similarly, there was no clear pattern among those who had changed their religion. This is interesting partly because it suggests that while Pentecostal warnings about traditional practice affect Christians' views on traditional practice in a general or abstract sense, they do not affect the interaction between family members quite as strongly, or at least not in a way that would illuminate a difference between Muslims and Christians. It is possible that when thinking about traditionalist family members in their hometowns rather than about traditional practice in the context of their life in Ede, the firm exclusion of traditional practice did not seem easier for Christians.

Certainly, family relationships played an important role in shaping the acceptance of other religions. Irrespective of gender and religion, people who had married someone of a different religion were more likely to agree to people of other religions being present, giving blessings or providing entertainment

---

[67] EDEADE134.
[68] EDEBHS115.
[69] EDETAL005.
[70] EDEOLU026.
[71] EDEEMG170.
[72] EDEESL143.
[73] EDEADE135.
[74] EDEADE139: 'Torí pé èṣìn yàtọ̀ sí àṣà láwùjọ Yorùbá'.
[75] Indeed, five respondents made reference to the importance of the deceased's religious beliefs in deciding how the ceremony should be carried out.
[76] Muslims were more likely to agree to people from other religions giving public blessings at a wedding or naming ceremony, and on the whole Christians were more likely to say 'it depends' and give conditions for their answers, such as 'If … it is not harmful or requiring me to violate my religious beliefs' (EDEADE111).

at weddings, funerals and naming ceremonies. This greater acceptance of religious difference at social occasions was particularly pronounced in the case of allowing people of other religions to attend a family funeral, to which 95 per cent of people who had married someone of a different religion would agree. It was also interesting to see that tolerance towards other religions at these occasions also correlated with greater willingness to attend traditional religious events such as the *Sàngó* Festival in Ede.[77] It is possible that this greater tolerance of traditional practices partly reflects the fact that many mixed marriages included at least one partner originally from Ede. But it does not seem unreasonable to assume that those who negotiated religious divides in their marital lives were generally more willing to tolerate others' religious practices (see chapter 10).

When we asked respondents to explain why they would go to celebrations by people of other religions, many respondents referred to the importance of community. They explained that they attended such occasions either to foster better relations between religions – one respondent said such occasions bring about 'good relationship'[78] and another said they 'teach lessons to humanity'[79] – or to improve their own knowledge about other religions: one Christian respondent attended 'to gain more knowledge about them'.[80] Others drew on a seemingly humanist or secular idea of unity, such as 'as a human being, I love everyone'.[81] Referring to the perceived closeness of Islam and Christianity explored above, many respondents also stated that Muslims and Christians 'are serving the same God',[82] or even, somewhat hyperbolically, 'There's no difference between Muslims and Christians.'[83]

The most common justification for tolerating religious difference at social occasions focused on different forms of social unity and communal identity, particularly the family (*ẹbí* or *mọ̀lébí*). Here a number of respondents used stock phrases or sayings, such as 'religion does not cause conflict. We are the

---

[77] For example, 94 per cent of those who said they would go to the *Sàngó* festival would attend different religions' celebrations (compared to 74 per cent of those who would not go to *Sàngó* festival). Similarly, 88 per cent of those who would go to *Sàngó* festival would agree for people from other religions to give a blessing at a wedding (compared to 49 per cent of those who would not attend the *Sàngó* festival).

[78] EDEADE113.

[79] EDEFPE103.

[80] EDETAL031.

[81] EDEAUD149.

[82] EDEESL148.

[83] EDEESL153: 'Ko si iyatọ larin Musulumi ati ọmọ leyin Kirisiti'.

same,'⁸⁴ and 'We are all related.'⁸⁵ Another respondent explained that they could allow traditional worshippers to provide entertainment at a funeral because 'friends and family can be from a different religion, we cannot cast them out',⁸⁶ while another said they would allow it 'because we are the same family'.⁸⁷ This confirms the suggestion in previous chapters that although religion plays an important role in shaping family relations, the opposite is also the case: in the context of religiously mixed families and especially extended families, religious difference is condensed and often bridged by shared identity and mutual obligation.

Respondents also emphasised the importance of a feeling of community within the town for various forms of sociality across religious boundaries. Suggesting a form of social solidarity similar to that shaped by family ties, one respondent referred to the town as the source of unity, saying 'we are people of the same town'.⁸⁸ However, not all respondents understood their participation in the practices of others as an act of tolerance legitimised or justified by higher-order values. Emphasising the importance of collaboration and cooperation for social wellbeing, some respondents actively valued the existence of different religions within the community for its own sake. As one respondent pointed out, religious difference also featured in notions of achievement, contentment and pleasure: 'Other religions may contribute because a single person cannot do the work of many people. This is happiness.'⁸⁹

'We are all One' but 'I Prefer my own Religion': Religious Difference in Marriage and the Family

The frequency of religious difference within families, as discussed above and in chapters 9 and 10 of this book, is often cited as an explanation for high levels of religious tolerance in south-western Nigeria. Therefore we wanted to find out what proportion of the people of Ede live in religiously mixed nuclear families, and how they perceive inter-religious families to shape their own attitudes towards religion.⁹⁰

---

84 EDETAL010: 'Esin ko fa ja. Ikanna ni wa'.
85 EDEOLU084: 'Gbogbo wa omo iya ni wa.'
86 EDETAL001: 'ore, ebi le wa ninu elesin miran, a gbodo le won'.
87 EDEPOL043: 'Nitori wipe ebi kan na ni waa'.
88 EDEOLU068: 'Toripe ara ilu kanna ni wa'.
89 EDEOLU006.
90 In our Ede survey we asked solely about parents and spouses with different religions, but in our revised survey, administered elsewhere in Yorubaland, we have asked respondents for more detail on changes and differences of religion among other important family members such as siblings, grandparents and children.

We looked in particular at religious differences between respondents and their parents and spouses, and we found a relatively high level of religious difference within families. Among our respondents, 10 per cent had a father of a different religion from themselves, and 9 per cent had a mother of a different religion.[91] Respondents with parents of a different religion were split fairly evenly between men and women and between indigenes and non-indigenes of Ede, but the majority consisted of Christians with Muslim fathers and mothers, which points to a higher rate of conversion to Christianity than to Islam, discussed in more detail below.

Moreover, 15 per cent of respondents reported that one or both of their parents had changed religion.[92] Twenty-one per cent of these respondents whose parents had changed religion had themselves changed religion, which is much higher than the rate among the whole population of respondents in Ede, of whom only 7 per cent reported having changed their religion. Although we cannot determine the causality of this correspondence between parent and child conversion from our survey data, it may suggest that if an individual's parent has changed her or his religion, they themselves are more likely to change their religion. This cross-generational influence would seem to confirm the reservations of Muslim and Christian leaders that intermarriage, which often entails conversion, affects the stability of familial religious identity.[93]

Among our respondents, religious differences within marriages were also high compared to other parts of the world where such numbers are available (see chapter 10). Eight per cent of our respondents reported that they were or had been married to someone of a different religion,[94] and 14 per cent (but including some of those in a religiously mixed marriage) said that either they or their spouse had changed their religion (whether before or after marriage). Depending on the exact calibration of these numbers, especially the inclusion of past marriages, between 14 and 20 per cent of our respondents were, or had

---

[91] In both cases this was because either the respondent or their parent had changed religion.

[92] Ten per cent of respondents reported that their father had changed his religion, and 9 per cent reported that their mother had changed her religion (some respondents reported that both their parents had changed religion, which is why the overall percentage of respondents with one or more parents who had changed religion is lower than the percentage for individual parents).

[93] In our Ede survey, we did not ask for the reasons why respondents' parents had changed their religion. However, in our subsequent revised survey, we did ask this question, and encountered some cases in which a parent had been convinced to convert to a child's religion. So children's conversions or differences of religion may also influence the previous generation, as well as vice versa.

[94] We asked respondents for details of up to four marriages, including those that had resulted in separation, divorce or widowhood, as well as ongoing marriages.

been, in a marriage where husband and wife did not have the same religion, or where one partner had converted.

As suggested in chapter 10, roughly half of our respondents said that they would be reluctant to marry someone of a different religion, owing to family difficulties or incompatibility, and lack of love and understanding within the marriage. At the same time, the survey responses reflected the widespread notion that if a husband and wife do not practise the same religion, the wife should convert to her husband's religion. Twelve per cent of respondents said they would be willing to marry someone of another religion, but only if the prospective spouse would convert to their religion. It was mostly (though not entirely) men who gave this answer, and indeed, three male respondents affirmed directly that they were the head of the household (*aláṣe*), and so their spouse must practise their religion. Thus although these respondents were not willing to *be married to* someone of a different religion, they did not seem to envisage insuperable cultural or social differences arising from the person's different religious background, as long as they would agree to convert. Implicit in this answer is, again, the sense of ultimate compatibility between people who are more alike than different.

A small number of those who said they could consider marrying someone of a different religion described a sense of the matter being out of their control, 'in God's hands',[95] but the largest number of these respondents explained how love conquered everything; if there was love, they could overcome any obstacles that a religiously mixed marriage might present (see chapter 10). Another group of respondents talked about how it was possible to marry someone of a different religion – and here they referred to Christianity or Islam – because 'we worship the same God' or 'we are all one'. Responses here variously described this sense of unity as being both *because of* and *in spite of* religion. Thus, for instance, one respondent invoked the religious similarities between the two religions, while still valorising Islam: 'Because the two religions preaches the words of Allah. The Dos and Don'ts of almighty Allah.'[96]

And finally, a large number of respondents simply noted that intermarriage was acceptable to them because superior forms of belonging subsumed religious difference. Statements such as 'we are all related'[97] or 'we are one'[98] affirmed the importance of a broader community – whether family, town or Yoruba identity – whose values could help to overcome religious differences.

---

[95] EDEOLU078: 'O wa ni owo Olorun'.
[96] EDEBHS134.
[97] EDETAL016 'omo iya kan naa ni wa'.
[98] EDEOLU089: 'okan naa ni wa'.

Conclusion

In conclusion, this chapter confirms and deepens insights into Ede's religious demography. While the vast majority of people identify as Muslim, there is a significant Christian community, and large sections of the population who identify as monotheists also participate in traditional practices in varying degrees. In addition, Islam is closely linked to indigeneity, and many highly educated immigrants to Ede are Christians. Education and migrant status are also closely associated with conversion from Islam to Christianity, although there are small numbers of converts to Islam too. Most converts to Christianity are based in the town's educational institutions.

While conversion for marriage and as a result of personal contact with others was common among converts to both religions, Christians also gave explicitly religious reasons for their conversion. This may reflect the rhetoric of Pentecostalism as well as the accessibility of Christianity to both Yoruba and English speakers. But while respondents' own or family members' conversions were generally described positively, the conversion of others in general was often seen as reflecting baser concerns, including greed. This ambivalence about conversion may reflect its association with migration, education and upward mobility, as well as with a lack of personal fortitude.

Reflecting different social experiences, attitudes towards traditional religion varied among both Muslims and Christians. This difference reflects both debates about this topic within many Pentecostal churches and the fact that many of Ede's Christians are non-indigenes, and thus under less pressure from family members to maintain such rites. However, as migrants most Christians also have less access to the benefits associated with Ede's traditional practices, and it is also possible that they emphasise the uncompromising nature of their faith in order to assert an alternative form of authority.

In contrast to the contrasting views and experiences shaped by different access to education and indigeneity, Muslim and Christian attitudes to the other monotheist religion were similar. Each firmly acknowledged the other religion's status as a religion. Positive views and participation in aspects of the other monotheist religion were generally associated with personal experience and different forms of sociality, such as the perceived good character of people of the other religion, aspects of religious practice, shared theology and religious commitment. As we did not ask about negative views, it is difficult to assess to what degrees the toleration of the other religion is really a form of endurance, but chapters 5 to 7 suggest that this applies at least in some cases. For other respondents, however, religious diversity contributes to wellbeing and even happiness; an attitude clearly outside the concept of toleration alone.

Despite the fact that many citizens of Ede participate in others' religious events and have friends and relatives of other religions, there are no universally accepted templates of inter-religious sociality, beyond an emphasis on both the similarity of the world religions and the shared community at the familial or town level. While about half of our respondents thought it acceptable for those of other monotheist religions to participate actively in social events associated with their own religion, this idea was associated with problems and disorder by other respondents who wanted religious outsiders to be passive. Clearly, ideas about the social and spiritual benefit of religious difference or, on the other end of the spectrum of engagement, the need to tolerate such difference, differ widely.

In Ede's extended families, as well as in more intimate relationships such as between parents and children or husbands and wives, religious difference is relatively high. But while some respondents were determined to avoid the introduction of religious difference into their (nuclear) family life, others suggested that such forms of difference could be managed through gendered forms of compliance, i.e. wives' acceptance of their husbands' religion, which was understood as partly constitutive of mutual tolerance. Yet others again side-stepped reflections on tolerance by arguing that religious difference was of little importance if there was love between spouses.

While some of our respondents' attitudes and experiences are shaped by their religion and its association with education and indigeneity, other responses point to the importance of personal encounters and observations. Individuals do not necessarily have one fixed approach to inter-religious interactions, and they may adjust their views or practices depending on situations or relationships they encounter. Understanding the nature of difference and the means of overcoming it differently in each situation, they may stress the value of respect for others in their encounters with Yoruba customs, praise 'normal' behaviour by religious others during religious celebrations, and point to the desirability of love in marriage. Although there are stock phrases and stereotypical dispositions that respondents use to analyse these situations (such as 'we are all calling on the same god'), and although their understanding of their own experiences may be shaped by social difference in the town, they also reflect on their own personal experiences to evaluate ways of behaving.

Many of the respondents to our survey reflected on the importance of 'unity' despite differences – and this 'unity' could take different, overlapping forms at different times: respondents made claims such as 'Ede is one room' (see chapter 1), Muslims and Christians 'worship the same god', or thought of themselves as '[a]s [a] family friend or fellow townsman'[99] in order to overcome religious

[99] EDEADE112.

difference. At first glance this stress on communal unity appears to resonate with David Laitin's argument that Yoruba religious tolerance is the result of a widespread devotion to the 'ancestral city'. However, while Laitin argues that the individual commitment to the hometown, which forms the basis of religious tolerance, is largely the result of British and local elite manipulation of local values and symbols,[100] our survey suggests that this argument needs to be turned from its head to its feet. Of course kingship, supported by the colonial state and valued in Yoruba elite discourse plays an important role in transcending (or transgressing) religious difference. But as this chapter has illustrated, in Ede belonging is also closely associated with differential access to material and political resources for Muslims and Christians, and by extension with explicit Muslim–Christian differences.

In contrast, many aspects of religious accommodation are rooted in the lived experience of mixed families and residential communities, which is – or can be – extended to encompass the community of the town. As many people are confronted with religious difference in the negotiation of basic forms of sociality, the sharing of religious celebrations primarily reflects the importance of everyday encounters and negotiations within the family and neighbourhood. Tolerance is practised where a sense of a broader 'togetherness' sometimes enable the citizens of Ede to overcome potential religious divisions. Beyond that, people understand religious difference as a positive aspect of their own lives, and they may even recognise their own ability to overcome difference as part of their own identities.

But our survey also suggests the importance of other forms of community beyond the level of the town. Thus, there are two ways in which being Yoruba is used as a unifying identity by the citizens of Ede. Firstly, it is one of several communal identities that can be used to overcome the potential for religious division – as, for instance, in the case of the respondent who gestured to shared Yoruba origins through the figure of *Olódùmarè*: 'Unity is what we need. Either Muslim or Christian or traditional Yoruba religion we come from *Olódùmarè*.'[101] But secondly, Yoruba-ness is also closely associated with traditional practice and customs. While those who refuse to participate in traditional practice see it as a (rival) religion, those who accept it tend to highlight its customary or cultural nature as a Yoruba (ethno-national) practice. Indeed, where traditional practice is discussed as a generally shared aspect of a cultural or ethno-national heritage it appears more acceptable than when it is explored as a ritual practice ensuring the spiritual wellbeing of a smaller

---

[100] D.D. Laitin, *Hegemony and Culture: Politics and Religious Change among the Yoruba* (Chicago and London: University of Chicago Press, 1986).
[101] EDEOLU002.

group of people, such as a family. Respondents' 'cultural work'[102] in relation to Yoruba identity constructs it both as closely associated with traditional customs, and as an identity that allows respondents to overcome other differences. Whether the notion of religious toleration is appropriate in a given context thus also reflects individual perceptions of Yoruba identity.

Of course, respondents also form identities based on non-religious spaces, institutions and interactions. But nonetheless all our respondents had a clear sense of a religious identity that was simultaneously also shaped by other social positions, such as being a member of a particular family, or being a husband, wife or child of someone who practises a certain religion. Respondents also perform 'cultural work' to decide what it means to be a Christian or Muslim in Ede, but these identities tend to be centred more on the family, friendship networks or the town. Respondents' dual senses of the reasons why people convert – for personal, spiritual reasons and for practical reasons with sociological explanations – point to these overlapping ways in which religious identities and inter-religious encounters can be experienced. It is as if respondents conceptualise both individual agency and broader social forces shaping identities and experiences – an echo (though not necessarily directly) of the notion of *orí*, which contains within it ideas of both predestination and one's personal choice to make efforts to follow a pre-ordained path.[103] To be a Muslim or Christian in Ede can be both a communal identity, shaped by one's experience of living in this majority Muslim town, or by the history and expectations of one's lineage, and an intensely personal, private experience.

In conclusion, while the town offers space for religious difference, the relationship between Ede's Muslims and Christians is shaped in complex ways by its institutions. While chapters 2 and 3 of this book illustrate that kingship is an important institution for facilitating peaceful religious coexistence, our survey also highlights that the importance of indigeneity within Ede means that belonging is associated with aspects of religious difference and disagreement. In contrast the everyday encounters of Muslims and Christians, as neighbours, colleagues and friends, play a much more important role in shaping mutual tolerance – and encounters 'beyond tolerance'. Explanations

---

[102] J.D.Y. Peel, 'The cultural work of Yoruba ethnogenesis', *History and Ethnicity*, ed. E. Tonkin, M. McDonald and M. Chapman (London: Routledge, 1989), pp. 198–215.

[103] *Orí* literally means 'head', but here is used in the sense of fate, or the *orí* each person is traditionally imagined to select before arriving on Earth, and which determines one's path in life. By consulting one's *orí* through *Ifá* a person may 'be able to tread the path already laid out for him in heaven', albeit in conjunction with that person's own efforts 'to bring to fruition what has already been predestined for him in heaven by the choice of a good *orí*': W. Abimbola, *The Study of Yoruba Literature* (Ile-Ife: University of Ife Press, 1977), pp. 113–16.

emphasising the togetherness of members of different religions therefore also extend to the wider 'Yoruba' identity, and to familial and other forms of shared experience. In this sense the religious differences in Ede are shaped both by different forms of coexistence and encounter that include but are not limited to toleration, and by forms of community that transcend religious difference at different levels.

CHAPTER 12

Outlook: Religious Difference, the Yoruba, and Beyond

Insa Nolte and Olukoya Ogen

Drawing on the case study of Ede and south-west Nigeria, this book offers an understanding of inter-religious relations that challenges the notion that Muslim–Christian difference is inherently conflictual. We suggest that the dominant role ascribed to conflict arises from the assumption that the experiences of the global North, where the increase of Muslim–Christian conflict has been an important feature of the religious encounters between clearly bounded groups, is paradigmatic for the rest of the world. As a result, interfaith debates and practices centre on the need for mutual toleration.[1] However, in Africa, both the growth of intra-religious mobilisation in some contexts, and the close social relations between members of different religions in others, illustrate that conflict – and the need for toleration – is only one form of inter-religious engagement.

In order to understand the full implications of the growing political importance of religion, we must recognise that in Africa and the global South, the social diversity and creativity subsumed under functioning forms of rationality in the global North are often 'promiscuously visible'.[2] Examples of the wide range of practices that shape Ede's mixed religious landscape certainly include practices of toleration and low-level conflict, particularly in the context of clearly bounded religious groups (chapters 5–7, 8). It is especially in these cases that religious boundaries are produced in relation to other forms of identity, such as descent and belonging, and in relation to social or institutional hierarchies. In other words, it appears that both potential conflict and the need for tolerance are of particular importance where religion is closely linked to social or institutional structures. In such contexts, practices of tolerance do not solely reflect explicitly normative values but also rely on practical

---

[1] R. Forst, 'The limits of toleration', *Constellations* 11:3 (2004), 312–25.
[2] J. Comaroff and J. Comaroff, *Theory from the South or, how Euro-America is Evolving Toward Africa* (London and Boulder: Paradigm Publishers, 2012), p. 6.

strategies that reflect entrenched social interests. In other words, tolerance does not exist independently of relations of power, and is thus itself subject to criticism from different vantage points: as chapter 8 illustrates, even toleration on an equal level between two important groups may alienate those who do not feel included by the resulting compromises.

The social embeddedness of both religious competition and the practices of tolerance designed to limit or prevent conflict confirm analyses that emphasise the importance of social difference, the state and its constituent elites in the emergence of religious conflict in other parts of Nigeria. This resonates strongly with detailed studies of religious conflict in northern Nigeria, including the emergence of the terrorist group Boko Haram. As Murray Last points out, religious dissidence has long been an important feature of Islamic politics in northern Nigeria. However, separatist Muslim communities can mobilise on a large scale only when the real concerns articulated do not lead to containment or transformation.[3] While not all religious sectarianism arises in response to state and local elites, the failure of such elites to produce socially embedded responses contributes to the collapse of existing modes of toleration.[4]

Just as religion should not be interpreted as being 'about' something else, religious toleration is not primarily a form of social practice aimed at something else. Certainly the recognition of the transcendence and heteronomy of the other can reflect a trace of the divine and thus constitute a form of ethical and religious agency.[5] However, where the social existence of others represents a real or potential threat to quests for recognition and self-realisation, it may be understood as being removed from divine provision. In such contexts, the refusal to acknowledge reciprocity and the denial of others' right to justification can (however mistakenly, we contend) appear as a valid religious choice.

As set out in the introduction, the existence of many forms of inter-religious engagement 'beyond tolerance' suggests that we understand the full range of possibilities inherent in religious coexistence only when we pay attention to the wide spectrum of responses to it. Other important forms of inter-religious engagement include multiple practice and membership (chapters 2–4, 9–11), transgression (3–4), and mediation and imitation (9–11, also in chapters 6–7). While this book is not the place to explore in detail how its description of the

---

[3] M. Last, 'From dissent to dissidence: The genesis & development of reformist Islamic groups in northern Nigeria', *Sects & Social Disorder: Muslim Identities & Conflict in Northern Nigeria*, ed. R.A. Mustapha (Woodbridge: James Currey, 2014), pp. 18–53.

[4] R.A. Mustapha, 'Conclusion: Religious sectarianism, poor governance & conflict', *Sects & Social Disorder: Muslim Identities & Conflict in Northern Nigeria*, ed. R.A. Mustapha (Woodbridge: James Currey, 2014), pp. 199–222.

[5] See E. Levinas, *Totality and Infinity: An Essay on Exteriority* (Pittsburgh, PA: Duquesne University Press, 1969).

productive use of these forms of encounter might contribute to, or transform, global debates on interfaith relations, there is evidence of multiple religious practice and membership in different historical contexts.

Historical research on the mutual engagement of different religions over the *longue durée*, to which we return in the final section of this conclusion, highlights that different forms of religious coexistence have existed in a range of largely non-European contexts where religion was not primarily realised in closely bounded and homogenous communities. But equally, contemporary data on religion in the global North suggest that multiple religious practices exist in individualised religious worship beyond Nigeria.

The contrasting nature of these examples suggests that the temporality of the Yoruba religious landscape cannot be clearly ascertained within the frameworks that explicitly or implicitly inform much research on Africa. Clearly many Yoruba Muslims and Christians understand the continuing existence of traditional practice as illustrating that local practices are somehow 'behind' European-derived forms of modernity, as having 'not yet' reached the forms of religious homogeneity associated with the global North. At the same time, the comparison with multiple religious practices in the US suggests not only that the forms of contemporary Yoruba engagement with difference studied in this book have global equivalents, but that they are 'ahead' of trends that are only now emerging in the global North.

In the following section of this conclusion, we make some suggestions for the wider implications specifically for the Yoruba that can be drawn from this book. However since the Yoruba experience of religious coexistence is not unique, we also consider the book's findings in the light of comparable or cognate studies across time and space, to offer tentative contributions to the academic debate on religious multiplicity and coexistence beyond tolerance more generally.

Religious Difference and the Yoruba

Unlike J.D.Y. Peel's study of the interplay of Christianity, Islam and traditional practice among the Yoruba, which illuminates the dominant expression of these religions,[6] this book explores the way in which these religions – and the differences between them – are put to work within the town of Ede. Describing not only conventional forms of religious mobilisation but also the social meanings ascribed to multiple religious practice, transgression, mediation and imitation, this book does not focus exclusively on the form and content of the

---

[6] J.D.Y. Peel, *Christianity, Islam, and Orisha Religion: Three Traditions in Comparison and Interaction* (Oakland CA: University of California Press, 2016).

coexisting religions; it also explores the implications of religious multiplicity and difference. Beyond the study of Islam or Christianity, the finely grained, intimate description of the wide range of practices related to religion in Ede invites more general reflection on the different social pulls on the expression of religion in different contexts, among different groups and different genders in Yorubaland as a whole.

By the early twentieth century, local practices throughout Yorubaland were transformed both by the rationality of the colonial state, which relied on traditional institutions such as *ọba*ship for local governance, and by the joint opposition of Islam and Christianity to many of the practices associated with *òrìṣà* worship. But while the monotheist religions shared important attributes, they also had very distinct, and separate, histories of local and global expression. The arrival of Islam, Christianity, and the colonial state within a relatively short period meant that by the first half of the twentieth century, Yoruba communities were introduced to a trio of influences that complicated any form of binary opposition between one dominant religion and its other, or between religion and the state.

The arrival of three competing universalising discourses constituted an important constellation because it differed in significant ways from other colonial or conversion processes. In contrast to many European and colonial societies, including parts of Africa and even northern Nigeria, colonial rule in south-west Nigeria did not privilege a religiously legitimated elite. As neither religion nor a perceived lack of it was associated with political power, it was not routinely mobilised for social protest, or subject to calls for reform. In the context of the Nigerian state, holding on to traditional practice remained important because it conferred a legitimacy that was independent of the state, while the accommodation of both Islam and Christianity pre-empted protest from any one religion. Thus even as twentieth-century *ọba*s drew on traditional notions of being the heads of all religions, the ongoing importance of multiple religious practice and even the transgression of religious boundaries was a thoroughly modern strategy for power (chapters 2 to 3). Today, the popularity of both *Tìmì* Muniru Adesola Lawal and many members of the Adeleke family among the people of Ede also reflects their ability to project charisma and authority that transcends religious boundaries (chapter 9).

Moreover, neither Islam nor Christianity was clearly associated with an exclusive ideological or social position. Yoruba Christians, subject to different missionary influences from the beginning, benefited from the privileged relationship to the state and the wider world that Western education and mission church networks offered. But at the same time, they sought to include Yoruba Muslims in their re-imagination of the Yoruba nation. Meanwhile, the dearth of research on Yoruba Islam means that the historical influence of different religious traditions has not been traced in detail, but the religious rivalry with northern Nigerian Muslims and the educational competition with Yoruba Christians meant that Yoruba Muslims looked towards both their ethnic compatriots and their co-religionists for solidarity and support. In Ede, as the Tablighi Jamaat illustrates, some Muslims are very sceptical of Christian practices, but the overall development of the town nonetheless owes much to the Muslim appropriation of Western schooling and the high level of education obtained by many Muslims (chapters 6–7).

As the triple pull of the two monotheist religions and the secular rationality of the state (and its 'traditional' representatives) limited large-scale identification and mobilisation, closely bounded religious groups tended to be most successful at the local level or within a limited demographic. As the differences between Ede's Muslim compounds illustrate, difference was considered acceptable even in the creation of Islamic spaces (chapter 5). At the larger social level, the multiple tensions that shaped Islam and Christianity meant that both religions were sites of significant social, political and religious differentiation. As examples ranging from Baba Abiye's prayer mountain to the 'counter crusade' of Ede's more conservative Muslims illustrate, both religions became sites of imitation, competition and innovation, buoyed by an effervescent creativity (chapters 6–7).

Yet all encounters with religious others are shaped by social hierarchies and fissures; including considerations about belonging, family background, access to education and especially gender. As the patrilineal logic of Yoruba marriage and the asymmetry of gendered forms of subjectivity in Islam and Christianity enable especially marriages between Muslim men and Christian women, the mediation or transcendence of boundaries between the different religions of their extended families is a female – or even wifely – task (chapters 9–10). As the recognition of religious others relies at least in part on gendered difference, it does not always reflect the understanding that all human beings are equal participants in the web of social relations that constitutes the town.

For Ede's citizens, then, their town exists as a community poised between the desire for unity and heterogeneity and the centrifugal force of difference. Certainly the acceptance of those of other and even competing religions implies the possibility of 'mutual recognition' of complementary burdens and contributions, even if that burden is not always evenly shared.[7] But at the same time, the appreciation and acceptance of internal difference confirms that community is also always a space created by retreat from the familiar and

---

[7] A. Honneth, 'Integrity and disrespect: Principles of a conception of morality based on the theory of recognition', *Political Theory* 20:2 (1992), 187–201: 192.

disagreement with the common.[8] Thus when the heads of Islamic compounds in Ede insist that non-Muslim women should cover their hair to collect water from wells within the compound, they assert their compound as a Muslim space that is marked by difference from non-Muslims, but they simultaneously acknowledge that non-Muslim women should be able to share in the use of its resources (chapter 5).

Beyond Ede, social and religious differences are also part of positive visions of community that exist independently of the town, both at the level of a shared Yoruba identity and in the bonds shaped by neighbourliness, family and friendship (chapter 11). Here mutual recognition derives from the insight that religion is always potentially more than a marker of difference or a form of social practice. Inherently transformative in nature, religion is also a powerful site of action, open to investment and appropriation in more than one way.[9] Respect for religious others is based on the widespread understanding that religion really matters because it can transform the lives of individuals and the various communities to which they belong.

Finally, the religious arguments and practices deployed within Ede also reflect the townspeople's participation in wider debates, both in response to Nigerian and Yoruba politics, and in the engagement with trends and movements within global Muslim and Christian communities. As national and even global debates centred on Nigeria confirm religion as a locus of meaningful political repertoires and politics as a site of religious import,[10] local practices and debates that intersect with such wider understandings remain disputed and subject to change. As different forms of Yoruba religious expression have successfully expanded into national and global space, it remains to be seen whether the creative engagement with religious difference will inspire others too.

Outlook: Future Areas of Research

As academic debate on religious coexistence beyond tolerance is only just emerging, it is important to clarify that this book does not claim an exceptional status for the Yoruba on the basis of unique cultural or historical dispositions that validate multiplicity and difference in ways unknown or impossible in other contexts. While there are no directly comparable analyses, existing

---

[8] J.L. Nancy, *The Inoperative Community* (Minneapolis and London: University of Minnesota Press, 1991).

[9] R. Marshall, *Political Spiritualities: The Pentecostal Revolution in Nigeria* (Chicago and London: University of Chicago Press, 2009), p. 22.

[10] Marshall, *Political Spiritualities*, especially pp. 211–37.

studies of multi-religious societies and forms of religious encounter suggest areas of further research and reflection that may contribute to the establishment of a field of study that focuses on religious encounter and mutual engagement both comparatively and in greater detail.

In a reflection on Muslim–Christian encounters in precolonial and colonial Africa, John Voll argues that Muslim–Christian conflict across Africa increased in the post-independence period, when 'European imperial rule was replaced by relations in which the two different communities confronted each other directly within the framework of independent states'.[11] This explanation certainly captures the rise of religious conflict across Nigeria from the mid-1970s and early 1980s onwards, and while south-west Nigeria constitutes one of many exceptions to the process, anecdotal evidence suggests that inter-religious, and indeed Muslim–Christian, relations were far more cordial in the 1950s and 1960s than they are today. Given the occasional sharp tone of the confrontations between Muslims and Christians discussed in chapters 6 and 7, and taking account of other debates in the wider Yoruba context, more detailed research on Muslim–Christian relations in relation to the areas of competition identified in this book, and in particular education, public presence and conversionary activity, is needed.

In cross-temporal comparison, Susan Bayly's historical anthropology of southern India offers an interesting and detailed exploration of a religious constellation of similar complexity to that in contemporary Yorubaland.[12] Describing the economic and political pressures and everyday practices that influenced the adoption of Islam and Christianity in predominantly Hindu India between 1700 and 1900, Bayly explains that important practices such as ceremonial processions often brought together members of different religions. At the same time, powerful Muslim and Hindu rulers sometimes sponsored the ceremonies of religious minority groups including Christians. However, over time, dynamics from both without and within the different communities that were part of southern India's religious commonwealth contributed to the emergence of more sharply defined religious boundaries.

Bayly's emphasis on the internal dynamics of religious groups is certainly relevant for south-west Nigeria. The fact that many Muslims in Ede – and other Yoruba towns – live in compounds that are envisioned as exclusively Islamic spaces, i.e. without challenge or disturbance by non-Muslims, illustrates both

---

[11] J. Voll, 'African Muslims and Christians in world history: The irrelevance of the "clash of civilizations"', *Muslim–Christian Encounters in Africa*, ed. B. Soares (Leiden: Brill, 2006), pp. 17–38.

[12] S. Bayly, *Saints, Goddesses and Kings: Muslims and Christians in South Indian Society, 1700–1900* (Cambridge: Cambridge University Press, 2004).

the ability of multi-religious societies to accommodate spaces of exclusive religious practice and the high value ascribed to religious boundaries by many Muslims. Where this limits the agency of Christians, boundary-making has resulted in enduring rivalry, and as especially Pentecostal Christians also increasingly emphasise the need for distance from non-Christians, it is certainly possible that the competing exclusivity of Islam and Christianity will contribute to the hardening of Muslim–Christian boundaries in the future.

However, in south-west Nigeria, another dynamic also comes into play: the widespread awareness of conflict in other parts of Africa and indeed Nigeria has certainly dampened enthusiasm for a greater separation of Muslims and Christians. Many people believe that the religious crises of northern Nigeria have validated Yoruba ways of life and in particular Yoruba Islam. During our research in Ede, we were often told, both by Christians and by Muslims, that 'Boko Haram is not religion [but] politics and selfishness,'[13] or that 'Boko Haram ... only hide under the cloak of religion.'[14] In local debates, even relatively minor failures of mutual recognition, such as an imam's or pastor's refusal to pray at a function organised by another religious group or an open refusal to socialise with those of other religions, may provoke rhetorical comparisons with radical groups. Overall, then, the negative example of Boko Haram may also contribute to maintaining Yoruba (and other) practices of toleration.

J.D.Y. Peel's recent book on the engagement between Christianity, Islam and traditional practice in Yorubaland also suggests that the continuing importance of non-violent forms of encounter reflects the fact that the two monotheist religions 'coexist ... within a framework of shared community values'.[15] This argument certainly resonates with our study of Ede, even as the implication of a shared framework, undoubtedly reflecting the broader scope of his analysis, appears far more static than the interactions between Muslims, Christians and traditionalists revealed by the diverse chapters in this book. While the multiplicity of forms in which members of different religions engage with each other suggests some resilience to an escalation of conflict, it also reveals that the potential for conflict exists in some areas of interaction. Given the very multiplicity of local practices, even smaller-scale shifts in personal lives or public affairs may affect the overall balance of practices in unexpected ways: the apparent continuity of coexistence offers no absolute guarantee for the future.

---

[13] Interview with Chief Jonathan Adebunmi Adeleke. 16 May 2012. Ilupeju, Ede.
[14] Interview with Alhaji Salaudeen Adedokun Olayiwola. 17 May 2012. Islamic Institute, Agbangudu, Ede.
[15] Peel, *Christianity, Islam, and Orisha Religion*, p. 2.

Beyond such political pressures, the existence of positive attitudes towards religious difference at varying levels of community suggests that many people perceive religious difference as productive. Some of our chapters point out that this appreciation of religious difference is closely linked to practices that predate the arrival of Islam and Christianity, including ọbaship and chieftaincy. The enduring appeal of authority based on multiple religious practice and the transgression of religious boundaries implies that despite the relatively limited presence of Yoruba traditional practice in Ede during the period of our research, its place in local practice is assured. While some towns, like Ede, appear to go through periods in which traditional practice is less present, others have experienced a revival and modernisation of traditional religious practice. Beyond neighbouring Osogbo and its famous Ọ̀sun festival, the establishment of explicitly traditionalist primary and grammar schools in the Oyo town of Igboho is a paradigmatic case in point.

But the personal appreciation of religious multiplicity can also exist independently of any dispositions associated with traditional practice. A recent US survey by the Pew Forum reveals that 24 per cent of Americans sometimes attend services of a faith different from their own. Since the definition of a different faith in this survey included different Christian denominations, this mostly captures intra-Christian practice, but it also shows an openness of many US Christians to Eastern and New Age spiritual practices.[16] The Yoruba attitudes discussed in this book and in forthcoming reflections of the 'Knowing Each Other' survey in general differ from the US in the degree of their ability to transcend boundaries between religions,[17] but the Pew findings nonetheless confirm that multiple religious practice is not limited to the Yoruba or even African context. Further quantitative and comparative research is crucial for comparative reflection on the implications of such practices.

Finally, while this book's emphasis on coexistence beyond tolerance illuminates the potential productivity of religious difference in itself, it calls for further research and reflection on the study of Islam and Christianity (and especially the anthropologies of Islam and Christianity). Both approaches have been instrumental in reinvigorating the study of religious practice, but as they demarcate boundaries that keep Christianity and Islam separate, they do not offer a useful frame of reference for this book and the wider project to

---

[16] Pew Forum on Religion and Public Life, 'Many Americans mix multiple faiths', *Pew Forum* (2009), < http://www.pewforum.org/2009/12/09/many-americans-mix-multiple-faiths/>, accessed 19 July 2016.

[17] I. Nolte, R. Jones, K. Taiyari and G. Occhiali, 'Exploring survey data for historical and anthropological research: Muslim–Christian relations in southwest Nigeria', *African Affairs* 115:460 (2016).

which it seeks to contribute. However, as both approaches have also generated critiques that focus on the compromised alterity of secular study, it is worth reflecting on the potential contribution of the study of religious multiplicity to the study of Islam and Christianity.

Both Asad's original intervention advocating the study of Islam as a 'discursive tradition' rather than a fixed faith[18] and recent critical reflections on the anthropology of Christianity[19] emphasise that anthropologists' understanding of their subjects is limited by the privileged relationship between Christianity – the religion primarily implicated in the emergence of the category of the 'religious' – and secular academic discourse. While we accept this problem as intrinsic to the study of religion and its others, we contend that the compromised alterity of secular study is most problematic in contexts where it confronts religion directly and only on the basis of implicit comparative reflection: it is in such contexts that unstated notions deriving largely from European and Western historical practice are most likely to misrecognise what Muslims, Christians, and indeed practitioners of other religions, know, do and hope for.

Where inquiry also focuses on the contestation, negotiation and transcendence of religious categories and practices, and on the multiplicity of religious encounters, a close engagement with how religious boundaries are made, tolerated, transcended and put to use in everyday life can expand the conceptual apparatus of the researcher. We believe the study of African religious practices is ideally situated to encourage a more widely shared understanding of knowledge production as deeply collaborative, as revelatory about what is studied, *and* as potentially transformative of the methods and forms of reflection that constitute it.

---

[18] For a summary of the most important points made by Asad, see T. Asad, 'The idea of an anthropology of Islam', *Qui Parle* 17:2 (2009), 1–30.

[19] See for example R. Marshall, 'Christianity, anthropology, politics', *Current Anthropology* 55:10 (2014), 344–56.

APPENDIX 1

Ede Anthem

Ìlú Ẹdẹ Màpó Àrógun
Ìlú Ọba Tìmì Àrólé
Ìlú àwon aj'ó lógun
Ati ṣetán lati gbée ga,

Ọmọ Ẹdẹ Màpó Àrógun
Ọmọ ajì làlà ọ́ṣọ ni
Fọjọ́ gbogbo dára bí egbin
K'á so'wọ́pọ̀ ká gbélu waga,
Ìsọ̀kan ṣà l'agbára wa,

Gbogbo ohun tó bá ti dára,
Ṣe-bí Ẹdẹ ni wọ́n fi n wé,
Fàlà sòdò béléwú báwo,
Wọn á bi'ra wọn ṣ'o dára bí t'Ẹ́dẹ,
Wọn sì dá'hùn pé ó dára bí t'Ẹ́dẹ,

Bó ṣe gúsù,
Bó ṣ àríwá,
Ìlà oòrùn tàbí 'wo oòrùn,
Kò sí-bì kan tó d à-bí ilé,
Torí ilé làbọ̀ sinmi oko,

À' m bẹ Ọ, Ọba Olúwa,
Gbàdúrà wa lórí ìlú wa,
Kí ìlú Ẹdẹ kí ó ta wọ́n yọ,
Kí Ọlọ́run o ràn wá lọ́wọ́
Àmín

Ede, the town of Màpó Àrógun
The town of (Ọba) Tìmì
The town of great warriors
We are ready to lift it to greatness

Descendants of Ede Màpó Àrógun
Descendants of those who cherish beauty

Beautiful everyday like a zebra
Let us join hands to lift our town to greatness
In unity lies our strength

Everything that is good
Is usually compared to Ede
In dispute about the standard of things,
People often ask if it is as good as Ede
Their reaction is that it is as good as Ede

In the South
In the North
In the East or West
There is no place like home
Because home is the place of rest after work

We are praying to You, God
Accept our prayers over our town
For Ede to triumph over others
May God help us
Amen

APPENDIX 2

Songs of Ede

These songs were collected from Hameed Nasiru Akinlade of Akinlade Cultural Group after the group's performance at Ede Mapo Arogun Day (Ede annual festival held on 30 November 2013).

First song

Ẹdẹ Màpó Àrógun, Ìlú ńlá
Ẹdẹ Màpó Àrógun, Ìyàkùn àgbò
Ẹdẹ Màpó Àrógun ìlú Tìmì
Ìlú tí a mọ̀ fún sùúrù tí kìí ṣagídí
Ìlú ti a mọ̀ nílùú ẹ̀sìn, a dúró déédé,
Mùsùlùmí ìlú Ẹdẹ kéwú wọ́n tún ńkírun
Onígbàgbọ́ ìlú Ẹdẹ wọ́n dòpọ̀ Jésù mú
Ẹlẹ́sìn ìbílẹ̀ ńṣe tiwọn láì díra lọ́wọ́
Ṣẹri pé Àgbàlé gbajúmọ̀, ó ní láárí
Àgbàlé gbajúmọ̀, a ma ntoto
Àgbàlé gbajúmọ̀ ó mohun tó yẹ
Tìmì Àgbàlé àkọ́kọ́ tán j'ásíwajú Ẹdẹ
Ipa rere tán fi lélẹ̀ kò ti ẹ̀ parẹ́
Tìmì ò dédé j'ọba l'Ẹ́dẹ, ẹ tẹ́tí ẹ gbọ́
Ọ̀rọ̀ ló se bí ọ̀rọ̀, ẹ síwèé ìtàn wò
Àwọn jàgùdà ọlọ́sà ní ń yọ Ẹdẹ lẹ́nu
Wọ́n jíwa léwúrẹ́ kó, wọ́n ńkó wa nírúgbìn lọ
Wọ́n ń pawá lọ́mọ, wọn tún fẹ wa láya
Òkìkí kàn délùú Ọ̀yọ̀ ní bi t'Ólúkòso ti ń jọba
B'Ólúkòso ti gbọ́rọ̀ yìí ló bá fárígá, n ló bá bínú
Ìbínú yìí pọ̀ púpọ̀jù tó fi jẹ́ wípé
Lalala bùlà bùlà bùlà bùlà niná ń yọ lẹ́nu Ólúkòso
Wéré wéré wàrà ǹsàsà lọbá bá ránṣẹ́ sí Tìmì
Kówá lọ gbàwọ́n sílẹ̀ lọ́wọ́ ọlọ́sà ìlú Ẹdẹ
Akíkanjú ni Tìmì tẹ́lẹ̀ jagun jagun tún ni
Ó ti rogun láìmọye ìgbà tó darí wálé láì farapa
Tìmì Àgbàlé Ọlọ́fà Iná

Tìmì Àgbàlé Ọlọ́fà ìjà, akíkanjú lógun
Aláyà bí àrà ni Tìmì Àgbà
Jagun jagun l'Àgbàlé a wí fún ni kó tó dáni
Ó fojú ọlọ́sà rí màbo nígboro Ẹdẹ
Ó sewọ́n kása kàsa, ó tún sewón kàsà kàsà
Ó fọfà iná se kísà fúnwọn ní wọn bá sálọ
Ọ̀pá kan soso mà ni Tìmì òò
Ọ̀pá kan soso tí ńdagba màálúù nígbó
Kò fólè kò fọ́le ló jẹ́ kó láwọn ọlạ́sà lugbó
Iná pẹ̀lú ẹ̀tù wọn ò lè gbé káriwo má sọ
Ààỳá pẹ̀lú ẹ̀tù wọn ò lè gbé káriwo má sọ
Aáyán pẹ̀lú adìyẹ wọn ò lè bárawọn gbé
Kẹ́nìkan má finú ilé sílẹ̀ fún ẹnìkan
Ìgbà tí a lé ọlọ́sà lọ tan nìlú Ẹdẹ rójú
Ìgbà yí la tó mọ̀pé Tìmì ò rorò
Oní fààjì ni Tìmì bóbá dọjọ́ àrìyá, Ẹdẹ kó ni mára
Ẹdẹ ló nìlù ló leré Ẹdẹ lólorin
Ẹdẹ Màpó Àrógun ò kéré níbi fààjì ò.

Ede Mapo Arogun, a big town
Ede Mapo Arogun, the town of *Tìmì*
A town known for patience
Her people are not stubborn
A town known for diverse religions and upright people
Muslims in Ede understand the Qur'an and observe the hours of prayer
Christians in Ede hold fast unto Jesus
The traditionalists do not hinder themselves
You can see that Agbale is popular and successful
Agbale is popular and knows what is right
Agbale is popular and knows what is just
The first *Tìmì* of Ede was Agbale
His landmark achievements are evergreen
Tìmì's ascension to the throne was not by coincidence
It has a history
Robbers were terrorising Ede
They stole our goats
They harvested our crops
They killed our children
They took our wives
News of these robbers got to Oyo
Where Olukoso was the King

Olukoso heard our ordeals
Anger seized him
In a fit of anger, fire oozed from his mouth
Olukoso immediately summoned *Tìmì*
To go and liberate Ede people from the robbers who seized the town
Tìmì was a brave man and a warrior
He had gone to war many times and had come home unhurt
Tìmì Agbale, the one with arrow of fire
Tìmì Agbale, the one with arrow of war
A brave man in war
Tìmì Agbale, a thunderbolt at heart
Agbale was a warrior who forewarned before he struck
He dealt terribly with the robbers in Ede
He dealt with them as he wanted
The robbers took to their heels
Tìmì was a lone staff
A lone staff that controls a herd of cattle in the forest
Tìmì would not tolerate thieves
He was not a friend to the indolent
Fire and gunpowder do not mix without a deafening sound
Bullets and gunpowder do not mix without a loud sound
Cockroach and hen cannot dwell together in the same house
Without one leaving for the other
Ede became peaceful after the robbers were sent parking
We knew afterwards that *Tìmì* was humane
Tìmì is sociable
He relates well during festivities
Ede is known for drumming, entertainments and songs
Ede Mapo Arogun is not a novice when it comes to enjoyment

Brief note

Generally, the song is used to describe some of the qualities of the people and town of Ede. The first three lines explain the greatness of the town founded by *Tìmì*. From lines four to eight, the song eulogises the humble character of the town and the religious devotion of its people, Muslims, Christian and traditionalists alike. From line nine to the end, the song narrates the historic feats of *Tìmì* Agbale when he was called upon by the *Aláàfin* of Oyo to protect the town from constant harassment by thieves. He was said to have driven away the thieves and ensured that the people of the town lived in peace and harmony. The story shows that *Tìmì* Agbale left good legacies for the people of the town to follow, including honesty, patience, tolerance and hard work. The song is also used to demonstrate that, as well as providing strong leadership for the town, *Tìmì* Agbale was fun-loving, and he enjoined the people of Ede to socialise and be merry.

Second song

Tó bá jẹ́ teré aráyé ti gbà p'Ẹ̀dẹ lóleré
Orin àgbọ́ fikọ́gbọ́n ìlù tó fa kíki
Ẹdẹ Màpó Àrógun Ọlọ́fà-Iná
Ẹdẹ Màpó Àrógun o ìlú Àgbọ́nrán
Ẹdẹ Màpó Àrógun o Ìyàkùn àgbò
Ẹdẹ ló leré taráyé ń wí kìí se lásán
Ati sèbà f'áwọn àgbà kí a tó jáde
Wọ́n ní ká mí lọ wọ́n ní kò mà ní séwu
Ẹdẹ Màpó tẹrí yẹn o kò dúró lásán
Ọmọ awo lóle yé o, ògbẹ̀rì ò mọ
Ògbẹ̀rì ò lè mò Ọmọ awo lóle yé
Ìdí pàtàkì t'Ẹ́dẹ fi ńgbayì lóde
Ẹ farabalẹ̀ kí ẹ wá gbálàyé ọ̀rọ̀
Ìbà nì gbín se lójọ́sí tó fi ńgungi
Ìbà làkèrése tó fi ńràyè lábàtà o
Ẹdẹ Màpó Àrógun ò fi t'àgbà seré
Ẹlẹ́gbẹ́ mo ní, ẹ jé á jọ sọ̀túmọ̀ Ẹdẹ
Kóle tàn sárá'yé pẹ̀lú àlejò
Ẹdẹ Màpó Àrógun
Ẹ́ – tówà níbẹ̀rẹ̀ – Ẹ kó wa mára
D – tó tún wà níbẹ̀ – Délẹ̀ ìléŕí
Ẹ – tó tún sìkẹta – Èyin àgbàgbà o

When it comes to entertainment
The whole world knows Ede as the master entertainers
Songs laced with wisdom
Drumming that is danceable
Ede Mapo Arogun *Ọlọ́fà-Iná*
Ede Mapo Arogun, the town of Agbọnran
Ede Mapo Arogun, *Ìyàkùn Àgbò*
That Ede are the master entertainers which people attest to is not untrue
We have paid homage to the elders before we set out from home
We have received their blessings that all will be well
Ede Mapo that you see is not ordinary

The secret is known only to the initiated
The uninitiated do not know
The uninitiated will not know
It is only the initiated that know
The main reason why Ede's performances are applauded
Be patient to listen to our explanations
The snail paid homage in those days
It received the skill to climb trees
The homage that the toad paid gave it unfettered access to operate in the swamp
Ede Mapo Arogun does not disrespect the elders
My colleagues let us say the meaning of Ede
For the whole world and foreigners to know Mapo Arogun
The first letter 'Ẹ'[1] means 'you join hands with us'
The 'D' is 'to reach the promised land'
The last 'Ẹ' is 'you our elders'

Brief note

The song is used to show that the people of Ede are foremost in singing good music accompanied with drumming. This is why they are honoured outside the town. The people are also believed to have been accorded this respect because of the honour they give to the elderly. They appreciate older people, and this is why they want them to open their arms and take the younger ones to the Promised Land – a developed city.

Third song

Ẹ jẹ́ ká sowọ́pọ̀ gbogbo wa l'Ẹ́dẹ
Ẹ jẹ́ ká sowọ́pọ̀ gbogbo wa l'Ẹ́dẹ
Ẹ̀ bá jẹ́ ká fifé báragbé àkójá òfin ni
Ìfẹ́ ló ye kó so wápọ̀ gbogbo wa l'Ẹ́dẹ
Bí a bá fọmọdé kalẹ̀ gẹ́gẹ́ bí asíwájú
Kódà bó s'àgbà la fà kalẹ̀ pé kó solórí
Ẹ má jẹ̀ẹ́ ká fọwọ́ lẹ́rán ma wò wọ́n níran
Àjèjé ọwọ́ kan niwọ́n ní ò le gbẹ̀rù dórí
Ààfi ká sowọ́pọ̀ kájọ báwọn gbe
Ẹ má jẹ̀ẹ́ ká wo ti lágbájá tóti bú wa rí

---

[1] 'Ẹ' begins a phrase 'Ẹ kó wa mọ́ra' (you join hands with us). 'D' begins the phrase 'Dé ilẹ̀ ìlérí' (to the promised land), and 'Ẹ' begins the phrase 'Ẹ̀yin àgbààgbà ò'(you elders).

Ẹ má jẹ́ẹ́ ká wo ti tàmẹ̀dú tó tí sẹ̀ wá rí
Níbi ayé lajúde àwa ọmọ Ẹdẹ Màpó
Sá wa lóyẹ ká máa wùwà bóò-ba-o-pá
Sá wa lóyẹ ká máa wùwà bóò-ba-o-bùú-lẹ́sẹ̀
Sá wa lóyẹ ká máa wùwà inúnibíni
Sá wa lóyẹ kẹ́nìkan sẹ̀ kámá le gbàgbé
Sá wa lóyẹ kẹ́nìkan sẹ̀ kámá le lámòójúkúrò láàrin wa
Ahán pẹ̀lẹ́nu ń jà, ókúkú ń parí
Ẹja pẹ̀lómi ńjà wọ́n ń parí ẹ̀, ó ńtán
B'álágbàfọ̀ b'ómi sọ̀tá dandan ni kó parí
Màpó Àrógun ẹ tẹ́tí gbọ́
Màpó Àrógun ẹ jẹ́ ká ronú gidigidi
Àwa laráyé ńwò, àwa laráyé ńrí
Gẹ́gẹ́bí olùkọ́ àgbà tí ń kọ́ni lọ́gbọ́n.

Let's join hands together, all of us at Ede
Let's join hands together, all of us at Ede
Let's live together in love
The practice of love renders law redundant
Love is what should bring us together in Ede
If we elect a young person to be our leader
Or an adult as our head
We should not fold hands and watch them unconcerned
A single hand cannot lift a load to the head
We have to join hands with them to move forward
We should forget about so-and-so that once abused us
We should forget about somebody else that once annoyed us
Because we are in the age of civilisation
We the people of Ede Mapo Arogun
Should we be the ones running after each other?
Should we be the ones willing to kill each other?
Should we be the ones that are always angry at the slightest provocation?
Should we be the ones that cannot forgive and overlook each other's wrongdoings?
Should we be the ones that are unable to forget each other's wrong doings?
The tongue and the mouth usually quarrel
They settle it among themselves
Fish and water also quarrel and they settle it
When a washman quarrels with water, it is a must that he settles it
Mapo Arogun, please listen and listen good
Mapo Arogun, let us think deeply

The world is looking at us
Because we are the people they see
As master teacher that teaches others

Brief note

The song shows the importance of living in peace and harmony in Ede, irrespective of differences that may exist among its people. In particular, it calls on people competing for positions at different levels of governance to exercise restraint, put aside their differences and work together with whoever is elected to bring about peace in the town. It is also an admonition to the people to live by showing good character and positive examples.

Hameed Nasiru Akinlade
Akinlade Cultural Group, Ede
1 December 2013

APPENDIX 3

Oríkì of the Tìmì of Ede, present and past

Oríkì Tìmì Munirudeen Adésǫlá Lawal Láminísà (2007–)

Láminísà ǫmǫ kúdú-ǹdú tó sewé gèru-gèru[1]
Ọ̀pọ̀lọ̀pọ̀ ògùn arumǫ gàlè gàlè
Láminísà ní bobá lọ́pọ̀ ògùn
Láminísà ní bobá lékèé- kò ní jẹ́ kó jẹ́
Ọmǫ pèrè ńdi-ọ̀pẹ-ọ̀kọ̀ọ̀kan làá he-ìrà
Àgbà tó bá he méjì ló sòjóró
Ọmǫ palé-ntogun-jìgan ntogun
Ọmǫ-arógun mọ́-sàá-àrọ̀nì wǫn ò fiyè ogun nù
Ọmǫ àrọ̀nì tí kò gbélé, Olúkòyí-Kòsin mi ogun-ún lǫ
Ọmǫ ẹ̀sǫ́ rógunjó jàgìnmì
Bí baba wǫn bá tijí, etí ogun níí mórí lé
Ọmǫ-Oníkòyí tí kìí gbọfà léyìn,
Iwájú ni baba won fíí gbọta
Ọmǫ-Oníkòyí tó gbọfà léyìn, ojo ló ṣe
Ọmǫ ẹni tó kú nílé-tagbé rogun rèé sin
Ọmǫ Tìmì Àgbàlé Ọlọ́fà-Iná
Ọmǫ ẹ̀sǫ́ Ìkòyí, ǫmǫ ajídá gbẹ̀du àkàlà

Laminisa, a leafy sweet potato[2]
Enormous charms that intoxicates
Laminisa says: "if you have many charms
And you are not forthright; the charms would lose their efficacy"
A heritage of war-happy
Arǫni,[3] who always thinks of war

---

[1] Oríkì taken from *First Year Coronation Anniversary Ceremony programme/souvenir of HRM, Ọba Munirudeen Adesola Lawal* (Ede: n.p., 5 March 2009). The editors of this book wish to thank the Tìmì of Ede, Tìmì Munirudeen Adesola Lawal Laminisa, for his permission to reproduce his *oríkì* and those of his predecessors.

[2] Translation by Olusanya Komolafe.

[3] In Yoruba mythology, *àrọ̀nì* is believed to be the Yoruba god of charms. Hence a very powerful juju man is said to be *àrọ̀nì*.

Aroni, who does not stay at home
Olukoyi, who does not cease to go to war
A heritage of war happy
When their father woke up
He headed to the war front
A heritage of Olukoyi, who would not be hit by bullets at the back
Their father would rather be hit by bullets in the chest
A heritage of Olukoyi who is shot at the back is a coward
A heritage whose corpse is taken to war front for burial
The child of Tìmì Àgbàlé Ọlọ́fà-Iná
A heritage of Ikoyi
The child of one who woke up to beat drum of war

Oríkì Tìmì Tìjání Ọládòkun Oyéwùsì (1976–2007)

Tìjání Ọládòkun Àjàgbé Oyéwùsì.[4]
Ọmọ Àgbánrán gbá ke ń ja.
Ọmọ sọ'gbó di ilé.
Ọmọ sọ̀'gbẹ́ dì ìgboro, ọmọ s'àtàn d'ọjà.
Ọmọ sọ inú ìgbẹ́ di ìgbéjọ́, ó dá ọmọ lẹ́kun à fojú di.
Ọmọ àrúnse kúta, órí ilé sí Mọ́sálásí, fìlà funfun, èwù funfun,
sòkòtò funfun bí Olósà ńlá.
Ọmọ Lálémo, ọmọ ẹ̀sọ́ Ìkòyí, ọmọ dììlẹ̀ dogun, Ọmọ ọ̀-sùn lẹ́dẹ̀-la obìnrin kàkà,
Ọmọ a pa ẹran kárí ayaba.
Ọmọ Oníkòyí, tó gbọ́ ohùn ogun yọ̀ sẹ̀sẹ̀,
Àgbọ́nrán Ìkọ̀tún o jà nífọ́n, o jà l'Éjìgbò,
O fi ẹnu òsà gbolẹ̀ aara,
Àgbọ́nrán fi Olójo se ìkówó wolé, àrí sọ igbánù ní Ìbòkun,
Ọkùnrin gbọin gbọin nígbó Aágba,
Ọkùnrin kìtìkìtì ní igbó Ìrágbìjí,
Ó l'árá Ìdó g'òkè ọ̀sun.
Ọmọ Ẹ̀sọ́ Ìkòyí, òbùrìn bùrìn fọhùn ogun yànmùyànmù.

Tijani Oladokun Ajagbe Oyewusi[5]
The child of Agbọnran

---

[4] *Oríkì* taken from *Eighth Day Fidau Prayer and Final Burial Ceremony programme/souvenir of Oba Tijani Oladokun Oyewusi* (Ede: n.p., 5 September 2007).
[5] Translation by Olusanya Komolafe.

The child of him who turned forest into living home
The child of him who turned wilderness into city, and dung hill into market
The child of him who turned bush into court
And restrained the stubborn of insolence
The disease-stricken-child-mosque became home
White cap, white cloth, white trousers like worshippers of *Òsà-ńlá*[6]
The child of Lalemọ, the child of Ikoyi warrior
The child of him who was always prepared ahead of war
The child of he who slept astride amidst women
The child of him who killed goat for each of his queens
The child of Onikoyi, a war monger who was always elated at the eavesdrop of war
Agbọnran Ikọtun,
You fought at Ifon[7]
You fought at Ejigbo[8]
The one who was sighted and the people of Ibokun threw away their dishes
A fearless man in the forest of Aagba[9]
A threat in the bush of Iragbiji[10]
He pursued Ido people across River Osun
The child of Ikoyi warrior,
A war monger who sang songs of war even as he walked

Oríkì Tìmì John Adétóyèṣe Láoyè (1946–1975)

Adétóyèṣe Àkànjí Erin, Atóíbọ-bí-orí ọmọ 'Mọ́wáare[11]
A-jà-bí-ìjí-wọ̀'lú, ọmọ Odẹfúnmkẹ́.
Eégún gbè ẹni wéré, Adétóyèṣe, Òrìṣà gbè ẹni wàrà.
Òrìṣà ni baba mi, Àkànji, bí o bá ti mọ̀ 'ọ́n ísìn,
Bẹ́ẹ̀ ni Adétóyèṣe Àkànji Erin ígbè ẹni mọ
B'ó bá gbé mí títítí, Àkànji, k'o má padà lẹ́hìn mi.
Má mì kùkùté, o ò gbọdọ̀ mi kùkùté.
Ẹn'tí nṣe Kúkúrú-bí-ikú, ara 'ẹ̀ ńi ńṣe.
Dẹ́mudẹ́mu kò da'gbọn.

---

[6] The Yoruba god of creation.
[7] A town in Osun State, south-western Nigeria.
[8] A town in Osun State.
[9] A town in Osun State.
[10] A town in Osun State.
[11] From A. Babalola, *Àwon Oríkì Bòròkìnní* (Ibadan: Hodder & Stoughton, 1975), pp. 124–5.

Àjànàkú jẹ ìdí òro gùdùgùdù.
"Máà bẹ́ mi l'óri sọnù; èmi ò sí n'nu wọn."
"Èmi ò sí ń'nú onírìkíṣí, onírìkíṣí abirunípàkọ́-jọ̀ǹlọ̀kìjọñlọki."
Ọ̀rọ̀ fi ẹni dùgbẹ̀dùgbẹ̀ fi ẹni nù.
Ọ̀rọ̀ fi ẹni dùgbẹ̀dùgbẹ̀ bí ẹn'ti ò ní tán mọ́.
Ọ̀rọ̀ mbọ̀ wá ítán, ojú á t'ẹlẹ́gàn, a sì tì ẹni tí nyọnusọ.
O bá wọn níwájú, o kí wọn, kí wọn.
O sì bá wọn lẹ́hìn, o ṣààlọ̀.
Ààlọ̀ kò tẹ́ wọn lọ́rùn bí àfojúdi.
Àfojúdi ni k'o maa ṣe sí pọñpọlọ orí baba wọn.
A kì íkí ẹrú baba ẹni k'á nà tán.
Adétóyèṣe Àkànjí, bi o bá ká'ṣẹ kan, k'o nà'kan.
Dààmú-dààbò, o dààmú àlejò, o dààmú onílé.
Àkànjí Ògún ti ídààmú afúnọ̀jámápọn'mọ.
Nlẹ́ Àkànjí, dákun má dààmú mi.
Mo f'Ọlọ́run Ọba bẹ̀ ọ́, Àkànjí k'o má dààmú mi.
Máà j'ébi ó pa mi, ewé orí igi kò j'óòrùn pa'gi
Makănjúọlá Olóríire l'ó d'ádé.
Àkànjí Olóríire l'ó dádé.
Ọba tí mbẹ l'óyè tí ìlú fi ntòrò kinkin.
Olóriire l'ó d'ádé, Adétóyèṣe ọmọ 'Mọ́wáare.

Adetoyese Akanji, mighty elephant.[12]
One can worship you, as one worships his head.
Son of Moware.
You enter the town like a whirlwind.
You, son of Odefunke.
Egungun blesses quickly when you worship him.
Orisha blesses more quickly when you worship him.
My father Akanji is an orisha.
The more devoutly you worship him.
The greater blessings you receive from Adetoyese Akanji.
Bless, and bless me continuously;
Akanji, and do not leave me unblessed.
Do not attempt to shake a tree trunk.
One who shakes a tree trunk, shakes himself.
One who tries to undo you, you who are as short as death,
He will only undo himself.

---

[12] From E. Olunlade, *Ede: A Short History* (Ibadan: General Publications Section, Ministry of Education, 1961). Translation by *Tìmì* Laoye.

A wine tapper cannot tap wine from a cocoa-nut palm.
An elephant eats up the entire roots of an oro tree.
Do not behead me, I am not among them.
I am not among the conspirators.
Conspirators, the hair on whose heads is ugly and ruffled.
A serious case may worry one – but it will come to an end.
A serious case worries one, as if it will never be settled.
The case will be settled, and the slanderers and gossipers
Will be put to shame.
You met them in the front, and you greet and greet them.
You met them behind you, and you greet and greet them.
Your being courteous does not please them, like being insolent.
Keep on being insolent to them and their fathers!
It is unusual for one to greet his father's slave and prostrate.
You Adetoyese Akanji, bend one foot to greet them,
You leave the other unbent!
You, a notorious confuser! You confused everybody by your appearance!
Akanji you confused all those
Who tie cloth around their waists, without carrying a child.
I beg you in the name of God, the great king, confuse me not!
Do not allow me to starve.
The leaves on a tree, do not allow the tree to feel the scorching sun.
You are a lucky person to wear the crown.
A person who is on the throne
When the town prospers,
Is a lucky person to wear the crown.

Oríkì Tìmì Sànúsí Àkàngbé (1934–1946)

Atilọ́lá Arọ́wọ́gbádàámú[13]
Ó burú ó ju gbèsè lọ
Atilọ́lá ìjí jà roro kan ọ̀run
Alágẹmọ se jẹ́jẹ́ ó kù
Àgbà tí kò ta wàrà òhun fún rarẹ̀ lómọ̀
Egúngún olójèé lójú tí bará Ìbàdàn lẹ̀rù
Mọ́jọ̀ọ́lágbé Ìbíyẹmí Arọ́wọ́gbádàámú
Kósírú erin nínú igbó
Ní Sókótó ní lẹ̀ Zàmfàrà ni

---

[13] Collected from Pa Kareem Ayanleke, the Palace Drummer at the Palace of the *Tìmì* of Ede, 24 December 2013.

Kòsírú erin nínú igbó.

Atilọla Arọwọgbadaamu[14/15]
More frightening than debt
Atilọla, a tempestuous whirlwind that destroys even to the sky
"A quiet going chameleon dies,"
He says: "a slow to act adult would have himself to blame"
A copper masked masquerade that frightens the people of Ibadan
Mọjọọlagbe Ibiyemi Arọwọgbadaamu
No other animal like the elephant in the forest
Whether in Sokoto or Zamfara[16]
There is no animal like the elephant in the forest

Atilọ́lá Ar'ọ́wọ́-gbá'dà-mú, kò ṣ'ẹ̀hìn Ọlọ́run.[17]
Ohun gbogbo kò ṣ'ẹ̀hìn Ọlọ́run, Atilọ́lá Ar'ọ́wọ́ gbádàmú.
Ó kúrò ní kòkòrò kan, Atilọ́lá Òdí o, àgbàlagbà Ifẹ̀
Àkééke, ó kére, kò kéré, ó kúrò ní kòkòrò kan.
Kétékété l'à íjìnnà s'éégún, gbọ̀ọ̀rọ̀gbọọrọ l'a íjìnnà s'éjò.
Aṣọ pupa kò ṣe ípa l'áró, pàṣípààrọ̀ obìnrin kò ṣe íṣe.
Etí mẹ́ta kò yẹ'rí, ènìà mẹ́ta kò dúró ní méjìméjì.
Atilọ́lá, o lé eégún wọ ilé Ọjọrọ.
Ará ilé Bísíkù kò l'eégún, Atilọ́lá l'eégún wọn.
Tìmì l'orò ibẹ̀.
A-ṣe-ọ̀kan-lékè ọkùnrin
Ikú ijó ọmọ Adédigba, ìjà ní ìlú, ọmọ amìgborotìtì
Alagbalúgbú irókò ti f'ẹwọn igba idi.
Okúta le, olóko dá a sí.
Ọ̀ràn burúkú ṣ'òde páro.
Obìnrinkóbìnrin kò j'ọmọ ẹni ó jọ'ni.
O b'eégún jà, o dá eégún, o b'óòṣà jà, o sì dá òòṣà
O b'Ọlọ́run Ọba jà, Ọlọ́run Ọba nìkan l'ó dá ọ.
Ẹni t'Ọlọ́run dá kò ṣe ífarawé.
Tìmì ọkọ ìyá Gbóyè, Atilọ́lá ọmọ Búsàrí.
Alóyúnogungbẹndu, ọmọ Búsàrí.

---

[14] This is a praise-name. It could be literally translated as a person with broad palm suited to holding a cutlass. The name suggests a person with a huge frame who is highly skilled in the use of the cutlass at war.

[15] Translation by Olusanya Komolafe.

[16] Sokoto and Zamfara are states in Northern Nigeria. Both states are far from Ede. The picture being created here is that a person like *Tìmì* Sanusi Ajagbe cannot be easily come by.

[17] From Babalola, *Àwon Oríkì Bòròkìnní*, pp. 123–4.

Oyèwálé, a f'ọ̀ràn-gbogbo-jẹ́-hòo-hòo
Ikú ijó ọmọ Tinúomi, ìjà ńlá ọmọ amìgborotìtì
Èèwọ̀ ọ̀pọ̀lọ́ ká ìlú, ọkọ Ìbídùn.
Ẹrú Búsàrí, a-kọ́-'lé-f'ọtí, Tìmì ọmọ Ìyá Ọlọ́bẹ̀.

Atilola, whose hand befits holding a sword.[18]
Nothing happens, without the knowledge of God.
Atilola, whose hand befits holding a sword.
Nothing happens, without the knowledge of God.
It is no ordinary insect,
It matters not how tiny the scorpion is,
It is not an ordinary insect.
Atilola hail! You elder of Ife!
One stays at a great distance from a masquerade,
One stays at an even greater distance from a snake.
It is unusual to dye a red cloth in indigo.
One cannot exchange one's wife for another's.
Three ears do not befit the head.
Three people can never stand in twos.
Atilola, you once drove an Egungun into Ojoro's compound.
The people of Bisiku compound have no Egungun.
But you Atilola, you are their Egungun.
You are their oro also.
You are a man who always surpasses other men.
Graceful and perfect dancer you are, son of Adedegba.
You are like a big fight, that shakes the city vigorously.
You are like a mighty Iroko tree, that has a chain round its stem.
If a rock is hard – the farmer gives it up.
A bad event casts a spell of silence on the area.
A bad woman prevents a child from resembling its father.
You wrestled with the Egungun – and you dashed the Egungun to the ground.
You wrestled with the orisha – and you dashed the orisha to the ground.
You wrestled with God – but God created you.
One who is created by God cannot be imitated.
Timi, you are the husband of Gboye's mother.
You are heavily pregnant with war,
Oyewale who answers yes to every question.
Everybody in the town is aware that it is forbidden to eat a frog.
You husband of Ibidun. You servant of Busari,

---

[18] From Olunlade, *Ede: A Short History*. Translation by *Tìmì* Laoye.

Who built a special house to keep drinks.
You Timi, son of Iya Olobe.

Oríkì Tìmì Ìpínloyè (1924–1933)

Àlàó ọmọ Ṣàngórẹ̀míl̩ẹ́kún.[19]
Ìgbá ti kékeré p'ẹtún, ọmọ Abídogun.
Ó ńtàn ara rẹ̀ jẹ, afaséegbèjò ńtàn ara rẹ̀ jẹ.
Kulukuọlá, Eégúndẹbí.
Orò gorí ọparun jókõ, Lóógun jìgan bí ọdẹ aperin.
Ò-fò-fẹ̀rẹ̀-dá-ìlú-dó.
A b'ọwọ́-gbọ-gbọ-gbọ tí íy'ọmọ 'ẹ̀ l'ọfin.
Ìjímèrè ṣe burúkú dìgbàró tí ígb'áláwà ṣánlẹ̀.
Eégúnlẹ́gi, o tó baba lójú adẹ́mu.
Ọkùnrin gbọ̀ngbọ̀n bí 'ọjọ́ kan'rí'.
Ò-dúró-ní-ìloro-kàn 'wákùn-l'ókè.
Ọkùnrin gbọ̀ọ̀rọ̀gbọ̀ọ̀rọ̀ bí ẹrù eèsún.
Abáwọn-rẹ́-má-f'ìdí-hàn-wọ́n.
Àwòdì òkè kò jẹ́ f'ìdí 'ẹ̀ hàn gúnnugún.
Kóńkótó gbé'lùjù fọ̀ ohùn ọkùnrin.
O ntúruku, ntúruku, erin turuku 'ẹ̀ lásán.
Ẹfọ̀n túruku 'ẹ̀ lásán.
Títuruku àjànàkú bọ̀ t'ẹfọ̀n mọ́lẹ̀.
Eégúndẹbí o borí wọn ní'lé, o borí wọn l'ógun.
Òrìṣà nlá kò s'ẹni à á yín'mú sí.
Bí o yín'mú sí baba Ọdẹjidé, a gbá wọn ní'gi l'ẹ́nu.
O fìdí ọ̀kọ̀ s'ọmọ l'órí, baba Oyèníwọ̀n.
Bí yíó bá wọn jà, Ilé Igbó ni íti ílo.
Bí yíó wọ̀ odò, ariwo, bí yíó gòkè odò, ariwo.
Ò-f-'ẹsẹ̀-méjèèjì-s'omi-rúkú-rùkù-rúkú, Baba Oyèníwọ̀n.
A-b'àiyà-piri-piri-bí-ẹni-y'Ògún.
A- b'àiyà-gbinrin-gbinrin-bí-alágbẹ̀de-ṣẹ̀- Ògún.
Ẹṣin ò gbọdọ̀ dá a, ènìà ò gbọdọ̀ bá a jà.
Akọkọlúkọ yèrèpè tí íso l'ẹ́hìnkùlé Ọ̀tún Omidé.
Ará ilé Ọ̀tún kò gbọdọ̀ já a; bẹ́ẹ̀ ni Ìkọ́làbà kò gbọdọ̀ bẹ̀ ẹ́ wò
A-lé-oníl̩é-wọ̀-ilé-kèrikèri.
A-lé-babaláwo-máà-dúró-mú-'Fá.
Ò-roko-roko-já-'mọdò-l'áiyà.
Ò-roko-roko-gb'ọ́wọ́-fújà-lé-kùkùté, ọkọ Ṣọlápé.

---

[19] From Babalọla, Àwon Oríkì Bòròkìnní, pp. 121–2.

A-b'oko-níhin A-b'okolóhún.
Ìsánsábá a-b'odòláàrin-oko.
Ikú tí íy'ọmọ l'ójú pókí, ọmọ Abídogun.
Ìpínloyè ọmọ Abídogun.
Afìiti-já-'gbà Akiri-má-dá'lé-sí.
Ò-fò-fẹrẹ-dá-'lu-dó, Ò g'ẹranko-gidigan.
Abá'ni-jà-máà-jẹbi, ọmọ Ọyakúnlé.
Pípele ni ó npele, Àlàó o ò ní kú.

Alao, son of Sangoremilekun,[20]
Young locust trees
Develop branches from their shoots.
He deceived himself!
He who collects water with a sieve deceives himself.
Kulukuola, Egundebi.
The Oro mounts up a bamboo stick and sits on it.
Warrior as fierce as an elephant hunter.
You jump up suddenly – and your enemies abandon their town.
You have long long hands,
With which you rescue your children from a ditch.
The baboon, having robbed your farm,
Stands prepared to dash you to the ground.
If you want to tie it with a chain.
Egunlegi, you appear tall even to the palmwine tapper,
On top of his tree.
You, a man as high as noon
Standing in the town gate your head touches the lintel.
You are as stout and tall as a bunch of bulrushes.
Though you agree with them,
Yet they will never know your secret.
The hawk soaring on high
Will never betray his secret to the vulture.
The Konkoto bird lives in the wilderness
And its cry sounds like the cry of man.
It scatters the dust! The elephant scatters the dust in vain.
The buffalo scatters the dust in vain.
Yet the scattering of the dust by the elephant is greater
Than that of the buffalo.
You Egunlegi, are greater than they at home,

---

[20] From Olunlade, *Ede: A Short History*. Translation by *Tìmì* Laoye.

And greater than they at the battlefield.
You cannot make faces at Orishanla.
If anyone dares to make faces at Adejide's father
He will be hit on the mouth with a stick.
You father Oyeniwon struck a man
With the handle of your spear.
Wherever he is, he is ready to fight them.
He will fight them even from Ile-Igbo.
If you want to enter a river, an alarm is raised.
And when you have crossed to the other side
Another alarm is raised.
You, father of Oyeniwon, stir the river vigorously with your two feet.
Your chest is as heavy as the Ogun stone.
Your chest gives a metallic sound,
Like an anvil beaten by a hammer.
He must not be knocked down by a horse,
No man must quarrel with him.
The burning nettle bears fruit behind Otun Omides house
But the people of Otun Omide's house must not pluck its fruit.
And Ikolaba himself must not touch it.
You drove a man, and we ran quickly into his house.
You drove an Ifa priest, and he forgot to carry his oracle.
You worked on your farm, and the brook itself was frightened.
You worked and worked and when you were tired
You rested your hand on a tree stump, husband of Solape.
Your farms are here and there, separated by a brook.
You are like death, who plucks a man's eyeballs suddenly.
You son of Abidogun, Ipinoye, son of Abidogun.
Merely by turning your body you broke into a garden.
There is no house you cannot enter when strolling.
You jump up quickly and your enemies abandon their town.
You rode on a mighty high animal.
You quarrelled, but were never found guilty.
Son of Oyakunle,
You are increasing in strength,
Alao, may you never die.

Oríkì Tìmì Oyèlékan (1899–1924)

Kò gbàgbé ẹnìkan.[21]
Ọlọ́run Ọba kò gbàgbé ẹnìkan.
Olúsomíró Ayílóyè.
Kò gbàgbé ẹnìkan.
Ìjí já'ko, ó yan, Olúsomíró Ayílóyè.
A-kọ̀ìn- kọ̀ìn ẹkùn.
B'ólóde kò kú, òde kò hù gbégi.
A kì í gb'àkàkà lọ́wọ́ akítì.
Ayílóyè, ta ni ígbà ọlá baba ọmọ lọ́wọ́ ọmọ?
A-dákájéjẹ́ m'èyí tí yíó ṣe.
Ọ̀rọ̀ gbogbo ní'kùn àgbà l'ó wà.
Ò-w'ọ̀ràn-péẹ́-f'oju-nù, baba Oyèkọ́lá.
Ọ̀-pa-bàbà-m'ẹ́ṣin-l'ẹ́ṣẹ̀, baba Lárewájú.
Ẹṣin nj'oko, bàbà nmì pẹkẹpẹkẹ.
Olúsomíró Ayílóyè
Atabatin olúbodè ní'gbà ìjà.
Òkuta giri, gbòǹgbò giri.
Agídí gbòǹgbò, ọkọ Odùníkẹ̆, tí íta l'áwùjọ ọ̀kúta.
O f'ìjà f'Ọlọ́run-jà, o f'ọwọ́ l'érán.
A-f'òtítọ́-inú-tú-ẹru-ìkà-palẹ̀.
Ìjí já'ko, ó yan, akọ̀ìnkọ̀ìn ẹkùn.

He remembe rs everybody.[22]
God the great king never forgets anybody.
Olusomire Ayiloye,
He forgets nobody, God the great king never forgets anybody.
When a monkey goes to raid a farm, creeps stealingly.
Olusomiro Ayiloye, the leopard, marches majestically.
Unless the landlord dies, the front of his house never grows weedy.
Ayiloye, my father, none can take from you the honour you inherited
From your father.
You are silent, but you know what you want to do.
An elder's secret remains in his belly.
You look at a serious matter,
And take away your eyes.
You put copper rings round your horse's neck.
When the horse eats grass, they make a jingling sound.

---

[21] From Babalọla, Àwon Oríkì Bòròkìnní, p. 121.
[22] From Olunlade, Ede: A Short History. Translation by Tìmì Laoye.

Olusomire, Ayiloye.
The brave defender of the town gate during a fight.
Closely tight rocks, closely tight roots.
A stubborn root grows amongst rocks.
You allow God to fight for your,
And rest your head on your hand.
When the monkey goes to raid a farm, he creeps stealthily.
But the leopard marches majestically.

Oríkì Tìmì Mọsùnlóyè (1892?–1899)

A dòòyi ká Gbẹ̀dẹ̀dile, Onílé-omi.[23]
A dòòyi ká a, apá ò k'ósẹ̀, a dòòyi ká a.
Ò-fi-bàbà-lù-ọmọ-pa.
Àgùnfọn kò foríbalẹ̀ f'ẹnìkan.
Apá bàmùbàmù kò ká bùtùbútù.
Bùtùbútù ni baba bàmùbàmù.
P'ẹran bọ 'rí, p'ẹran bọ 'Fá
A-b'ẹ̀hìn-ààrò-gelemọ̀-gelemọ̀
Ọkọ Olókun, Tìmì ọkọ Òmìnì.
Ẹ̀hìnkùlé l'ọ̀tá wà.
Gbẹ̀dẹ̀dile, ilé l'aṣeni ibá 'ni gbé.
À bá mọ̀ ilé ọlọ́ràn.
A kò lè mọ̀ ilé aṣeni.
Ẹni tí nṣe'ni kì ínílááří.
Ènia tí nṣe'ni kò ní ṣòkòtò.
Ẹni ti nṣe'ni kì íjẹ́ ǹkankan.
Eégún gbé ẹni jéjé, ọkọ Olókun.
Òrìṣà gbè ẹni wàrà, òrìṣà ni baba mi Ìṣọ̀lá.
B'o bá ti mọ̀ ọ́n ísìn, bẹ́ẹ̀ ni Gbẹ̀dẹ̀dile ígbè ẹni mọ.
Kòkòrò jowójowó n'nu owó ni ígbé.
Kòkòrò jobìjobì n'nú obì ni íwà.
Ẹ̀hìnkùlé l'ọ̀tá wà, ilé l'aṣeni íbá ni gbé.
À bá m'ojú ọlọ́ràn, a kò m'ojú ẹn'tí nṣe'ni.
Ẹn'tí nṣe 'ni kì ínílááří.
Ẹn'ti nṣe 'ni kì ító ènìà.
Gbẹ̀dẹ̀dile, o f'òkè ṣe.
Ò-fi-bàbà-lù-ọmọ-pa.

---

[23] From Babalọla, *Àwon Oríkì Bòròkìnní*, p. 120.

They try to surround him,[24]
But the girth of a baobab tree cannot be encompassed by two arms.
You killed a child with a copper rod.
The crown bird bows down for nobody.
The flat piece of wood used to beat mud floors level
Is unable to beat dry dust level.
Dry dust is the father of the flat wood.
You killed animals to sacrifice to your head.
You killed animals to sacrifice to Ifa.
The back of your heart is filled with dry meat.
Gbededile, you husband of the goddess of the sea.
Timi, you are the husband of Omimi,
Ones enemy is behind the house.
One who undoes another stays in the same house with him.
You may know the house of the complainant,
But you cannot know the house of the one who will undo you.
One who undoes another can never prosper.
One who undoes another has no trousers.
One who undoes another has nothing at all.
If you worship Egungun, you will be rewarded quickly.
If you worship Orisa, you will be rewarded quickly.
My father Isola is an orisa.
The more you serve him, the greater the reward you shall receive.
Worms that live on cowries are usually found inside cowries shells.
Worms that live on Kola nuts are usually found inside kola nuts.
One's enemy always stays behind one's house.
The one who undoes one always stays under the same roof with you.
You will never recognise the one who will undo you.
One who undoes another shall never prosper.
One who undoes another shall never be great.
Gbededile, you are a mountain.
You killed a child with a copper rod.

Oríkì Tìmì Lánṣebe (unknown–unknown)

Atińṣọlá, Láṣebìkan, Ò-rí-máà-dé'lé-wí[25]
"J'óníbi ó ṣe'bi, j'óníkà ó ṣe ìkà;
Àt'ìbi-àt'ìkà kò tò íjẹ bí òótọ́

---

[24] From Olunlade, *Ede: A Short History*. Translation by Timi Laoye.
[25] From Babaḷọla, *Àwon Oríkì Bòròkìnní*, p. 119.

Atińṣọlá A-tó-íjẹ-bí-ire.
A-jí-rẹ́rin-ọ̀kinkin A-d'àgbàlàgbà-ṣiyan-àgbìgbò.
Ohun t'ó s'àgbìgbò t'ó fi dẹkun ẹ̀rín írín.
B'ó bá ṣe gúnnugún, a wonkoko m'órí ẹyin.
Ọ̀kanṣoṣo àràbà ó t'ẹ́gbẹ̀rún ọ̀ṣúnṣún.
Atińṣọlá, o tó'gba nínú ọmọ 'Lámọdi.
'T'ẹ̀ṣín-t'ọ̀kọ̀ ní mbẹ l'ọ́fun òwíjọ́.
Atińṣọlá, Ọba, nìkanṣoṣo ni ígbà ẹni lọ́wọ́ ẹn'tí nṣe 'ni.
Ọ̀kanṣoṣo àwòdì n'yíó run adìẹ tán.
Ògudugudu a-hó-bí-ìlù-Ìjẹ̀ṣà.
Ò l'ẹ́ṣin-ní-màdu-màdu, ab'ìrìn-ẹṣin-tìkọ̀- tìkọ̀.
Oníṣe-Ògún.
Ẹ̀fúùfù lẹ̀lẹ̀ là igi má là òkúta.
Ò-ṣ'oògùn-ṣe-múnimúni.
Sálúbàtà ọkùnrin, òbalẹ̀súnkẹrẹrẹ.
Atińṣọlá Okunlabí Láṣebìkan Òrímáàdéléwí.
A lé kùruu, ó nsá, àwõdì õkĕ
Ọ̀kanṣoṣo àwõdì n'yíó run adìẹ tán
Ọ̀kanṣoṣo mẹ̀mbẹ́ borí ìlù mọ́lẹ̀
Atińṣọlá Okunlabí, o borí wọn ní'lé, o borí wọn l'ógun.

Atinsola, Lasebikan.[26]
You cannot talk about your encounters on the battlefield,
When you return home.
Let the evil one continue with his evil doing,
Let the wicked one continue in his wickedness.
Evil doing and wickedness are not as profitable as kindness.
The Okinkin bird starts laughing as soon as he wakes up.
The Agbigbo behaves like a spoilt child.
Whatever could prevent Agbigbo from laughing,
Would make the vulture die on his eggs.
A single white silk cotton tree
Is worth two thousand osunsun trees.
Lansebe, my father, you are worth more than two hundred
Of the other descendants of Lamodi.
The throat of an accuser pours forth javelins and spears.
It is God alone who can save one from such destroyers.
A single hawk can devour all the chicken.
Your drums sound like Ilesha drums.

---

[26] From Olunlade, *Ede: A Short History*. Translation by *Tìmì* Laoye.

Your checked horse has a rocking gait.
A strong wind cannot rend rocks,
But can break trees into pieces.
Powerful wizard, who can render a crowd helpless
With his medicines
The sandals of the hero noisily stamp the ground.
Atinsola Ogunlabi Lasebikan, you cannot talk about your encounters
In the battlefield, when you return home.
Drive a kite, and it will fly away.
Drive a hawk, and it will fly away.
Yet a single hawk can devour all your chicken.
The full sound of the Bembe drum.
Drowns the sound of the other drums.
Atinsola you surpass them at home.
And at war you surpass them also.

Oríkì Tìmì Olúnlóyè (unknown–unknown)

Kò hù gbẹ́gi, b'ólóde ò kú, òde kò hù gbẹ́gi.[27]
Olúnrebi ọmọ Baṣọ̀run, Òyanugbàagbàagbọ́kùnrin mì.
Ó wù'ràwọ̀ k'ó mọ́lẹ̀ tó òṣùpá, ẹni a f'ọlá fún òun l'ọlá yẹ.
Òyanugbàagbàagbọ́kùnrin mì.
Igbó méje, òdàn méje, òkè n'yíó r'ẹ̀hìn igbó.
Ò-sùn-tẹẹrẹ-t'Ewégbèmí, A-sùn-tantantan-máà-díyàn-ogun.
Ò njagun níwájú, ó mbààlẹ̀ lẹ́hìn.
Nítorí k'ọmọ kéékèèké ó má baà jagun mọ́.
Àbídẹ́kunìyá, Olúnlóyē baba mi, Ab'eegun-gbogbo-íle-bí-oṣé-irin.
Ògbágbá wọ̀ ilẹ̀, ó k'àtiyọ, ọmọ Tinúomi.
Eèkàn tagìrì wọ̀ ilẹ̀, ọkọ Awònù.
Àrẹàgo ni ífi ṣe ìyá, Aríléwọlá ni ífi ṣe baba.
Mú'nú ṣe ìkà, m'óde ṣ'òótọ́, b'ó bá pẹ́ títí.
Ohun tí íbi'ni kò ní ṣàìbi'ni.
Ikú ṣ'ọkọlóbìnrin d'àpọ́n.
Ab'ẹ̀hìn-ọrùn igb'ódòdó-fùkẹ̀fùkẹ̀.
Múnimúni nù un, jagunjagun nù un nì.
Timi nù un nì.
Ọmọ Baṣọ̀run, egúngún mbọ̀, ẹbọra mbọ̀.
Ọmọ Baṣọ̀run, Ò-yà-ẹnu-gbàagbàa-gb'ọ́kùnrin mì.

---

[27] From Babalọla, Àwon Oríkì Bòròkìnní, p. 115.

Weeds will never grow.[28]
If the landlord is not dead, weeds will never grow in front of the house.
Olunrebi, descendant of the Basorun,
He opened his mouth widely and swallowed a hero.
Stars want to shine as brightly as the moon,
But honour only becomes him, whom honour is accorded.
Seven forests, and seven grassfields.
Hills will survive grassfields.
He slept by the slender body of Ewegbemi.
He slept soundly, unmindful of war.
Fighting a battle in front,
He marked out the battlefield behind him
So that the young generation might no longer
Have to fight any wars.
The last born of his mother, Oluloye,
My father, whose bones are as strong as iron rods,
A peg firmly driven into the ground, in haste.
Husband of Awonu,
You made Arinago to be your mother,
And Arilewola to be your father.
One may try to be wicked inwardly and kind outwardly,
But soon justice will overtake him!
The death of the wife makes the husband a bachelor.
The back of your neck befits a red scarf.
Olugbodi, rain is the husband of the corn plant.
Your horse storms onto the battlefield.
Here comes the captor,
Here comes the warrior,
Here comes the Timi, son of the Basorun,
Here comes the Egungun,
Here comes the powerful spirit, son of the Basorun,
Who opened his mouth widely, and swallowed a hero.

---

[28] From Olunlade, *Ede: A Short History*. Translation by *Tìmì* Laoye.

Oríkì Tìmì **Abibu Lágúnjú (1847–1900)**[29]

Adúkeeṣi, ẹrẹbẹ-l'ókun, idì ọmọ apàṣà.[30]
Ẹrú Ọba kùru.
B'ó pẹ́ títí, àlejò á d'onílé.
Ọ̀bẹ ṣìlò mbá' ni ṣiré, à ní kò mú.
Ó ṣe bí eré, bí eré ó npa'ni l'ọ́wọ́ gbẹgbẹgbẹ.
Àṣẹ̀ṣẹ̀rú ewé òbíṣèrè mb'ẹlẹ́kọ ṣ'ọ̀rẹ́ gúnmọ́-gúnmọ́.
B'ó bá gbó tán, a maa ta wọ́n l'ọ́wọ́ kakaka.
Kékeré ẹkún, ọdẹ ni; àgbàlagbà ẹkùn, ọdẹ ni.
Ọ̀kanṣoṣo ẹkùn, ó bù igba ọdẹ jẹ.
Ẹkùn p'ẹran f'ìrù gbá'lẹ̀ gẹẹrẹrẹ.
Ọ̀rẹ́ Dípẹ̀, awo Ìdàhọ̀mì.
Ẹni à bá kì, kì, kì, nwọn ò kì.
Ẹni à bá yìn, yìn, yìn, nwọn ò yìn.
Òòṣà t'ó pàdé alákìsà l'ójà, t'ó rín, rín, rín, t'ó bú gbaragada.
Òòṣà t'ó dá alákìsà, b'ó pẹ́ títí a sọ ọ'dalàṣọ.
Abá òwú kò gbọdọ̀ fẹgẹ lójú iná.
B'ó bá fẹgẹ lójú iná, iná a maa mú u jẹ.
O jagun òjò, jagun èwọ.
O fa'jú alápatà, Adúkeeṣi, o fa'jú agbẹ́ran.
Òrògbòǹkù ọsàn tí íbọ́ lù ọmọ láàrin òru.
Okú ọ̀pọ̀lọ́ w'ọlọ́bẹ tirigi.
Adéṣínà, baba mi, wò ohun olóhun bínńtín-bínńtín.
Olóòórọ́ ní: "Bí nwọn bá nlọ l'óde, ẹnu wọn kì ìdákẹ́."
Nwọn a ní: 'Baba, gba dúdú kí ng fún ọ ni funfun.'
Ò bá gba àlàbá, kí ng fún ọ ní yùnkùn.
Olóbũ t'oun t'afojúdi, Ọbagùn t'àìgbọdọ̀rìn.
Akìrun kò mọ̀kan-mọ̀kàn, ó mbá wọn rìn lásán.
"Olúgbọ́n, ó ní ng kí ọ, Arẹ̀sà ó ní ng kí ọ."
O ḿ b'ó dé'lé k'ó ní ojú Olúgbọ́n yíó rí i.
B'ó dé'lé k'ó ki Arẹ̀sà pé:
Ojú Arẹ̀sà yíó já a pẹ̀lú.
Òníṣujọlà, Adúkeeṣi, abiṣugbọrọgbọrọ l'oko.
Adéṣínà, baba mi, abàgbàdokọ̀ọ̀rùkọ̀ọ̀rù l'ẹ́gàn.
O ní nkan gbàǹdù-gbàǹdù ní'lé, nwọ́n ní: 'Nítorí kí ni?'

---

[29] In Olunlade's *Ede: A Short History*, the end date of *Tìmì* Lagunju's reign is given as 1892, which is when he was deposed. However, since in many Yoruba traditions an *ọba* is considered to reign until his death, we have given the dates of his reign here (and throughout the book) as ending with his death in 1900.

[30] From Babalọla, *Àwon Oríkì Bòròkìnní*, pp. 116–17.

O ní : 'Nítorí ọ̀tẹ̀ Àgbàlé, bí yíó baà dé'.
K'Ádéṣínà, baba mi, k'ó ba rí'hun gbàǹdùgbàǹdù fi si wọn l'ẹ́nu.
Ẹ̀fúùfù Àkẹ̀sán fẹ́, kóró'sàn mejì l'ó bọ́.
Ayíká dé'bi ọsàn, ó he ọ̀kan.
Ayíká dé'bi ọsàn, o he ọ̀kan.
Olóòóróọ́ l'ó dé'bẹ̀ tí kò rí rárá.
Ayíká pa tiẹ̀ pẹ̀rẹ́, ó fún Dójútẹleẹ́gàn, ọmọ Ṣàbi.
Ayíká pa tiẹ̀ pẹ̀rẹ́, ó fún Dójútẹleẹ́gàn, ọmọ Ṣàbi.
T'àwọn méjèèjì d'àbààbọ̀, ti Dójútẹlẹ́gàn wá d'odidi.
Nwọn ní ohun mẹ́ta l'a kì ímú wọ̀ ilé ba.
Mẹ́tẹ̀ẹ̀ta l'Adúkeeṣi mú wọ̀ ilé ọba lọ.
O ṣán kúkúmọ́ jooro wọ̀ ilé ọba.
A kì íṣán bàntẹ́ wọ̀ ilé Òsì Ìwẹ̀fà.
O ṣán bàntẹ́ wọ̀ ilé Òsì Ìwẹ̀fà.
A kì ímu tábà d'Ákẹ̀sán, Olóòóróọ́ mu tábà Ákẹ̀sán.
O fá'rí kodoro, o ṣ'òṣùká èwọ̀n rìbìtì.
O gbé yangí ká pòòyì Ákẹ̀sán lẹ́ẹ̀mẹ́fà lemọ-lemọ.
Ẹrú ọba kùru, idì ọmọ apàṣà.
Ọ̀kanṣoṣo ẹkùn, ó bù igba ọdẹ jẹ.

Adukesi – all the body except the teeth is black.[31]
A hero at sea.
An eagle that kills choice game.
Faithful servant of the great king.
A stranger becomes a companion only after a while.
You play with a carving knife and think it is blunt.
Playfully, playfully, it makes a deep cut.
It is easy to wrap your maize pap into ibisere leaves when they are young.
When they are old, they became rather stiff and hard to handle.
A leopard cub is a hunter.
A grown up leopard is also a hunter.
A single leopard can destroy ten score hunters.
When the leopard kills, its tail drags playfully on the ground.
Friend of Dipe, confident of Dahomey.
One who should be greeted and greeted, is not greeted.
One who should be praised and praised, is not praised.
The god who met a man in rags at the market,
Smiled and smiled, and burst into laughter.
The god who created a man in rags will also create a garment for him.

---

[31] From Olunlade, *Ede: A Short History.* Translation by *Tìmì* Laoye.

Cotton wool dare not be careless near fire,
If it is careless the fire will eat it up.
You cut marks on the face of the butcher,
Adukesi, you cut marks on the face of the goat thief.
You are like big ripe fruit that fell on a child at midnight.
A dead frog gazes at the man holding a knife contemptuously.
Adesina, my father, you do not care for another man's property.
Oloro says: as they are going their own way, they will never
Keep their mouth shut.
They keep on saying: father take the black, and I give you the white,
When you take the blue, then I give you the blue black.
The Olobu with his insult.
The Obagun who pretends he is forbidden to walk out.
The Akirun in his ignorance keeps company with them.
The Olugbon said: I should salute you.
The Aresa said: I should salute you.
You said: when you get back tell Olugbere, woe betide him.
You said: when you get back tell the Aresa, woe betide him.
You have yams in the market, Adukesi.
And on the farm you have long long yams
My father you have maize with fat cobs on your forest farm.
You pile up food in the palace.
We asked you why and you said:
When the people of Agbale begin their plot
I shall have food to feed you.
The wind blew at Akesan,
And only two fruit fell down.
Ayika got to the tree and picked one.
Ayika got there quickly and picked one.
But when Oloro came, there was no fruit left.
Ayika split his fruit in two
And gave half to Dejutelegan, son of Sabi
Had a whole fruit.
It was forbidden to enter the palace of the king with three things,
But Adukesi entered the palace with all three.
It was forbidden to enter the palace in working clothes.
He entered the palace in his working clothes.
It was forbidden to enter the palace in a loincloth,
He entered the palace in a loincloth.
It was forbidden to use tobacco on Akesan market,
He used tobacco on Akesan market.

He shaved his head clean and made a pad of iron chains,
And went round Akesan market six times carrying a big stone on his head.
The king's servant in truth.
An eagle which kills choice game.
A single leopard who destroys ten score hunters.

Bibliography

Abimbola, W., *The Study of Yoruba Literature* (Ile-Ife: University of Ife Press, 1977).
Adebanwi, W., *Yorùbá Elites and Ethnic Politics in Nigeria: Ọbáfẹmi Awólowo and Corporate Agency* (Cambridge: Cambridge University Press, 2014).
Adebayo, I., 'The role of traditional rulers in the Islamization of Osun State (Nigeria)', *Journal for Islamic Studies* [South Africa] 30 (2010), 60–77.
Adedoyin, I., *The Place of Ogbomosho in the History of Nigerian Baptists* (Ibadan: Penthouse Publications, 2005).
Adedoyin, I., and J.T. Ayorinde, *A Study in the Growth of the Nigerian Baptist Convention and Moses Oladejo Stone and the Beginning of Baptist Work in Nigeria* (Ibadan: Nigerian Baptist Book Store, 1998).
Adegbola, A., *Ile-Ife: The Source of Yoruba Civilisation* (Lagos: Oduduwa International Communications, 2009).
Adejumo, A., 'The practice and worship of Ṣàngó in contemporary Yorubaland', *Ṣàngó in Africa and the African Diaspora*, ed. J. Tishken, T. Falola and A. Akinyemi (Bloomington: Indiana University Press, 2009), pp. 44–62.
Adelegan, F., *Nigeria's Leading Lights of the Gospel: Revolutionaries in Worldwide Christianity* (Bloomington IN: Westbrow Press, 2013).
'Adeleke finally defects to APC', *Nigerian Tribune* (1 June 2014).
Adeleke, D., 'A speech by Dr Deji Adeleke-Adeleke University, Ede, Osun State, on the inauguration of the Board of Trustees of Adeleke University', *Adeleke University* (n.d.), <http://www.adelekeuniversity.edu.ng/news/?id=1e12f77a-0d13-49ce-a85d-21d9bee97d3f>, accessed 11 December 2013.
Adeleke-Sanni, M., 'Tribute', *Celebration of Life, Funeral and Outing Services* (n.p., 2009).
Adepoju, O., *Esin* (n.p., 1978).
Adesegun, A.A., 'Christian education in the Seventh-Day Adventist Church in Remo, Ogun State, Nigeria, 1959–2004', unpublished PhD thesis (Ibadan: Department of Religious Studies, University of Ibadan, 2009).
Adesoji, A., 'The Boko Haram uprising and Islamic revivalism in Nigeria', *Africa Spectrum* 45:2 (2010), 95–108.
Agiri, B.A., 'Early Oyo history reconsidered', *History in Africa* 2 (1975), 1–16.
Ajayi, J.A., *Christian Missions in Nigeria, 1841–1891: The Making of a New Elite* (London: Longman, 1965).
Ajayi, S.A., *Baptist Work in Nigeria, 1850–2005: A Comprehensive History* (Ibadan: Book Wright Publishers, 2010).

Akande, F., 'Baba Abiye', The Making of the Prophet: The Testimony of Prophet Samson Oladeji Akande (Ede: Gospel Promotion Outreach, 2002).
Akinade, A.E., 'The precarious agenda: Christian–Muslim relations in contemporary Nigeria', Journal of Islam and Christian–Muslim Relations (2002).
Akinjobi, T., 'The role of sheikhs and imams in the promotion of Islam in Edeland', Crowns and Turbans in the Promotion of Islam in Osun State: Essays in Honour of HRM Oba Raufu Olayiwola Olawale, Adedeji II, Akinrun of Ikirun, ed. S. Oyeweso (Abuja: Mega Press Ltd, 2012), pp. 194–217.
Akinyemi, A., 'The place of Ṣàngó in the Yorùbá pantheon', Ṣàngó in Africa and the African Diaspora, ed. J. Tishken, T. Falola and A. Akinyemi (Bloomington: Indiana University Press, 2009), pp. 23–43.
Akomolafe, C., 'A comparative study of principals' administrative effectiveness in public and private secondary schools in Ekiti State, Nigeria', Journal of Education and Practice 3:13 (2012), 39–45.
Alabi, S.A., 'Islam in Ede, 1850–2000', unpublished BA Long Essay (Ile-Ife: Department of History, Obafemi Awolowo University, 2008).
Ali, J.A., 'Islamic revivalism: A study of the Tablighi Jamaat in Sydney', unpublished PhD thesis (Sydney: University of New South Wales, 2006).
al-Ilori, A.A., Mujiz Tarikh Nigeria (Beirut: n.p., 1965).
Anglican Diocese of Osun, Outline History of Churches in the Diocese of Osun Anglican Communion (Osogbo: Safesight Publishers, 2007).
Apter, A., Black Critics and Kings: The Hermeneutics of Power in Yoruba Society (Chicago and London: University of Chicago Press, 1992).
Asad. T., 'The idea of an anthropology of Islam', Qui Parle 17: 2 (2009), 1–30.
Atanda J., ed., W.H. Clarke's Travels and Explorations in Yorubaland, 1854–1858 (Ibadan: University of Ibadan Press, 1972).
—, Baptist Churches in Nigeria, 1850–1950: Accounts of Their Foundation and Growth (Ibadan: University of Ibadan Press, 1988).
—, First Baptist Church, Oke-Apaso, Ede, Osun State: A Century of Practical and Expansive Evangelism in Edeland, 1900–2000 (Osogbo: A Centenary Celebration Souvenir printed for the Church by Ademola Printing Press, 2000).
Awolalu, J.O., Yoruba Beliefs and Sacrificial Rites (London: Longman, 1979).
Babalola, A., The Content and Form of Yorùbá Ijala (Oxford: Clarendon Press, 1966).
—, Àwon oríkì bòròkìnní (Ibadan: Hodder & Stoughton, 1975).
Babatunde, J., 'I never dreamt of being the king – Timi, paramount ruler of Ede', Vanguard (10 March 2013), <http://www.vanguardngr.com/2013/03/i-never-dreamt-of-being-the-king-timi-paramount-ruler-of-Ede>, accessed 19 February 2014.
Badejo, D.L., 'Ṣàngó and the elements: Gender and cultural discourses', Ṣàngó in Africa and the African Diaspora, ed. J. E. Tishken, T. Falola and A. Akinyemi (Bloomington: Indiana University Press, 2009), pp. 111–34.
Bakare, S., 'Sango in the Church', Daily Sketch (27 October 1974), pp. 1–2.
Barber, K., 'How man makes God in West Africa: Yoruba attitudes towards the Orisa', Africa 51:3 (1981), 724–45.
—, 'Discursive strategies in the texts of Ifá and in the "Holy Book of Odù" of the African Church of Òrúnmìlà', Self-Assertion and Brokerage: Early Cultural Nationalism in West Africa, ed. K. Barber and P.F. de Moraes Farias (Birmingham: Birmingham University African Studies Series, 1990), pp. 196–224.

—, 'Oríkì, women and the proliferation and merging of Òrìsà', *Africa* 60:3 (1990), 313–37.

—, *I Could Speak until Tomorrow: Oriki, Women and the Past in a Yoruba Town* (Edinburgh: Edinburgh University Press, 1991).

Barnes, S., *Patrons and Power: Creating a Political Community in Metropolitan Lagos* (London (IAL): Manchester University Press, 1986).

—, 'Ritual, power, and outside knowledge', *Journal of Religion in Africa* 20:3 (1990), 248–68.

Bascom, W., 'The principle of seniority in the social structure of the Yoruba', *American Anthropologist* 44 (1942), 37–46.

—, *Ifa Divination: Communication Between Gods and Men in West Africa* (Bloomington: Indiana University Press, 1969).

Bayly, S., *Saints, Goddesses and Kings. Muslims and Christians in South Indian Society, 1700–1900* (Cambridge: Cambridge University Press, 1989).

Beier, U., 'Festival of the images', *Nigeria Magazine* 45 (1954), 14–20.

—, *A Year of Sacred Festivals in One Yoruba Town*, ed. D.W. MacRow (Lagos: Nigeria Magazine Special Publication, 1959).

Bender, D.R., 'Agnatic or cognatic? A re-evaluation of Ondo descent', *MAN* 1:5 (1970), 71–87.

Biedelman, T., *Colonial Evangelism: A Socio-Historical Study of an East African Mission at the Grassroots* (Bloomington: Indiana University Press, 1982).

Bop, C., 'Inter-religious marriages in Dakar, Thies, and Ziguinchor, Senegal', *Inter-Religious Marriages among Muslims: Negotiating Religious and Social Identity in Family and Community*, ed. A. An-na'im (New Delhi: Global Media Publications, 2005), pp. 163–216.

Brenner, L., 'Muslim divination and the history of religion of Sub-Saharan Africa', *Insight and Artistry in African Divination*, ed. John Pemberton III (Washington and London: Smithsonian Institution Press, 2000), pp. 45–59.

Burton, F.A., 'Tablighi Jamaat: an indirect line to terrorism', *STRATFOR* (23 January 2008), <http://www.stratfor.com/weekly/tablighi_jamaat_indirect_line_terrorism>, accessed 30 August 2012.

Caballero, C., R. Edwards and S. Puthussery, *Parenting 'Mixed' Children: Negotiating Difference and Belonging in Mixed Race and Faith Families* (York: The Joseph Rowntree Foundation, 2008).

Cannell, F., 'Introduction: The anthropology of Christianity', *The Anthropology of Christianity*, ed. F. Cannell (Durham NC and London: Duke University Press, 2006), pp. 1–50.

Chopra, R., and J. Punwani, 'Discovering the other, discovering the self: Inter-religious marriage among Muslims in the Greater Bombay area, India', *Inter-Religious marriages among Muslims: Negotiating Religious and Social Identity in Family and Community*, ed. A. An-na'im (New Delhi: Global Media Publications, 2005), pp. 45–162.

Clarke, P., *Mahdism in West Africa: The Ijebu Mahdiyya Movement* (New York: Weatherhill Incorporated, 1995).

Clarke, W.H., *Travels and Explorations in Yorubaland, 1854–1858*, ed. J.A. Atanda (Ibadan: Ibadan University Press, 1972).

Cole, J., and L.M. Thomas, eds., *Love in Africa* (Chicago and London: University of Chicago Press, 2009).

Collins, T., *The Baptist Mission of Nigeria, 1850–1993: A History of the Southern Baptist Convention Missionary Work in Nigeria* (Ibadan: Associated Book-Makers Nigeria Ltd, 1993).

Comaroff, J., and J. Comaroff, *Theory from the South or, How Euro-America is Evolving toward Africa* (London and Boulder CO: Paradigm Publishers, 2012).

Cooper, B., *Evangelical Christians in the Muslim Sahel* (Bloomington and Indianapolis: Indiana University Press, 2006).

Danmole, H.O., 'Religious encounter in Southwestern Nigeria: The domestication of Islam among the Yorùbá', *Òrìṣà Devotion as World Religion: The Globalization of Yorùbá Religious Culture*, ed. J.K. Olupona and T. Rey (Madison: University of Wisconsin Press, 2007), pp. 202–17.

Davidson, J., and Widman, T., 'The effect of group size on interfaith marriage among Catholics', *Journal for the Scientific Study of Religion* 41:3 (2002), 397–404.

Dokun, L., 'Islam in Ede', unpublished BA Long Essay (Ibadan: Department of Arabic and Islamic Studies, University of Ibadan, 1974).

Drewal, M.T., *Yoruba Ritual: Performers, Play, Agency* (Bloomington: Indiana University Press, 1992).

Duval, L.M., *Baptist Missions in Nigeria* (Richmond VA: Educational Department of Foreign Mission Board of Southern Baptist Convention, 1928).

Eades, J.S., *The Yoruba Today* (Cambridge: Cambridge University Press, 1980).

Egwaikhide, F., V. Isumonah and O. Ayodele, *Federal Presence in Nigeria: The 'Sung' and 'Unsung' Basis for Ethnic Grievance* (Dakar: CODESRIA, 2009).

Eighth Day Fidau Prayer and Final Burial Ceremony programme/souvenir of Oba Tijani Oladokun Oyewusi (Ede: n.p., 5 September 2007).

Ellis, S., and G. ter Haar, 'Religion and politics in Sub-Saharan Africa', *The Journal of Modern African Studies* 36:2 (1998), 175–201.

Fadipe, N.A., *The Sociology of the Yoruba* (Ibadan: Ibadan University Press, 1970 [1939]).

Fafunwa, A.B., *History of Education in Nigeria* (Ibadan: NPS Educational, 1977).

First Year Coronation Anniversary Ceremony programme/souvenir of HRM, Oba Munirudeen Adesola Lawal (Ede: n.p., 5 March 2009).

Forst, R., 'The limits of toleration', *Constellations* 11:3 (2004), 312–25.

Gbadamosi, T.G.O., '"Odu Imale': Islam in Ifa divination and the case of predestined Muslims', *Journal of the Historical Society of Nigeria* 8:4 (1977), 77–93.

——, *The Growth of Islam among the Yoruba, 1841–1908* (London: Longman, 1978).

Giddens, A., and Pierson, C., *Conversations with Anthony Giddens: Making Sense of Modernity* (Cambridge: Polity Press, 1998).

Godlas, A., *Sufism – Sufis – Sufi Orders, Islam and Islamic Studies Resources* (n.d.), <http://islam.uga.edu/Sufism.html>, accessed 25 September 2014.

Green, C.S., *New Nigeria: Southern Baptists at Work in Africa* (Richmond VA: Educational Department of Foreign Mission Board of Southern Baptist Convention, 1936).

Griswold, E., *The Tenth Parallel: Dispatches from the Faultline between Christianity and Islam* (London: Penguin Books, 2010).

Guyer, J., 'Traditions of invention in Equatorial Africa', *African Studies Review* 39:3 (1996), 1–28.

Habermas, J., 'Religion in the public sphere', *European Journal of Philosophy* 14:1 (2006), 1–25.

Habermas, J. et al., *An Awareness of What is Missing: Faith and Reason in a Post-Secular Age* (Cambridge: Polity Press, 2010). First published in German as *Ein Bewußtsein von dem, was fehlt* (Frankfurt/Main: Suhrkamp. 2007).

Haynes, J., 'Religion, ethnicity and civil war in Africa: The cases of Uganda and Sudan', *The Round Table* 96:390 (2007), 305–17.

Hock, K., ed., *The Interface between Research and Dialogue: Christian–Muslim Relations in Africa* (Berlin et al.: LIT Verlag, 2004).

Honneth, A., 'Integrity and disrespect: Principles of a conception of morality based on the theory of recognition', *Political Theory* 20:2 (1992), 187–201.

Huntington, S.P., 'The clash of civilizations?' *Foreign Affairs* 72:3 (1993), 22–49.

Ibrahim, J., 'Civil society, religion and democracy in contemporary Africa', *Civil Society and Authoritarianism in the Third World*, ed. B. Beckman, E. Hanson and A. Sjorgen (Stockholm: Stockholm University, PODSU, 2001), pp. 183–95.

Isola, B.R., 'Islam and society in Ede, 1817–1976', unpublished BA Long Essay (Lagos: Department of History, Lagos State University, 1993).

Isumonah, V., and F. Egwaikhide, 'Federal presence in higher institutions in Nigeria and the North–South dichotomy', *Regional and Federal Studies* 23:2 (2013), 169–88.

Janson, M., *Islam, Youth, and Modernity in the Gambia: The Tablighi Jama'at* (Cambridge: Cambridge University Press for the International African Institute, 2013).

Johnson, S., *The History of the Yorubas: From the Earliest Times to the Beginning of the British Protectorate* (Lagos: CMS Bookshops, 1921).

Jolly, N., 'Inter-religious marriage: Literature review', unpublished literature review for the Knowing Each Other project (n.p., 2012).

Khan, M.M., and M.T. Al-Hilali, *Interpretation of the Meanings of the Noble Qur'an* (Riyadh: Darussalam Publishers and Distributors, 1996).

Kriger, C.E., 'Mapping the history of cotton textile production in precolonial West Africa', *African Economic History* 33 (2005), 87–116.

Laitin, D.D., *Hegemony and Culture: Politics and Religious Change among the Yoruba* (Chicago and London: University of Chicago Press, 1986).

Langer, A., 'Situational importance of ethnicity and religion in Ghana', *Ethnopolitics* 9:1 (2010), 9–29.

Laoye, J.A., *The Story of My Installation* (Ede: Aafin Timi Ede, 1956).

Laoye, A., The 7th Timi of Ede, *An Address of Welcome delivered to the Islamic Congress held at Ede on the 3rd & 4th August* (n.p., 1963).

Lasisi, R., 'Oyo–Yoruba and Ilorin relations in the 19th century', *Readings in Nigerian History and Culture*, ed. G.O. Oguntomisin and S.A. Ajayi (Ibadan: Hope Publications, 2002), pp. 254–70.

Last, M., 'From dissent to dissidence: The genesis & development of reformist Islamic groups in northern Nigeria', *Sects & Social Disorder: Muslim Identities & Conflict in Northern Nigeria*, ed. R.A. Mustapha (Woodbridge: James Currey, 2014), pp. 18–53.

Launay, R., *Beyond the Stream: Islam and Society in a West African Town* (Berkeley: University of California Press, 1992).

Law, R., *The Oyo Empire, c. 1600–c. 1836: A West African Imperialism in the Era of the Atlantic Slave Trade* (Oxford: Clarendon Press, 1977).

—, 'Making sense of a traditional narrative: Political disintegration in the Kingdom of Oyo', *Cahiers d'études africaines* 22:87/88 (1982), 387–401.

——, 'How many times can history repeat itself? Some problems in the traditional history of Oyo', *International Journal of African Historical Studies* 18:1 (1985), 33–51.
Lawal, O., 'Isiaka Adeleke: The central issue in Osun politics', *The Sun* (3 July 2013), <http://www.sunnewsonline.com/news/politics/isiaka-adeleke-the-central-issue-in-osun-politics>, accessed 12 December 2013.
Lawuyi, O., 'Islam, economy and political identity: An insight into religious identifications of the Yoruba', *Annals of the Institute of Cultural Studies* 6 (1995), 4–15.
Lawuyi, T., and T. Falola, 'The instability of the naira and social payment among the Yoruba', *Journal of African and Asian Studies* 27:3 (1992), 216–28.
Levinas, E., *Totality and Infinity: An Essay on Exteriority* (Pittsburgh, PA: Duquesne University Press, 1969).
Lloyd, P., 'The Yoruba lineage', *Africa* 25 (1955), 235–51.
——, 'Yoruba myths: A sociologist's interpretation', *Odù: Journal of Yoruba and Related Studies* 2 (1955), 20–8.
Loimeier, R., *Islamic Reform and Political Change in Northern Nigeria* (Evanston IL: Northwestern University Press, 1997).
——, 'Is there something like "Protestant Islam"?', *Die Welt des Islams* 45:2 (2005), 216–54.
——, 'Boko Haram: The development of a militant religious movement in Nigeria', *Africa Spectrum* 47:2/3 (2012), 137–55.
Lord, K., 'Implicit religion: A contemporary theory for the relationships between religion, state and society', *Journal of Contemporary Religion* 23:1 (2008), 33–46.
Mabogunje, A. 'The Yoruba home', *ODU* 5 (1985), 28–36.
Makinde, A.F.K., 'The institution of Shari'ah in Oyo and Osun States, Nigeria, 1890–2005', unpublished PhD thesis (Ibadan: Department of Arabic and Islamic Studies, University of Ibadan, 2007).
Mamdani, M., *Good Muslim, Bad Muslim: America, the Cold War, and the Roots of Terror* (New York: Pantheon, 2004).
Marshall, R., 'Power in the name of Jesus', *Review of African Political Economy* 52 (1991), 21–37.
——, *Political Spiritualities: The Pentecostal Revolution in Nigeria* (Chicago and London: University of Chicago Press, 2009).
——, 'Christianity, anthropology, politics', *Current Anthropology* 55:10 (2014), 344–56.
Masquelier, A., *Women and Islamic Revival in a West African Town* (Bloomington: Indiana University Press, 2009).
Masud, M.K., *Travellers in Faith: Studies of the Tablīghī Jamā'at as a Transnational Islamic Movement for Faith Renewal* (Leiden: Brill, 2000).
Matory, J.L., 'Rival empires: Islam and the religions of spirit possession among the Ọ̀yọ́-Yorùbá', *American Ethnologist*, 21:3 (1994), 495–515.
——, *Sex and the Empire that is no more: Gender and the Politics of Metaphor in Oyo Yoruba Religion* (Minneapolis and London: University of Minnesota Press, 1994).
Maxwell, D., *African Gifts of the Spirit: Pentecostalism & the Rise of a Zimbabwean Transnational Religious Movement* (Oxford: James Currey, 2006).
McCutcheon, R., 'The category "religion" in recent publications: A critical survey', *Numen* 42:3 (1995), 284–309.
McGuire, M.B., *Lived Religion: Faith and Practice in Everyday Life* (Oxford: Oxford University Press, 2008).

Metcalf, B.D., '"Traditionalist" Islamic activism: Deoband, Tablighis, and Talibs', *Social Science Research Council* (n.d.), <http://essays.ssrc.org/sept11/essays/metcalf.htm>, accessed 25 January 2013.

Meyer, B., '"Make a complete break with the past": Memory and post-colonial modernity in Ghanaian Pentecostalist discourse', *Journal of Religion in Africa* 28:3 (1998), 316–49.

——, '"Praise the Lord": Popular cinema and pentecostalite style in Ghana's new public sphere', *American Ethnologist* 31:1 (2004), 92–110.

Moosa, E., 'Worlds "Apart": The Tabligh Jamat under Apartheid, 1963–1993', *Journal for Islamic Studies* 17 (1997), 28–48.

Moraes Farias, P.F. de, '"Yoruba Origins" Revisited by Muslims: An interview with the Arọ́kin of Ọ̀yọ́ and a reading of the Aṣl Qabā'il Yūrubā of Al-Ḥājj Ādam al-Ilūrī', *Self-Assertion and Brokerage: Early Cultural Nationalism in West Africa*, ed. K. Barber and P.F. de Moraes Farias (Birmingham: University of Birmingham African Studies Series, 1990), pp. 109–47.

——, 'History as consolation: Royal Yorùbá bards comment on their craft', *History in Africa* 19 (1992), 263–97.

Muhammed, A., 'The Tabligh Jammaat influence in the midst of controversy', *Islam Online* (n.d.), <http://islamonline.net/en/529>, accessed 15 August 2012.

Mustapha, A.R., ed., *Sects & Social Disorder: Muslim Identities & Conflict in Northern Nigeria* (Woodbridge: James Currey, 2014).

Mustapha, R.A., 'Conclusion: Religious sectarianism, poor governance & conflict', *Sects & Social Disorder: Muslim Identities & Conflict in Northern Nigeria*, ed. R.A. Mustapha (Woodbridge: James Currey, 2014), pp. 199–222.

Nancy, J.L., *The Inoperative Community* (Minneapolis and London: University of Minnesota Press, 1991).

Ninalowo, A., 'Specifications on trade unionism: Democratization and contradictory realities', *Governance and Democratization in Nigeria*, ed. O. Dele, K. Soremekun and A. Williams (Lagos: Spectrum, 1995), pp. 147–65.

Nolte, I., 'Chieftaincy and the state in Abacha's Nigeria: Kingship, political rivalry and competing histories in Abeokuta during the 1990s', *Africa* 72:3 (2002), 368–90.

——, *Obafemi Awolowo and the Making of Remo: The Local Politics of a Nigerian Nationalist* (Edinburgh: Edinburgh University Press for the International Africa Institute, 2009).

——, 'Spirit: Histories of religion and the Word', *West Africa: Word, Symbol, Song*, ed. G. Casely-Hayford, J. Topp Fargion and M. Wallace (London: British Library, 2015), pp. 48–71.

——, 'Transformations of the customary: Christianity, Islam and Yoruba traditional rulers in southwest Nigeria', *Chiefship and the Customary in Contemporary Africa*, ed. J. Comaroff and J. Comaroff (Bloomington: Indiana University Press, forthcoming).

Nolte, I., R. Jones, K. Taiyari and G. Occhiali, 'Exploring survey data for historical and anthropological research: Muslim–Christian relations in southwest Nigeria', *African Affairs* 115:460 (2016).

Nwagwu, N.A., 'The state take-over of schools in Nigeria: A controversy', *Journal of Educational Administration* 17:1 (1979), 75–86.

Obadare, E., 'White-collar fundamentalism: Interrogating youth religiosity on Nigerian university campuses', *Journal of Modern African Studies* 45:4 (2007), 517–37.

Ogundele, W., 'Ulli Beier', *Centre for Black Culture and Understanding* (n.d.), <http://www.centreforblackculture.org/Ulli.htm>, accessed 8 September 2014.

Ogundiran, A., 'Material life and domestic economy in a frontier of the Oyo Empire during the Mid-Atlantic age', *International Journal of African Historical Studies* 42:3 (2009), 351–85.

Ogunmola, M., *A New Perspective to Oyo Empire History, 1530–1944* (Ibadan: Vantage Publishers, 1985).

Ohachenu, U., 'Learning from below: Indigenous non governmental grass root organizations in governance and democratization', *Governance and Democratization in Nigeria*, ed. O. Dele, K. Soremekun and A. Williams (Lagos: Spectrum, 1995), pp. 111–29.

Ojo, S.A., *History of African Church in Ede, Osun State* (Ede: Monec Printers, n.d.).

Okedara, J., and S.A. Ajayi, *Thomas Jefferson Bowen: Pioneer Baptist Missionary to Nigeria, 1850–1856* (Ibadan: John Archers, 2004).

Oladimeji, L.F., 'Tablighi movement in Nigeria: Conceptions and misconceptions', *Journal of the Faculty of Islamic Studies and Arabic* 5:81 (1999–2000), 73–9.

——, 'A sociological analysis of experiences of selected Jama'atut Tabligh in the Nigerian society', *Science and Religion in the Service of Humanity*, ed. A.P. Dopamu (Ilorin: LSI and NASTRENS, 2006), pp. 390–400.

——, 'Roaming about for God's sake: The upsurge of the Jama'atut Tablighi in Nigeria', *Degel: The Journal of FAIS* 7:52 (2007), 52–73.

——, 'The role of the Jama'tut-Tablighi in the promotion of adult and non-formal education among Muslims in Nigeria', *Education Crises in Nigeria: Arabic and Islamic Studies Perspectives*, ed. M.A. Muhbbu-Din (Jos: NATAIS Publication, 2007), pp. 16–28.

——, 'The Tabligh movement and Jehovah's Witnesses in Nigeria: A comparative analysis of their propagation strategies', *Fluorescence of Arabic and Islamic Studies in Nigeria*, ed. I.Z. Oseni (Ibadan: HEBN, 2008), pp. 90–9.

Oladipo, O., *The History of Osun State: From Zero to Hero*, Vol. III (Ibadan: Simlad Nigeria Ltd, 2010).

——, 'SANGO; The god of Thunder', TIA–This is Africa (17 April 2011), <http://tia-thisisafrica.blogspot.co.uk/2011/04/sango-god-of-thunder_17.html>, accessed 27 July 2013.

Olatunji, O.O., 'Classification of Yorùbá oral poetry', *Yorùbá Language and Literature*, ed. A. Afolayan (Ibadan: University of Ibadan Press, 1982), pp. 57–72.

——, *Features of Yorùbá Oral Poetry* (Ibadan: University of Ibadan Press, 1984).

Olukoju, E., 'The place of Chants in Yorùbá traditional oral literature', unpublished PhD thesis (Ibadan: University of Ibadan, 1978).

Olukoshi, A., 'Associational life', *Transition Without End: Nigerian Politics and Civil Society under Babangida*, ed. L. Diamond, A. Kirk-Green and O. Oyediran (Ibadan: Vintage Press, 1996), pp. 450–76.

Olunlade, E., *Ede: A Short History* (Ibadan: General Publications Section, Ministry of Education, 1961).

Olupona, J.O., *Kingship, Religion, and Rituals in a Nigerian Community: A Phenomenological Study of Ondo Yoruba Festivals* (Stockholm: Alimquist & Wiksell, 1991).

Olupona, J., *City of 201 Gods: Ilé-Ifẹ̀ in Time, Space, and the Imagination* (Berkeley: University of California Press, 2011).

Omoluabi, P., 'The psychosocial bases of violence, cultism and religious fanaticism in Nigerian tertiary institutions', *Citadels of Violence: A CDHR Publication on the State of the Campuses of Nigerian Tertiary Institutions*, ed. J. Ogunye, S. Jegede and J. Akinsola (Lagos: CDHR, 1999).
Opeloye, M., 'Evolution of religious culture among the Yoruba', *Culture and Society in Yorubaland*, ed. D. Ogunremi and B. Adediran (Ibadan: Rex Charles Publication in association with Connel Publications, 1998), pp. 139–48.
Osaghae, E., 'The role of civil society in consolidating democracy: An African comparative perspective', *Africa Insight* 27:1 (1997), 15–23.
Osoba, S., and A. Fajana, 'Educational and social development during the twentieth century', *Groundwork of Nigeria History*, ed. O. Ikime (Ibadan: Heinemann Educational Books, 1980), pp. 570–600.
Oyedeji, A., 'History of imamship in Ede', unpublished manuscript (n.p., n.d.).
Oyeweso, G., 'Traditions of origin and growth of Ede up to 1960', unpublished BA long essay (Ile-Ife: Department of History, University of Ife, 1982).
Oyeweso, S., 'The state and religion in a plural society: The Nigerian experience', *Islamic Culture* 63:4 (1989), 65–80.
—, *Eminent Yoruba Muslims of the 19th and Early 20th Centuries* (Ibadan: Rex Charles Publications in association with Connel Publications, 1999).
—, *Ede in Yoruba History* (Lagos: Multi Vision Publishing House, 2002).
—, 'Opening speech', *17th Ede day celebration*, Former Baptist High School, Ede (2010).
—, 'Historical development of Islam in Ede', *Islam and Society in Osun State: Essays in Honour of HRM Oba Raufu Olayiwola Olawale Adedeji II, Akinrun of Ikirun*, ed. S. Oyeweso and R.O. Olawale (Abuja: Mega Press, 2012), pp. 1–18.
—, 'Keynote address', *Everyday Religion and Tolerance in Ede, Southwest Nigeria* conference, Adeleke University, Ede, 5–6 December 2012.
Peel, J.D.Y., 'Olaju: A Yoruba concept of development', *Journal of African Studies* 2 (1978), 139–65.
—, *Ijeshas and Nigerians: The Incorporation of a Yoruba Kingdom 1890s–1970s* (Cambridge: Cambridge University Press, 1983).
—, 'Making history: The past in the Ijesha present', *Man* 19:1 (1984), 111–32.
—, 'The cultural work of Yoruba ethnogenesis', *History and Ethnicity*, ed. E. Tonkin, M. McDonald and M. Chapman (London: Routledge, 1989), pp. 198–215.
—, 'A comparative analysis of Ogun in precolonial Yorubaland', *Africa's Ogun: Old World and New*, ed. S.T. Barnes, 2nd edn (Bloomington: Indiana University Press, 1997), pp. 263–89.
—, *Religious Encounter and the Making of the Yoruba* (Bloomington: Indiana University Press, 2000).
—, 'Gender in Yoruba religious change', *Journal of Religion in Africa* 32:2 (2002), 136–66.
—, 'Review of *Sango in Africa and the African Diaspora*', *Africa* 81:2 (2011), 340–1.
—, *Christianity, Islam, and Orisha Religion: Three Traditions in Comparison and Interaction* (Oakland CA: University of California Press, 2016).
Pemberton, J., and F. Afolayan, *Yoruba Sacred Kingship: 'a power like that of the gods'* (Washington: Smithsonian Institution Press, 1996).

Pew Forum on Religion and Public Life, 'Many Americans mix multiple faiths', *Pew Forum* (2009), <http://www.pewforum.org/2009/12/09/many-americans-mix-multiple-faiths/>, accessed 19 July 2016.

Pew Forum on Religion and Public Life, 'Tolerance and tension: Islam and Christianity in Sub-Saharan Africa', *Pew Forum* (2010), <http://www.pewforum.org/files/2010/04/sub-saharan-africa-full-report.pdf>, accessed 11 February 2014.

Pinnock, S., *The Romance of Missions in Nigeria* (Richmond VA: Educational Department of Foreign Mission Board of Southern Baptist Convention, 1917).

Post, K., and G. Jenkins, *The Price of Liberty: Personality and Politics in Colonial Nigeria* (Cambridge: Cambridge University Press, 1973).

Rahim, A., *Islamic History* (Delhi: Royal Publishers and Distributors, 2003).

Rana, M.A., *Tablighi Jama'at: Discourse and Challenges* (Islamabad: Pak Institute for Peace Studies, 2009).

Reichmuth, S., *Islamische Bildung und soziale Integration in Ilorin (Nigeria) seit ca. 1800* (Münster: LIT Verlag, 1998).

Renne, E., *Population and Progress in a Yoruba Town* (Edinburgh: Edinburgh University Press, 2003).

Rizvi, S.M., 'Religious tolerance in Islam', *Ahlul Bayt Digital Islamic Library Project* (n.d.), http://www.al-islam.org/articles/religious-tolerance-islam-sayyid-muhammad-rizvi>, accessed 25 September 2014.

Roberson, C., *A History of Baptists in Nigeria, West Africa, 1849–1935 (with Appropriate Projections into Later Years)*, released in 1986 as Roberson Papers and kept as Private Collections at J.C. Pool Memorial Library, The Nigerian Baptist Theological Seminary Ogbomoso, Oyo State, Nigeria (n.d.).

——, 'The Bowen Papers: A Compilation of Private and Business Papers of Rev. Thomas Jefferson and his wife Laurenna Henrietta (Davis) Bowen', Private Collections available at J.C. Pool Memorial Library, The Nigerian Baptist Theological Seminary, Ogbomoso, Oyo State, Nigeria (n.d.).

Romain, J.A., *Till Faith Do Us Part: Couples who Fall in Love across the Religious Divide* (London: Fount Paperbacks, 1996).

Rotberg, R.I., *Missionary Researches and Travels* (London: Frank Cass and Company Ltd, 1968).

Sanneh, L., *Piety and Power: Muslims and Christians in West Africa* (Maryknoll NY: Orbis Books, 1996).

Schielke, J.S., and L. Debevec, eds., *Ordinary Lives and Grand Schemes: An Anthropology of Everyday Religion* (Oxford and New York: Berghahn, 2012).

Schwab, W.B., 'Kinship and lineage among the Yoruba', *Africa* 25:4 (1955), 352–74.

——, 'Continuity and change in the Yoruba lineage system', *New York Academic Science* 96 (1962), 590–605.

Shankar, S., *Who Shall Enter Paradise? Christian Origins in Muslim Northern Nigeria, ca. 1890–1975* (Athens OH: Ohio University Press, 2014).

Sikand, Y., 'The Tablighi Jama'at and politics: A critical re-appraisal', *ISIM Newsletter* 1:13 (2003), 42–3.

——, 'The Tablighi Jama'at's contested claims to Islamicity', *Indian Muslim Observer*, 24 June 2010 <http://indianmuslimobserver.com/2010/06/24/issues-the-tablighi-jamaats-contested-claims-to-islamicity/>, accessed 2 October 2014.

Soares, B.F., 'Introduction: Muslim–Christian Encounters in Africa', *Muslim–Christian Encounters in Africa*, ed. B.F. Soares (Leiden: Brill, 2006), pp. 1–16.

—, *Muslim–Christian Encounters in Africa* (Leiden: Brill, 2006).
—, 'An Islamic social movement in contemporary West Africa: NASFAT of Nigeria', *Movers and Shakers: Social Movements in Africa*, ed. S. Ellis and I. Kessel (Leiden: Brill, 2009), pp. 178–96.
Talal, A., 'Anthropological conceptions of religion: Reflections on Geertz', *Man* 18:2 (1983), 237–59.
Tamuno, T., *The Police in Modern Nigeria, 1861–1965: Origins, Development and Role* (Ibadan: University of Ibadan Press, 1970).
Taylor, C., *Sources of the Self: The Making of the Modern Identity* (Cambridge: Cambridge University Press, 1992).
Tijani, H.I., *Union Education in Nigeria: Labor, Empire, and Decolonization since 1945* (Basingstoke: Palgrave Macmillan, 2012).
—, 'Dr. Abubakar Ibiyinka Olorun-Nimbe: Islam, Western modernity and the making of a twentieth century elite', *Actors and Institutions in the Development of Islam in Lagos State*, ed. S. Oyeweso and M. Raheemson (Ibadan: Matrixcy Books, 2013), pp. 536–62.
Tishken, J., T. Falola and A. Akinyemi, *Ṣàngó in Africa and the African Diaspora* (Bloomington: Indiana University Press, 2009).
Turner, H., *History of an African Independent Church: The Church of the Lord (Aladura)* (Oxford: Clarendon Press, 1967).
Turner, S., '"These Young Men Show no Respect for Local Custom" – Globalisation and Islamic revival in Zanzibar', *Journal of Religion in Africa* 39:3 (2009), 237–61.
Vahed, G., and S. Jeppie, 'Multiple communities: Muslims in post-apartheid South Africa', *State of the Nation: South Africa 2004–2005*, ed. J. Daniel, R. Southall and J. Lutchman (Cape Town, HSRC Press, 2004), pp. 252–4.
Vardar, S., 'Inter-religious marriage in the Greater Istanbul municipality, Turkey', *Inter-Religious Marriages among Muslims: Negotiating Religious and Social Identity in Family and Community*, ed. A. An-na'im (New Delhi: Global media publications, 2005), pp. 217–91.
Voas, D., 'The maintenance and transformation of ethnicity: Evidence on mixed partnerships in Britain', *Journal of Ethnic and Migration Studies* 35:9 (2009), 1497–1513.
Voll, J., 'African Muslims and Christians in world history: The irrelevance of the "clash of civilizations"', *Muslim–Christian Encounters in Africa*, ed. B. Soares (Leiden: Brill, 2006), pp. 17–38.
Ware, R.T., *The Walking Qur'an: Islamic Education, Embodied Knowledge, and History in West Africa* (Chapel Hill NC: University of Carolina Press, 2014).
Welch, D., 'Ritual intonation of Yoruba Praise-Poetry (Oriki)', *Yearbook of the International Folk Music Council* 5 (1973), 156–64.
Zemmel, N.E., 'Intermarriage, variations on a theme: Examining the reality of mixed and conversionary marriage in contemporary Anglo-Jewry', unpublished PhD thesis (Birmingham: University of Birmingham, 1999).

Index

Note: Page numbers in italic indicate maps or illustrations; page numbers followed by *n* indicate a footnote with relevant number.

Abiodun, *Aláàfin* 37
Abudu, Alfa 43
Adebanwi, P.O. 156
Adebanwi, Wale 12
Adebesin, Ayo 179–80
Adekilekun, Mikail Hamzat 212–13, 214
Adekilekun, Musa 96–7
Adekilekun, Noah 43, 96–7
Adelekan, *Tìmì* 155
Adeleke family
   chieftaincy titles 194–5, 200
   interfaith marriage 190, 192–3, 195–6
   mutual support 202–3
   political success 193–5, 199–202
   popularity 260
   private resolution of conflict 203–4
   second generation religious plurality 196–202
Adeleke, Adedeji Tajudeen, Dr 50, 196, 197–8, 202
Adeleke, Esther Nnena (née Akpara) 190, 192–3, 195–6, 223–4
Adeleke, Isiaka, *Alhaji* 196, 199–202
Adeleke, Muniratu 191
Adeleke, Raji Ayoola 190–96
Adeleke, Rasheed 196
Adeleke-Sanni, Modupe 198
Adeleke University *19*, 172, 197–8
Adenusi, Adeniyi 183–4
Adepoju, Olanrewaju 67
Adeyemi II, Adeniran 64
Adhān (call to prayer) 41
Adio, Rasheed, *Alhaji* 24
Afolayan, D.T.T. 156
African Church 49, 158–9

Agbale, *Tìmì* (Agbale Olofa Ina) 33, 37, 67, 77, 269–72
Agbonran Gbakoya, Kubolaje, *Tìmì* 38
Agbonran II, *Tìmì* (Tijani Oladokun Oyewusi) 67, 195, 278–9
Ahmadiyya 45–6, 128, 182–4
Aina, Ayandiji 24
Ajani, A. 156
Ajani, J.A. 156
Akajewole Compound 104
Akajewole, Mas'ud Husain, *Alhaji* 46, 99, 104–5, 213
Akande, Samson Oladeji 22, 49, 110, 159–60
Akangbe, Sanusi, *Tìmì* 281–4
Akerele, Jacob Oyeboade 48, 155
Akpara, Esther Nnena *see* Adeleke, Esther Nnena
Al-Haramani Society 130, 144
Alágbára war (1860s) 44
Alapo Tiemi Tiemi 33–4
All Progressives' Congress (APC) 201
Anglican Church 49, 158, 232, 236
animals
   dogs and pigs unclean for Muslims 92
   Iléyá sacrifice (ram) 195, 198, 200, 222
   Ògún sacrifice 35
   Ṣàngó sacrifice 76, 78
Anke, Iyalode 191
Ansar-Ud-Deen Society 45, 104, 128, 129, 139, 218, 232
anthem, national 267–8
Apter, Andrew 61
Aregbesola, Rauf 201
Arohanran, Ojo, *Tìmì* 44, 96
àròni (god of charms) 277*n*3

INDEX

Atiba, *Aláàfin* 39
Awolowo, Obafemi 194
Àwòrò Ṣàngó 71, 72
Àyàn Àgalú (deity of drummers) 82–3

Baba Abiye *see* Akande, Samson Oladeji
Baba Abiye prayer mountain 22, 160, 261
Bàbá Kékeré (deputy of the *Tìmì*) 99
Bàbá Mọ́gbà (chief priest) 79
Babalola, Joseph Ayo 159
Babasanya Baptist Church 48–9, 155
Badawi, Hassan 127
Badejo, Diedre L. 77
Balewa, Sir Abubakar Tafawa 127
Bamigbaye, Ajeniju, *Tìmì*
   and Islam 40, 60–61, 95
   rise of *Ṣàngó* worship 31, 38–9, 59–60
   Ṣàngó predestination 36, 38, 59
   victory against Ibadan 40, 60–61
Bamigbaye Memorial Grammar School 167
Baptist Church 151–72
   arrival in Ede 48–9
   Babasanya Baptist Church 48–9, 155
   Celestial Church of Christ 50
   early history 153–6
   First Baptist Church 161
   joint Baptist-*Ṣàngó* service 70–72
   Oke Apaso Baptist Church 49
   opposition from Muslims and traditionalists 160
   outreach activities 171
   popularity 232
   schools 156–7
   social events and festivals 170–71
   Tìmì Laoye support 161
Barber, Karin 38, 60, 86
Bayly, Susan 263
behaviour
   characteristics liked or respected 242–5
   Muslim compounds 116
   Ṣàngó's powers 87
   Tablighi practices 137–8
Beier, Ulli 18–20, 35n17
Bello, Sir Ahmadu 127
Bible
   Corinthians on interfaith marriage 210
   Muslim familiarity with 17
blacksmiths 35, 46
Boko Haram 177, 264
Boram, Cecil 50n82
Bowen, Thomas Jefferson 153–4
Buremo Owon-laa-rogo 40, 41, 45, 61–2, 95, 96

call to prayer (*adhān*) 41
Caller to Prayer (*Mu'aḏḏin*) 99, 119
Catholic Church 49
Celestial Church of Christ 50
Central Mosque 17, *18*, 51, 63–4, 99, 198
Cherubim and Seraphim Church 51, 192, 195
Chief Imam 11, 14, 99–100, 101–2
Chief Imam (Federal Polytechnic) 181–2, 187
children
   conceived with help from *Ṣàngó* 87
   in interfaith marriages 209, 219, 220–21
Christ Apostolic Church 49, 159, 232, 236
   Ori-Oke Baba Abiye prayer mountain 22, 160, 261
Christian Association of Nigeria 200
Christianity
   Christian Religious Knowledge (CRK) 48, 167–8
   early churches 48–9
   educational role 11, 51, 156–9, 177, 227, 233, 260
   growth 50–51
   Healing Jesus Crusade 140–43, *141*, *142*
   Muslims' views on 242–5
   numerous denominations 50–51
   recognition of *Ṣàngó*'s powers 87
   and Tablighi Jamaat 140, 148–9
   viewed with scepticism 48
   see also Baptist Church; Muslim-Christian relations; Pentecostal Christianity
Christians
   changes of denomination 235–6
   characteristics 243–4
   in Ede 231, 232
   Federal Polytechnic Chaplain 181–2, 187
   growing number 172
   minority status in Ede 20–21
   Muslim compound tenants 102–3, 107, 110–113, 114, 115, 164–6, 172
   and traditional practice 241
   views of Islam 242–5
Church Missionary Society (CMS) 153, 158
Clarke, W.H. 48, 154
colonial medical service 192
colonialism 12, 45, 52, 167, 260
compounds
   advisers 100, 102–3
   see also Muslim compounds
conversion

ambivalence towards others'
motives 236–7, 252
changes of denomination within a
religion 235–6
childhood influence 196
concern over failure to appease òrìṣà 47
in interfaith marriages 22, 117, 224–5,
251
Muslim origins of leading Baptists 157
Muslim to Christian 234–5, 250, 252
parent and child conversion 250
reasons for 236, 252
relapses 49
to Christianity 48
to Islam 41, 43, 234
Cooper, B. 3
cotton 62
Cross, Messer 50n82
Crowther, Samuel Ajayi 153
crusades
Healing Jesus Crusade 140–43, *141*, *142*
Islamic counter-crusade 142–3, *142*
culture, and religion 237–41r

Daodu Lagunju Compound 102
daʿwa (proselytising) 109, 126, 132, 135
see also khurūj (missionary tours)
Deeper Life Bible Church 51, 170, 179, 232
Deobandi movement 125
Deputy Chief Imam (*Naibul Imam*) 99
Deputy of the Tìmì (*Bàbá Kékeré*) 99
Dokun, L. 102
dress codes
in schools 168–70
social functions 118
Tablighi Jamaat 137–8
drumming
Oníbàtá (drum players) 70, 71–2, 82–3
talking drums 44, 69

economic hardship, and rise in
religion 175–6
Ede 6
anthem 267–8
early history 32–6
foundation 33
Mapo Arogun Day songs 269–75
maps *5*, *19*
pluralist religious landscape 17–23
Ede Muslim Council 99
Ede Muslim Grammar School 52, 167
Ede-Ile 33, 38
education

and Christian conversion 234
Christian Religious Knowledge
(CRK) 48, 167–8
Christianity's influence 11, 50–51,
156–9, 177, 227, 233, 260
growth of Muslim institutions 16–17, 45,
98, 261
Islamic Religious Knowledge
(IRK) 167–8
Muslim resentment over Christian
bias 51
Muslim-Christian relations 167–70,
171–2
religious rhetoric and 175
and self-confidence for women 216–17
universities 171–2
see also Federal Polytechnic; schools
Egúngún festival 35, 65–6, *66*, 107–8
Eid al-Adha see Iléyá (Muslim festival)
elderly people, respect 137, 203, 237, 238,
272
elections (1979) 194
elections (2007) 201
Ẹlẹ́gùn Ṣàngó (dancers) 70, 72, 78, 79–80
Ellis, S. 177
Ellstrom, G.M. 50n82

Fadipe, L.O. 155
Fadipe, N.A. 8
Fakafaka movement 128, 145
family
gendered expectations 22, 193, 198, 199
Islamic religious obligations 104–5
Muslim wifely responsibilities 193,
195–6
religious plurality 190
see also kinship
family rites see traditional practice
Farias, P.F. de Moraes 92
Fatih, Muhammed, Imam 129
Fatihu Quareeb 45
Federal Polytechnic 173–87
Chief Imam and Chaplain 181–2
hierarchy of student
representation 180–82
intra-denominational conflict 179,
182–4
marginalisation of non-religious students 174–5, 185–6
MSSN-Ahmadiyya conflict 182–4
Pentecostalism 178, 179
positive inter-religious relations 176
religious group registration 181–2

festivals
and the Baptist church 170–71
Baptist-Ṣàngó joint service 70–72
considered inauthentic by Tablighi Jamaat 136
Ede Mapo Arogun Day songs 269–75
Ede as master entertainers 273–4
Egúngún 35, 65–6, 66, 107–8
Iléyá (Muslim festival) 32, 46, 195, 198, 200, 222
in India 263
masquerades 35–6
Muslim participation in Jumu'ah prayer service 71
Ògún worship 35
òrìṣà 18–20
Ṣàngó 60, 65–7, 76–80, 82–3
see also social functions
food
Islamic taboos 91–2
Ṣàngó taboos 76
Forst, Rainer. 3
Freeman, Thomas Birch 153
funerals 105, 136, 170, 246, 247

Gbadamosi, T.G.O. 11, 14
Gbamolada (chief) 43
Gbonka Ebiri (warrior) 37
gender
Ìyá Ṣàngó (possession priests) 77, 78
Muslim compounds and 116–19
and religious tolerance 207, 225–6, 253–4
Ṣàngó wives 77, 78, 80
wifely duties 193, 195–6, 223–4, 261
see also women
Ghana, religious tolerance 2
Gowon, Yakubu, General 167
Guyer, Jane 5–6

Habermas, Jürgen 175
Hadith 125, 131
Hasan, Mawlana In'amul 126, 127, 128
Hassan, Adeyemo, Imam 129
hijab 168–9
honours, chieftaincy titles 194–5, 200
humour, oríkì (praise poems) 91–2
hunters 34–5, 46

Ibadan
army 40, 44–5, 61–2
comparison with 21, 178
religious links to 72, 128–30, 153, 178, 199
University (College) 17, 191
Ifá divination
Abibu Lagunju 42
intermediary between humans and spiritual forces 9, 42
link with Islam 9
and religious predestination 38, 42, 59
Ṣàngó festival 78
Ifá verses 36, 82
Odù of Muslims (Odù Òtura Méjì) 42
ijtimā (annual gathering) 126, 127, 128
Iléyá (Eid al-Kabir or Eid al-Adha, Muslim festival) 32, 46, 195, 198, 200, 222
al-Ilori, Adam, Alhaji 148–9
Ilori, Joseph Abiodun 166
Ilorin 16, 34, 39
Ilyas, Mawlana Muhammed 124–5, 135
immigrants
effect on religious self-expression 21–2
and religious affiliation 227, 232, 252
sources 178
Imole Compound 97, 105–9
and Chief Imams 106
Christianity practised discretely 107
establishment 43, 45, 96–7
exclusively Muslim nature 101, 107, 108–9
and interfaith marriage 212–13
Islamic education 98
Ratibi mosques 106
and traditional religion 107–8, 109
India, religion 263
indigeneity 162–4, 165, 232–3
interfaith marriages 207–226
Baptist church and 171
Biblical verses 210
concerns over grandchildren's religion 219
conversion 22, 117, 224–5
in Daodu Lagunju Compound 114
decisions not to pursue 212–13
everyday married life 223–5
family concerns 217–19
father/husband reconciliation 220–21, 226
high incidence in Ede 208, 250–51
and marital love 214–16, 251
Muslim concerns 116–17, 213, 233
personal acceptance 112
pregnancy and reconciliation 209, 220–21

pressures from religious
  communities 211
Qur'anic verses 211, 213
reconciliation processes 209, 220–21,
  226
reluctance to pursue 251
social disadvantage of small marriage
  ceremony 218
and social functions 222–3
unequal gendered expectations 22,
  195–6
wifely duties 193, 195–6, 223–4, 261
women as mediators 209–210, 220–23,
  225–6
see also Adeleke family
Ipinloye, *Tìmì* 284–6
Islam
  ambivalent relationship with
    Ṣàngó 61–4
  arrival in Ede 21
  arrival in Yorubaland 11
  Christians' views on 242–5
  da'wa (proselytising) 109, 126, 132, 135
  dominant religion 231
  early discrimination 41
  food taboos 91–2
  growth in Ede 42–4, 97–8
  historical background 14–16
  and *Ifá* divination system 9
  intra-Muslim harmony 16
  Islamic Religious Knowledge
    (IRK) 167–8
  Jumu'ah prayer 71
  khurūj (missionary tours) 126, 130,
    131–3
  and kinship 101, 104–5, 119
  links with Ṣàngó òrìṣà 39–40
  Muslim groups 45, 45–6, 128, 139, 232
  new Islamic schools 169
  open-air lectures (*Wa'azi/da'wa*) 47,
    98, 109
  in *oríkì* praise poetry 85–6, 91–2
  peaceful co-existence with
    non-Muslims 15–16
  'Pentecostal Islam' 148
  Reformist Islam 125
  Sunna observance 131–2 and Yoruba
    custom 14–15
  see also Muslim-Christian relations;
    Muslim compounds; Muslims
Islamic (*Sharia*) law 44, 45, 243

Jàkúta day 76

Jimoh, Prince 67
Johnson, Samuel, *The History of the
  Yorubas* 33
Jumu'ah service 71

khurūj (missionary tours) 126, 130, 131–3
see also da'wa (proselytising)
kingship
  authority 9–10
  colonial era 52
  and council of traditional chiefs 31,
    98–9
  importance of Ṣàngó 18–19, 41, 57–8,
    73, 83
  and Muslim politics 99–100
  political and spiritual leadership 53–4,
    57–8
  religious leadership 26, 32, 41, 53–5,
    58, 260
  spiritual power 57–8
  Tìmì deputy (*Bàbá Kékeré*) 99
  Tìmì-in-Council 99
kinship
  and interfaith marriage 212–14, 217–19
  Muslim religious identity 101–2, 104–6,
    119
  and religious plurality 190
kola nuts 35, 76, 78
Kori, *Aláàfin* 33
Kubolaje Agbonran Gbakoya, *Tìmì* 38

La Jamah group 144
Ladipo, E.D. 156
Lagos
  comparison with 21, 197
  leaders 68
  religious links to 126–7, 128, 153–4
Lagunju, Abibu, *Tìmì*
  abilities as a warrior 44
  authority derived from Ṣàngó 63
  conversion to Islam 41
  encouragement of Muslim
    compounds 100
  Islamic predestination 42, 63
  opposition and exile 32, 44–5, 54
  oríkì (praise poem) 292–6
  spread of Islam 16, 31, 42–4, 63, 96–8
  suppression of traditional practice 43–4,
    54
Lagunju, Alfa 65, 66
Lagunju, Memudu 68–9, 114–15
Laitin, David D. 12, 254
Lalemo, *Tìmì* 36

Laminisa I *see* Lawal, Muniru Adesola, Tìmì, (Laminisa I)
lamps, Àtùpà Olójúmẹ̀rìndínlógún (sixteen-points-lamp) 78
land
  Muslim-Christian struggles 162–4
  Muslim dominance of old town 120–21
  religious topography 19, 63–4
Laniyi, Benjamin 156
Lansebe, Tìmì 289–91
Laoye, John Adetoyese, Tìmì
  Baptist-Ṣàngó joint service 70–72
  Christian identity 68
  early career and travels 50
  first Christian Ọba 32, 50
  and growth of Christianity 50–51, 114–15, 161
  infrastructure and resources 52
  Memudu Lagunju's court challenge 68–9
  Muslim resentment 51–2, 55
  and Muslim schools 52
  oríkì (praise poem) 279–81
  support for Christian education 50–51
  support for Ṣàngó worship 69–72
  and Ulli Beier 35n17
Lawal, Muniru Adesola, Tìmì, (Laminisa I)
  Iléyá festival 32
  Ọba of Ede 17, 31
  oríkì (praise poem) 277–8
  popularity 260
  research support 24
  Ṣàngó festival 60, 83
Lawal, Nureni, *Alhaji* 24
Lawani, Alfa 43
love 214–16, 251

magic, physical feats 79
Mapo Arogun Day songs 269–75
marital love 214–16, 251
marriage
  celebrations during Ṣàngó festival 65
  Muslim alliances 97
  polygamous marriage 215, 244
  wedding ceremonies 218
  see also interfaith marriages
Marshall, Ruth 143, 176
Matory, J. Lorand 18
mediation, in interfaith marriages 209–210, 220–23, 225–6
Metcalf, Barbara D. 125
migrants *see* immigrants
missionaries 48, 153–6, 167

Mọ́gbà (chief priests of Ṣàngó) 20, 37, 59, 80
mosques
  in Adeleke University 198
  Ede Central Mosque 17, 18, 51, 63–4, 99, 198
  land for a new Central Mosque 51
  Ratibi mosque and statue of Tìmì Oyewusi 67
  Ratibi mosques 106
  wells 106, 114, 118–19, 262
Mosunloye, Tìmì 288–9
Mountain of Fire and Miracles 179, 232
MSSN *see* Muslim Students' Society of Nigeria (MSSN)
Mu'addin (Caller to Prayer) 99, 119
Muhammed, Prophet 103–4, 132, 136, 144
Muslim-Christian relations
  beneficial encounters 4, 260–61
  in education 167–70, 171–2
  Healing Jesus Crusade 140–43, 141, 142
  inter-religious sociality 245–9, 253, 254
  land ownership struggles 162–4
  in Muslim compounds 107, 110–113, 114, 115
  mutual fascination 3
  mutual perceptions 242–5
  points of convergence 228, 243, 251, 252, 253–4
Muslim compounds
  Akajewole Compound 104
  Asafa Compound 43
  and Chief Imam selection 101–2
  Christian activities 114, 163
  Christian activities restricted 107, 110–113, 115
  Christian tenants 107, 110–111, 115, 164–6, 172
  Daodu Lagunju Compound 43, 102, 113–16
  Egúngún worship 36
  gender and 116–19
  historically important compounds 102
  importance 15
  Islamic space 263–4
  Lagunju's encouragement 100
  names and religions 35
  Owonlarogo Compound 95, 96
  Ratibi mosques 106
  religious outsiders and 101, 213
  religious tolerance 103–116
  Talafia Baba Abiye 110, 159

Talafia Imam Compound 43, 101, 109–113
  'the five compounds' 102
  and traditional practices 107–8, 109, 113, 115–16, 120
  wells 106, 114, 118–19, 262
  see also Imole Compound
Muslim Congress (TMC) 128, 136
Muslim Students' Society of Nigeria (MSSN)
  active on university campuses 177
  criticism of money collections 136
  Federal Polytechnic conflict with Ahmadiyya 182–4
  formation 128
  and pure Islam 108–9
  sisters' circle 148
  and Western-educated Muslims 128, 147
Muslims
  changes of denomination 235
  characteristics 242–3
  participation in the *Jumu'ah* prayer service 71
  persecution 96
  views of Christianity 242–5
  wifely responsibilities 193, 195–6

naming ceremonies 222, 246
Naibul Imam (Deputy Chief Imam) 99
Nasrul-Lahi-Fatih Society (NASFAT)
  popularity 129, 231, 235
  social meeting space 232
  spiritual equality 133, 147
  and Tablighi Jamaat 139
  and women 148
  and young people 147
national anthem 267–8
neoliberalism, and religion 175
New Oyo 39
nursing 191–2

ọbaship see kingship
Odù Òtura Méjì 9
Ògún (deity of iron) 34–5, 46
Ogunmola, M. 39–40
Olagunju, Abdul-Ganiyu 67
Olagunju, Imran Oluwasegun, Prince 114
ọlàjú (enlightened progress) 10–11
Olanrewaju, Muhammed Saheed, *Alhaji* 110, 112, 157
Olayiwola, Salahudeen, *Alhaji* 67, 157
Qlóya (devotees of Ọya) 70, 72, 83
Olunlade, E. 61–2

Olunloye, *Tîmì* 291–2
Olupona, Jacob 12, 58
Oníbàtá (drum players) 70, 71–2, 82–3
Oniye, Prince S.B. 50
oral literature
  central to Ṣàngó worship 75–6
  Ifá divination verses 36, 82
  three forms 81
  women's role 81
  see also oríkì (praise poetry)
orí (fate) 255
Ori-Oke Baba Abiye prayer mountain 22, 160
Oridoru masquerade 35
oríkì (praise poetry)
  ambivalence towards other religions 84–6, 93
  challenges to Islam and Christianity 86–93
  honouring the Mógba 80
  humour 91
  indispensable channel between òrìṣà and devotee 86
  in praise of Ṣàngó's powers 88–9
  on Ṣàngó's Muslim identity 85–6, 91–2
  of the Tîmì of Ede, past and present 277–96
òrìṣà
  Ede's deities 34–6
  festivals 18–20
  hidden from public view 17
  historical importance 18, 20
  Lagunju's opposition 43–4, 46
  multiplicity 8–9
  ongoing process of proliferation and merging 73
  see also Ṣàngó
Òsà-nlá (god of creation) 279n6
Ọsanyìn (lamp custodian) 83
Osogbo 19, 265
  Battle of (1838) 15, 34
Ọsun festival 19
Owonlarogo see Buremo Owon-laa-rogo
Ọya (Ṣàngó's wife) 70, 83
Oyelekan, *Tîmì* 287–8
Oyeweso, Siyan 24
Oyewusi, Tijani Oladokun, *Tîmì* (Agbonran II) 67, 195, 278–9
Oyo, *Aláàfin* 64, 269–72
Oyo Empire 15, 36, 37–9, 59

Pacific Farms 194
Patterson, Scott 156

Peel, J.D.Y. 4, 10–11, 259, 264
Pentecostal Christianity
    and break with the past 21
    conversion 236
    discouragement of socialising outside the group 179
    distance from non-Christians 264
    membership 232
    student membership 176, 178–9
    and traditional practice 241
'Pentecostal Islam' 148
People's Democratic Party (PDP) 201
political system
    Adeleke family success 193–5, 199–202
    Balógun 195
    Muslim community 98–103
    Tìmì-in-Council 99
polygamous marriage 215, 244
Polytechnic see Federal Polytechnic
praise poetry see oríkì (praise poetry)
prayer 242
    see also Baba Abiye's prayer mountain; Caller to Prayer (Mu'addin)
priests
    Àwòrò Ṣàngó 71
    Bàbá Mógbà (chief priest) 79
    Ìyá Ṣàngó (possession priests) 77, 78, 80
    magic feats 79
    Mógbà (senior priests) 20, 37, 59, 80
proverbs
    A man walks in front of his wife 77
    Be identical to me! 93
    Ede is one room 8
    Ifá, we met in the world 48
    It is not a single road that leads to the market 82
    The husband's religion is the wife's religion 209

Qadiriyya 45, 128
Qur'an
    on interfaith marriage 211
    on religious tolerance 104–5
    study 17
    Surah 109 15, 20, 103
    and Tablighi Jamaat 125, 131

Redeemed Christian Church of God (RCCG) 51, 232, 235–6
religious ambivalence 57–8, 72–3, 84–5, 92–3
religious boundaries 13–14, 58, 72, 257, 264
religious conflict 1–2, 179, 183–4, 257, 263
religious fundamentalism 176–7
religious multiplicity 6, 8–9, 30, 82, 121, 259–60
religious pluralism 4, 6, 193–5
religious sectarianism 258
religious tolerance
    Adeleke family 192–205
    in America 265
    Christian-Muslim 244
    competitive appeal 7, 172
    ethical and religious agency 258
    Federal Polytechnic 179–80
    Muslim-Christian 13
    ongoing multiple religious practices 260
    and gender 207, 225–6, 253–4
    and sociality 253–4
    spectrum 3
    Surah 109 15, 20, 103
    theoretical reflection on 3–4, 13–4, 32, 73, 93, 146–7, 255–6
religious topography 19, 63–4
religious transgression, Ṣàngó 26–7, 57–8, 73, 90–1
research areas for the future 262–6
research survey 23–4, 229–31
research workshop 24, 25
Roman Catholic Church 49
Royal Palace (Ede) 10, 17, 63–4

sacrifices
    Iléyá (ram) 195, 198, 200, 222
    Ògún worship (dog) 35
    Ṣàngó 76, 78
Sado, Alfa 43
Ṣàngó
    ambivalence towards other religions 84–6, 93
    association with ọbaship 18–19, 41, 57–8, 73, 83
    Bàbá Mọgbà (chief priest) 79
    Bamigbaye and the rise of Ṣàngó worship 31, 38–9, 59–60
    Baptist-Ṣàngó joint service 70–72
    civic and royal deity 58–61
    daily and weekly worship 76
    decline in worship 64
    deity of thunder, lightning and justice 36, 58–9
    double axe symbol (Oṣé Ṣàngó) 58
    early opposition to Islam 41

INDEX

facilitator and rival of early Islam 61–4
festivals 60, 65–7, 76–80, 82–3
help with problems 64
help with problems and failure to
  acknowledge 87–8
Ìyá Ṣàngó (possession priests) 77, 78,
  80
links with Islam 39–40
Mọgbà (senior priests) 20, 37, 59, 80
Muslim identity 85–6, 91–2
openness to other religions 81–4
possession of his followers 79–80
power to encourage good behaviour 87
principal òrìṣà of Tìmì of Ede 36–40, 73
reveals hidden truths 59
statue of Tìmì Agbale 67, 77
strength from other religious
  practices 54
taboos 76
thunderstones (èdùn àrá) ritual cleansing 36, 37n28, 59n7, 77, 78
Tìmì Laoye's support 69–72
transgressive power 26–7, 57–8, 73
work for and in the community 54
see also oríkì (praise poetry)
Sango, Aláàfin 33, 36–7, 38, 59
Sangodokun, Oyebanji, Chief 20
schools
  Baptist church 156–7
  Christian 50–51
  Christian (mission) schools 11, 51
  dress codes 168–70
  Muslim schools 52–3
  new Islamic schools 169
  Raji Adeleke's mixed religious
    education 191–2
scriptures
  central form of knowledge 17
  Fazail-il-Amal 136
  see also Bible; Qur'an
Seventh Day Adventist Church 50, 197, 232
Shankar, Shobana 3
Sharia (Islamic) law 44, 45, 243
smoking, Ṣàngó taboo 76
Soares, Benjamin F. 3–4
social functions
  Baptist Church approach 171
  inter-religious sociality 245–9, 253, 254
  interfaith families 222–3, 247–8
  non-Muslim women's dress code 118
  Tablighi Jamaat approach 136
  see also festivals
Sokoto Caliphate 15, 34, 39

songs
  Ede Mapo Arogun Day 269–75
  Ede as master entertainers 273–4
  greatness of Ede 269–72
  living in peace and harmony 273–5
  opposition to Lagunju 44
  opposition to Laoye 52
South Africa, Muslim minority 2
Springtime Development Foundation 197
statue, Tìmì Agbale (as Ṣàngó) 67, 77
Sudan, Janjaweed militia violence 2
Sufism 124, 125, 128
Surah 109 15, 20, 103
Suwari, Salim, Alhaji 15–16
Suwarian tradition 15–16

Tablighi Jamaat 123–49
  arrival in Ede 129–30
  arrival in Nigeria 126–8
  counter-crusade 142–3, 142
  Fazail-il-Amal 136
  history 124–7
  Islamic authenticity (debates
    about) 135–8
  missionary tours (khurūj) 126, 130,
    131–3
  no political agenda 125, 143–4
  non-materialist approach 136, 144
  personal piety and spirituality 134–5
  political issues 145–7
  relations with Christians 142–3, 148–9
  relations with other Muslim
    groups 137–40
  'tablighi' interpretation 131
  weekly meetings 130–31
  women 130, 148
  young people 130, 147–8
taboos 76, 116
Taiwo, T.A. 156
Tajudeen School 52
Talafia, Aminulah, Alhaji 102
Talafia Baba Abiye 110, 159
Talafia Imam Compound 43, 101, 109–113
Teacher Training College 51
ter Haar, Gerrie 177
thunderstones (èdùn àrá) 36, 37n28, 59n7,
  77, 78
Tijani, Daud Adekilekun, Alhaji 17
Tijani, Ibikunle 24
Tijaniyya Movement 45, 128, 129, 134, 232
Tìmì, role see kingship
  see also individual Tìmì
titles, chieftaincy titles 194–5, 200

tolerance *see* religious tolerance
Townsend, Henry 153
traditional practice
　against religious beliefs 238
　appreciation 238
　and the Baptist church 171
　compatibility with world religions 12–13, 231, 239–41
　decline 47, 64
　drumming 44, 69, 70, 71–2, 82–3
　Ede citizens' experiences 237–41
　mixed welcome at social functions 246–8
　in Muslim compounds 107–8, 109, 113, 115–16, 120
　views on continuing existence 259, 265
　and Yoruba identity 254–5
　see also òrìṣà; Ṣàngó
transgressive power, Ṣàngó 26–7, 57–8, 73
Tunolase, Moses Orimolade 192

Uganda, religious violence 1
unionism 192
Unity Party of Nigeria (UPN) 194
universities *19*, 171–2, 176–7, 197–8

Victory Life Ministries 232

Voll, John 263

water, mosque wells *106*, 114, 118–19, 262
wells *106*, 114, 118–19, 262
Winners Chapel 232
women
　crucial role in entertainment 80–81
　education and self-confidence 216–17
　maternal duties 215
　in Muslim associations 148
　in Muslim compounds 118, 120
　pressure to convert in interfaith marriages 251
　Tablighi Jamaat 130, 148
　wifely duties 193, 195–6, 223–4, 261
　wifely proverbs 77, 209
　see also interfaith marriages

Yoruba identity 12, 254–5
young people
　Pentecostal Christianity 176, 178–9
　Tablighi Jamaat 130, 147–8
　see also Federal Polytechnic; Muslim Students' Society of Nigeria (MSSN)
Yusuf, Mawlana Muhammad 126

Zumratul-Mu'minin Society 45

Previously published titles in the series

Violent Conversion: Brazilian Pentecostalism and Urban Women in Mozambique, Linda Van de Kamp (2016)

Beyond Religious Tolerance: Muslim, Christian & Traditionalist Encounters in an African Town, edited by Insa Nolte, Olukoya Ogen and Rebecca Jones (2017)

Faith, Power and Family: Christianity and Social Change in French Cameroon, Charlotte Walker-Said (2018)

www.ingramcontent.com/pod-product-compliance
Lightning Source LLC
Chambersburg PA
CBHW051558230426
43668CB00013B/1897